KOUJI MIURA

I retouch parts of the finalized
graphic novel even though my
friends ask, "Will the readers
even notice that?"

I do it for my own satisfaction.

Born March 28, Kouji Miura began her manga career in 2015 with the release of
Aozora Lover (Blue Sky Lover). Her previously published works include *Sensei, Suki
Desu* (I Love You, Teacher) and several one-shots. *Blue Box* was first published as
a one-shot in 2020 before it began serialization in *Weekly Shonen Jump* in 2021.

Blue Box

VOLUME 4
SHONEN JUMP Edition

STORY AND ART BY
KOUJI MIURA

TRANSLATION — **CHRISTINE DASHIELL**
TOUCH-UP ART & LETTERING — **MARK MCMURRAY**
DESIGN — **ALICE LEWIS**
SHONEN JUMP SERIES EDITOR — **ALEXIS KIRSCH**
GRAPHIC NOVEL EDITOR — **JACK CARRILLO CONCORDIA**

Printed in the U.S.A.

Published by VIZ Media, LLC
P.O. Box 77010
San Francisco, CA 94107

10 9 8 7 6 5 4 3 2 1
First printing, May 2023

viz.com

PARENTAL ADVISORY
BLUE BOX is rated T for Teen and is
recommended for ages 13 and up.
This volume contains mild language.

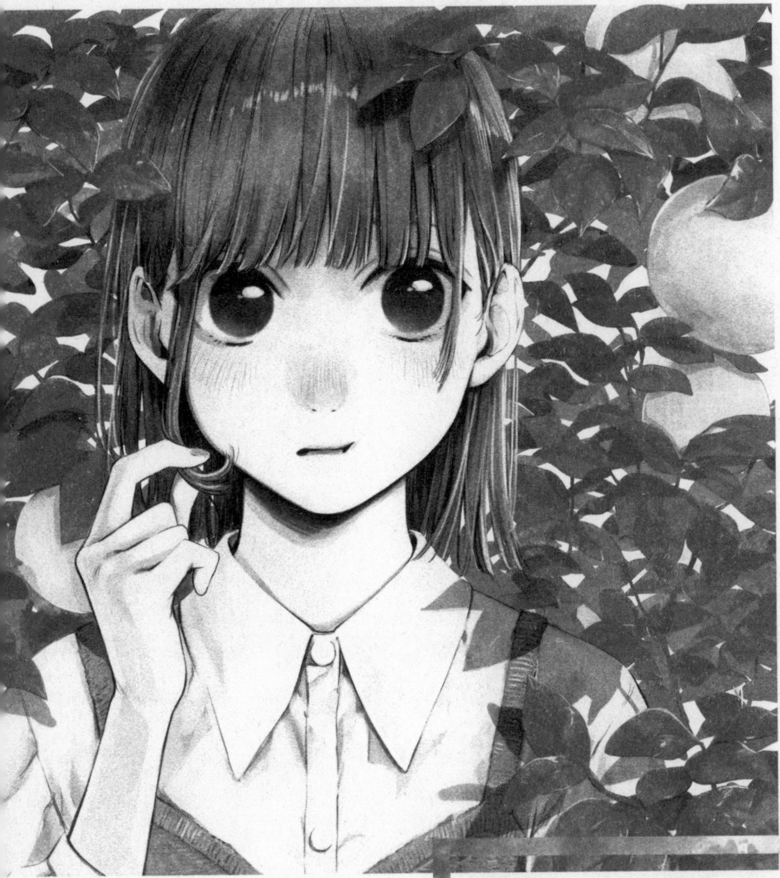

Blue Box

STORY AND ART BY
KOUJI MIURA

A Chance

4

Blue Box

Chinatsu Kano

The second-year MVP of the girls' basketball team. When her parents move abroad for work, she ends up living in the Inomata household.

Taiki Inomata

A first-year member of the badminton team. He has a crush on Chinatsu and wants to become an athlete worthy of standing by her side.

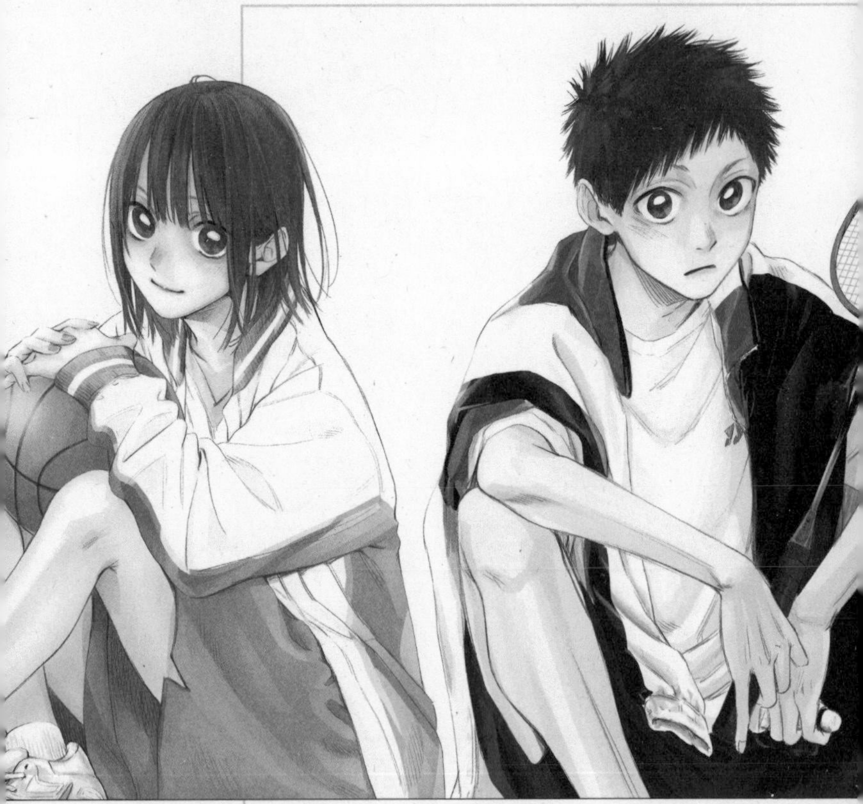

Hina Chono

A first-year member of the rhythmic gymnastics team who shows a lot of promise. She loves to tease Taiki.

Kyo Kasahara

A first-year member of the badminton team and one of Taiki's best friends. He's cool, calm, and collected and often gives Taiki advice.

Kengo Haryu

A second-year member of the badminton team. He's a classmate of and good friends with Chinatsu.

Shota Hyodo

One of the best players on the Sajikawa High School badminton team. He previously won the national tournament.

The Story So Far

When Taiki catches Chinatsu practicing alone in the gym, he falls for her hard. One day, he learns that Chinatsu's parents are moving abroad. Shaken, Taiki rushes to her side, but Chinatsu explains that she'll do anything to achieve her dreams of reaching nationals, even if it means staying behind in Japan without her family. Taiki's relief is soon replaced by stress when he finds out who Chinatsu will be living with—him! And so begins their secret living arrangement...

Chinatsu and Taiki continue to encourage each other's aspirations of becoming great athletes. While Chinatsu secures her spot and reaches the first step toward her dream, Taiki suffers a crushing defeat at the hands of Sajikawa's championship-level team. Unable to get over his loss, Taiki is wallowing in self-pity when Chinatsu pays him an impromptu visit.

Story

4

Contents

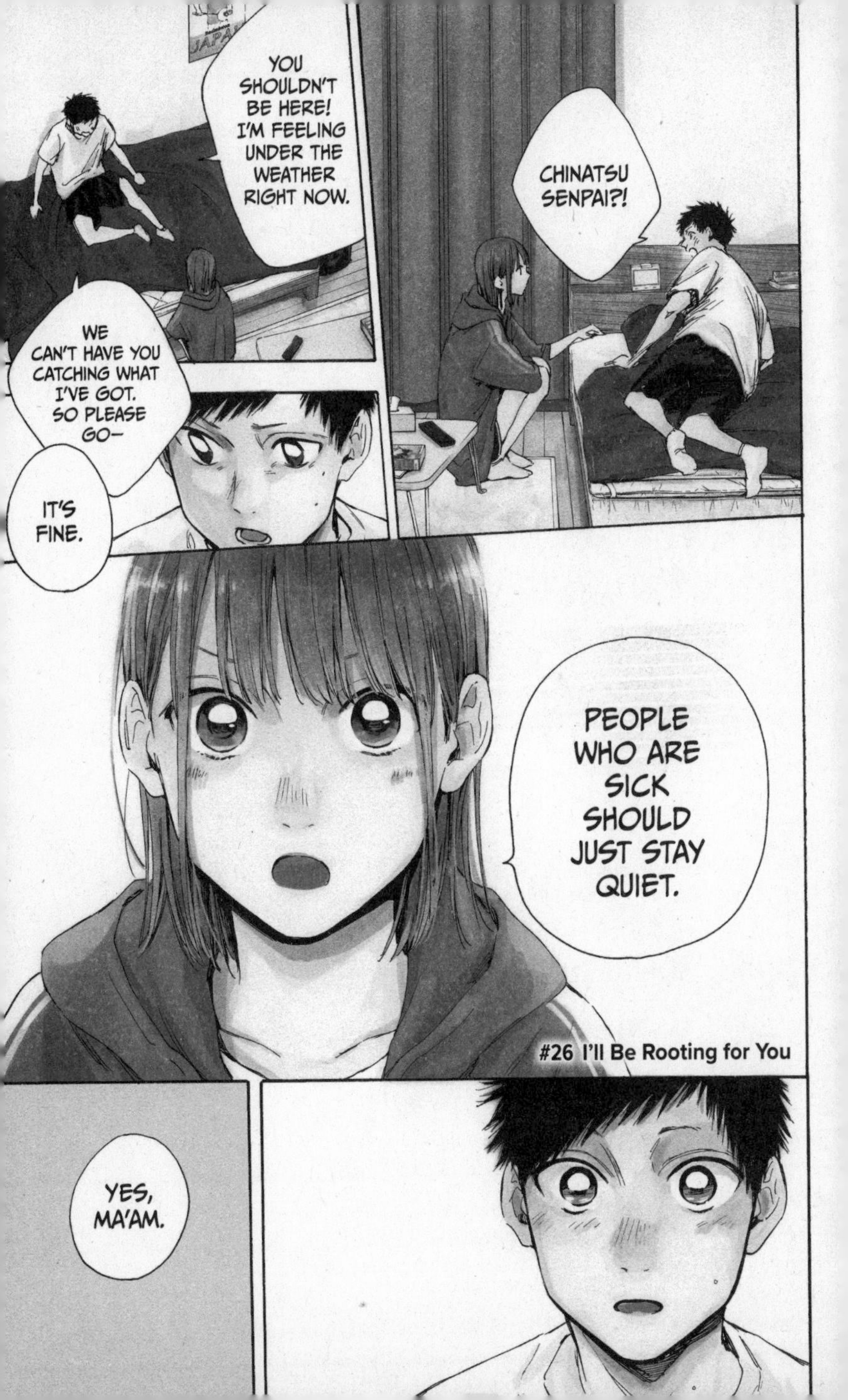
CHINATSU SENPAI?!
YOU SHOULDN'T BE HERE! I'M FEELING UNDER THE WEATHER RIGHT NOW.
WE CAN'T HAVE YOU CATCHING WHAT I'VE GOT. SO PLEASE GO–
IT'S FINE.
PEOPLE WHO ARE SICK SHOULD JUST STAY QUIET.
#26 I'll Be Rooting for You
YES, MA'AM.

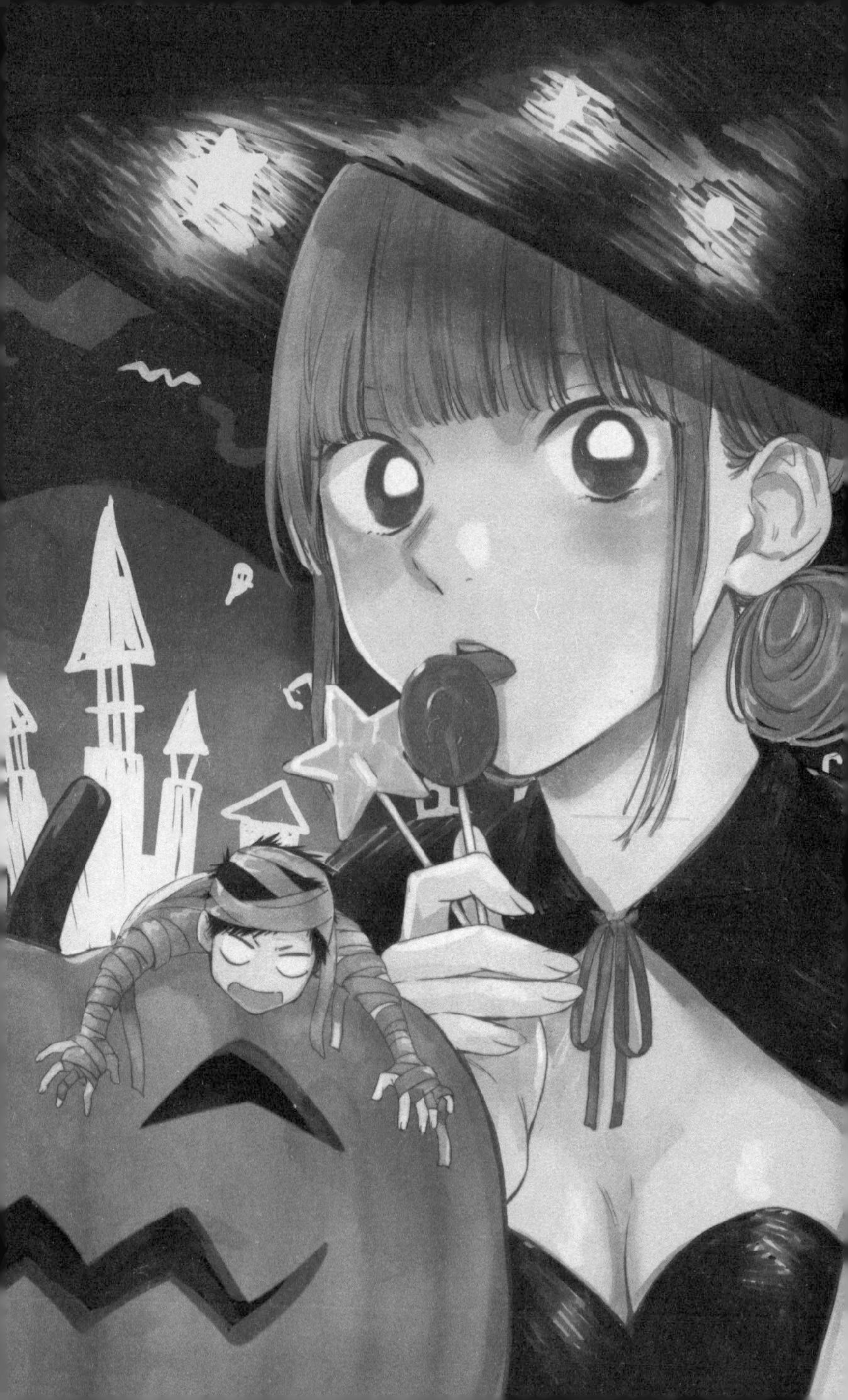

#26 I'll Be Rooting for You

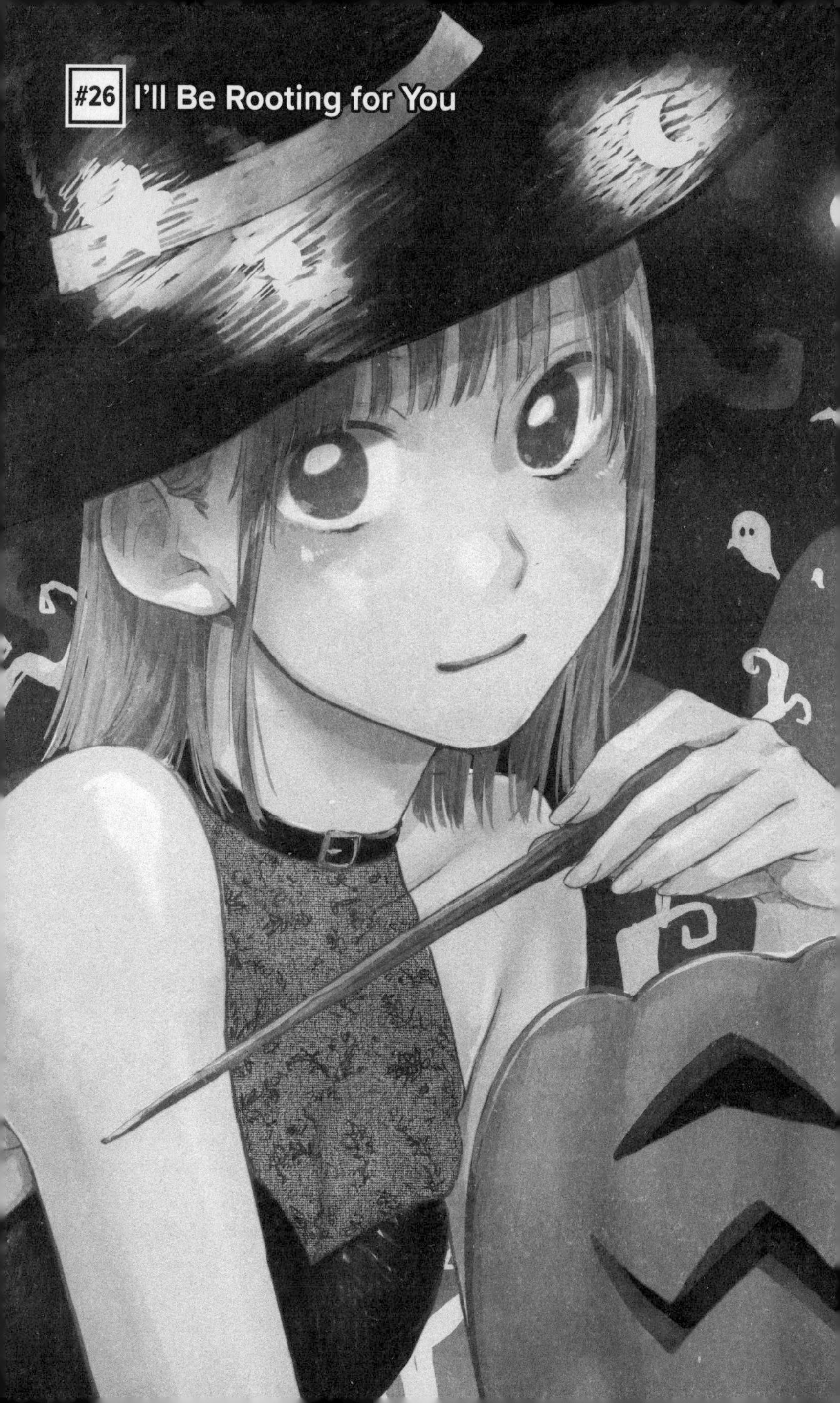

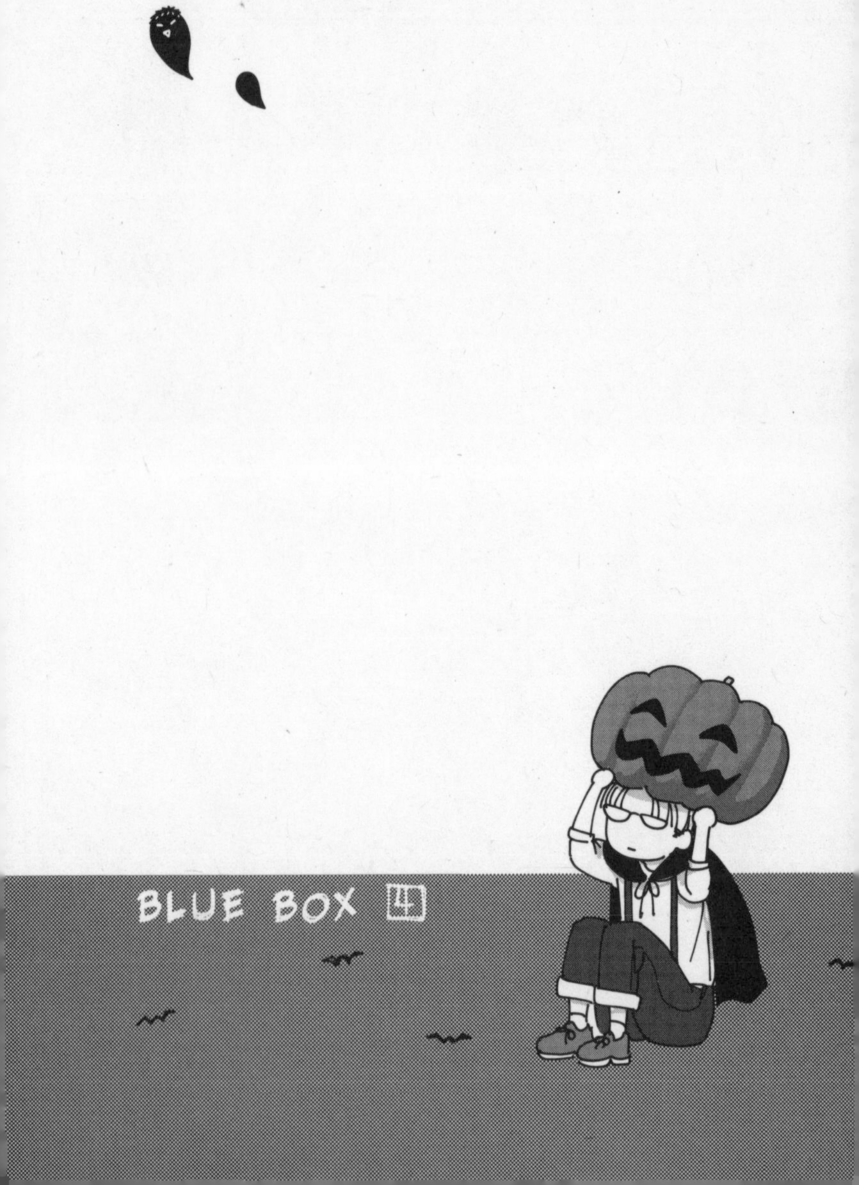
BLUE BOX 4

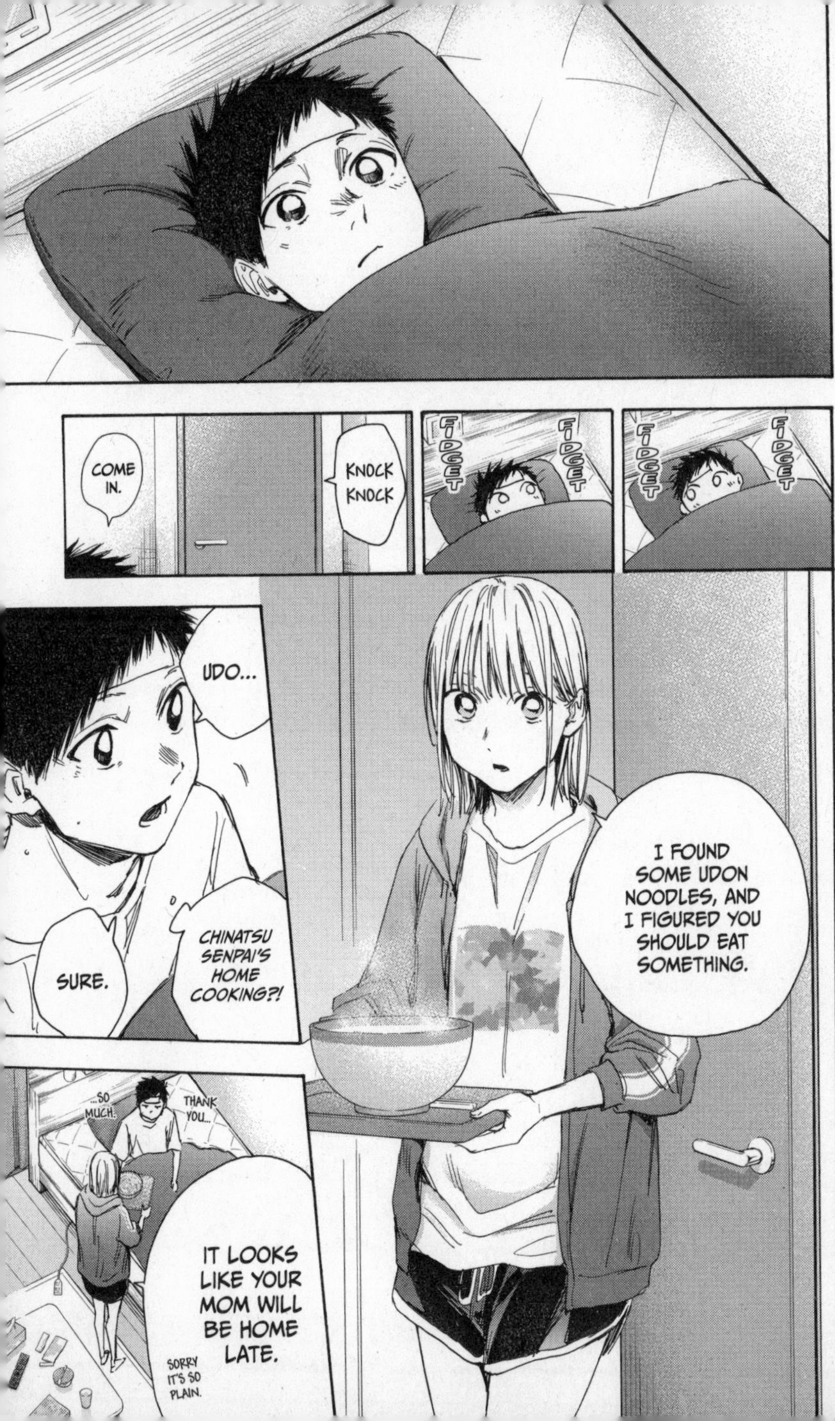
FIDGET
FIDGET
FIDGET
FIDGET
KNOCK KNOCK
COME IN.
I FOUND SOME UDON NOODLES, AND I FIGURED YOU SHOULD EAT SOMETHING.
UDO...
CHINATSU SENPAI'S HOME COOKING?!
SURE.
IT LOOKS LIKE YOUR MOM WILL BE HOME LATE.
SORRY IT'S SO PLAIN.
THANK YOU...
...SO MUCH.

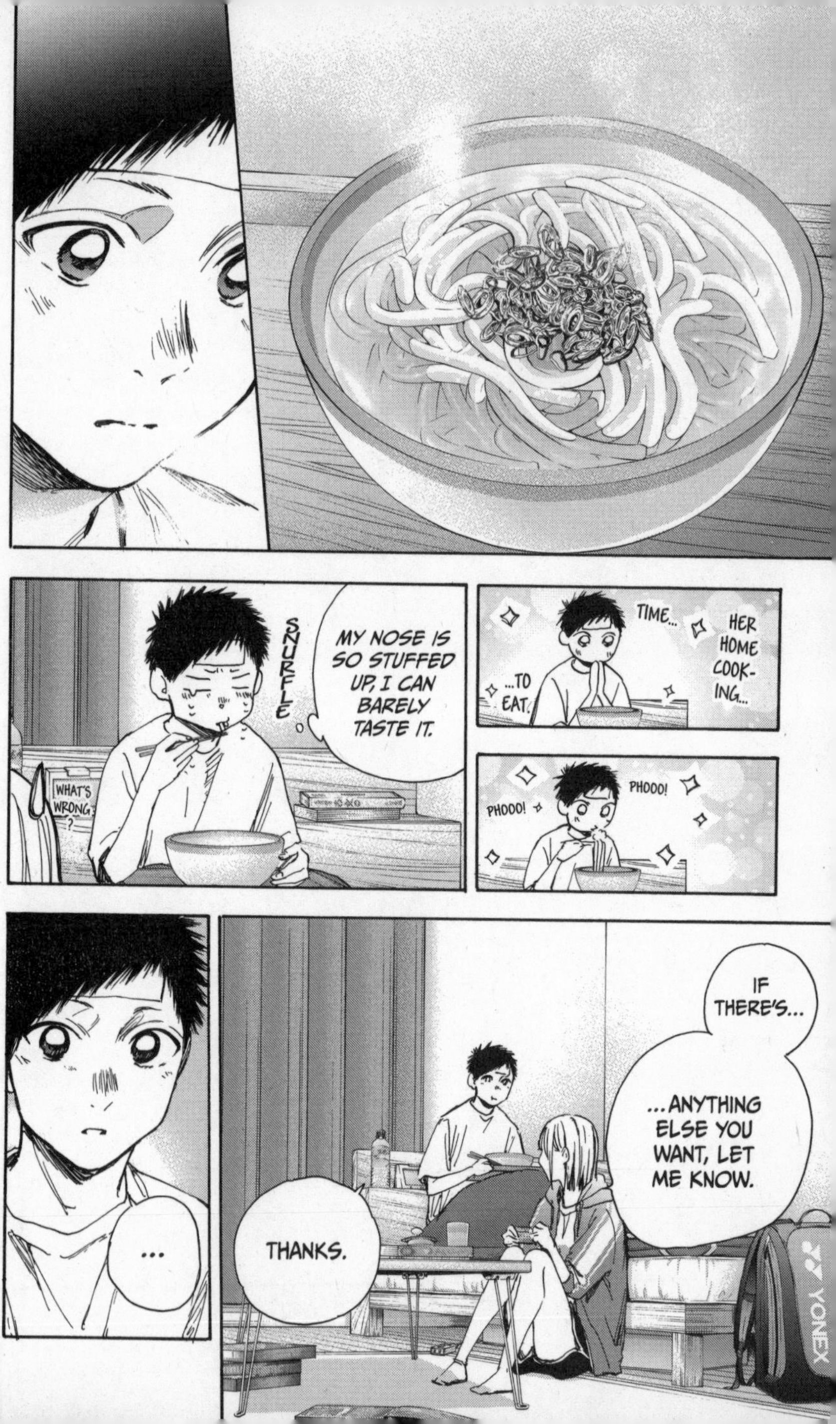
HER HOME COOKING...
TIME...
...TO EAT.
PHOOO!
PHOOO!
MY NOSE IS SO STUFFED UP, I CAN BARELY TASTE IT.
SNURFLE
WHAT'S WRONG?
IF THERE'S...
...ANYTHING ELSE YOU WANT, LET ME KNOW.
THANKS.
...
YONEX

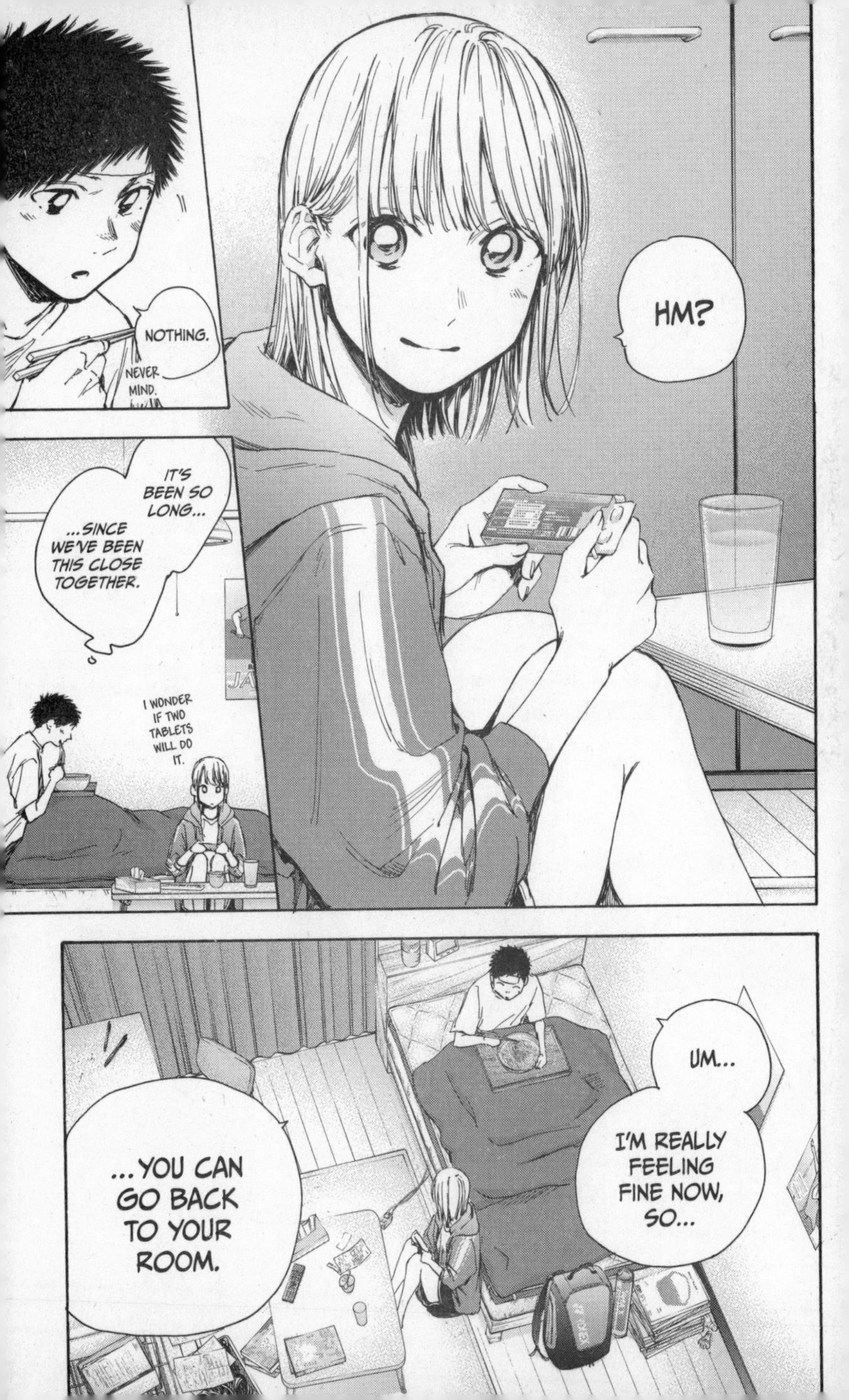
HM?
NOTHING.
NEVER MIND.
IT'S BEEN SO LONG...
...SINCE WE'VE BEEN THIS CLOSE TOGETHER.
I WONDER IF TWO TABLETS WILL DO IT.
UM...
I'M REALLY FEELING FINE NOW, SO...
...YOU CAN GO BACK TO YOUR ROOM.

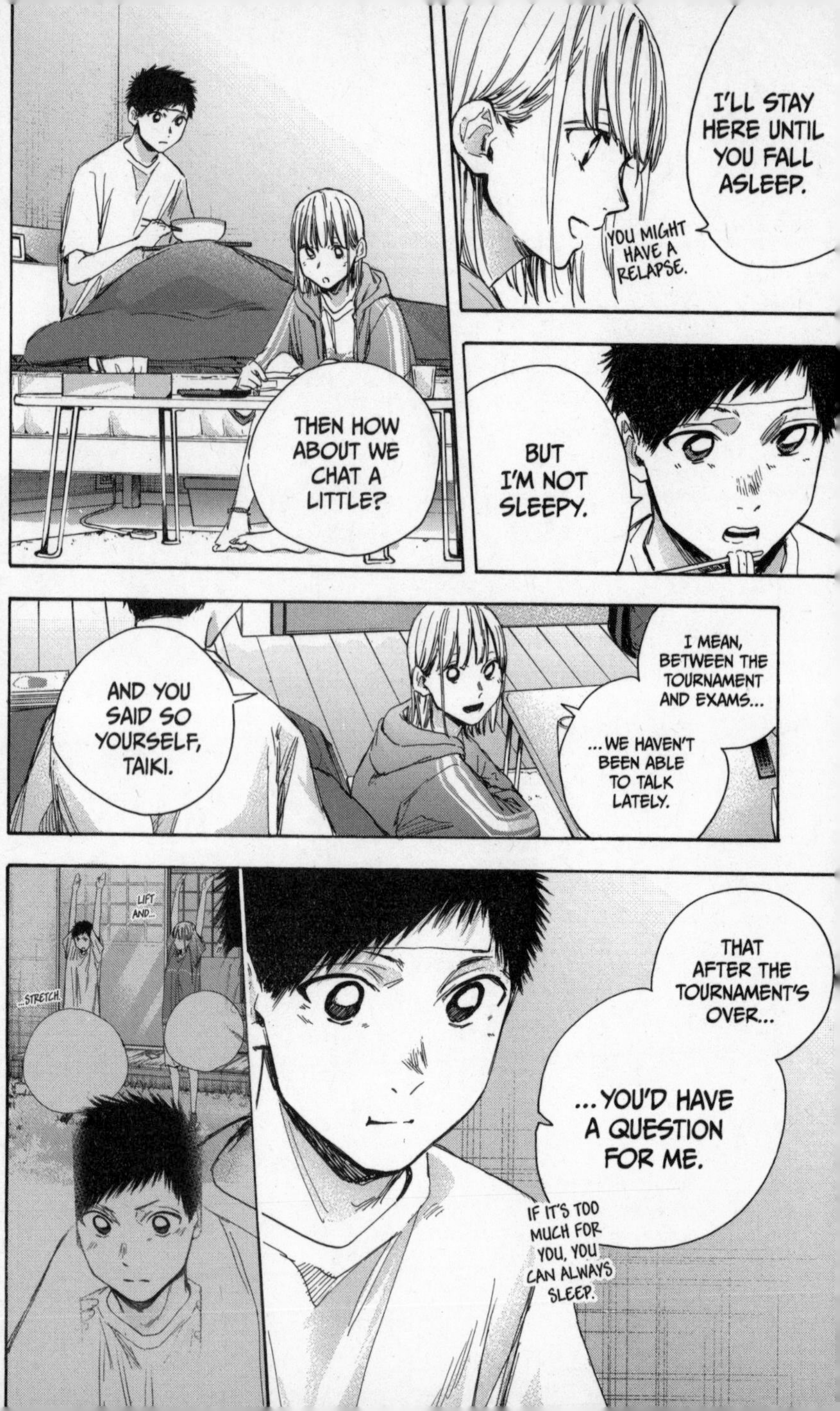
I'LL STAY HERE UNTIL YOU FALL ASLEEP.
YOU MIGHT HAVE A RELAPSE.
BUT I'M NOT SLEEPY.
THEN HOW ABOUT WE CHAT A LITTLE?
I MEAN, BETWEEN THE TOURNAMENT AND EXAMS...
...WE HAVEN'T BEEN ABLE TO TALK LATELY.
AND YOU SAID SO YOURSELF, TAIKI.
THAT AFTER THE TOURNAMENT'S OVER...
...YOU'D HAVE A QUESTION FOR ME.
IF IT'S TOO MUCH FOR YOU, YOU CAN ALWAYS SLEEP.
LIFT AND...
...STRETCH.

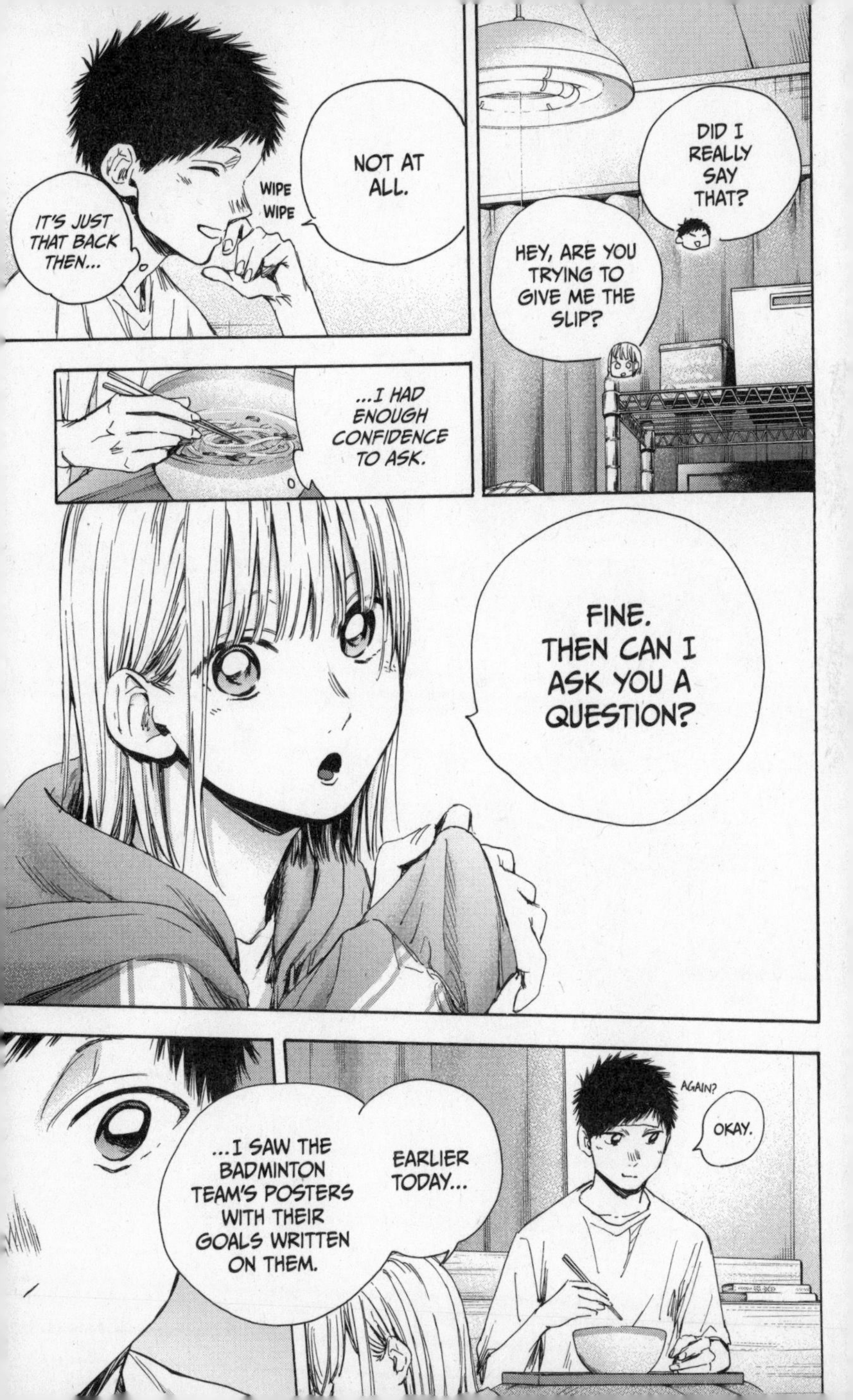
DID I REALLY SAY THAT?
HEY, ARE YOU TRYING TO GIVE ME THE SLIP?
NOT AT ALL.
WIPE WIPE
IT'S JUST THAT BACK THEN...
...I HAD ENOUGH CONFIDENCE TO ASK.
FINE. THEN CAN I ASK YOU A QUESTION?
AGAIN?
OKAY.
EARLIER TODAY...
...I SAW THE BADMINTON TEAM'S POSTERS WITH THEIR GOALS WRITTEN ON THEM.

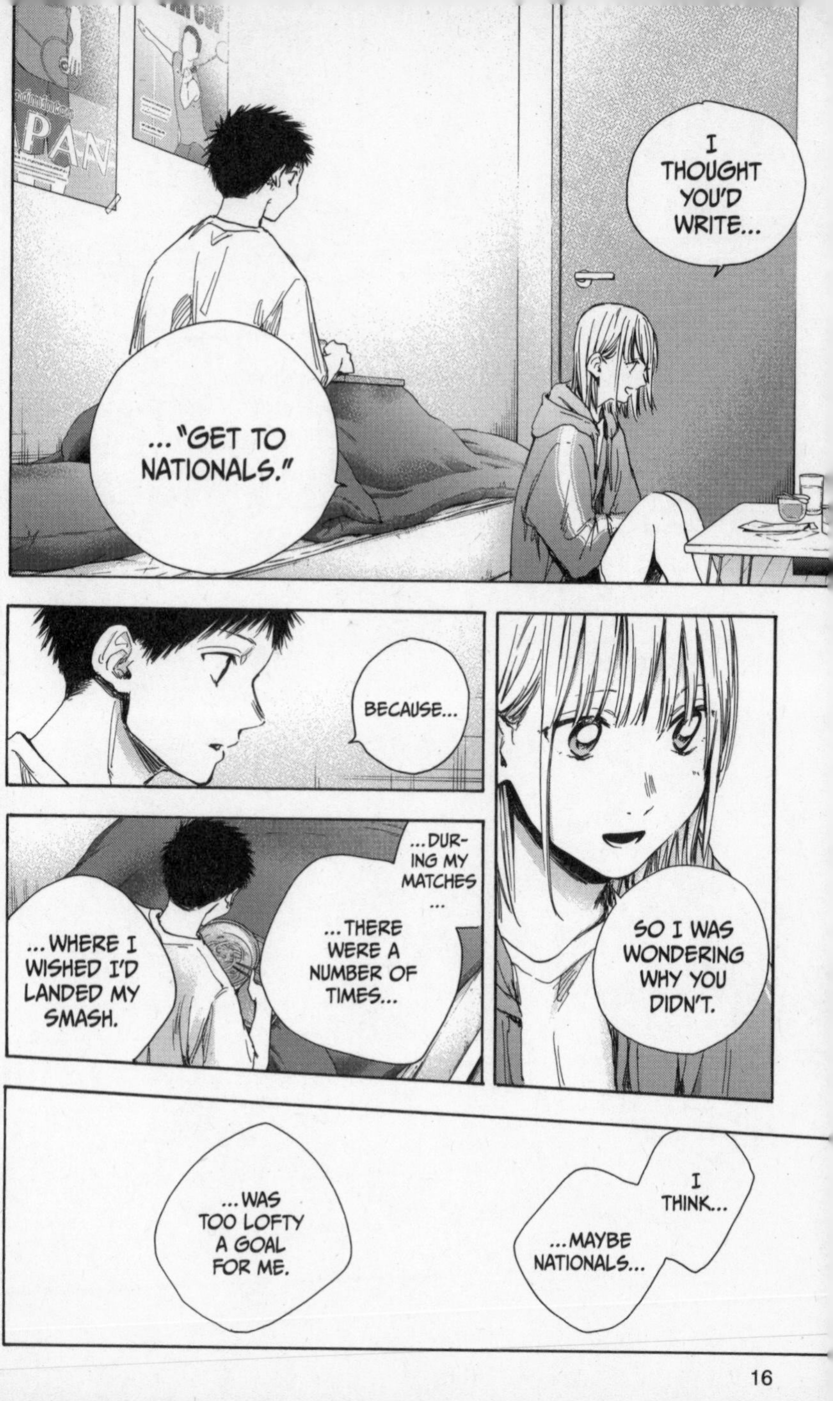
I THOUGHT YOU'D WRITE...
..."GET TO NATIONALS."
SO I WAS WONDERING WHY YOU DIDN'T.
BECAUSE...
...DUR-ING MY MATCHES...
...THERE WERE A NUMBER OF TIMES...
...WHERE I WISHED I'D LANDED MY SMASH.
I THINK...
...MAYBE NATIONALS...
...WAS TOO LOFTY A GOAL FOR ME.

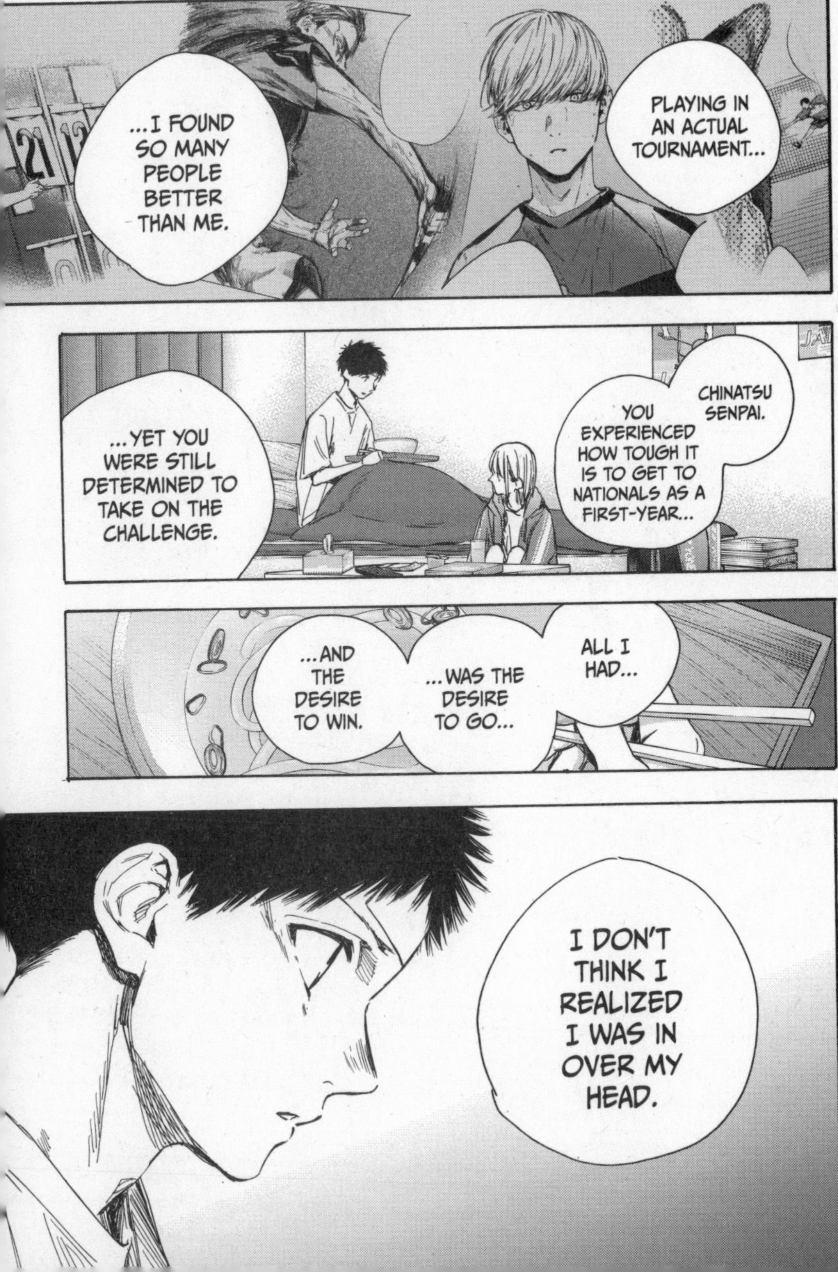
PLAYING IN AN ACTUAL TOURNAMENT...
...I FOUND SO MANY PEOPLE BETTER THAN ME.
CHINATSU SENPAI.
YOU EXPERIENCED HOW TOUGH IT IS TO GET TO NATIONALS AS A FIRST-YEAR...
...YET YOU WERE STILL DETERMINED TO TAKE ON THE CHALLENGE.
ALL I HAD...
...WAS THE DESIRE TO GO...
...AND THE DESIRE TO WIN.
I DON'T THINK I REALIZED I WAS IN OVER MY HEAD.

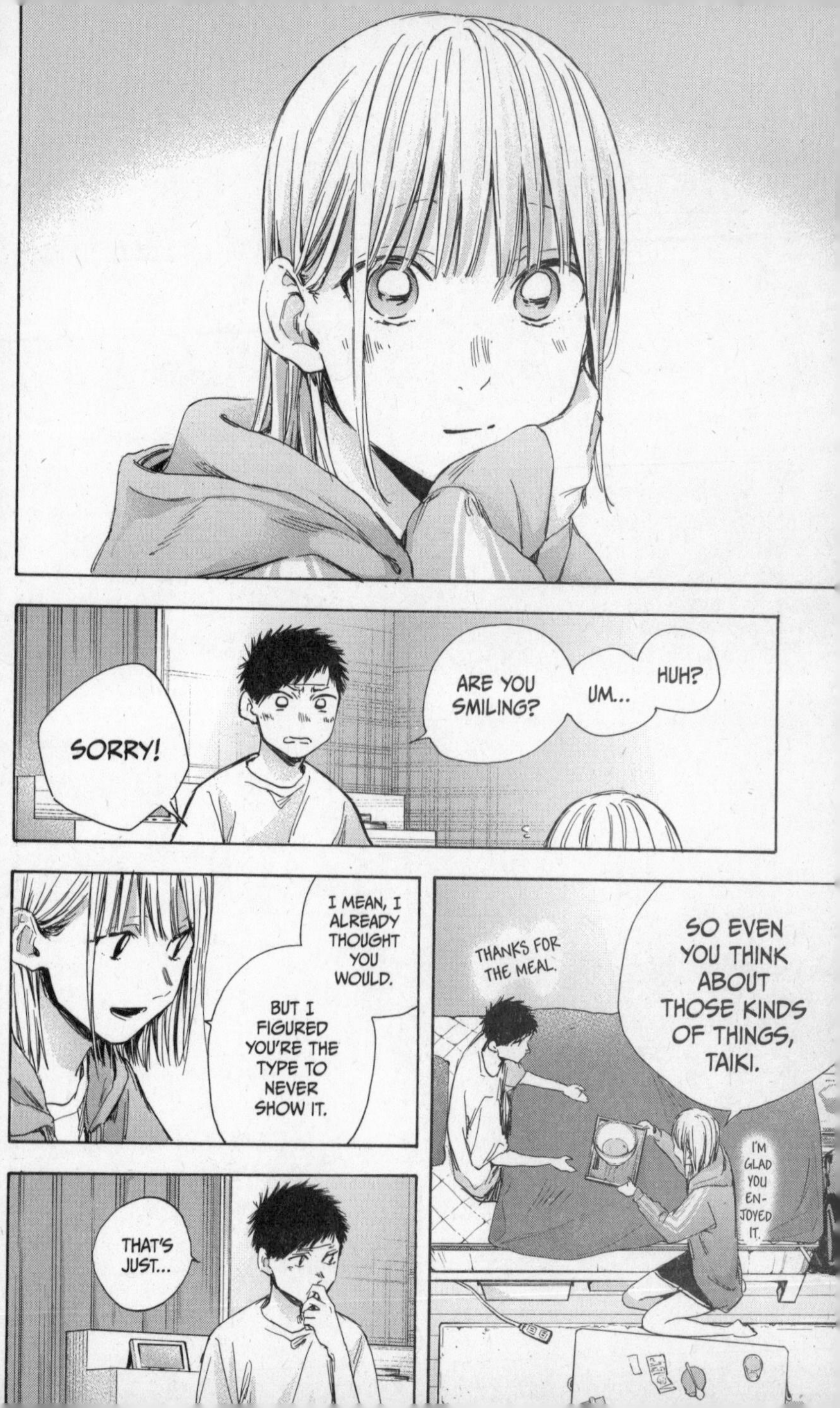
HUH?
UM...
ARE YOU SMILING?
SORRY!
SO EVEN YOU THINK ABOUT THOSE KINDS OF THINGS, TAIKI.
THANKS FOR THE MEAL.
I'M GLAD YOU EN-JOYED IT.
I MEAN, I ALREADY THOUGHT YOU WOULD.
BUT I FIGURED YOU'RE THE TYPE TO NEVER SHOW IT.
THAT'S JUST...

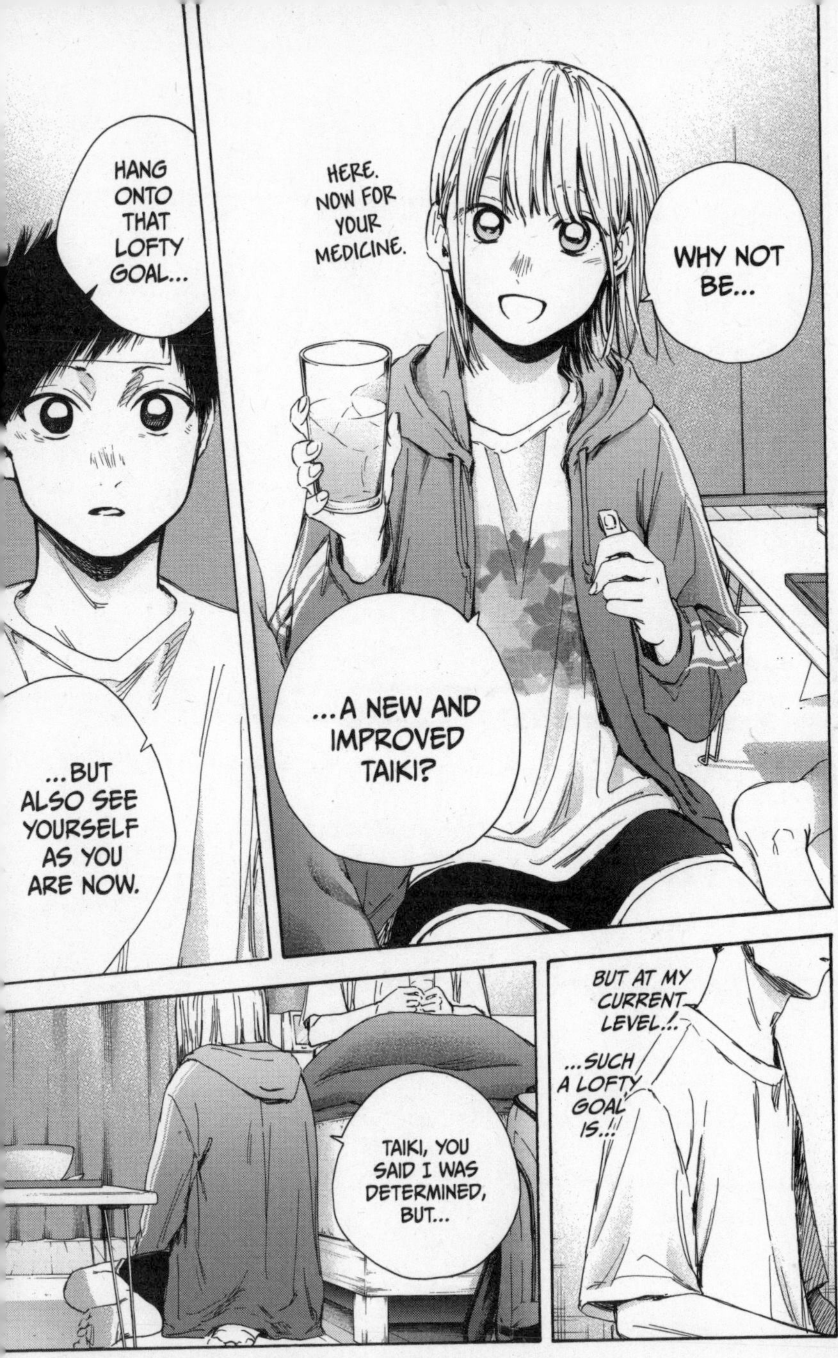
WHY NOT BE...
...A NEW AND IMPROVED TAIKI?
HERE. NOW FOR YOUR MEDICINE.
HANG ONTO THAT LOFTY GOAL...
...BUT ALSO SEE YOURSELF AS YOU ARE NOW.
BUT AT MY CURRENT LEVEL...!
...SUCH A LOFTY GOAL IS...!
TAIKI, YOU SAID I WAS DETERMINED, BUT...

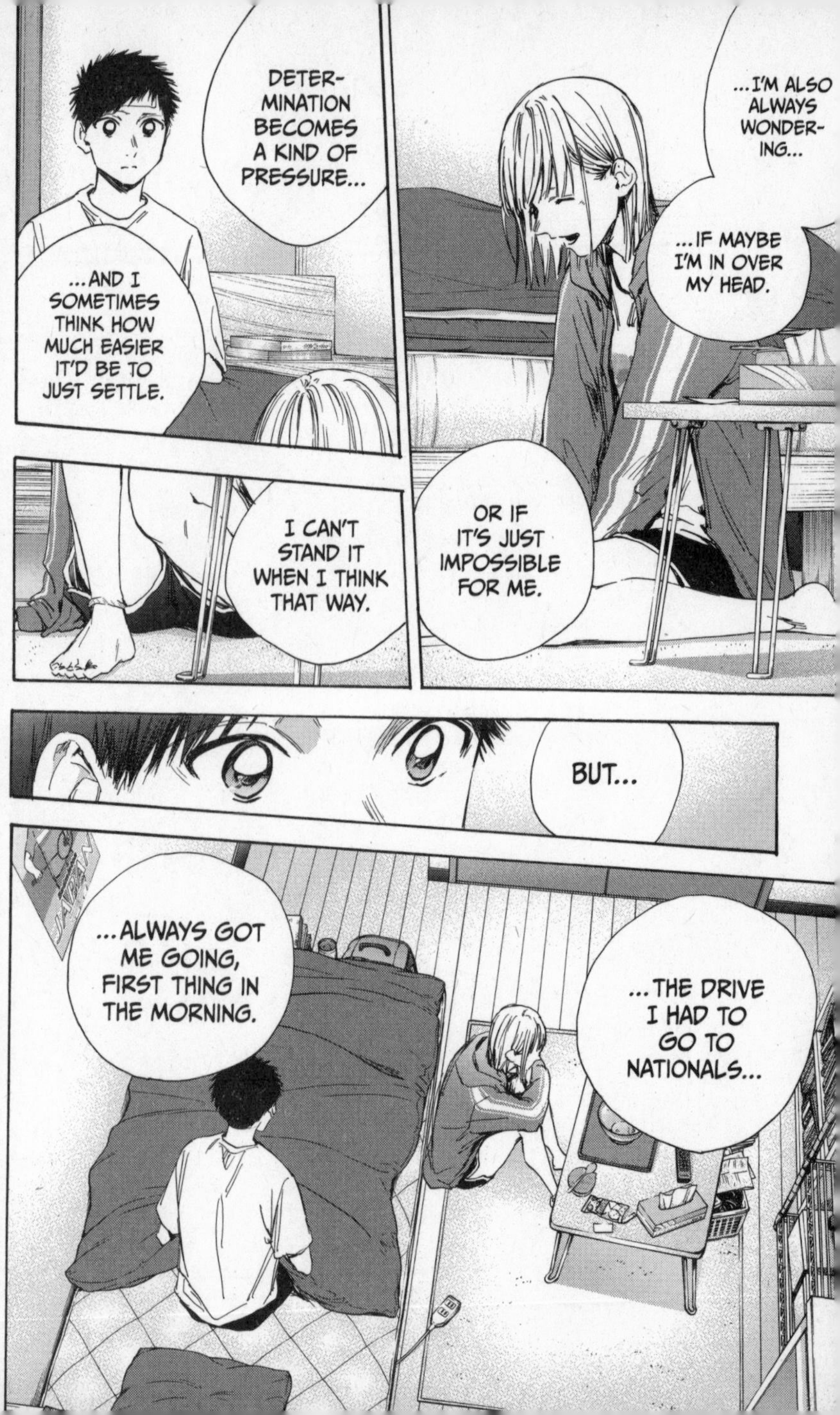
...I'M ALSO ALWAYS WONDERING...
...IF MAYBE I'M IN OVER MY HEAD.
OR IF IT'S JUST IMPOSSIBLE FOR ME.
DETERMINATION BECOMES A KIND OF PRESSURE...
...AND I SOMETIMES THINK HOW MUCH EASIER IT'D BE TO JUST SETTLE.
I CAN'T STAND IT WHEN I THINK THAT WAY.
BUT...
...THE DRIVE I HAD TO GO TO NATIONALS...
...ALWAYS GOT ME GOING, FIRST THING IN THE MORNING.

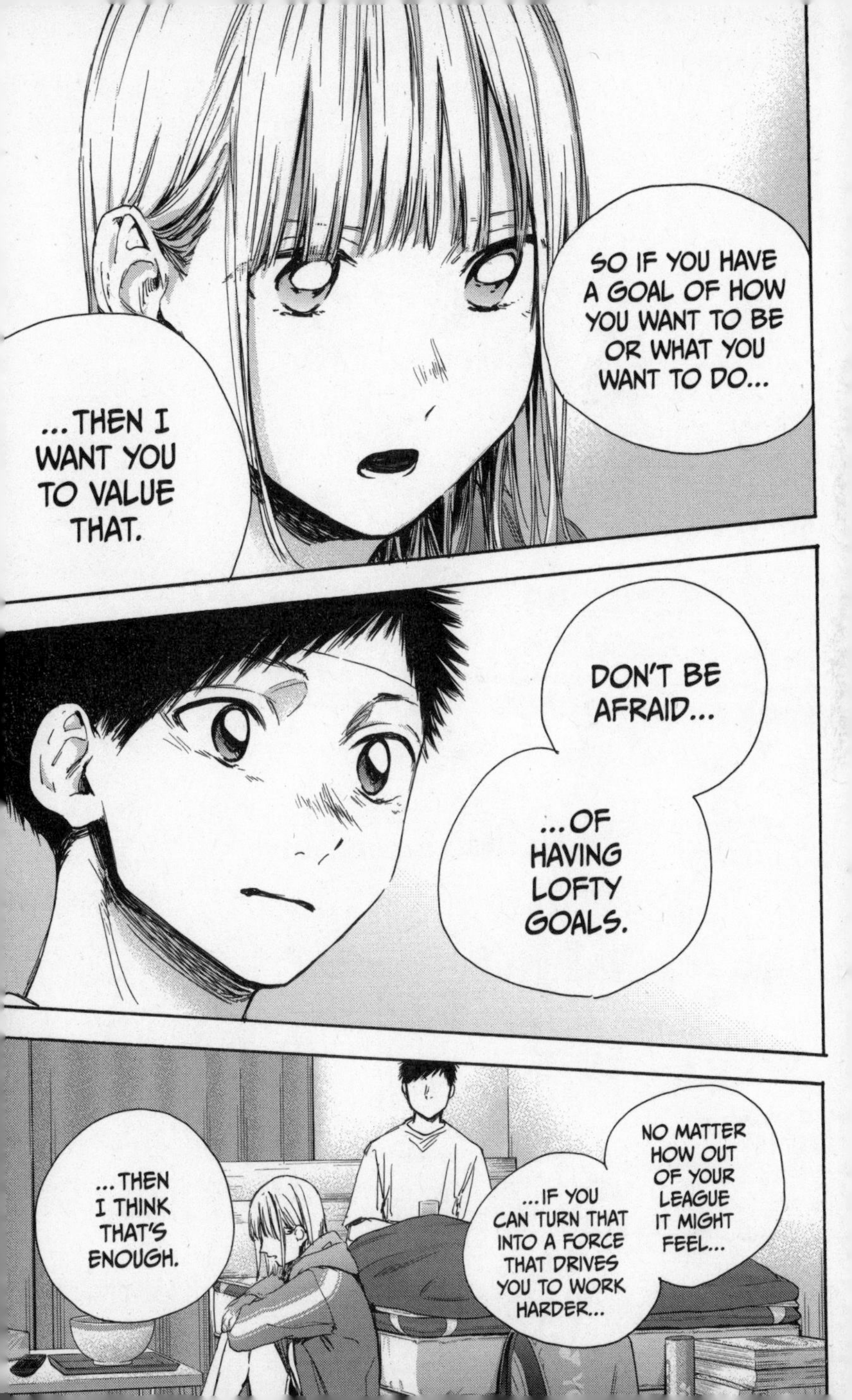
SO IF YOU HAVE A GOAL OF HOW YOU WANT TO BE OR WHAT YOU WANT TO DO...
...THEN I WANT YOU TO VALUE THAT.
DON'T BE AFRAID...
...OF HAVING LOFTY GOALS.
NO MATTER HOW OUT OF YOUR LEAGUE IT MIGHT FEEL...
...IF YOU CAN TURN THAT INTO A FORCE THAT DRIVES YOU TO WORK HARDER...
...THEN I THINK THAT'S ENOUGH.

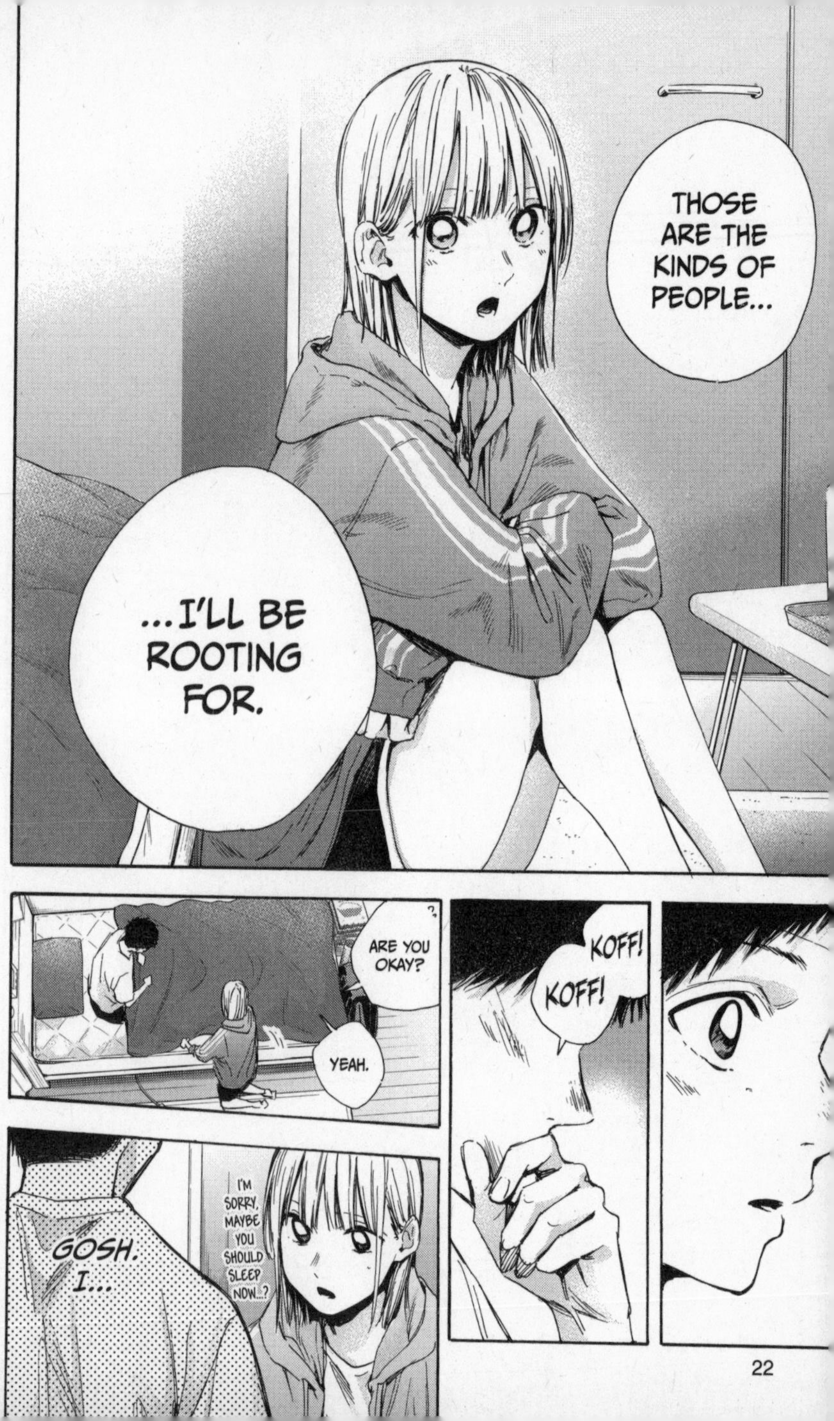
THOSE ARE THE KINDS OF PEOPLE...
...I'LL BE ROOTING FOR.
KOFF!
KOFF!
ARE YOU OKAY?
YEAH.
I'M SORRY, MAYBE YOU SHOULD SLEEP NOW...?
GOSH. I...

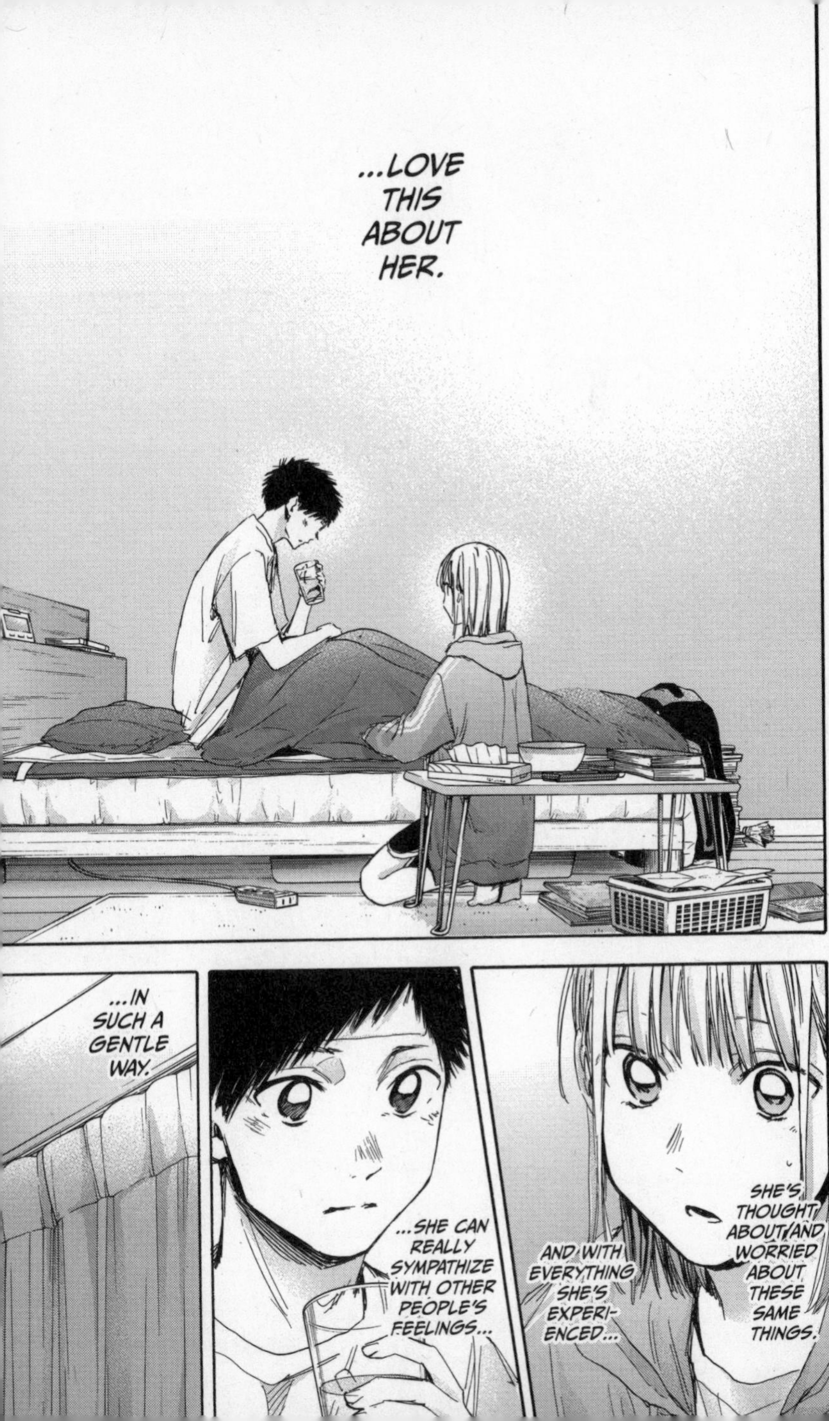
...LOVE THIS ABOUT HER.
SHE'S THOUGHT ABOUT AND WORRIED ABOUT THESE SAME THINGS.
AND WITH EVERYTHING SHE'S EXPERI-ENCED...
...SHE CAN REALLY SYMPATHIZE WITH OTHER PEOPLE'S FEELINGS...
...IN SUCH A GENTLE WAY.

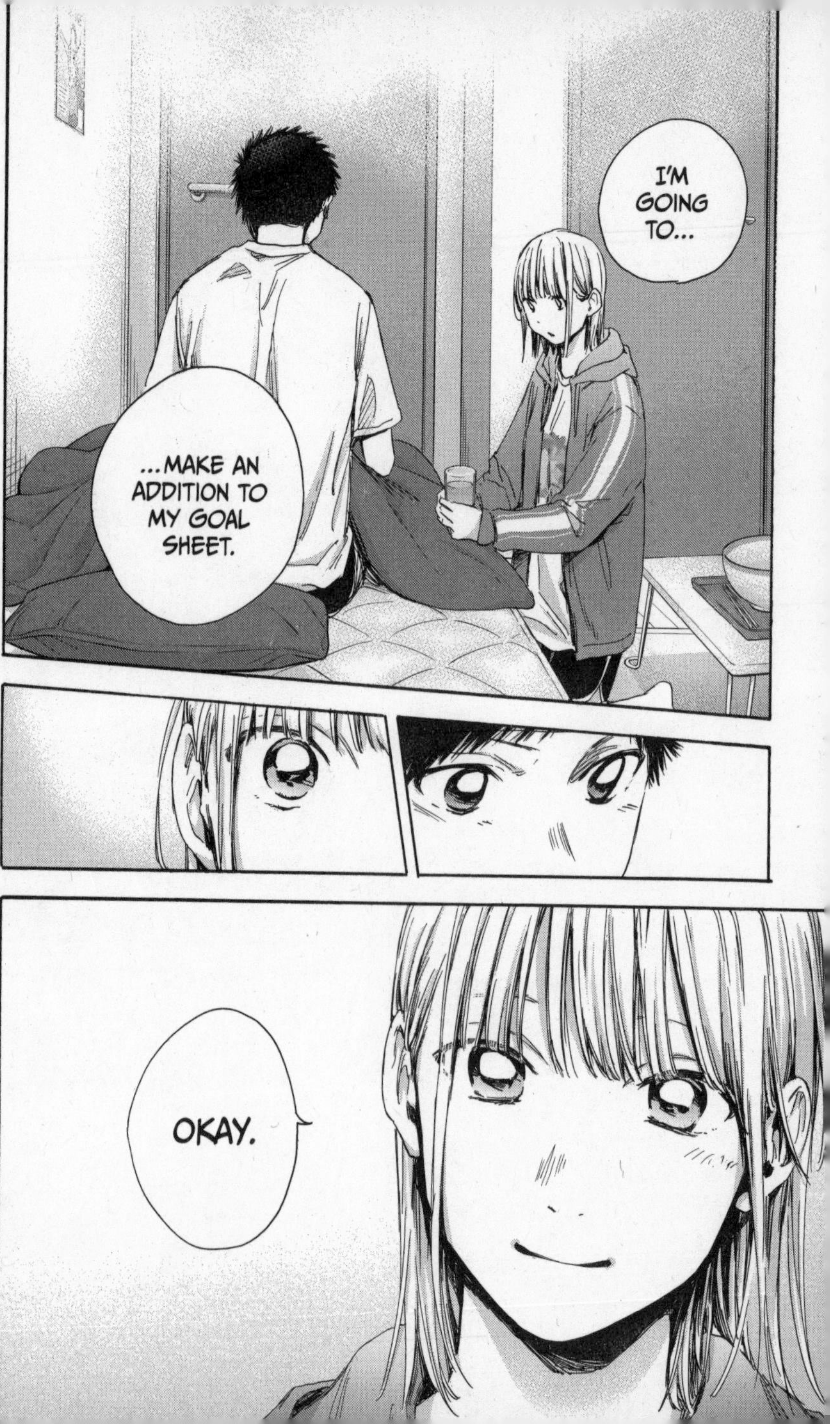
I'M GOING TO...
...MAKE AN ADDITION TO MY GOAL SHEET.
OKAY.

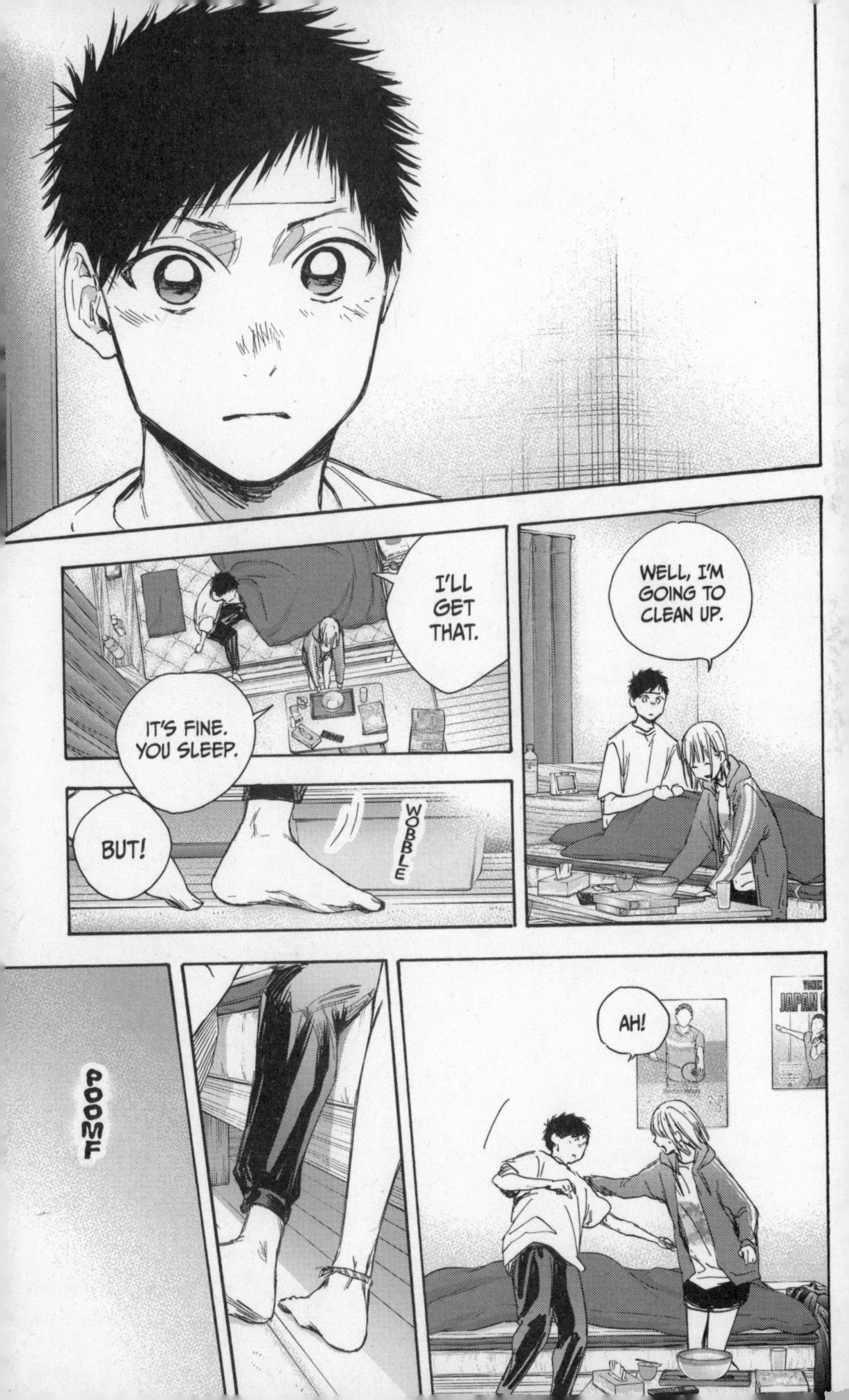
WELL, I'M GOING TO CLEAN UP.
I'LL GET THAT.
IT'S FINE. YOU SLEEP.
BUT!
WOBBLE
AH!
POOMF

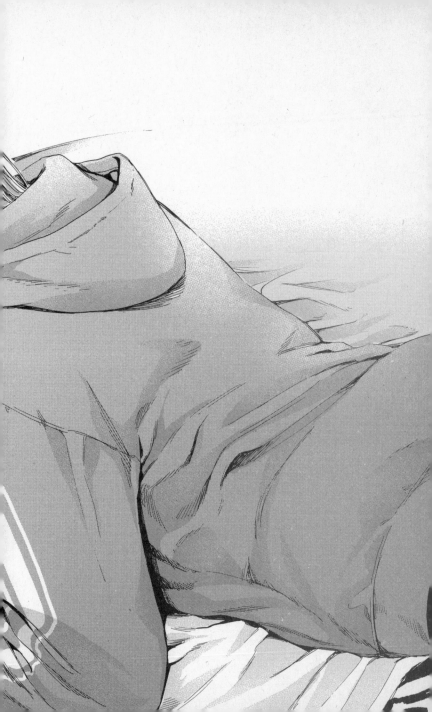

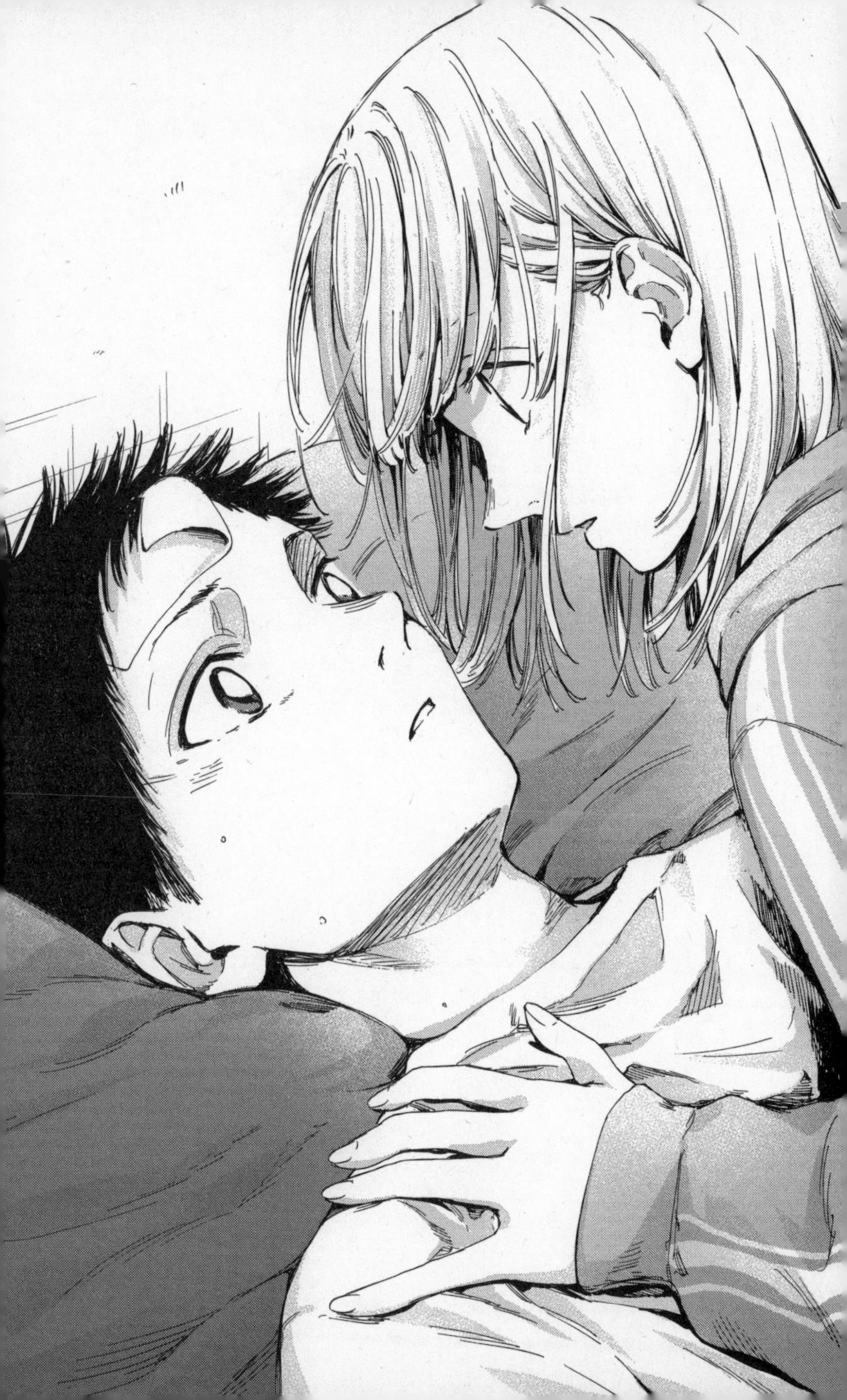

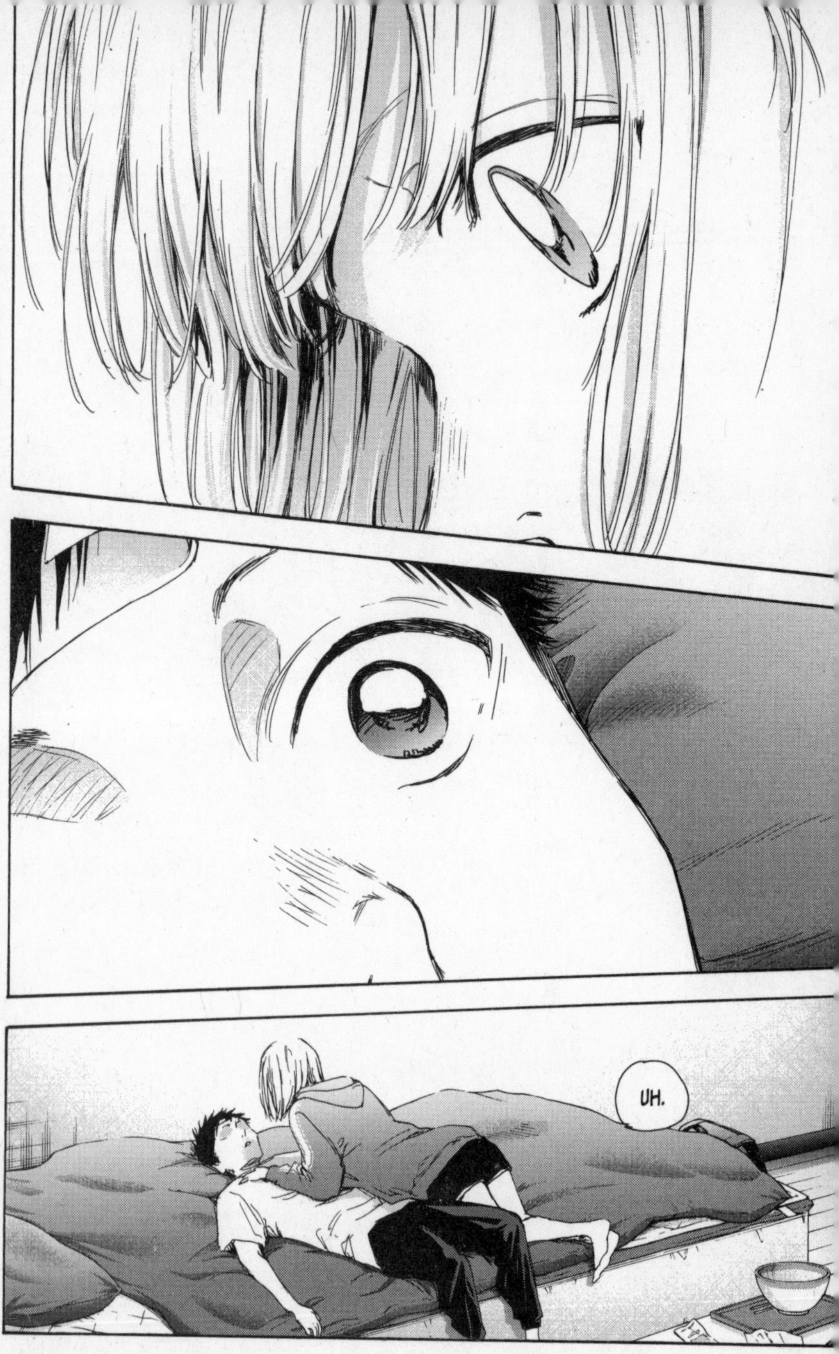
UH.

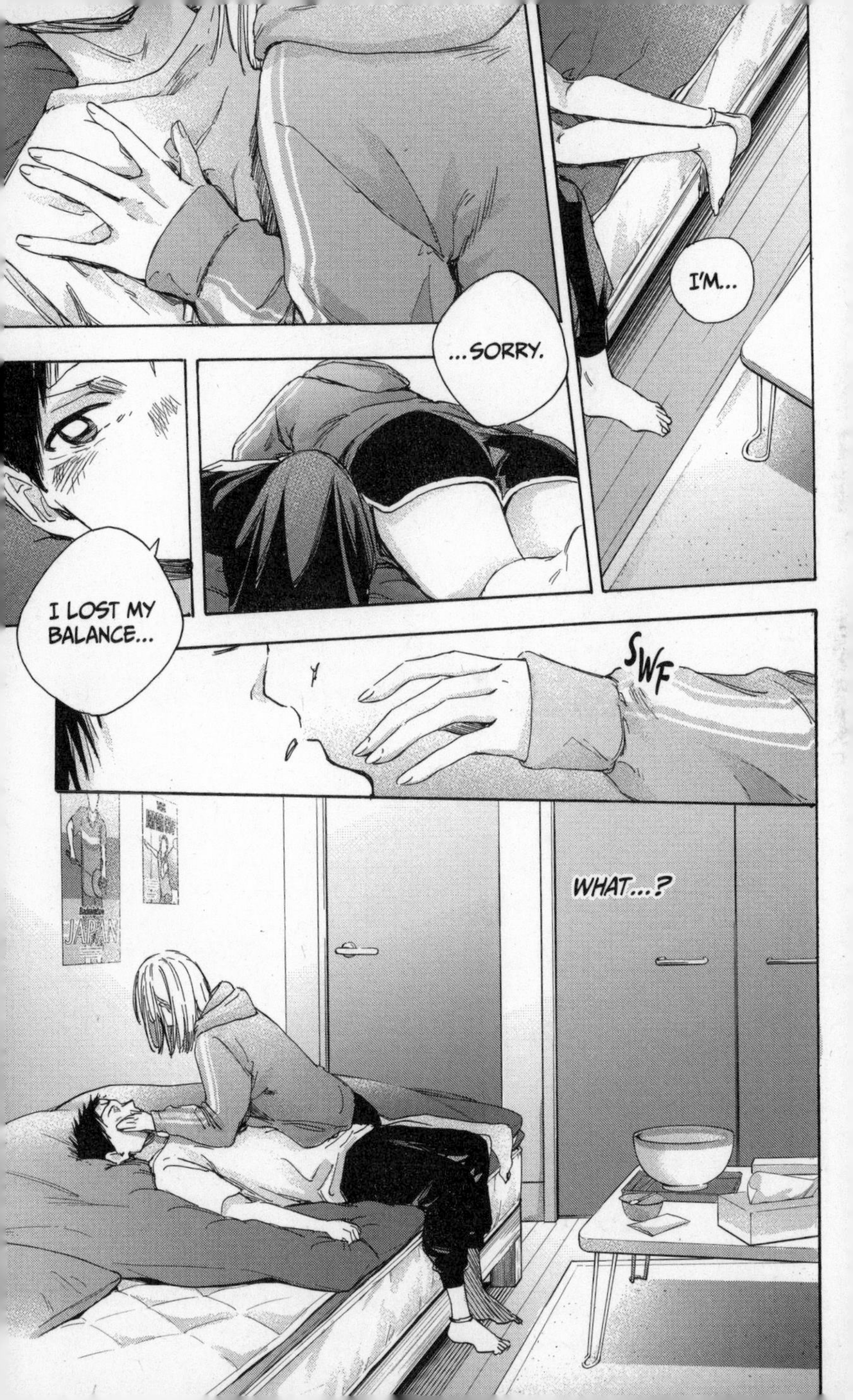
I'M...
...SORRY.
I LOST MY BALANCE...
SWF
WHAT...?
JAPAN

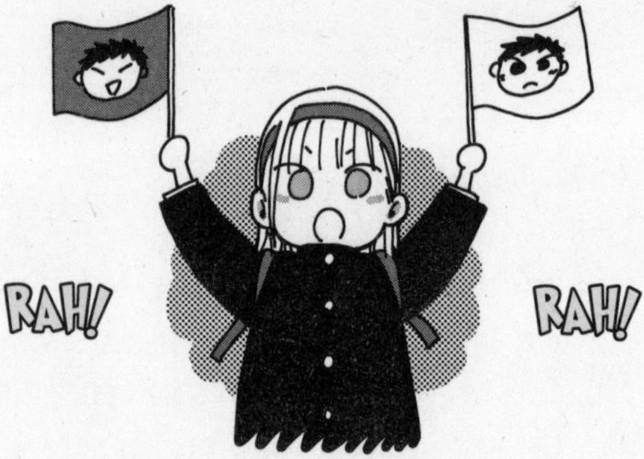
RAH!
RAH!

#27 A Chance

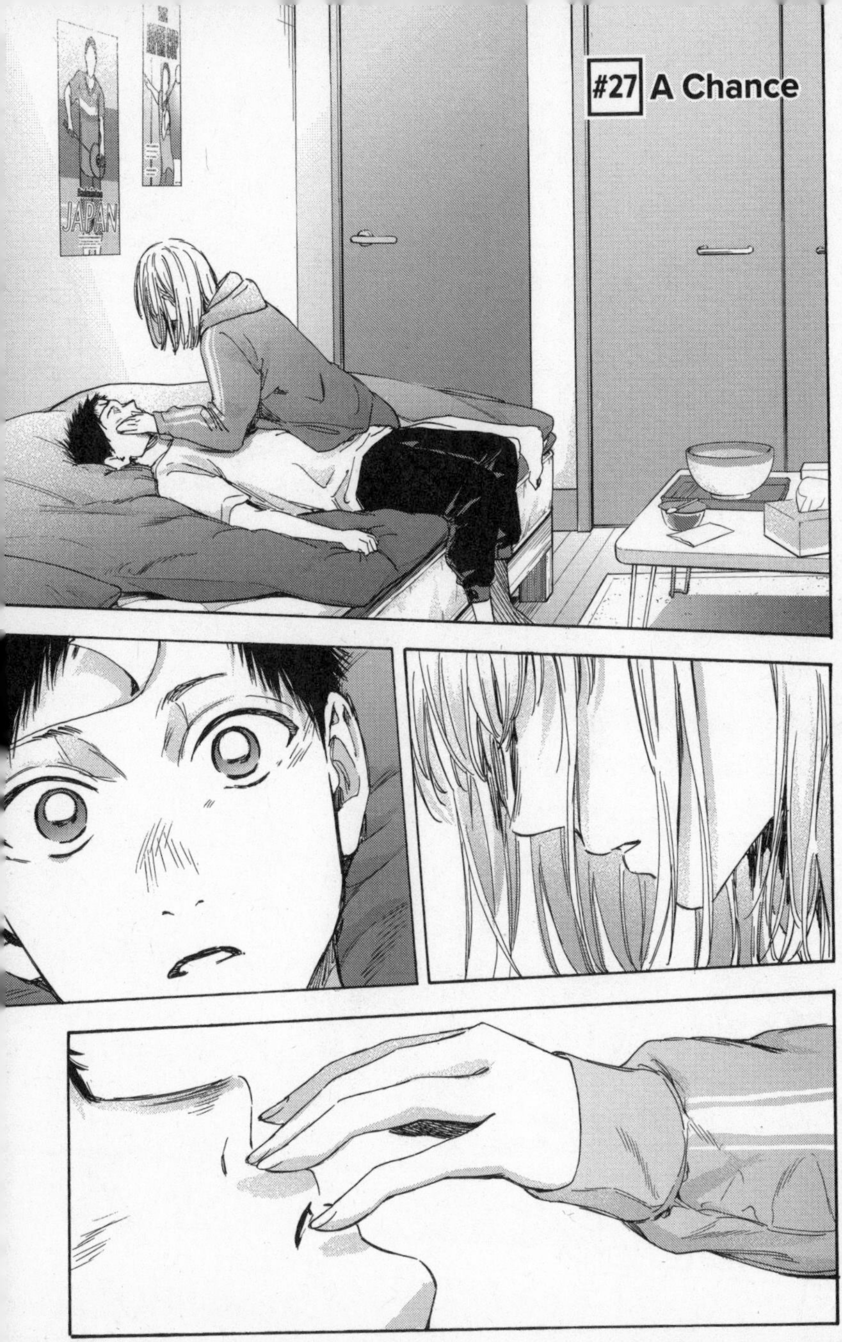
JAPAN

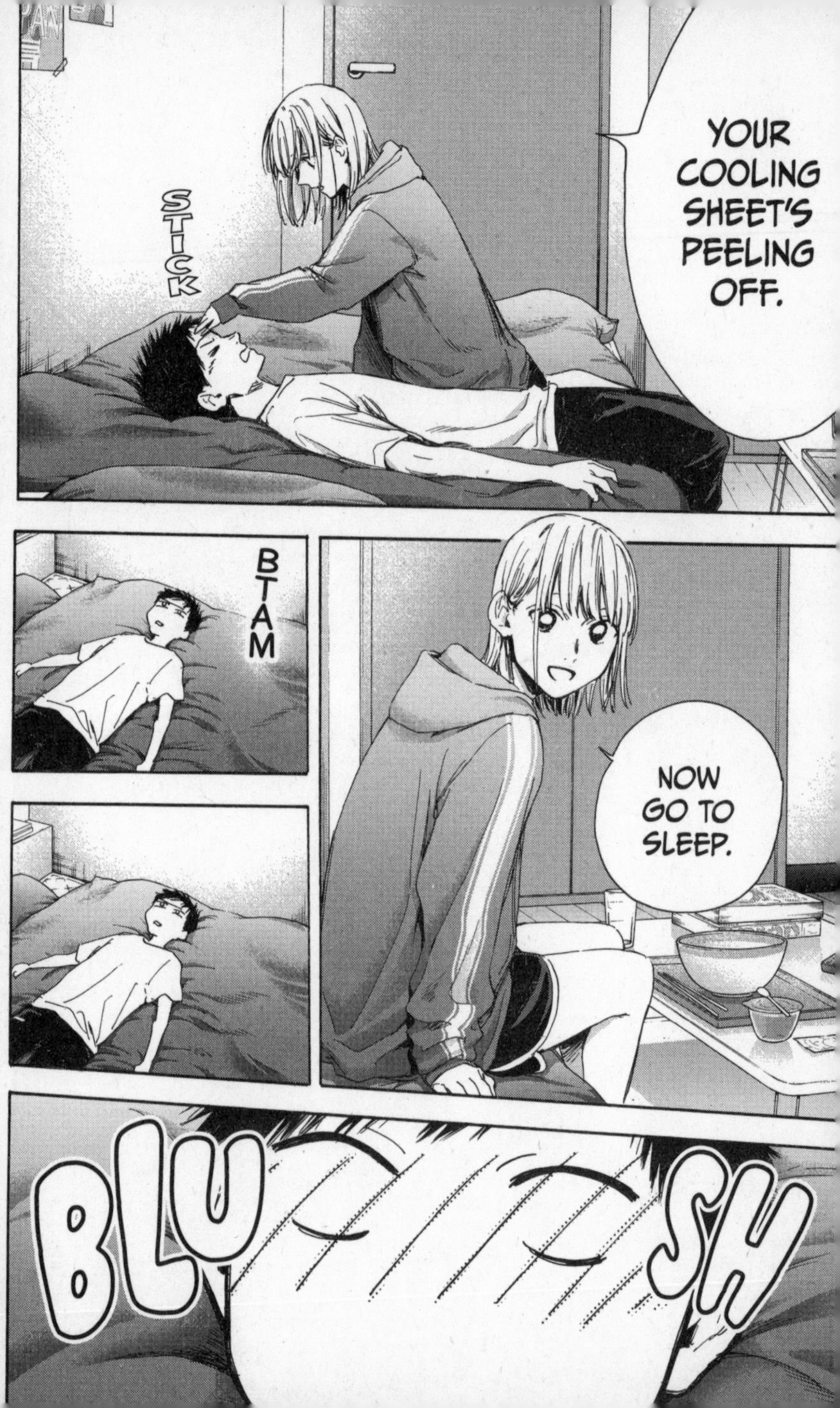
YOUR COOLING SHEET'S PEELING OFF.
STICK
NOW GO TO SLEEP.
BTAM
BLUSH

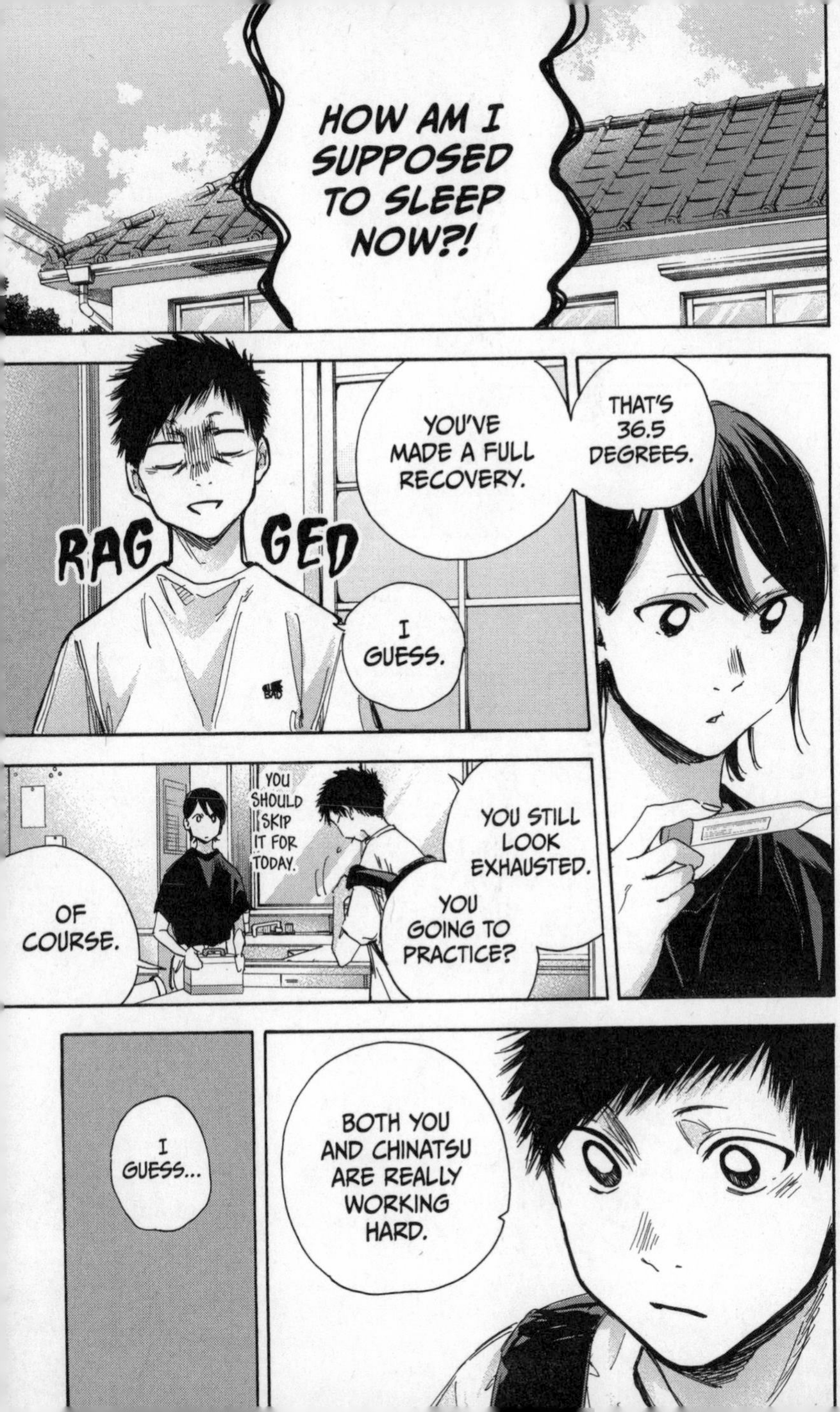
HOW AM I SUPPOSED TO SLEEP NOW?!
THAT'S 36.5 DEGREES.
YOU'VE MADE A FULL RECOVERY.
RAG GED
I GUESS.
YOU STILL LOOK EXHAUSTED.
YOU GOING TO PRACTICE?
YOU SHOULD SKIP IT FOR TODAY.
OF COURSE.
BOTH YOU AND CHINATSU ARE REALLY WORKING HARD.
I GUESS...

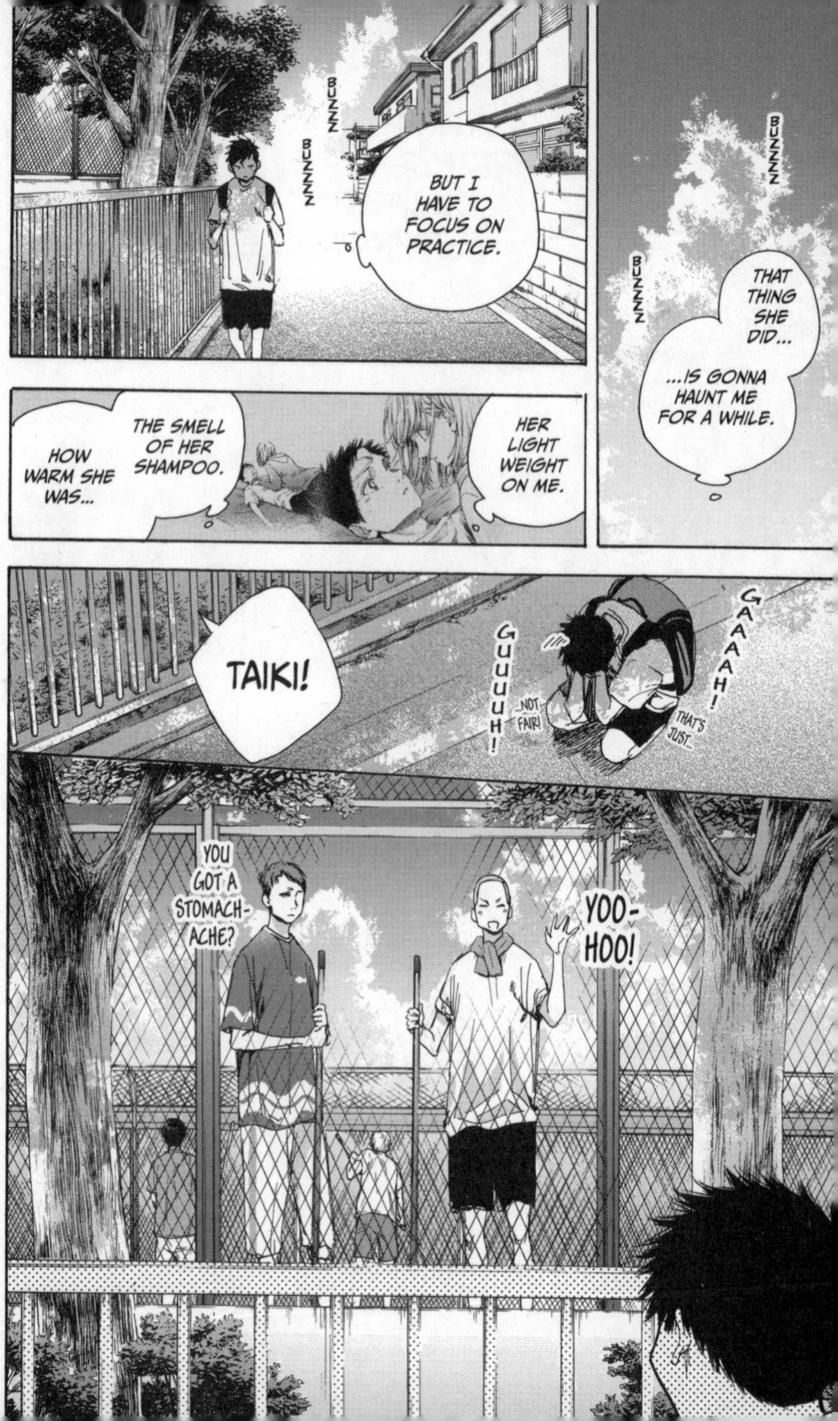
BUZZZ
BUZZZ
THAT THING SHE DID...
...IS GONNA HAUNT ME FOR A WHILE.
BUZZZ
BUZZZ
BUT I HAVE TO FOCUS ON PRACTICE.
HER LIGHT WEIGHT ON ME.
THE SMELL OF HER SHAMPOO.
HOW WARM SHE WAS...
GAAAAH!
THAT'S JUST...
...NOT FAIR!
GUUUUH!
TAIKI!
YOO-HOO!
YOU GOT A STOMACH-ACHE?

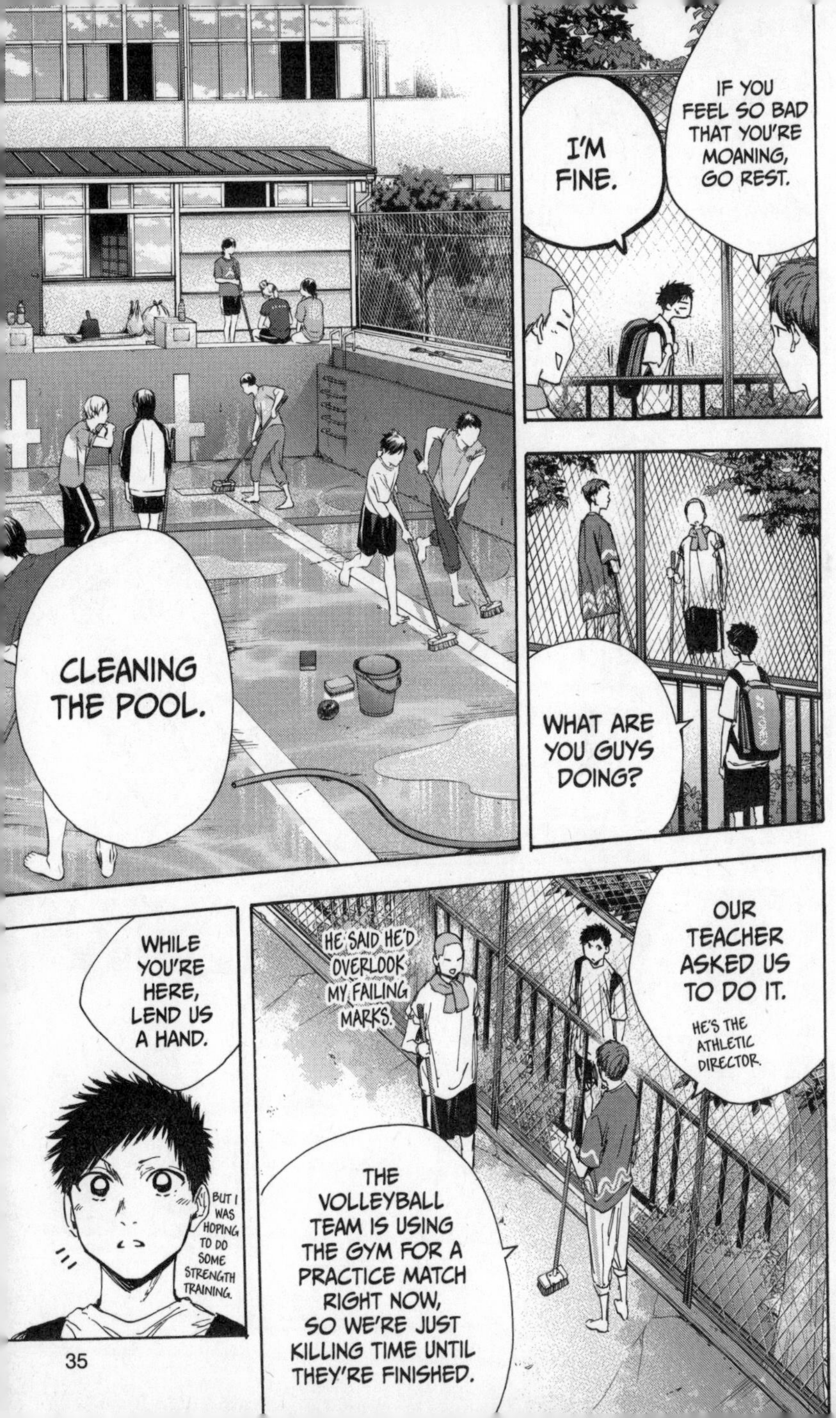
IF YOU FEEL SO BAD THAT YOU'RE MOANING, GO REST.
I'M FINE.
WHAT ARE YOU GUYS DOING?
CLEANING THE POOL.
OUR TEACHER ASKED US TO DO IT.
HE'S THE ATHLETIC DIRECTOR.
HE SAID HE'D OVERLOOK MY FAILING MARKS.
THE VOLLEYBALL TEAM IS USING THE GYM FOR A PRACTICE MATCH RIGHT NOW, SO WE'RE JUST KILLING TIME UNTIL THEY'RE FINISHED.
WHILE YOU'RE HERE, LEND US A HAND.
BUT I WAS HOPING TO DO SOME STRENGTH TRAINING.

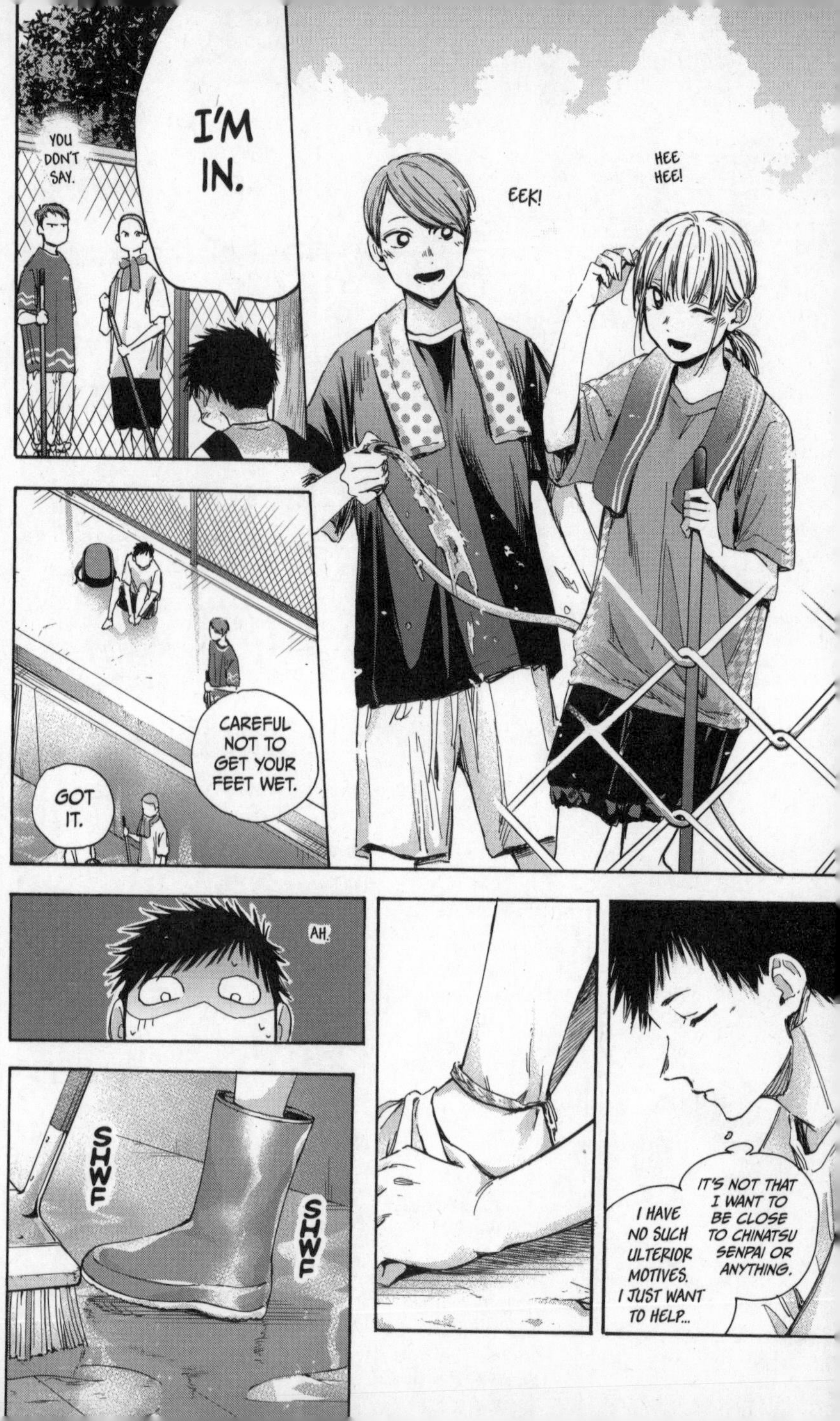
HEE HEE!
EEK!
I'M IN.
YOU DON'T SAY.
CAREFUL NOT TO GET YOUR FEET WET.
GOT IT.
IT'S NOT THAT I WANT TO BE CLOSE TO CHINATSU SENPAI OR ANYTHING.
I HAVE NO SUCH ULTERIOR MOTIVES. I JUST WANT TO HELP...
AH.
SHWF
SHWF

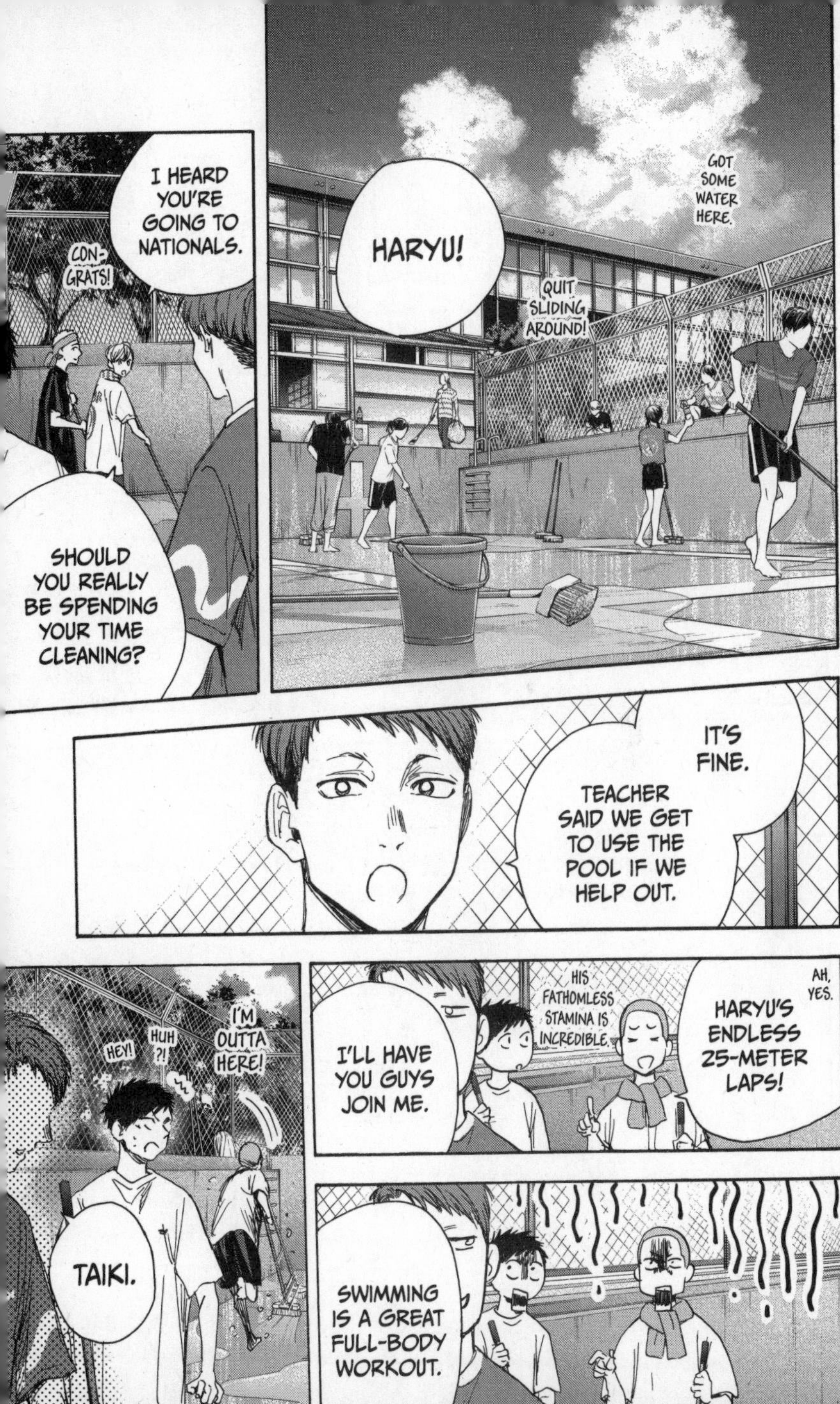
GOT SOME WATER HERE.
QUIT SLIDING AROUND!
HARYU!
I HEARD YOU'RE GOING TO NATIONALS.
CON-GRATS!
SHOULD YOU REALLY BE SPENDING YOUR TIME CLEANING?
IT'S FINE.
TEACHER SAID WE GET TO USE THE POOL IF WE HELP OUT.
AH, YES.
HARYU'S ENDLESS 25-METER LAPS!
HIS FATHOMLESS STAMINA IS INCREDIBLE.
I'LL HAVE YOU GUYS JOIN ME.
SWIMMING IS A GREAT FULL-BODY WORKOUT.
TAIKI.
I'M OUTTA HERE!
HUH ?!
HEY!

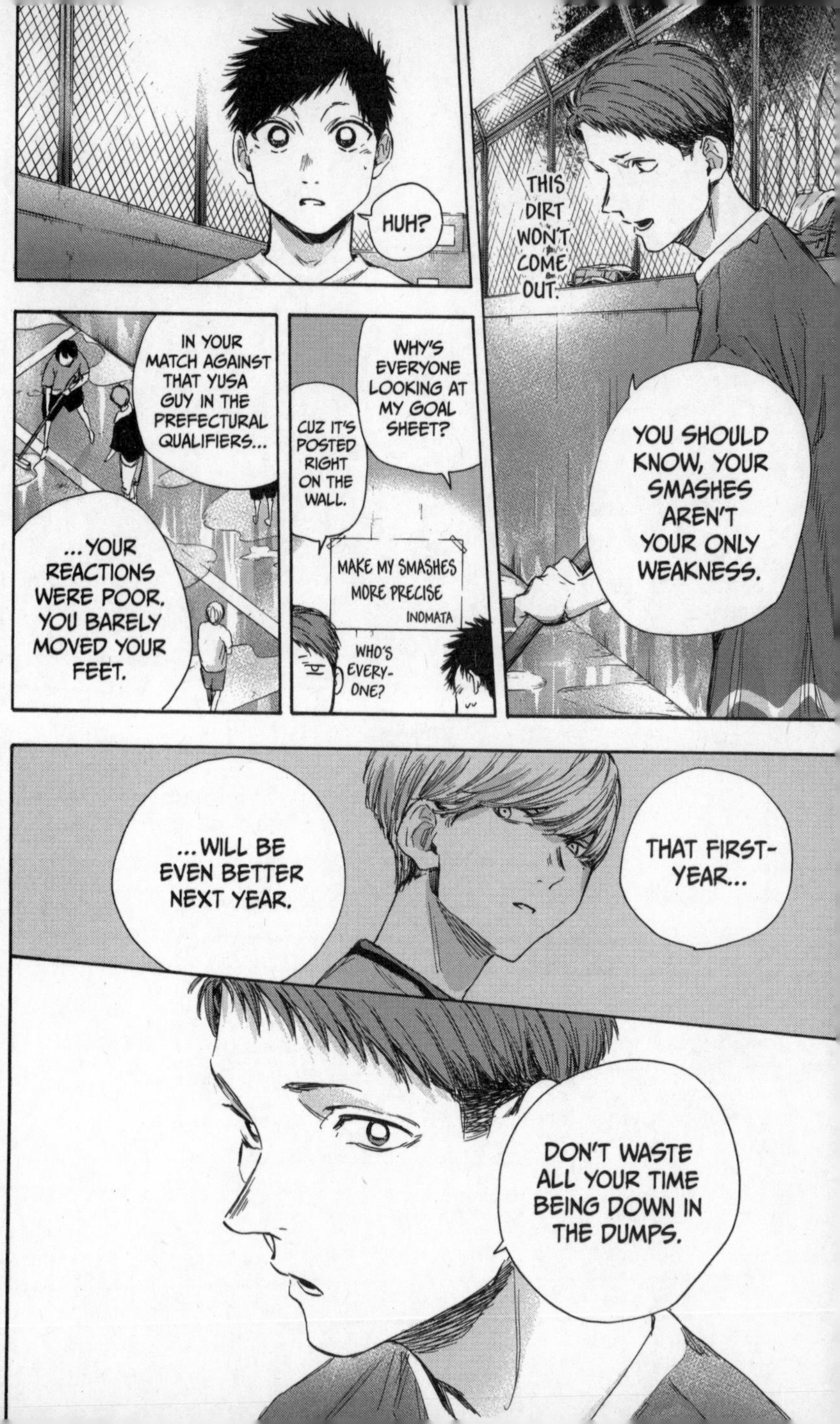
THIS DIRT WON'T COME OUT.
HUH?
YOU SHOULD KNOW, YOUR SMASHES AREN'T YOUR ONLY WEAKNESS.
WHY'S EVERYONE LOOKING AT MY GOAL SHEET?
CUZ IT'S POSTED RIGHT ON THE WALL.
MAKE MY SMASHES MORE PRECISE
INOMATA
WHO'S EVERYONE?
IN YOUR MATCH AGAINST THAT YUSA GUY IN THE PREFECTURAL QUALIFIERS...
...YOUR REACTIONS WERE POOR. YOU BARELY MOVED YOUR FEET.
THAT FIRST-YEAR...
...WILL BE EVEN BETTER NEXT YEAR.
DON'T WASTE ALL YOUR TIME BEING DOWN IN THE DUMPS.

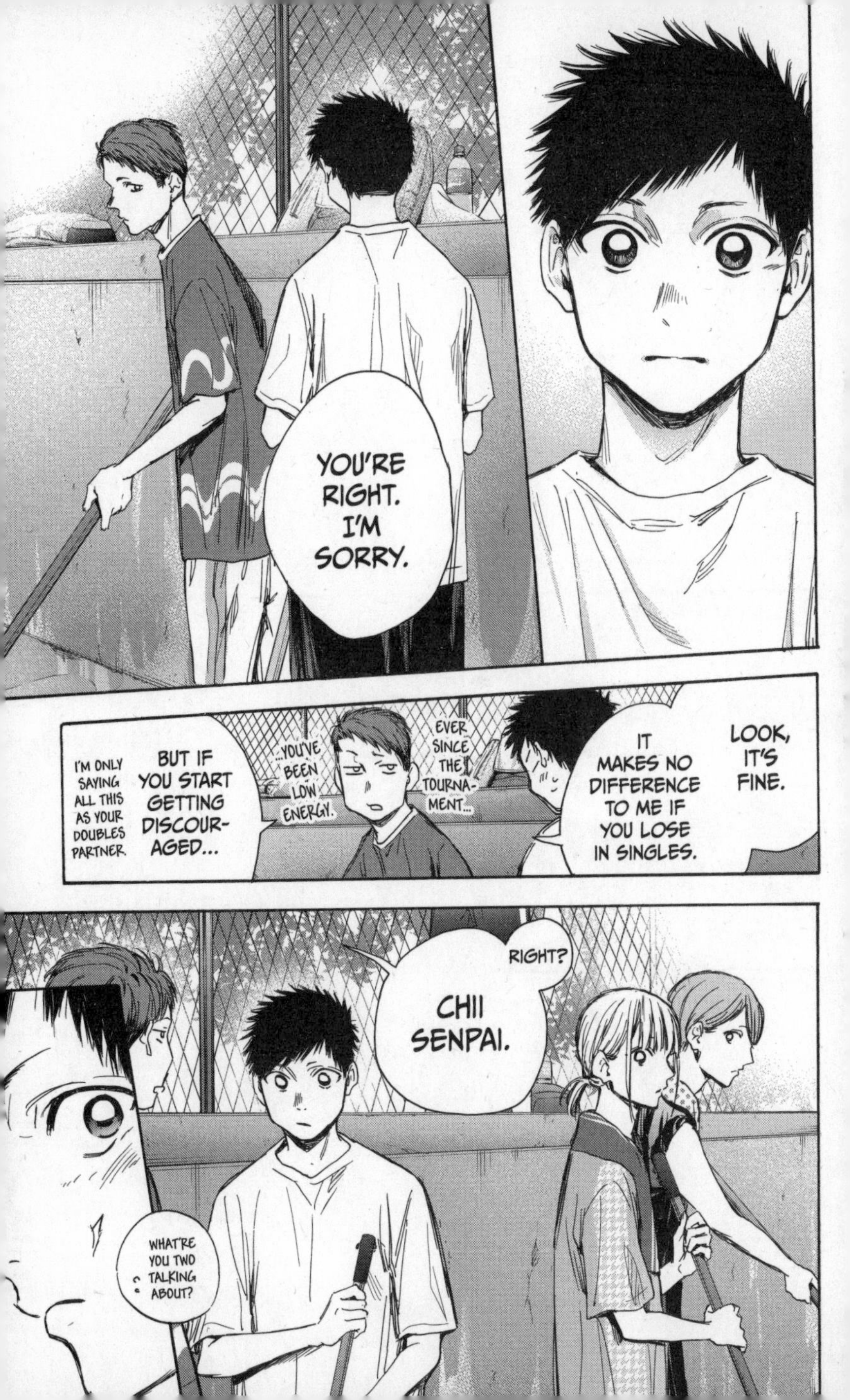
YOU'RE RIGHT. I'M SORRY.
LOOK, IT'S FINE.
IT MAKES NO DIFFERENCE TO ME IF YOU LOSE IN SINGLES.
EVER SINCE THE TOURNAMENT...
...YOU'VE BEEN LOW ENERGY.
BUT IF YOU START GETTING DISCOURAGED...
I'M ONLY SAYING ALL THIS AS YOUR DOUBLES PARTNER.
RIGHT?
CHII SENPAI.
WHAT'RE YOU TWO TALKING ABOUT?

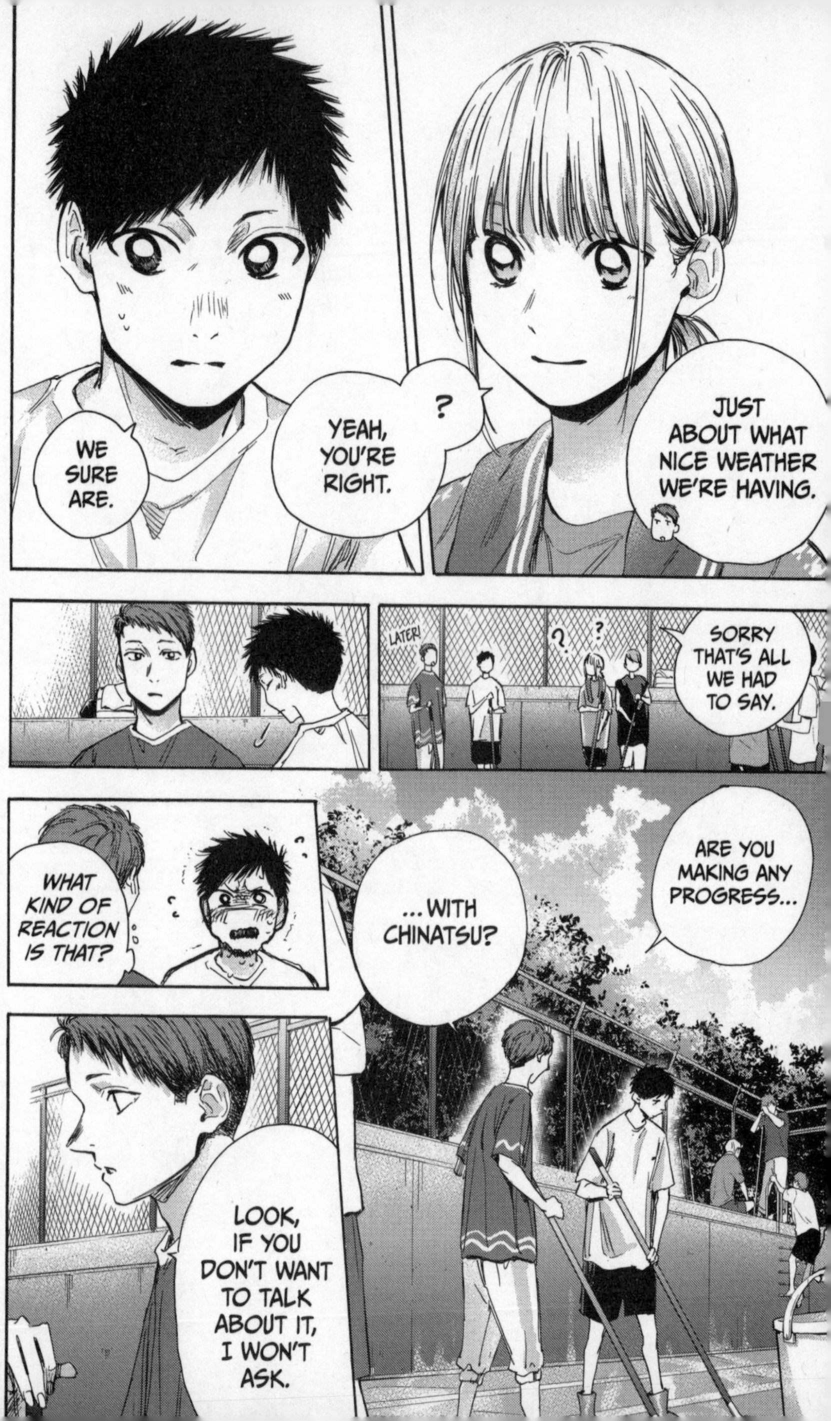
JUST ABOUT WHAT NICE WEATHER WE'RE HAVING.
?
YEAH, YOU'RE RIGHT.
WE SURE ARE.
SORRY THAT'S ALL WE HAD TO SAY.
? ?
LATER!
ARE YOU MAKING ANY PROGRESS...
...WITH CHINATSU?
WHAT KIND OF REACTION IS THAT?
LOOK, IF YOU DON'T WANT TO TALK ABOUT IT, I WON'T ASK.

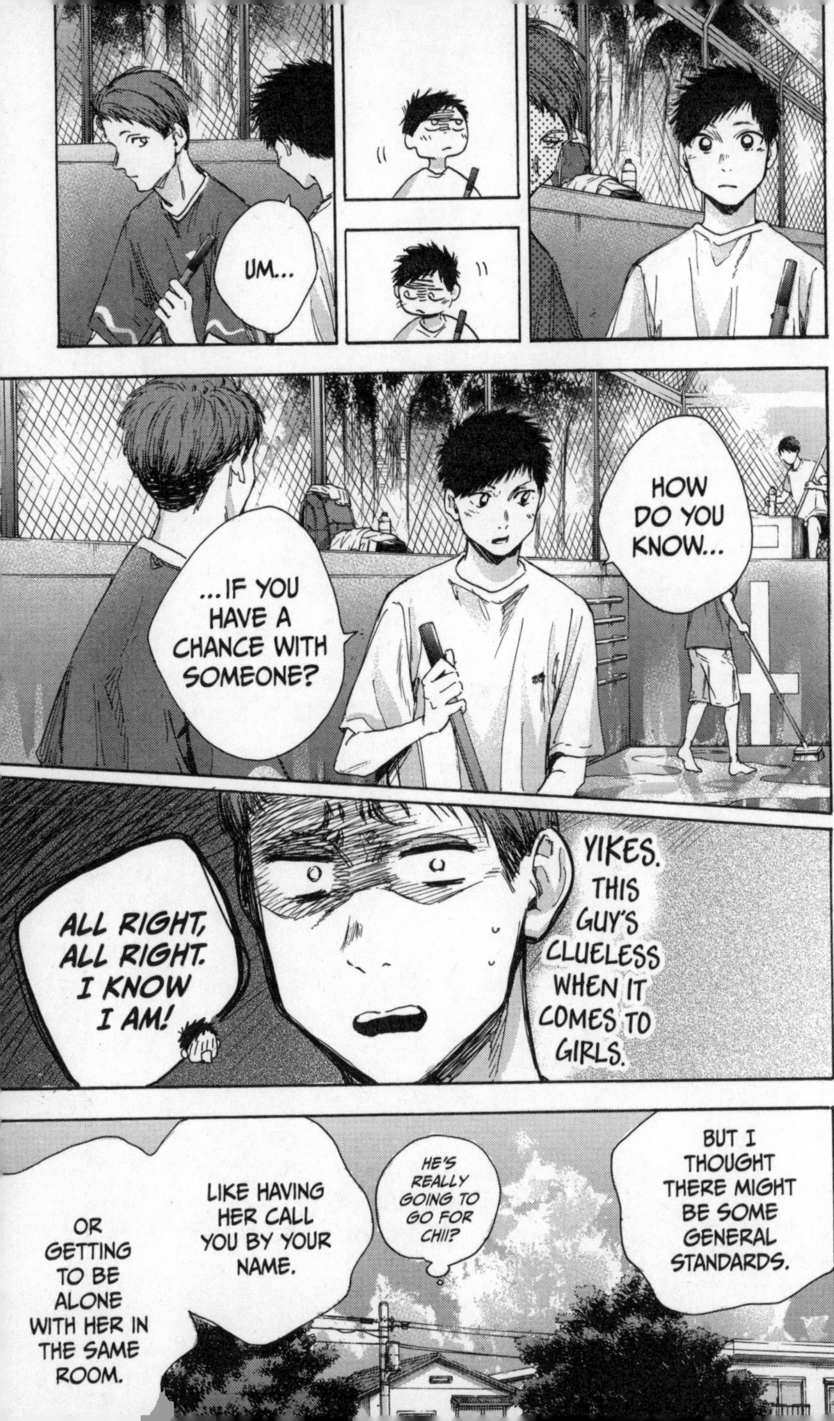
UM...
HOW DO YOU KNOW...
...IF YOU HAVE A CHANCE WITH SOMEONE?
YIKES. THIS GUY'S CLUELESS WHEN IT COMES TO GIRLS.
ALL RIGHT, ALL RIGHT. I KNOW I AM!
BUT I THOUGHT THERE MIGHT BE SOME GENERAL STANDARDS.
HE'S REALLY GOING TO GO FOR CHII?
LIKE HAVING HER CALL YOU BY YOUR NAME.
OR GETTING TO BE ALONE WITH HER IN THE SAME ROOM.

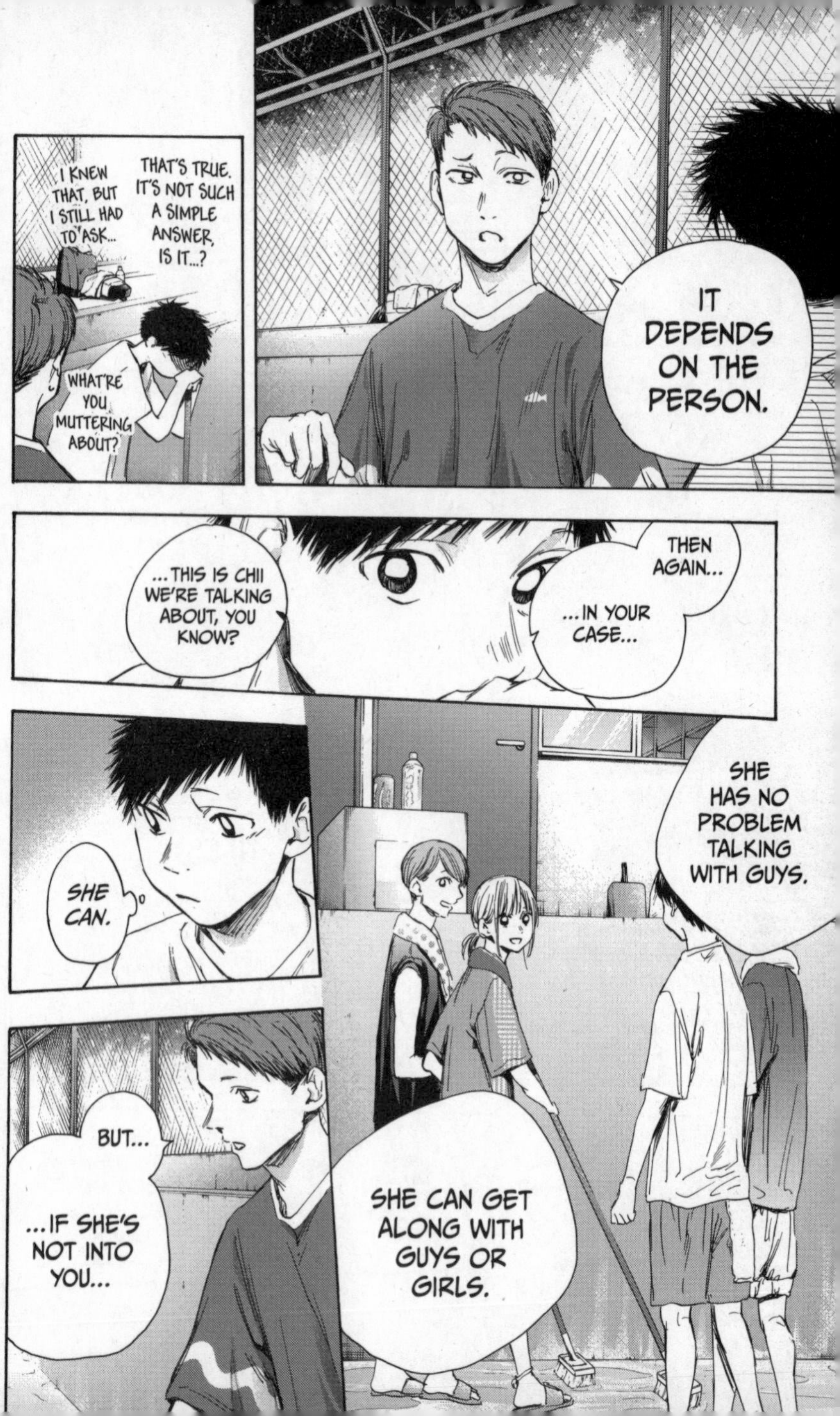
IT DEPENDS ON THE PERSON.
THAT'S TRUE. IT'S NOT SUCH A SIMPLE ANSWER, IS IT...?
I KNEW THAT, BUT I STILL HAD TO ASK...
WHAT'RE YOU MUTTERING ABOUT?
THEN AGAIN...
...IN YOUR CASE...
...THIS IS CHII WE'RE TALKING ABOUT, YOU KNOW?
SHE HAS NO PROBLEM TALKING WITH GUYS.
SHE CAN.
SHE CAN GET ALONG WITH GUYS OR GIRLS.
BUT...
...IF SHE'S NOT INTO YOU...

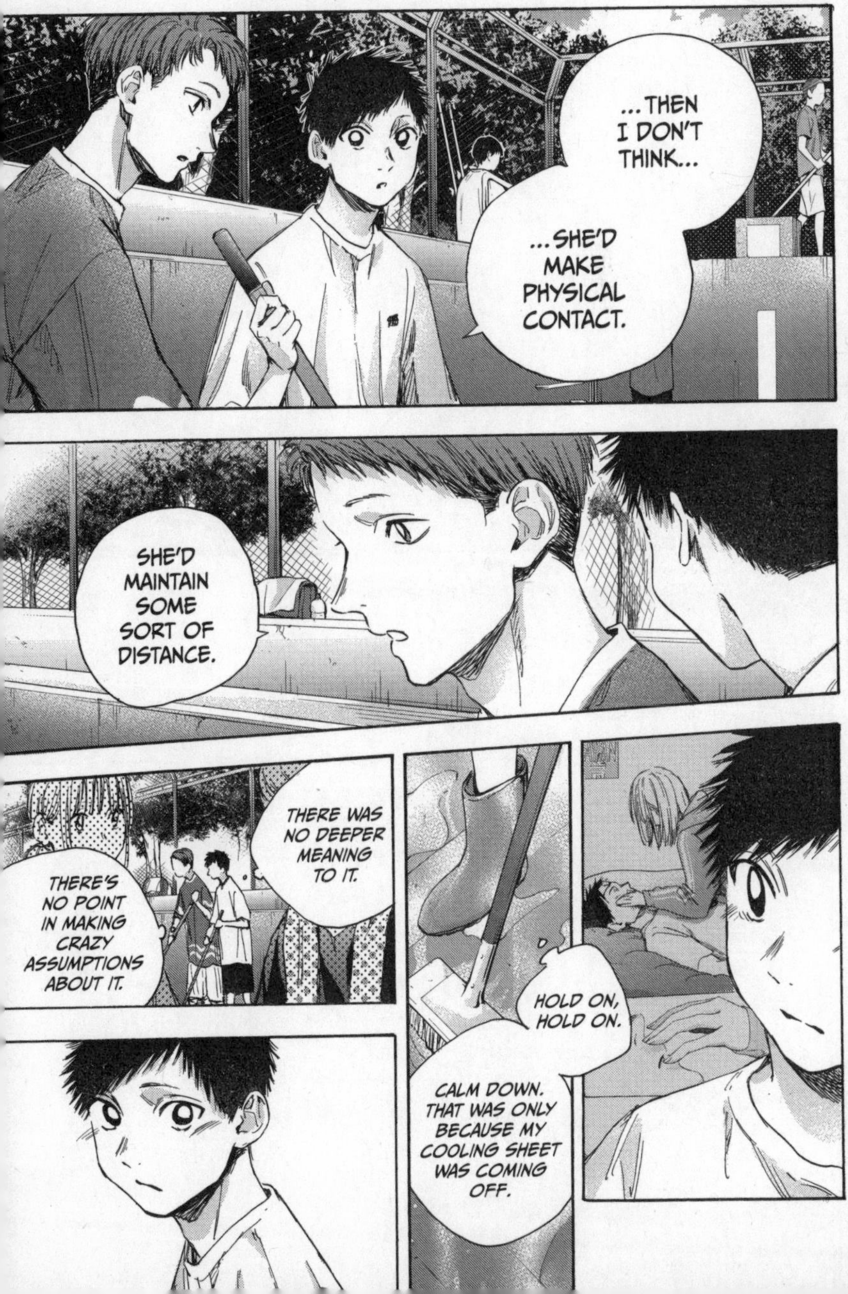
...THEN I DON'T THINK...
...SHE'D MAKE PHYSICAL CONTACT.
SHE'D MAINTAIN SOME SORT OF DISTANCE.
HOLD ON, HOLD ON.
CALM DOWN. THAT WAS ONLY BECAUSE MY COOLING SHEET WAS COMING OFF.
THERE WAS NO DEEPER MEANING TO IT.
THERE'S NO POINT IN MAKING CRAZY ASSUMPTIONS ABOUT IT.

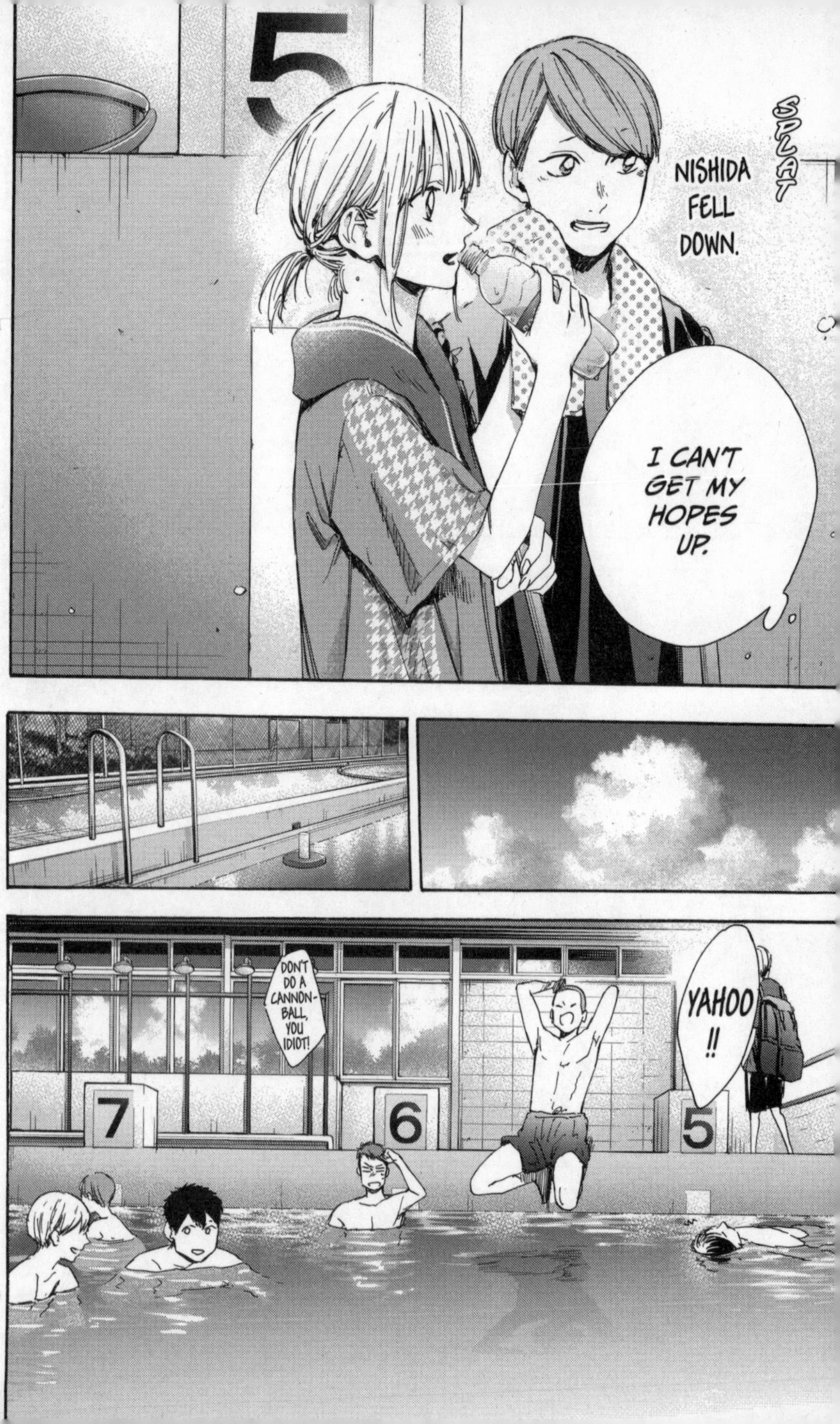
SPLAT
NISHIDA FELL DOWN.
I CAN'T GET MY HOPES UP.
YAHOO!!
DON'T DO A CANNON-BALL, YOU IDIOT!
5
7
6
5

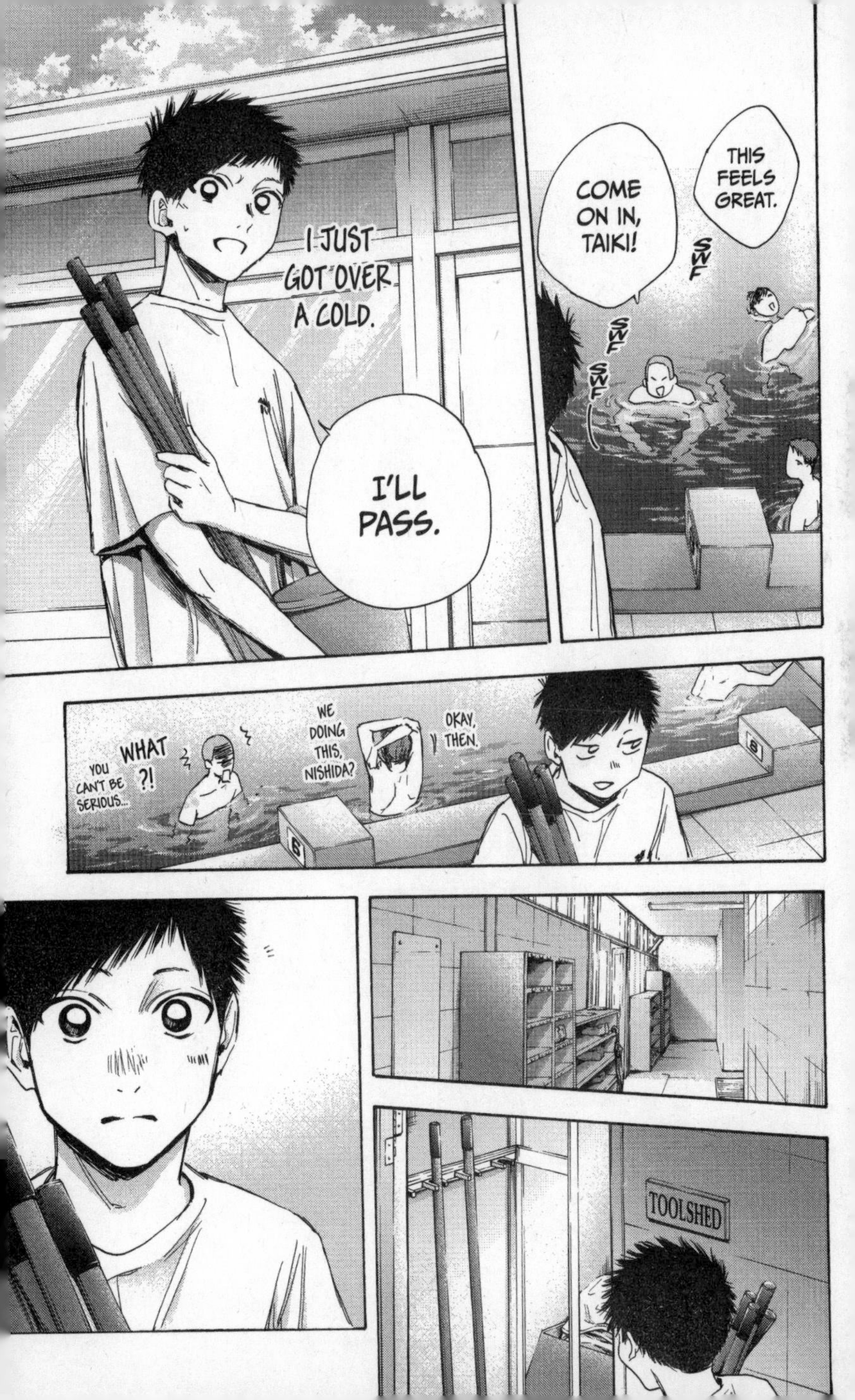
THIS FEELS GREAT.
COME ON IN, TAIKI!
SWF
SWF
SWF
I JUST GOT OVER A COLD.
I'LL PASS.
OKAY, THEN.
WE DOING THIS, NISHIDA?
WHAT ?!
YOU CAN'T BE SERIOUS...
TOOLSHED

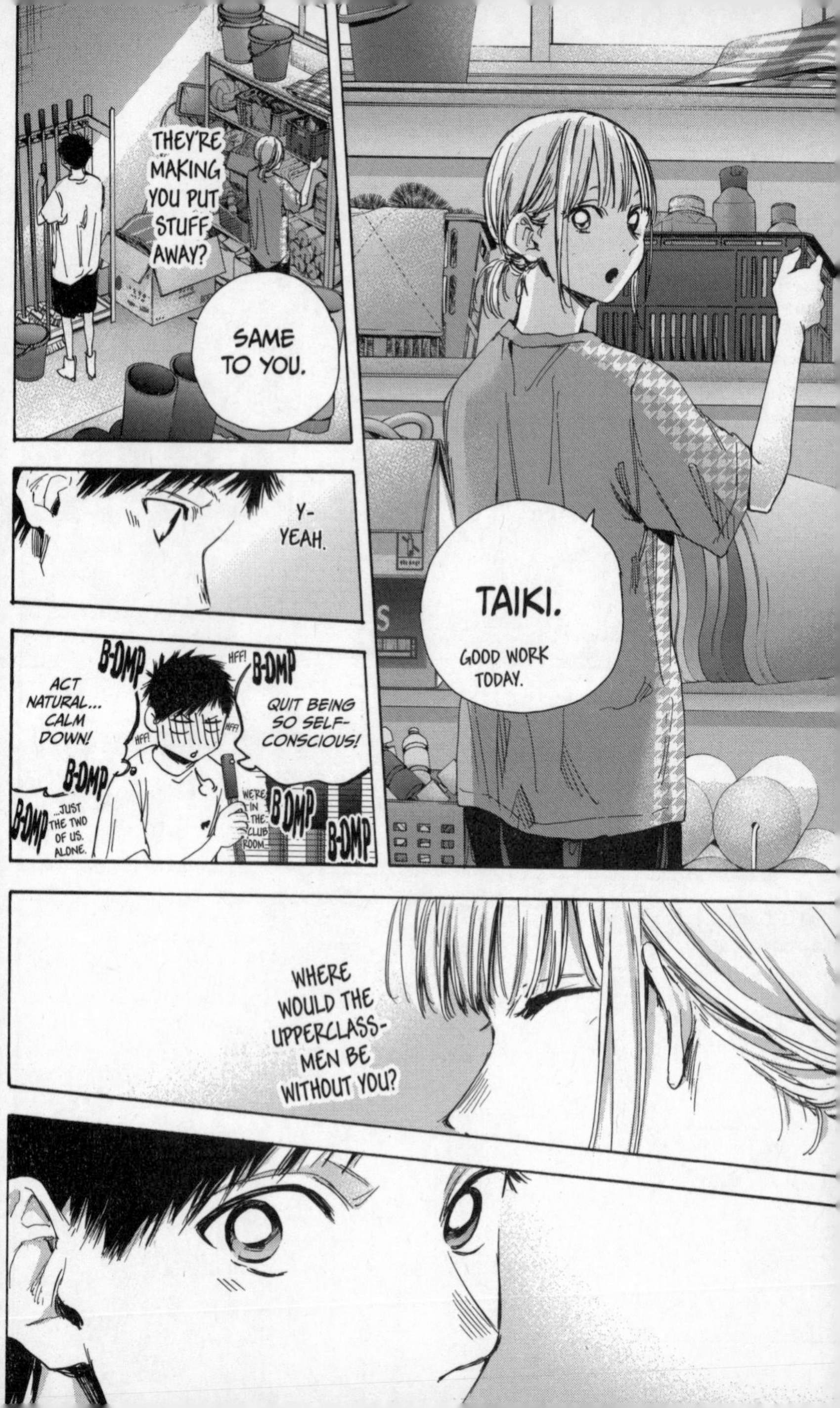
TAIKI.
GOOD WORK TODAY.
THEY'RE MAKING YOU PUT STUFF AWAY?
SAME TO YOU.
Y-YEAH.
B-DMP
HFF!
B-DMP
QUIT BEING SO SELF-CONSCIOUS!
ACT NATURAL... CALM DOWN!
HFF!
HFF!
B-DMP
WE'RE IN THE CLUB ROOM
B-DMP
B-DMP
B-DMP
...JUST THE TWO OF US. ALONE.
WHERE WOULD THE UPPERCLASSMEN BE WITHOUT YOU?

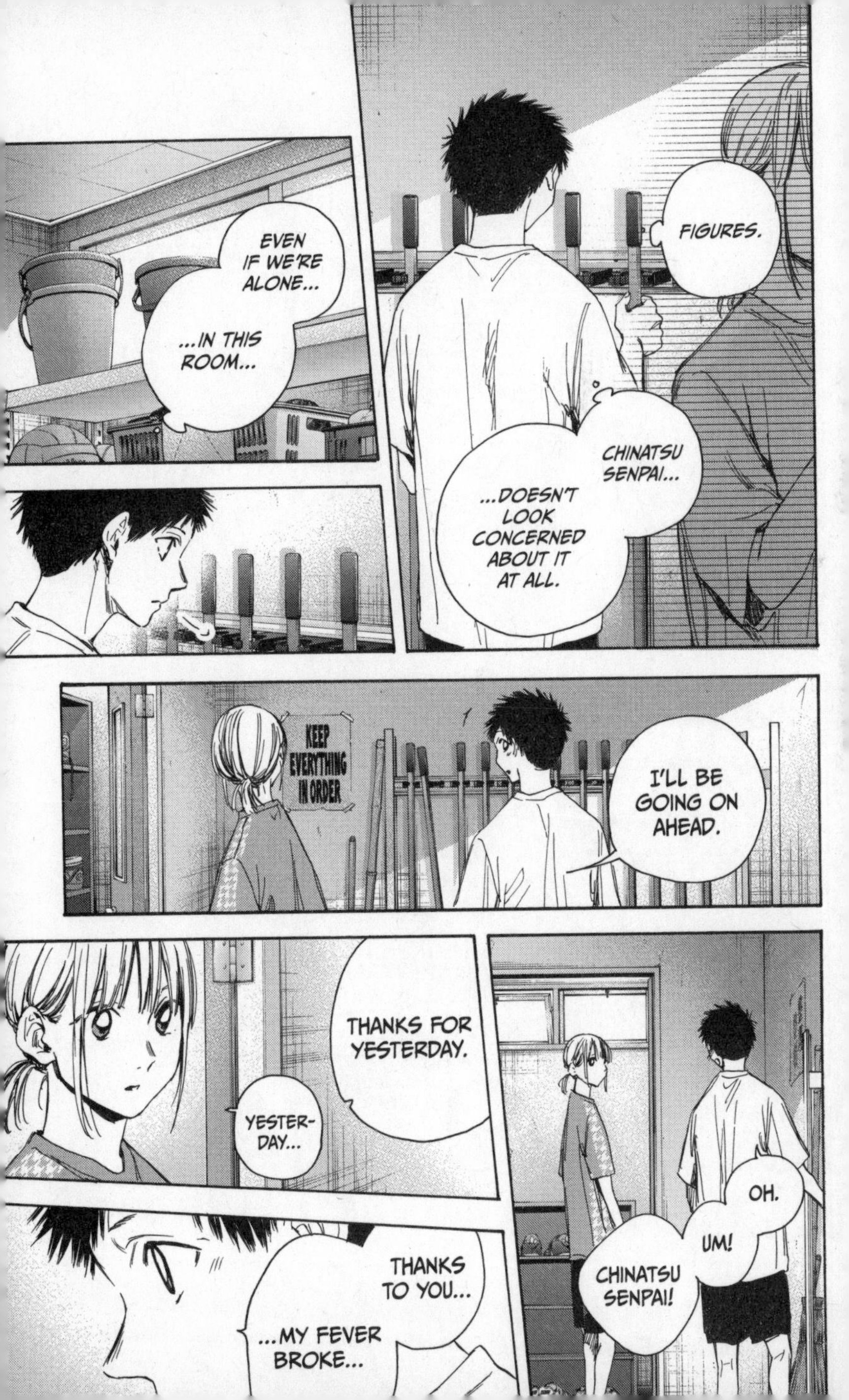
FIGURES.
EVEN IF WE'RE ALONE...
...IN THIS ROOM...
CHINATSU SENPAI...
...DOESN'T LOOK CONCERNED ABOUT IT AT ALL.
KEEP EVERYTHING IN ORDER
I'LL BE GOING ON AHEAD.
OH.
UM!
CHINATSU SENPAI!
THANKS FOR YESTERDAY.
YESTER-DAY...
THANKS TO YOU...
...MY FEVER BROKE...

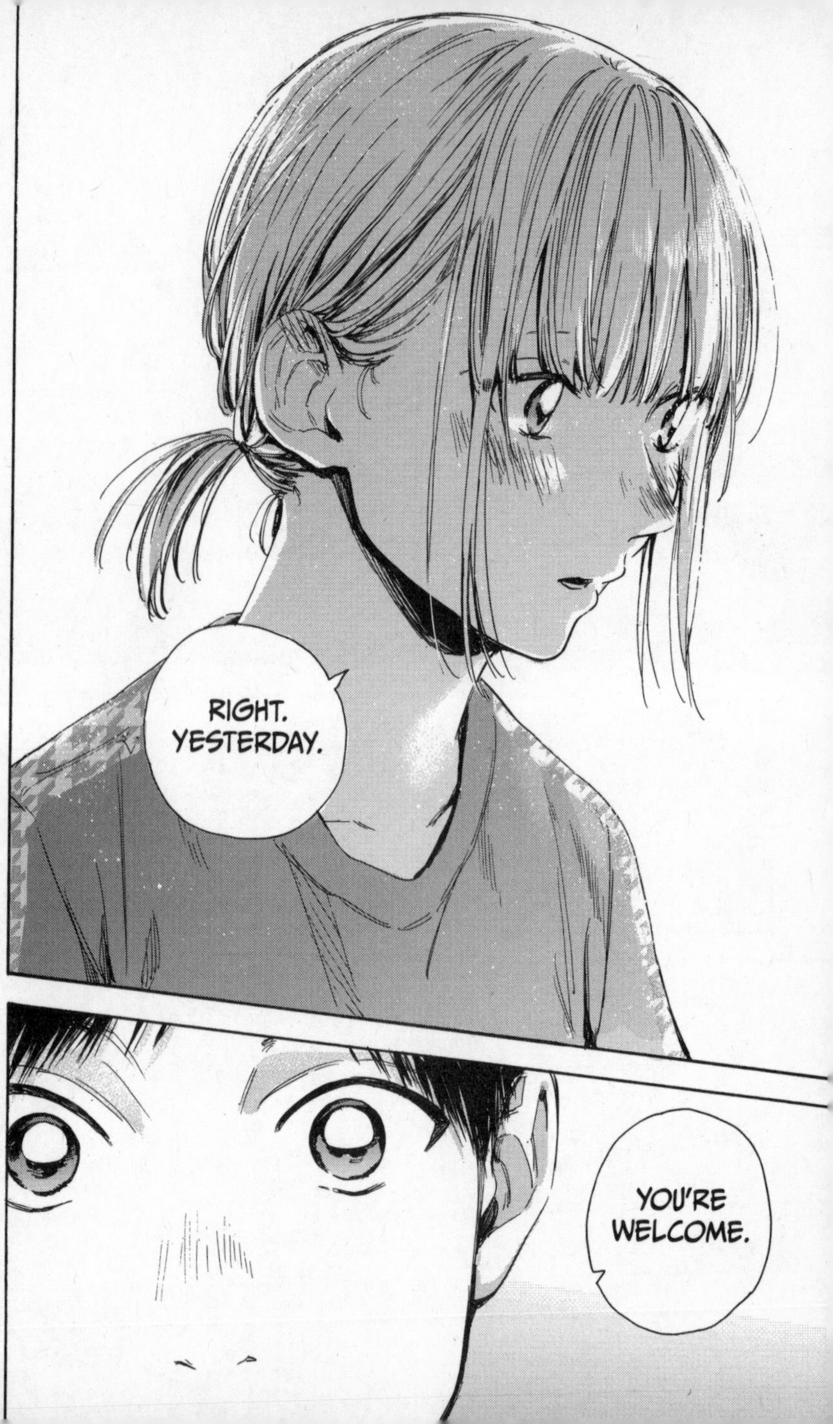
RIGHT. YESTERDAY.
YOU'RE WELCOME.

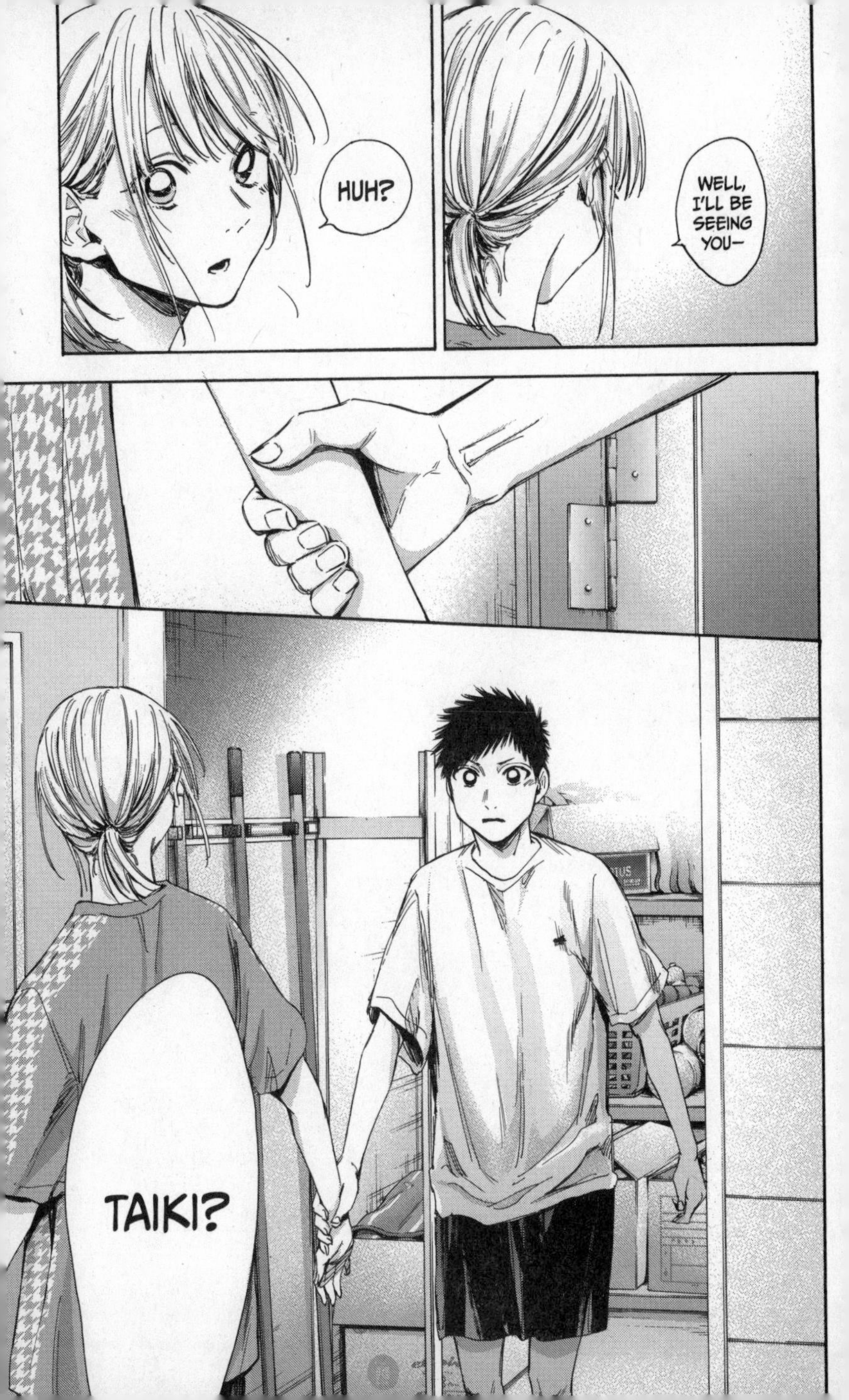
WELL, I'LL BE SEEING YOU—
HUH?
TAIKI?

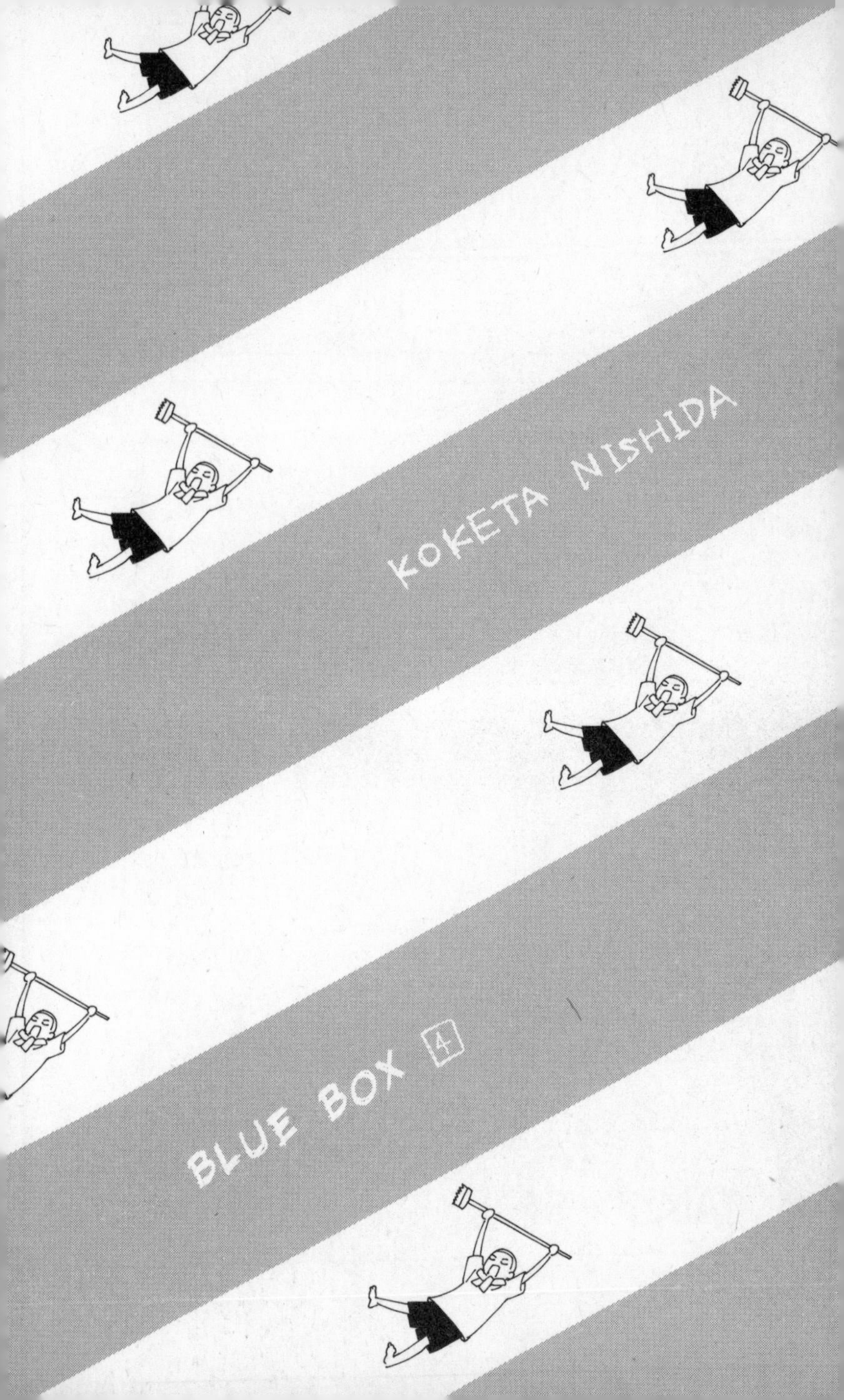
KOKETA NISHIDA
BLUE BOX 4

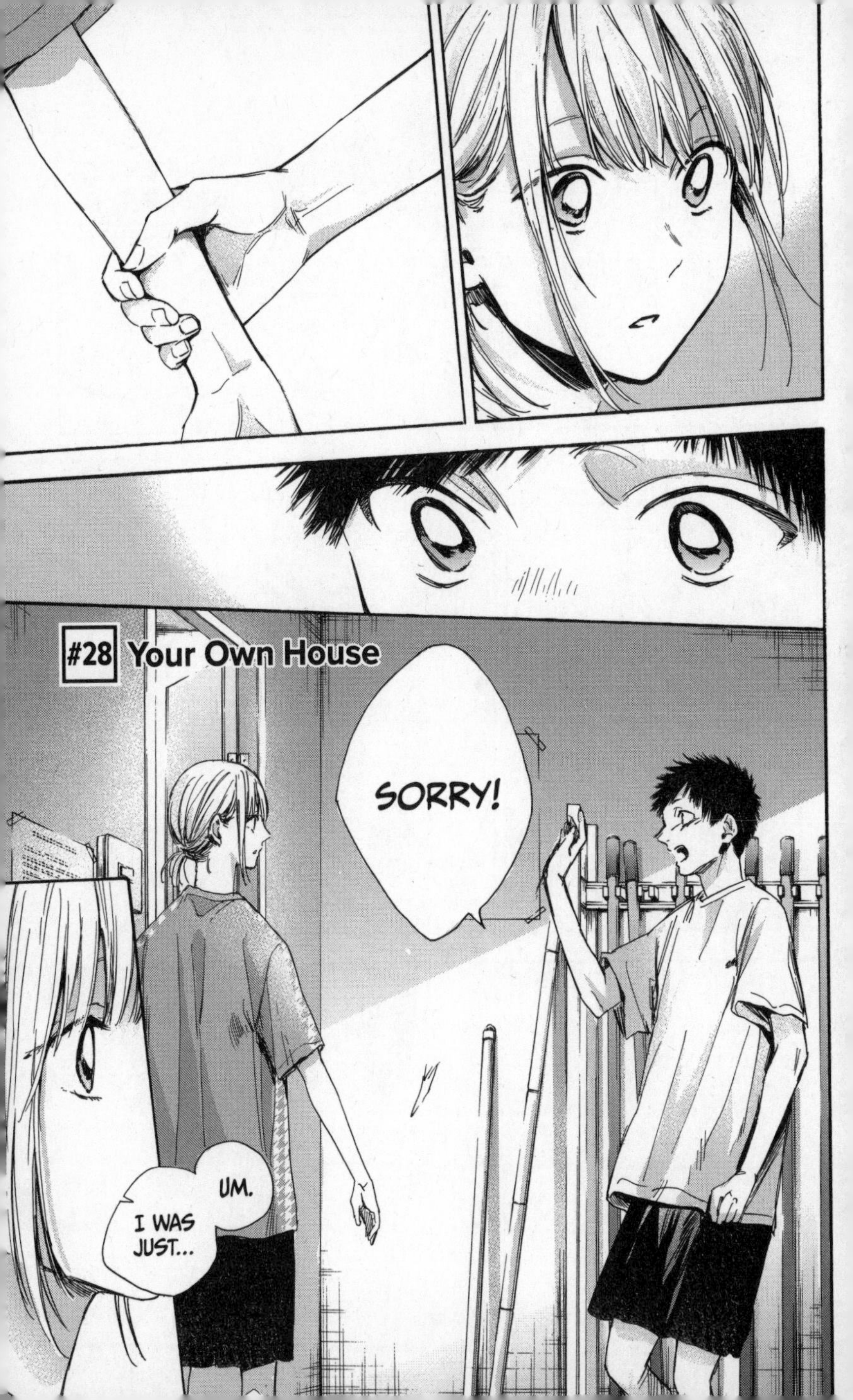
#28 Your Own House
SORRY!
UM.
I WAS JUST...

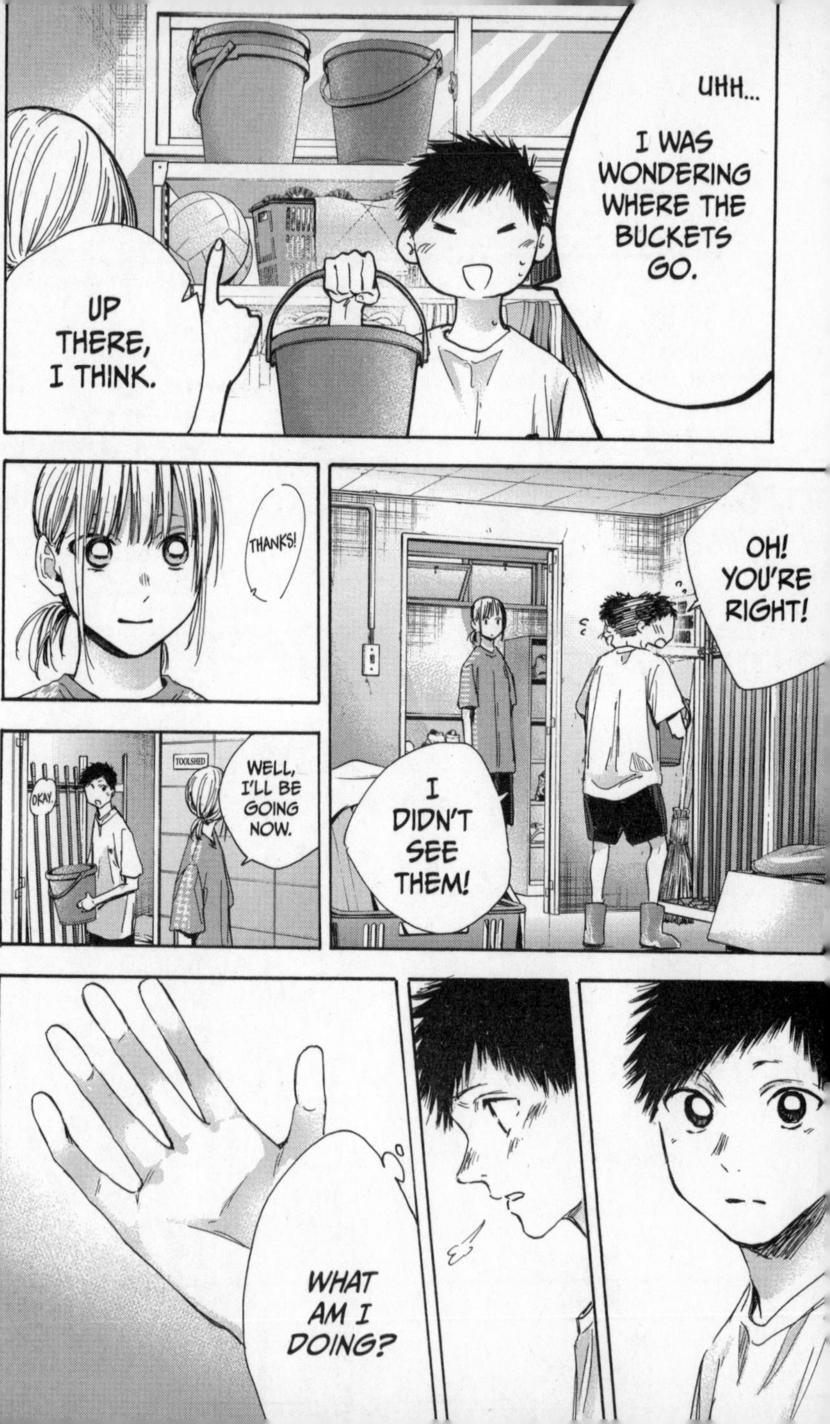
UHH...
I WAS WONDERING WHERE THE BUCKETS GO.
UP THERE, I THINK.
OH! YOU'RE RIGHT!
I DIDN'T SEE THEM!
THANKS!
WELL, I'LL BE GOING NOW.
OKAY.
TOOLSHED
WHAT AM I DOING?

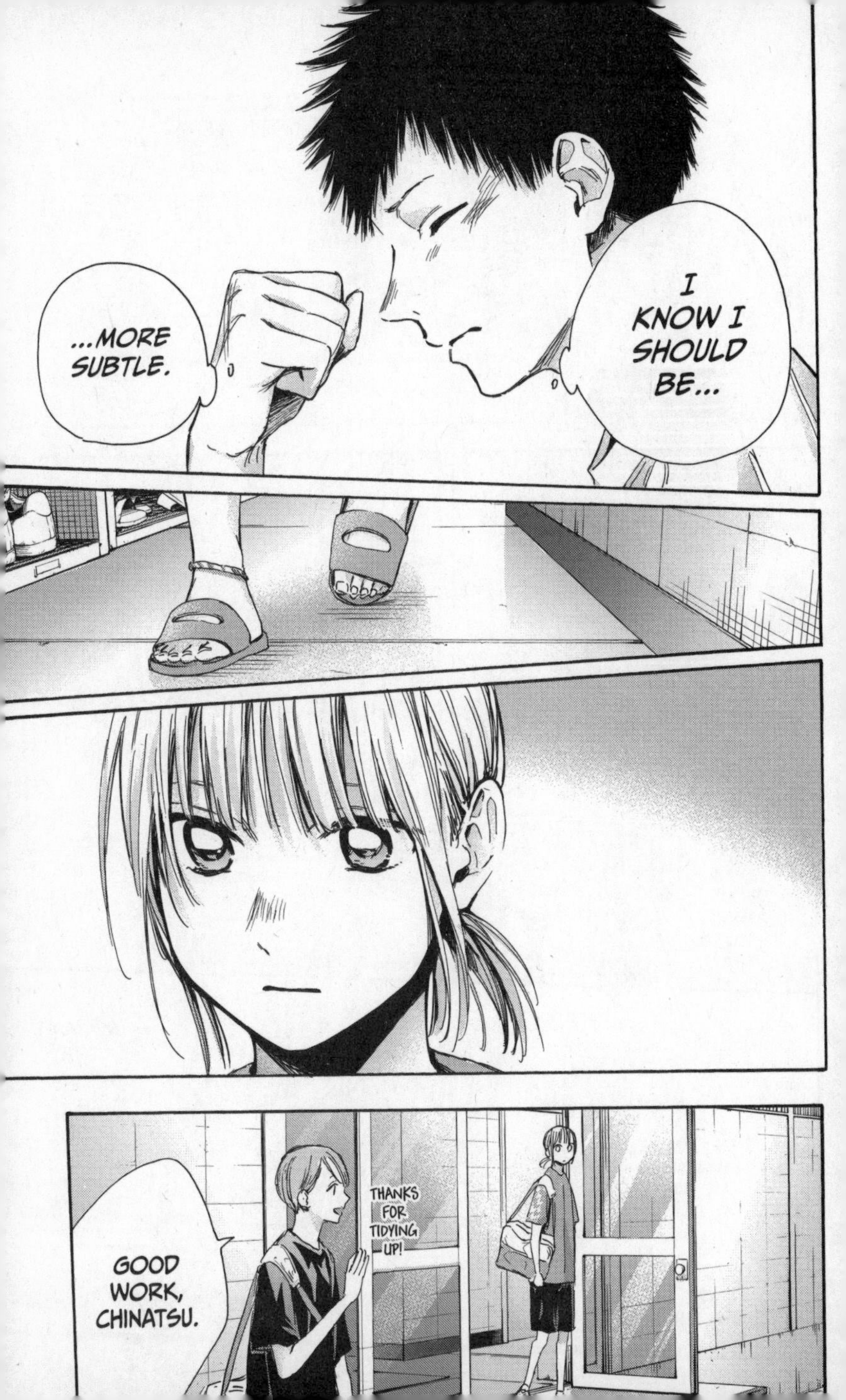
I KNOW I SHOULD BE...
...MORE SUBTLE.
THANKS FOR TIDYING UP!
GOOD WORK, CHINATSU.

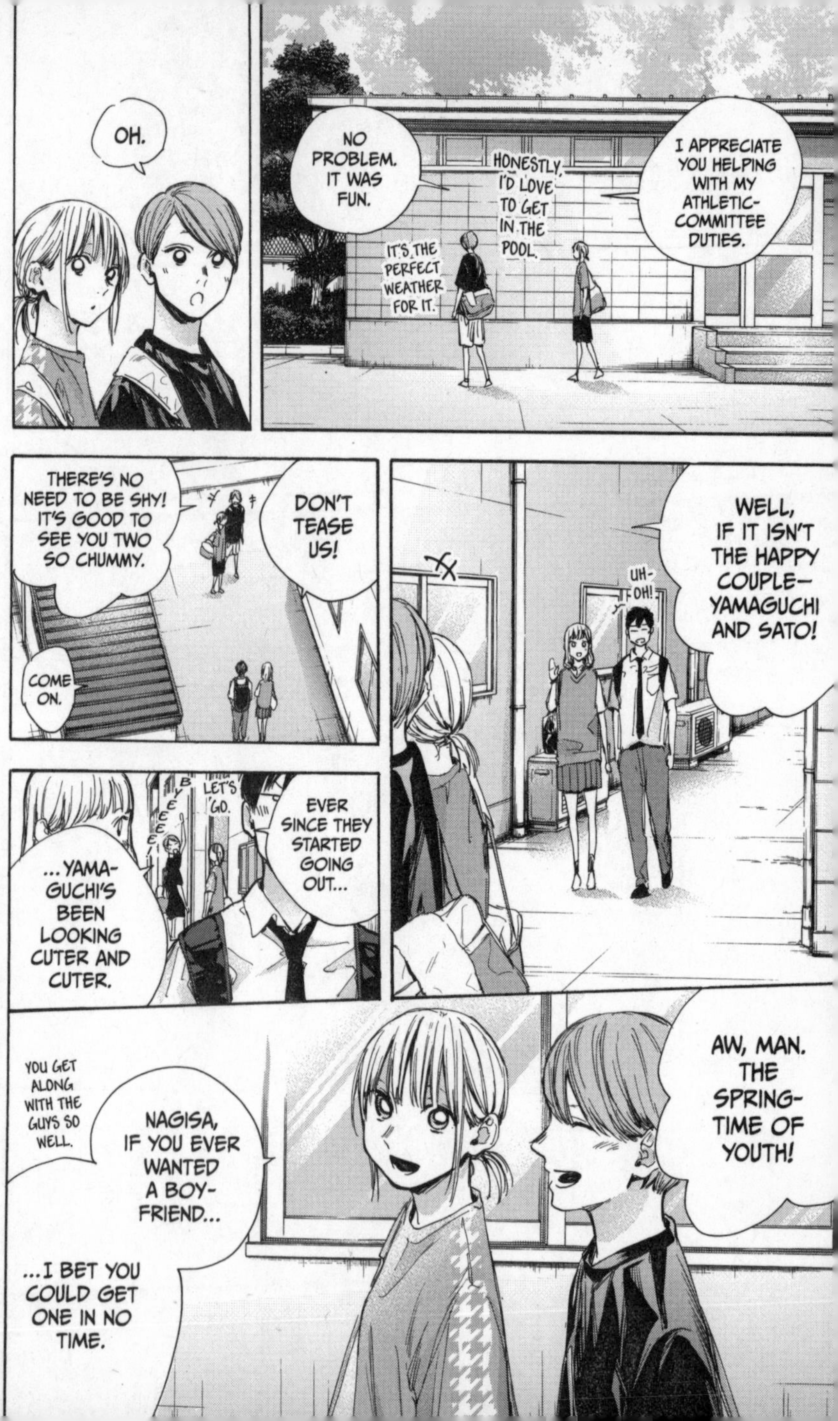
I APPRECIATE YOU HELPING WITH MY ATHLETIC-COMMITTEE DUTIES.
HONESTLY, I'D LOVE TO GET IN THE POOL.
NO PROBLEM. IT WAS FUN.
IT'S THE PERFECT WEATHER FOR IT.
OH.
WELL, IF IT ISN'T THE HAPPY COUPLE—YAMAGUCHI AND SATO!
UH-OH!
DON'T TEASE US!
THERE'S NO NEED TO BE SHY! IT'S GOOD TO SEE YOU TWO SO CHUMMY.
COME ON.
EVER SINCE THEY STARTED GOING OUT...
LET'S GO.
BYEEEE!
...YAMAGUCHI'S BEEN LOOKING CUTER AND CUTER.
AW, MAN. THE SPRINGTIME OF YOUTH!
NAGISA, IF YOU EVER WANTED A BOYFRIEND...
YOU GET ALONG WITH THE GUYS SO WELL.
...I BET YOU COULD GET ONE IN NO TIME.

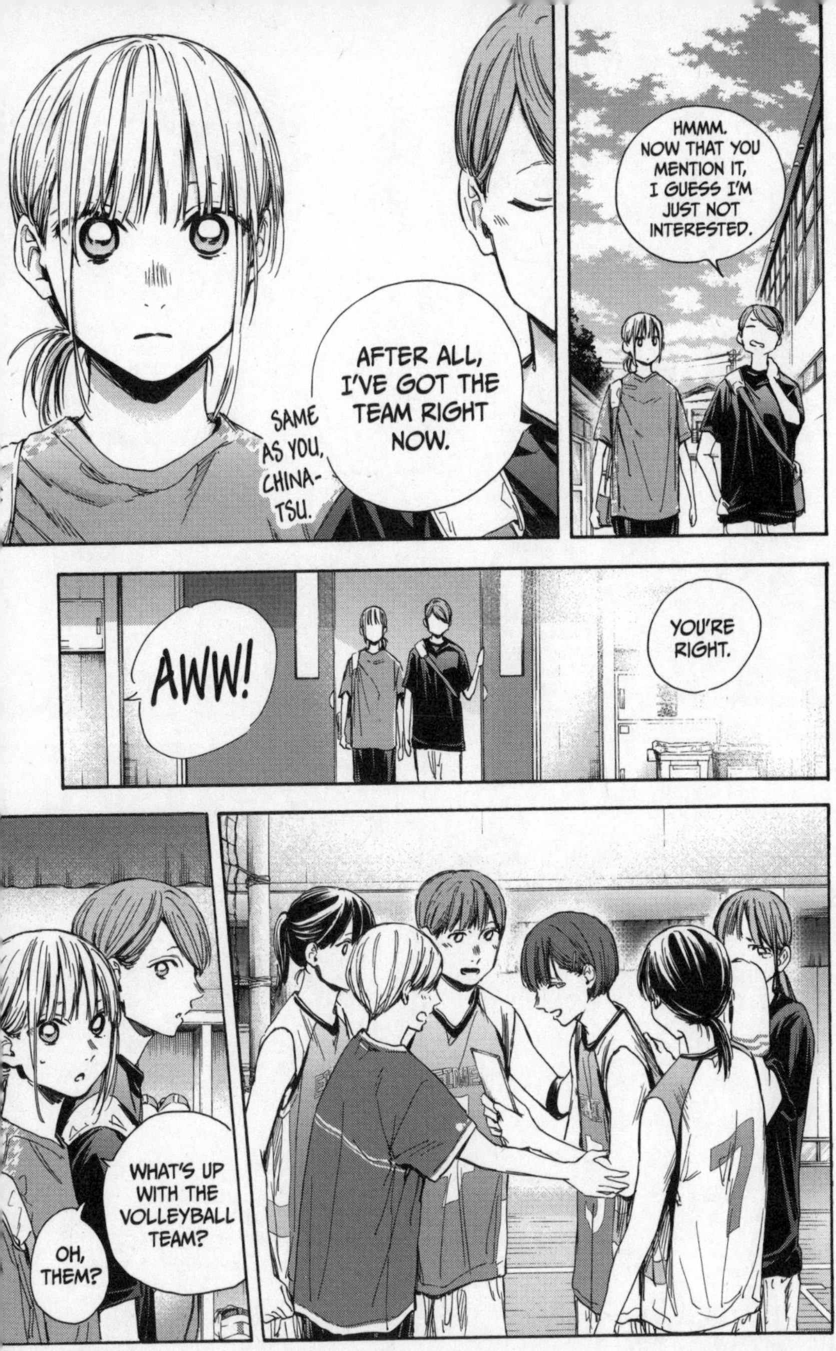
HMMM. NOW THAT YOU MENTION IT, I GUESS I'M JUST NOT INTERESTED.
AFTER ALL, I'VE GOT THE TEAM RIGHT NOW.
SAME AS YOU, CHINA-TSU.
YOU'RE RIGHT.
AWW!
WHAT'S UP WITH THE VOLLEYBALL TEAM?
OH, THEM?

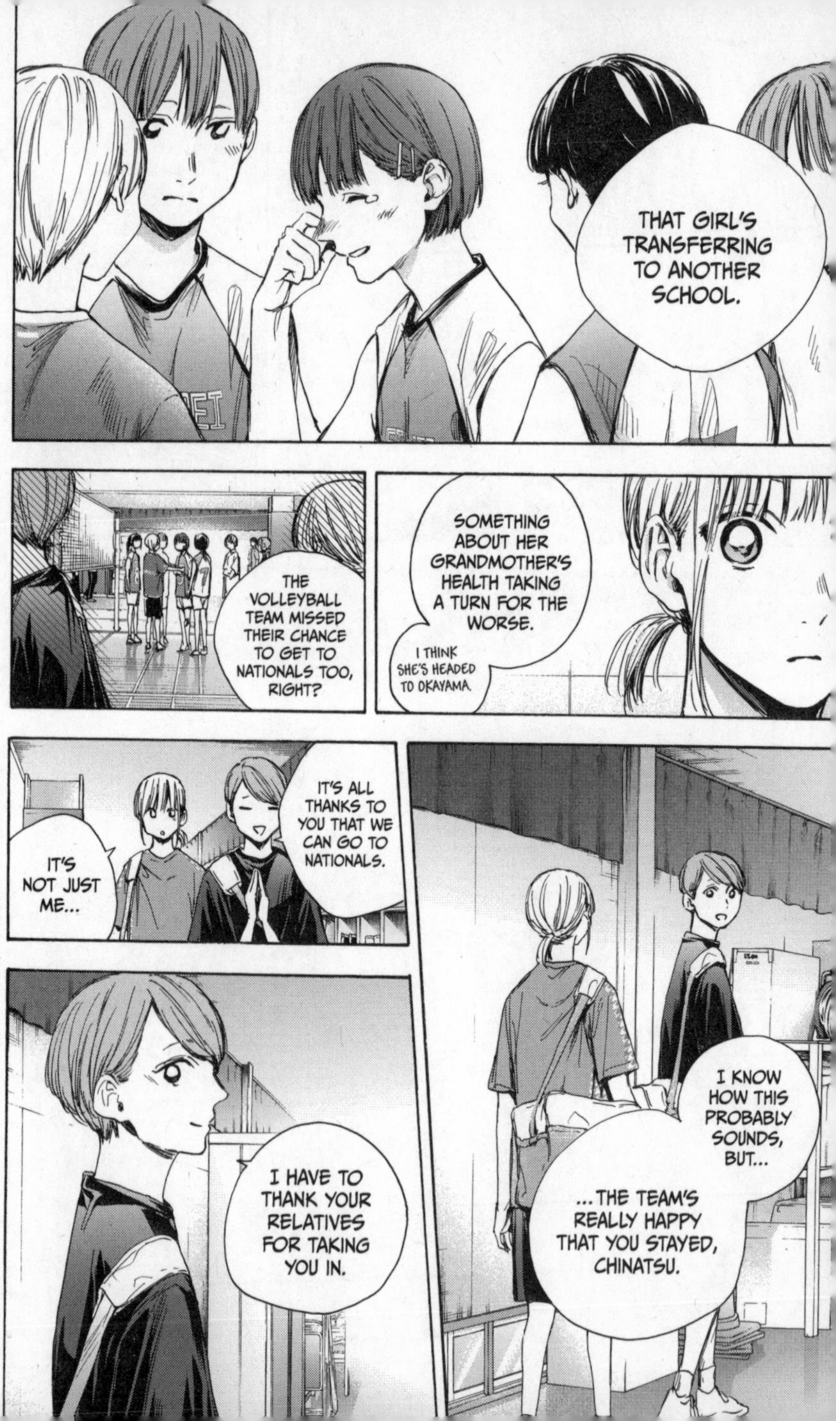
THAT GIRL'S TRANSFERRING TO ANOTHER SCHOOL.
SOMETHING ABOUT HER GRANDMOTHER'S HEALTH TAKING A TURN FOR THE WORSE.
I THINK SHE'S HEADED TO OKAYAMA.
THE VOLLEYBALL TEAM MISSED THEIR CHANCE TO GET TO NATIONALS TOO, RIGHT?
IT'S ALL THANKS TO YOU THAT WE CAN GO TO NATIONALS.
IT'S NOT JUST ME...
I HAVE TO THANK YOUR RELATIVES FOR TAKING YOU IN.
I KNOW HOW THIS PROBABLY SOUNDS, BUT...
...THE TEAM'S REALLY HAPPY THAT YOU STAYED, CHINATSU.

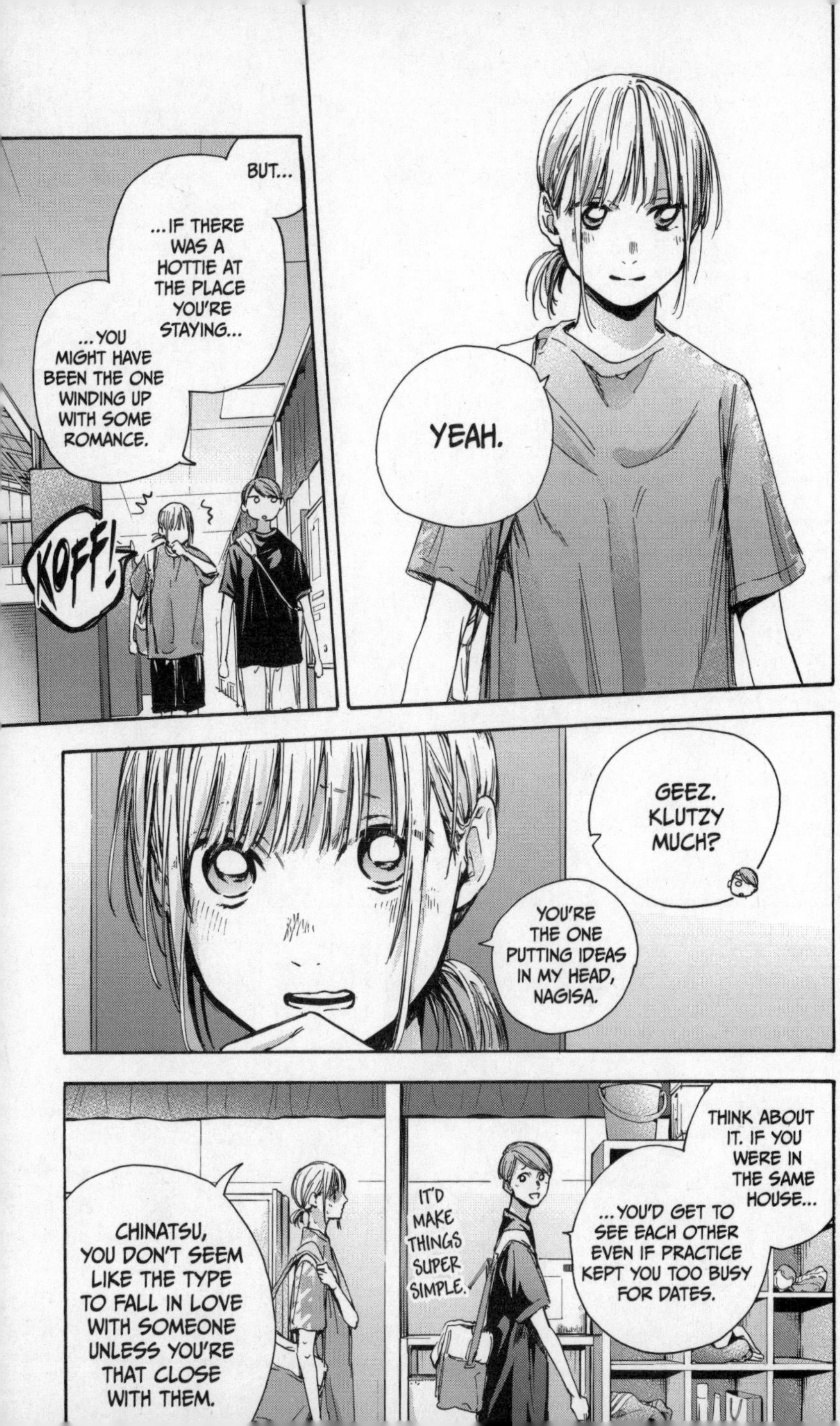
YEAH.
BUT...
...IF THERE WAS A HOTTIE AT THE PLACE YOU'RE STAYING...
...YOU MIGHT HAVE BEEN THE ONE WINDING UP WITH SOME ROMANCE.
KOFF!
GEEZ. KLUTZY MUCH?
YOU'RE THE ONE PUTTING IDEAS IN MY HEAD, NAGISA.
THINK ABOUT IT. IF YOU WERE IN THE SAME HOUSE...
...YOU'D GET TO SEE EACH OTHER EVEN IF PRACTICE KEPT YOU TOO BUSY FOR DATES.
IT'D MAKE THINGS SUPER SIMPLE.
CHINATSU, YOU DON'T SEEM LIKE THE TYPE TO FALL IN LOVE WITH SOMEONE UNLESS YOU'RE THAT CLOSE WITH THEM.

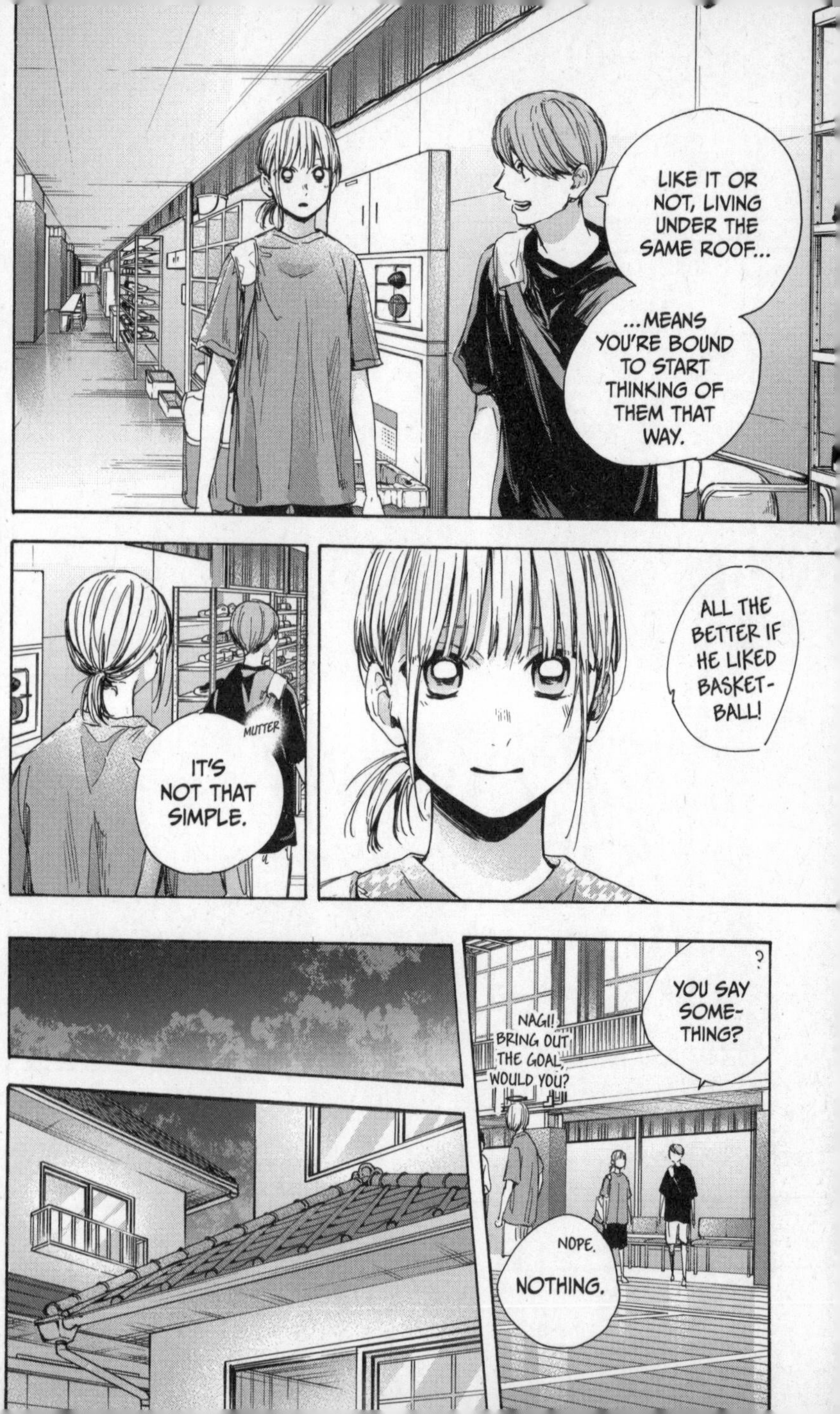
LIKE IT OR NOT, LIVING UNDER THE SAME ROOF...
...MEANS YOU'RE BOUND TO START THINKING OF THEM THAT WAY.
ALL THE BETTER IF HE LIKED BASKET-BALL!
MUTTER
IT'S NOT THAT SIMPLE.
?
YOU SAY SOME-THING?
NAGI! BRING OUT THE GOAL, WOULD YOU?
NOPE.
NOTHING.

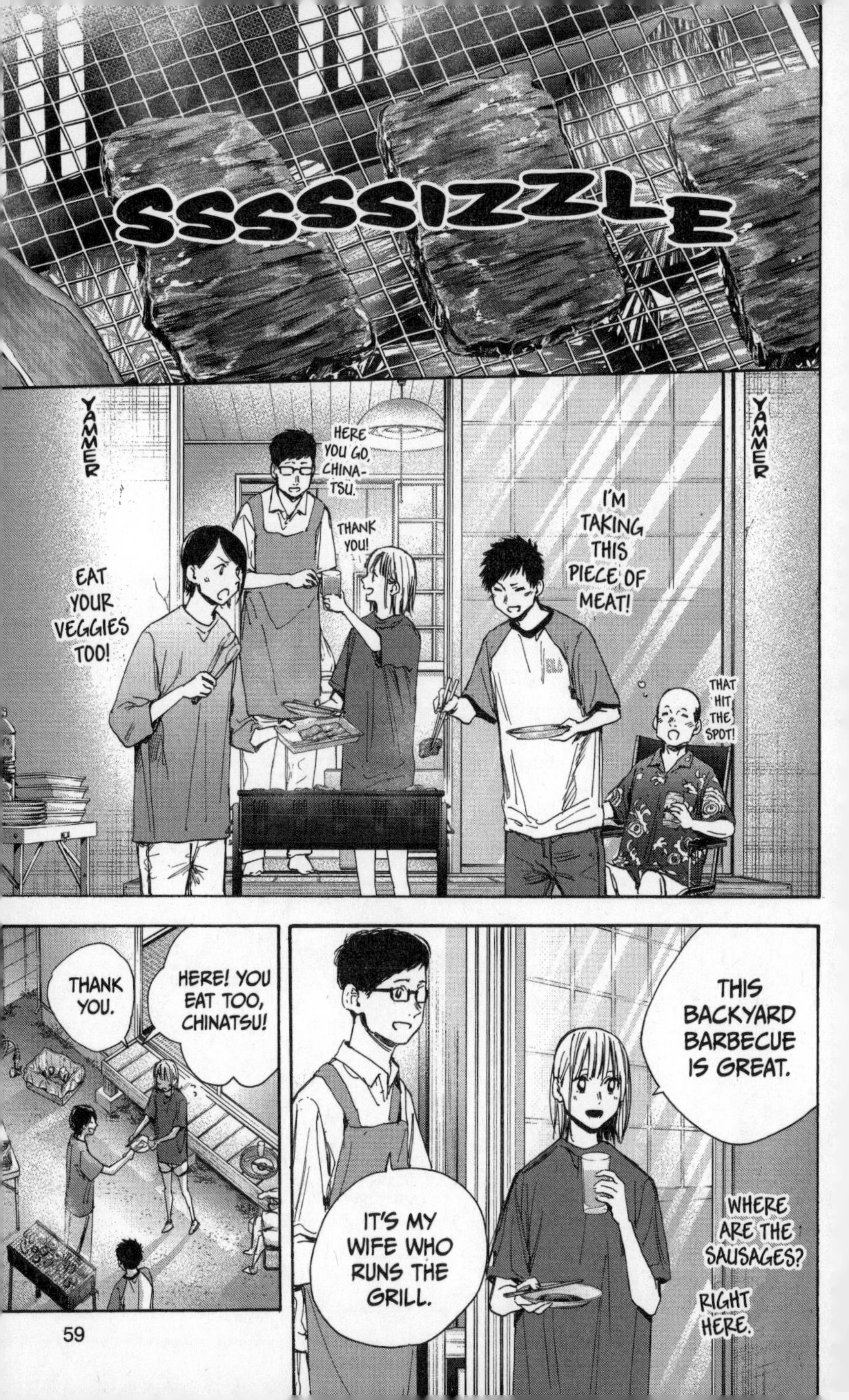
SSSSIZZLE
YAMMER
THAT HIT THE SPOT!
I'M TAKING THIS PIECE OF MEAT!
HERE YOU GO, CHINATSU.
THANK YOU!
EAT YOUR VEGGIES TOO!
YAMMER
THIS BACKYARD BARBECUE IS GREAT.
IT'S MY WIFE WHO RUNS THE GRILL.
WHERE ARE THE SAUSAGES?
RIGHT HERE.
HERE! YOU EAT TOO, CHINATSU!
THANK YOU.

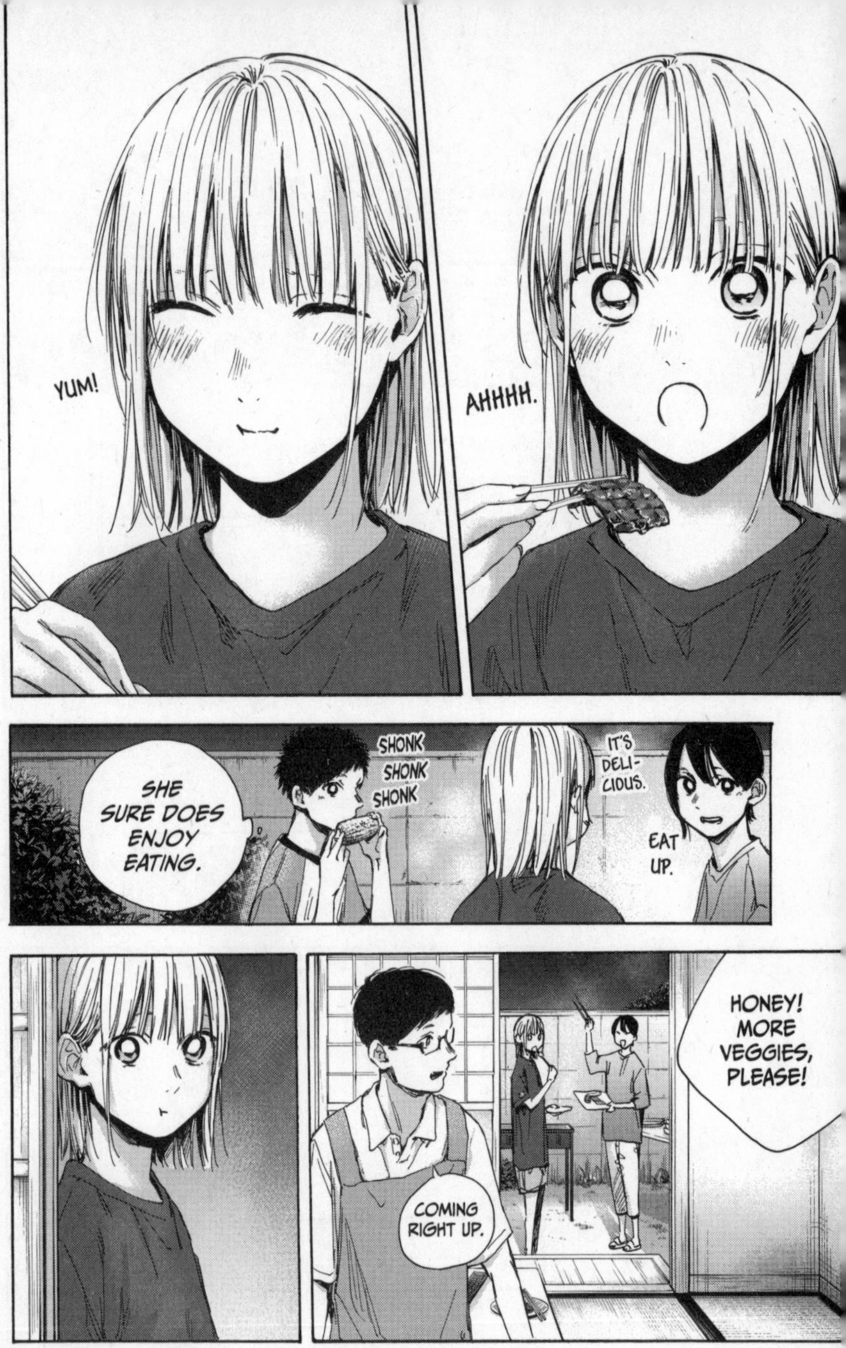
AHHHH.
YUM!
IT'S DELI-CIOUS.
EAT UP.
SHONK
SHONK
SHONK
SHE SURE DOES ENJOY EATING.
HONEY! MORE VEGGIES, PLEASE!
COMING RIGHT UP.

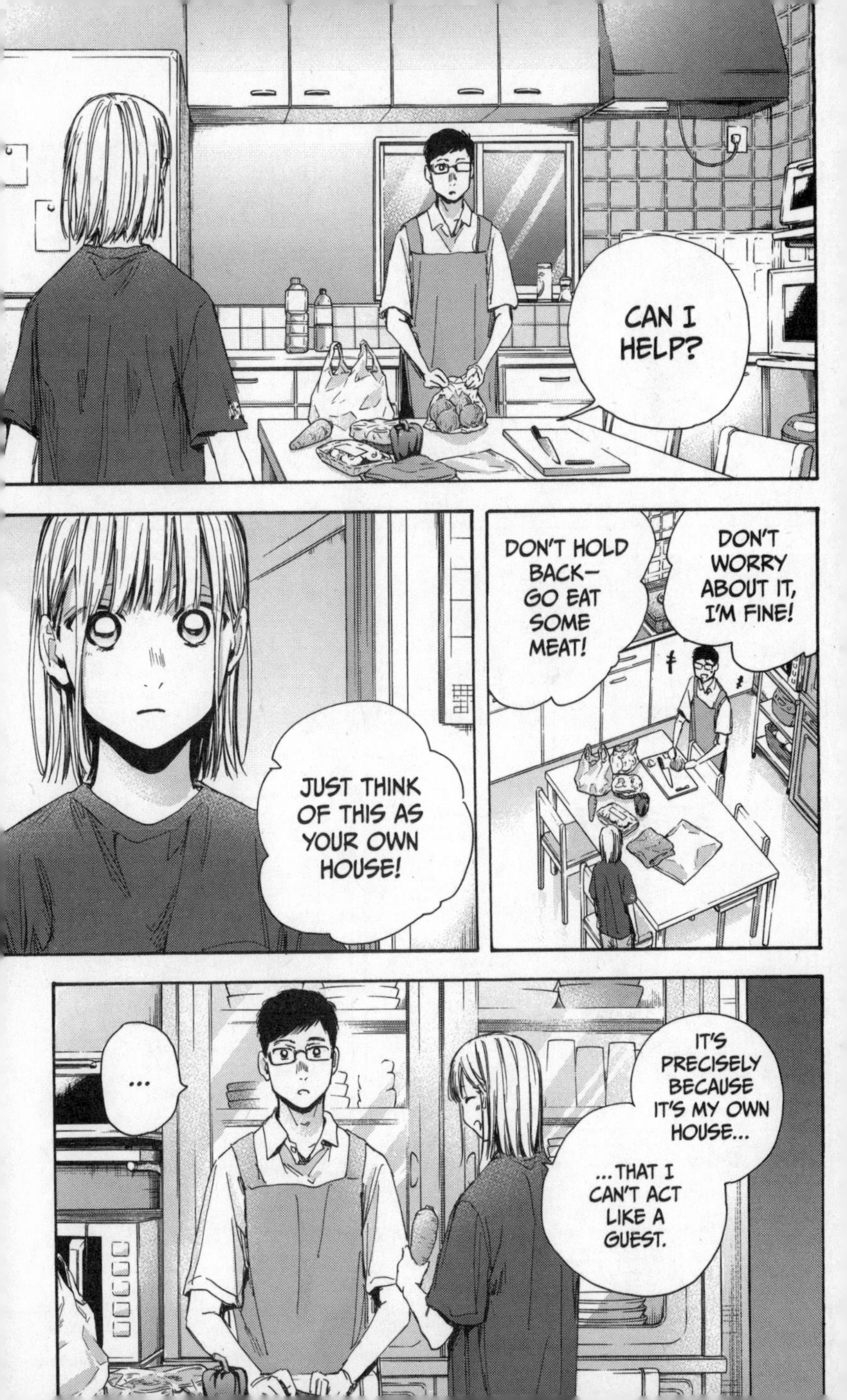
CAN I HELP?
JUST THINK OF THIS AS YOUR OWN HOUSE!
DON'T HOLD BACK— GO EAT SOME MEAT!
DON'T WORRY ABOUT IT, I'M FINE!
...
IT'S PRECISELY BECAUSE IT'S MY OWN HOUSE...
...THAT I CAN'T ACT LIKE A GUEST.

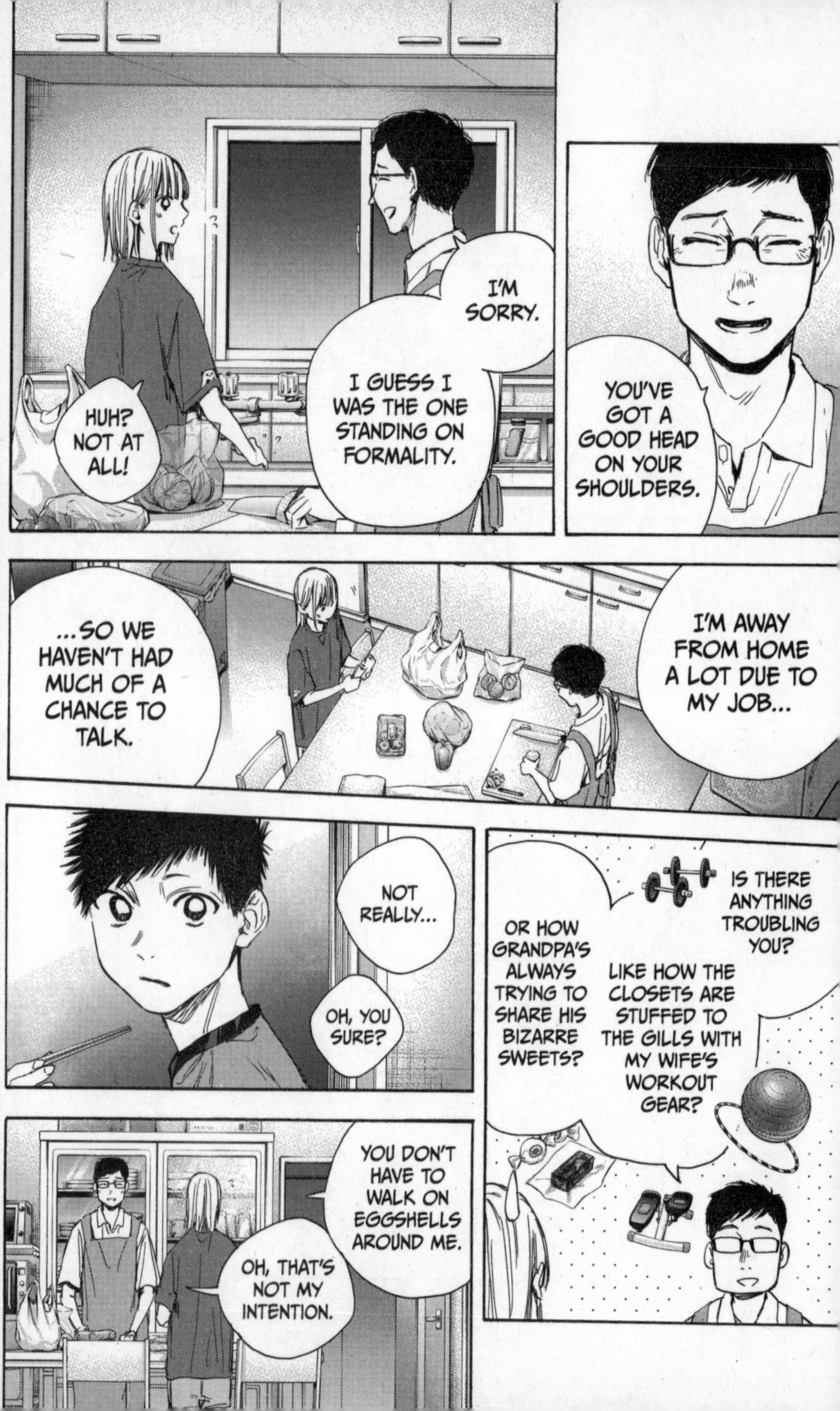
YOU'VE GOT A GOOD HEAD ON YOUR SHOULDERS.
I'M SORRY.
I GUESS I WAS THE ONE STANDING ON FORMALITY.
HUH? NOT AT ALL!
I'M AWAY FROM HOME A LOT DUE TO MY JOB...
...SO WE HAVEN'T HAD MUCH OF A CHANCE TO TALK.
IS THERE ANYTHING TROUBLING YOU?
LIKE HOW THE CLOSETS ARE STUFFED TO THE GILLS WITH MY WIFE'S WORKOUT GEAR?
OR HOW GRANDPA'S ALWAYS TRYING TO SHARE HIS BIZARRE SWEETS?
NOT REALLY...
OH, YOU SURE?
YOU DON'T HAVE TO WALK ON EGGSHELLS AROUND ME.
OH, THAT'S NOT MY INTENTION.

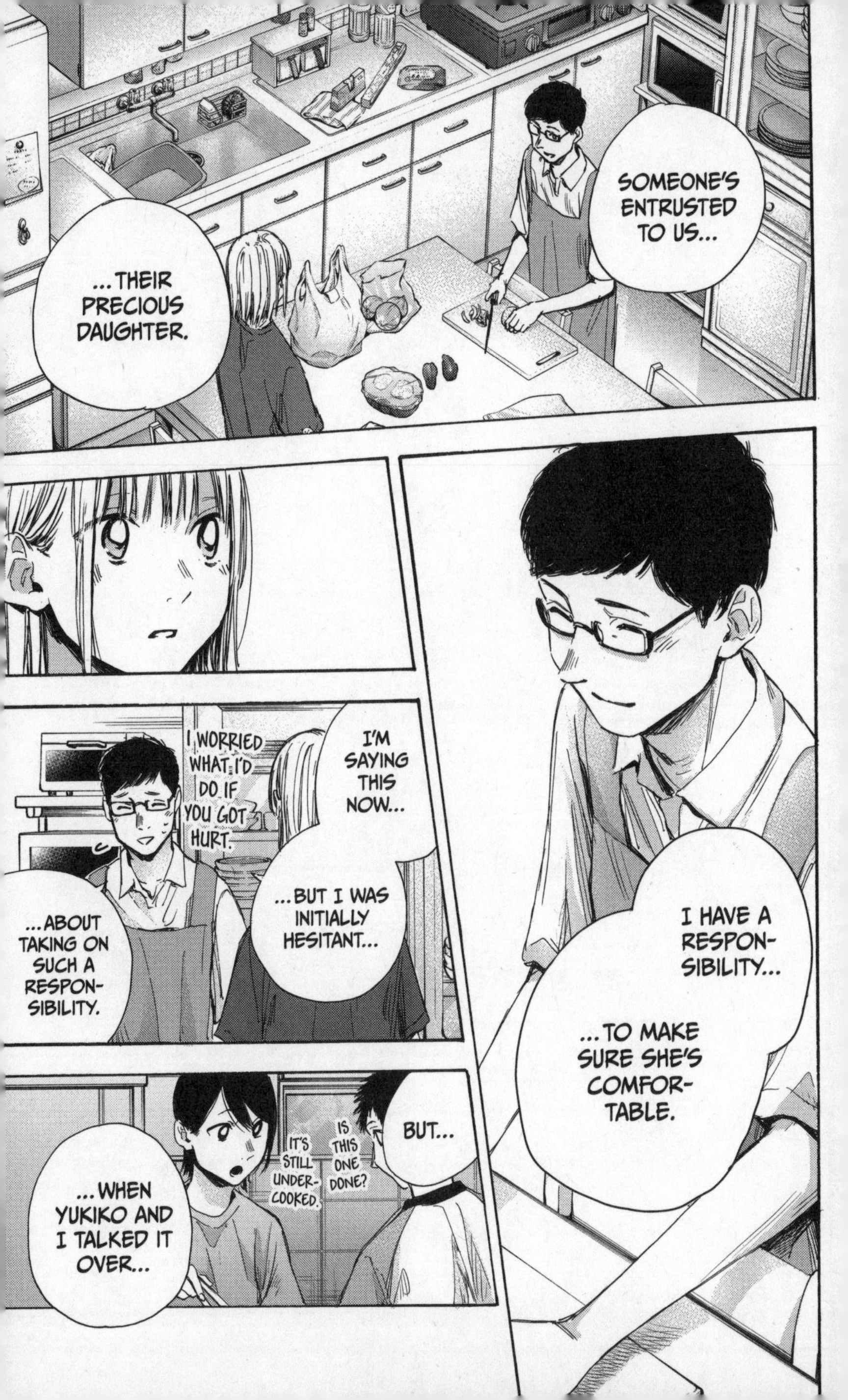
SOMEONE'S ENTRUSTED TO US...
...THEIR PRECIOUS DAUGHTER.
I HAVE A RESPON-SIBILITY...
...TO MAKE SURE SHE'S COMFOR-TABLE.
I'M SAYING THIS NOW...
...BUT I WAS INITIALLY HESITANT...
I WORRIED WHAT I'D DO IF YOU GOT HURT.
...ABOUT TAKING ON SUCH A RESPON-SIBILITY.
BUT...
IS THIS ONE DONE?
IT'S STILL UNDER-COOKED.
...WHEN YUKIKO AND I TALKED IT OVER...

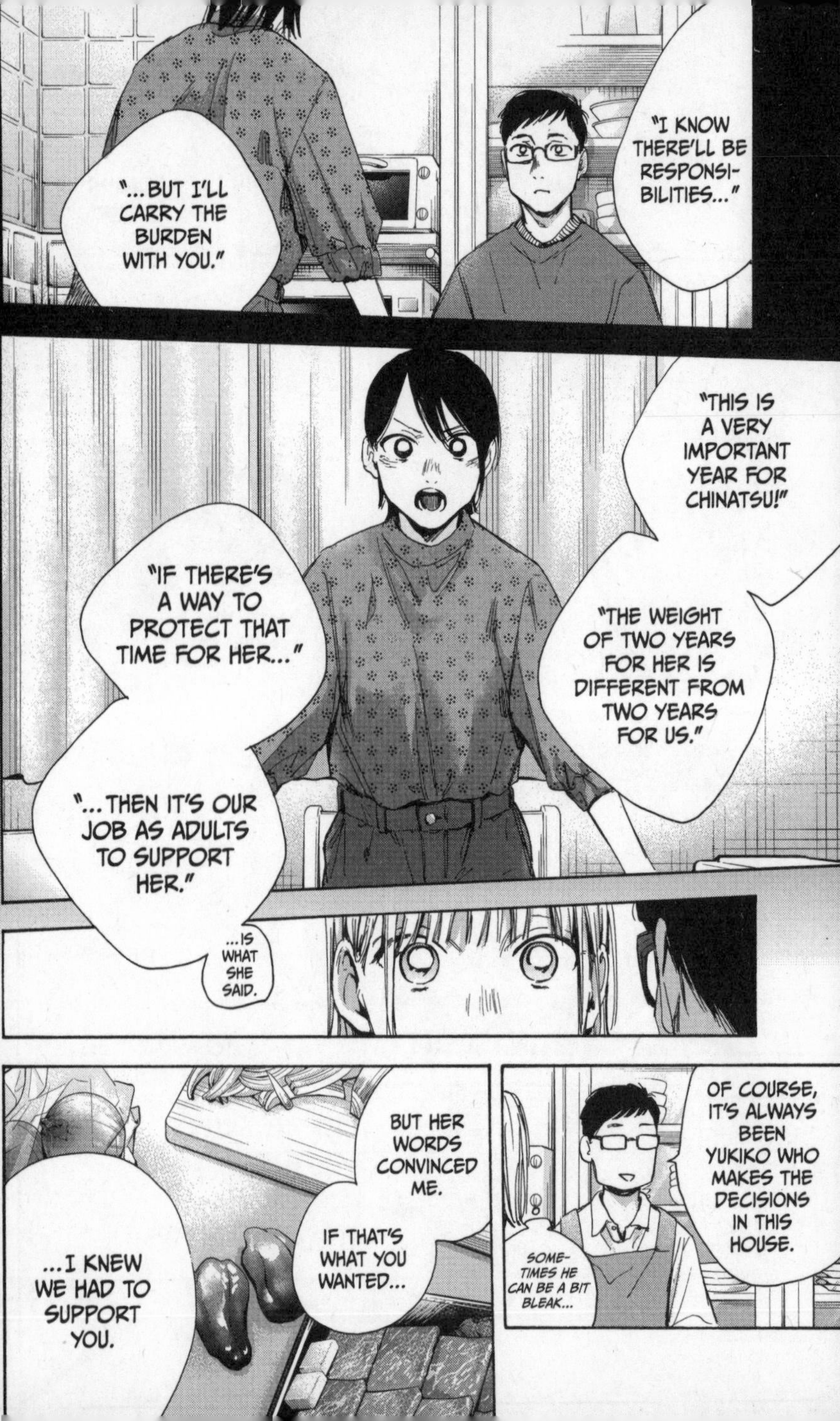
"I KNOW THERE'LL BE RESPONSI-BILITIES..."
"...BUT I'LL CARRY THE BURDEN WITH YOU."
"THIS IS A VERY IMPORTANT YEAR FOR CHINATSU!"
"THE WEIGHT OF TWO YEARS FOR HER IS DIFFERENT FROM TWO YEARS FOR US."
"IF THERE'S A WAY TO PROTECT THAT TIME FOR HER..."
"...THEN IT'S OUR JOB AS ADULTS TO SUPPORT HER."
...IS WHAT SHE SAID.
OF COURSE, IT'S ALWAYS BEEN YUKIKO WHO MAKES THE DECISIONS IN THIS HOUSE.
SOME-TIMES HE CAN BE A BIT BLEAK...
BUT HER WORDS CONVINCED ME.
IF THAT'S WHAT YOU WANTED...
...I KNEW WE HAD TO SUPPORT YOU.

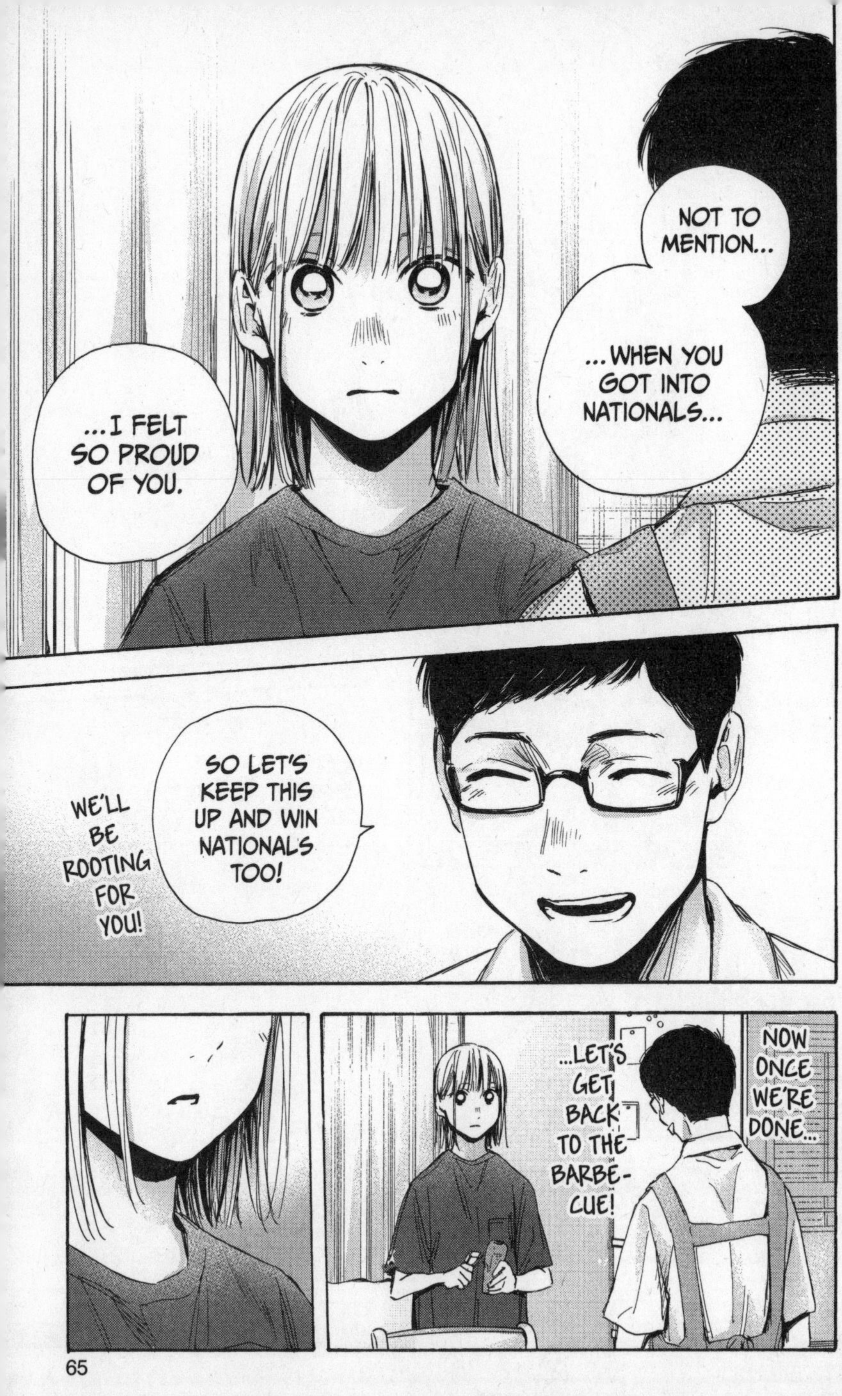
NOT TO MENTION...
...WHEN YOU GOT INTO NATIONALS...
...I FELT SO PROUD OF YOU.
SO LET'S KEEP THIS UP AND WIN NATIONALS TOO!
WE'LL BE ROOTING FOR YOU!
NOW ONCE WE'RE DONE...
...LET'S GET BACK TO THE BARBE-CUE!

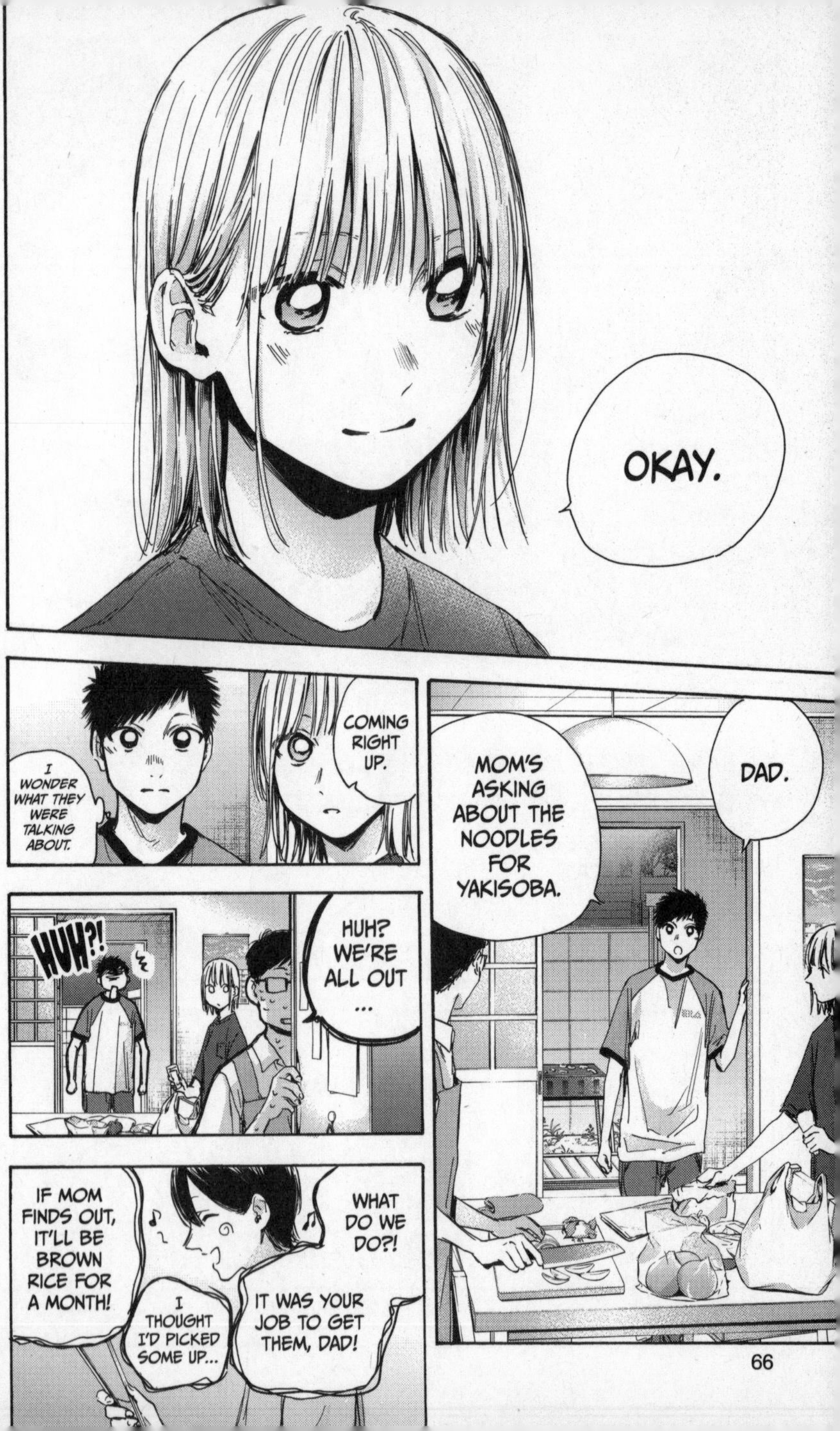
OKAY.
DAD.
MOM'S ASKING ABOUT THE NOODLES FOR YAKISOBA.
COMING RIGHT UP.
I WONDER WHAT THEY WERE TALKING ABOUT.
HUH? WE'RE ALL OUT ...
HUH?!
WHAT DO WE DO?!
IT WAS YOUR JOB TO GET THEM, DAD!
IF MOM FINDS OUT, IT'LL BE BROWN RICE FOR A MONTH!
I THOUGHT I'D PICKED SOME UP...

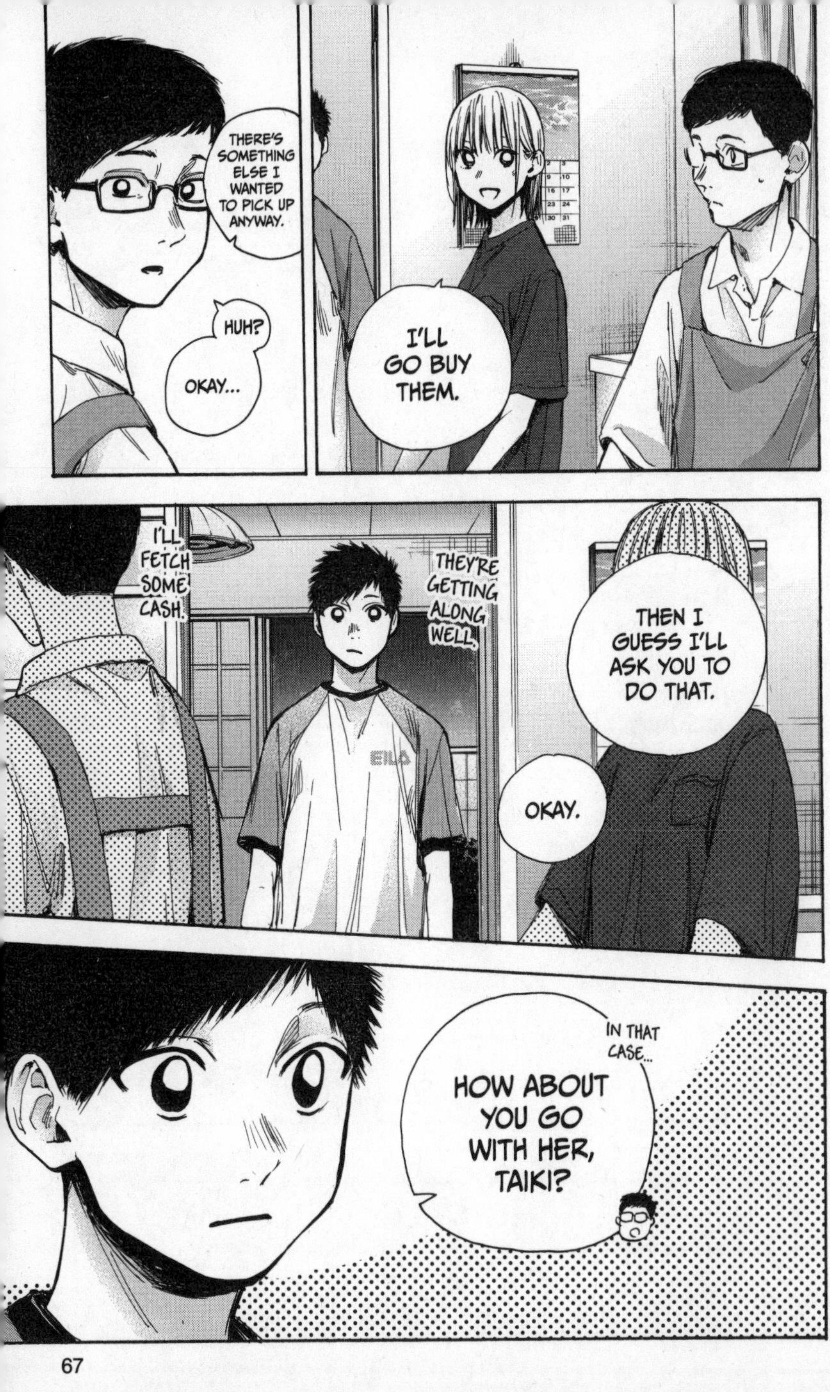
I'LL GO BUY THEM.
THERE'S SOMETHING ELSE I WANTED TO PICK UP ANYWAY.
HUH?
OKAY...
THEN I GUESS I'LL ASK YOU TO DO THAT.
OKAY.
THEY'RE GETTING ALONG WELL.
I'LL FETCH SOME CASH.
EILA
IN THAT CASE...
HOW ABOUT YOU GO WITH HER, TAIKI?

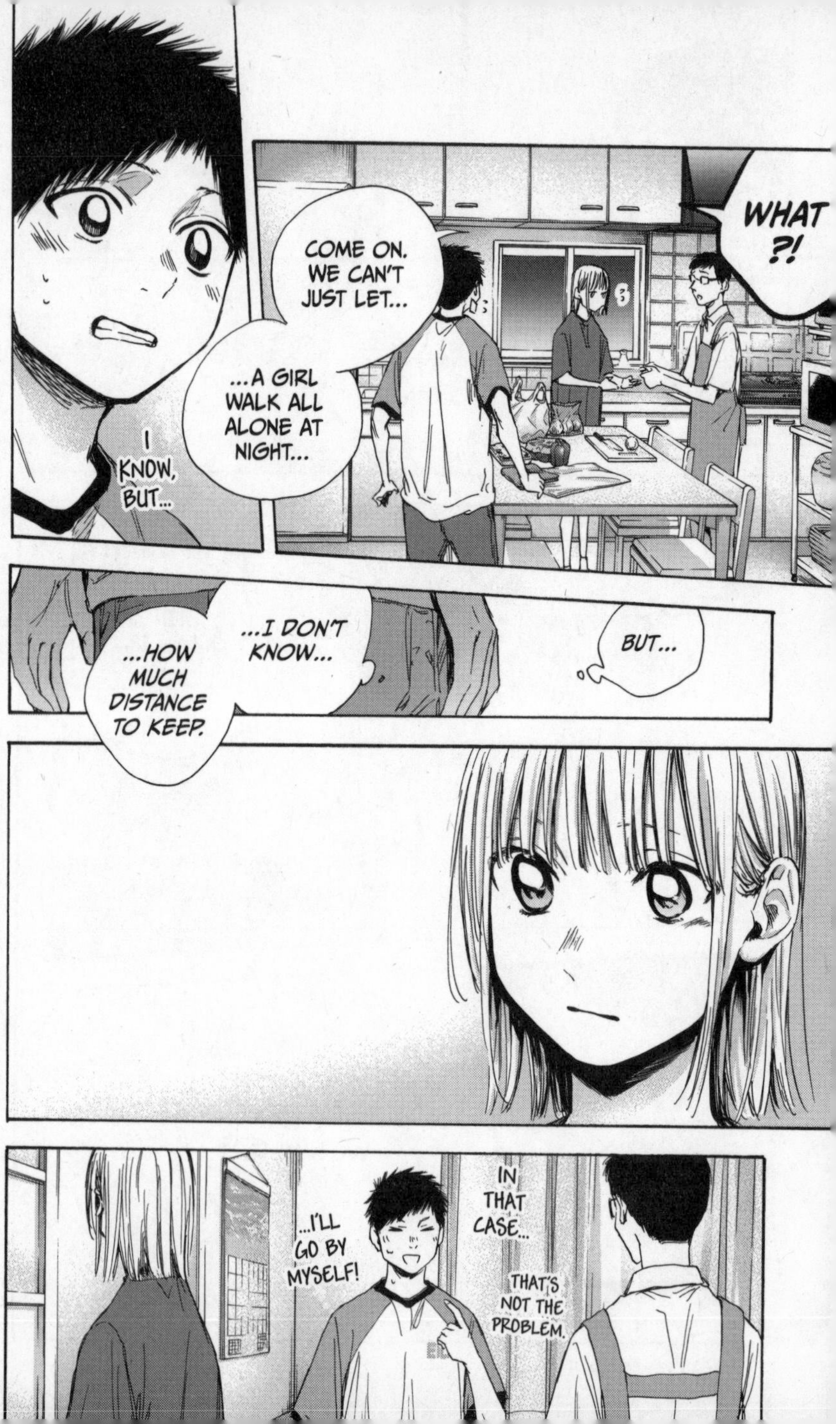
WHAT ?!
COME ON. WE CAN'T JUST LET...
...A GIRL WALK ALL ALONE AT NIGHT...
I KNOW, BUT...
BUT...
...I DON'T KNOW...
...HOW MUCH DISTANCE TO KEEP.
IN THAT CASE...
...I'LL GO BY MYSELF!
THAT'S NOT THE PROBLEM.

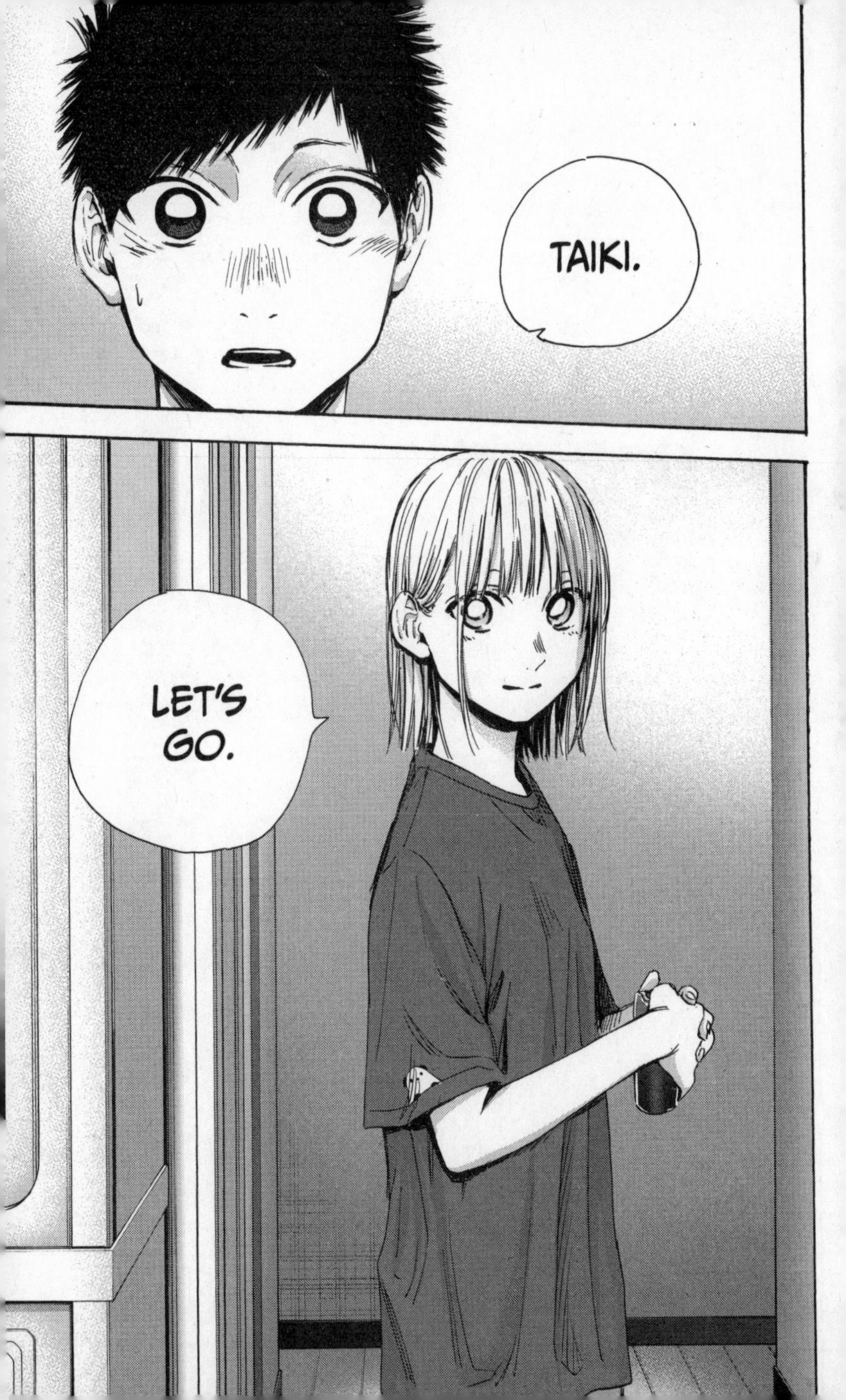
TAIKI.
LET'S GO.

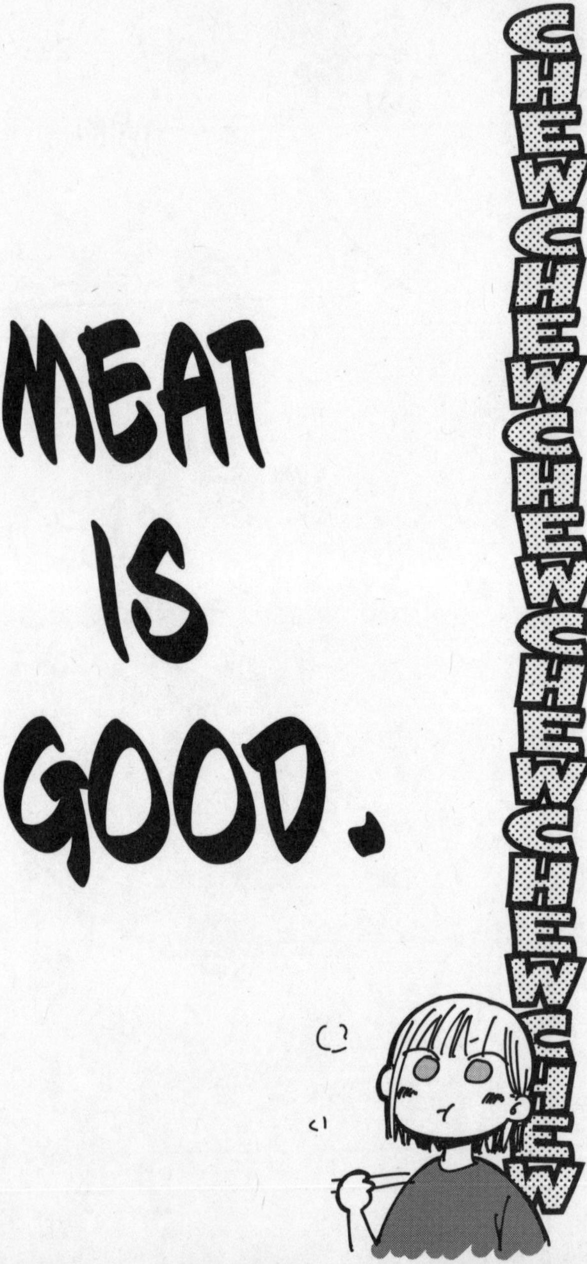
CHEWCHEWCHEWCHEWCHEWCHEW
MEAT IS GOOD.

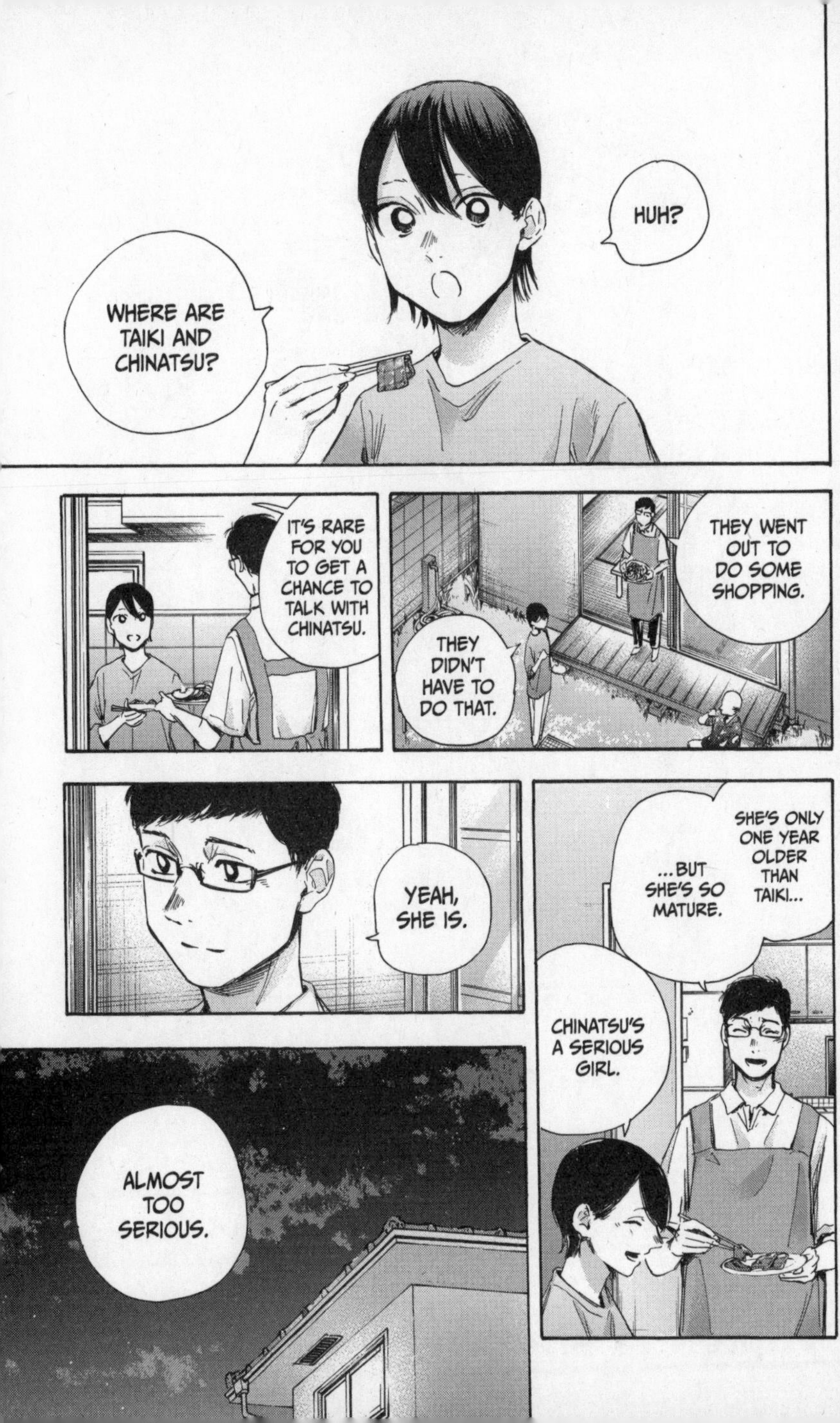

HUH?
WHERE ARE TAIKI AND CHINATSU?
THEY WENT OUT TO DO SOME SHOPPING.
THEY DIDN'T HAVE TO DO THAT.
IT'S RARE FOR YOU TO GET A CHANCE TO TALK WITH CHINATSU.
SHE'S ONLY ONE YEAR OLDER THAN TAIKI...
...BUT SHE'S SO MATURE.
CHINATSU'S A SERIOUS GIRL.
YEAH, SHE IS.
ALMOST TOO SERIOUS.

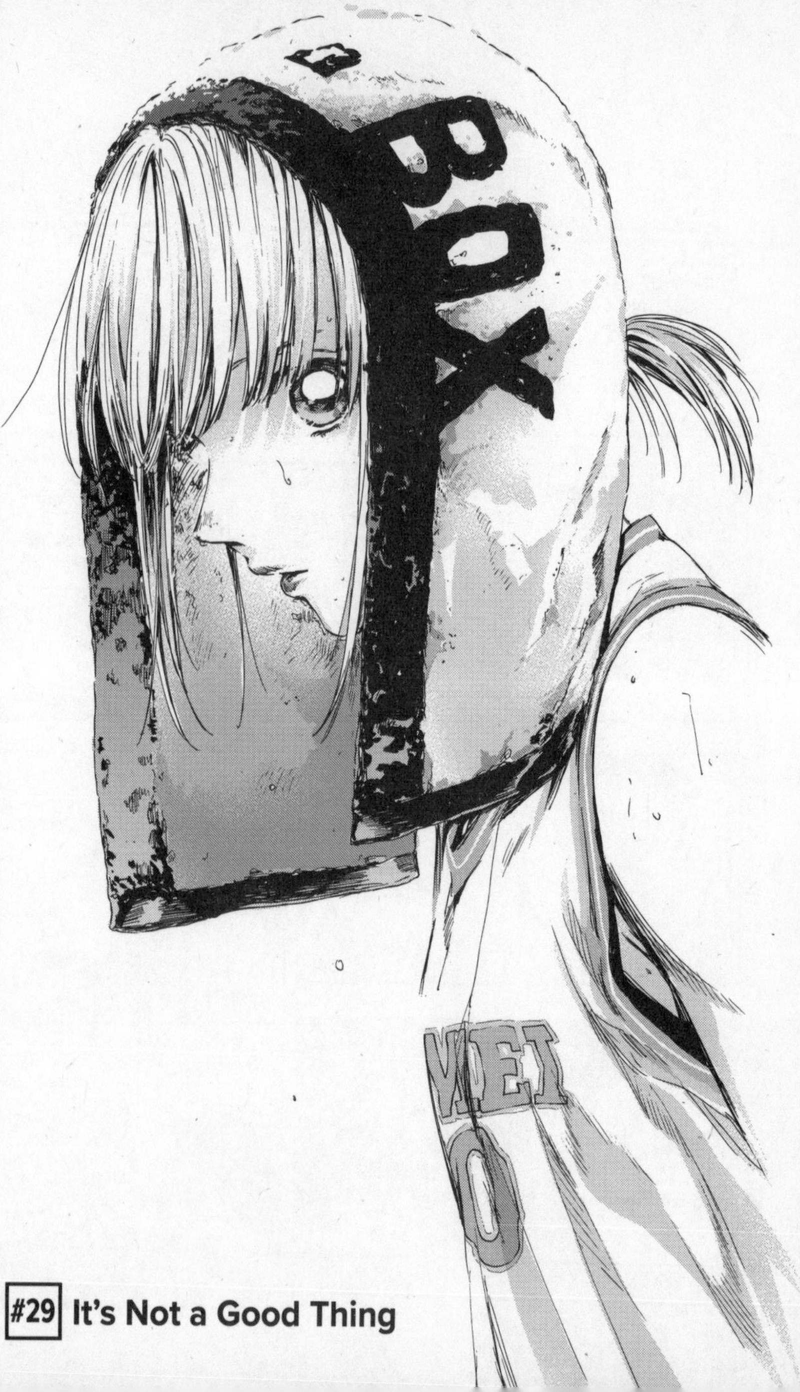
BOX
MEI
0

#29 It's Not a Good Thing

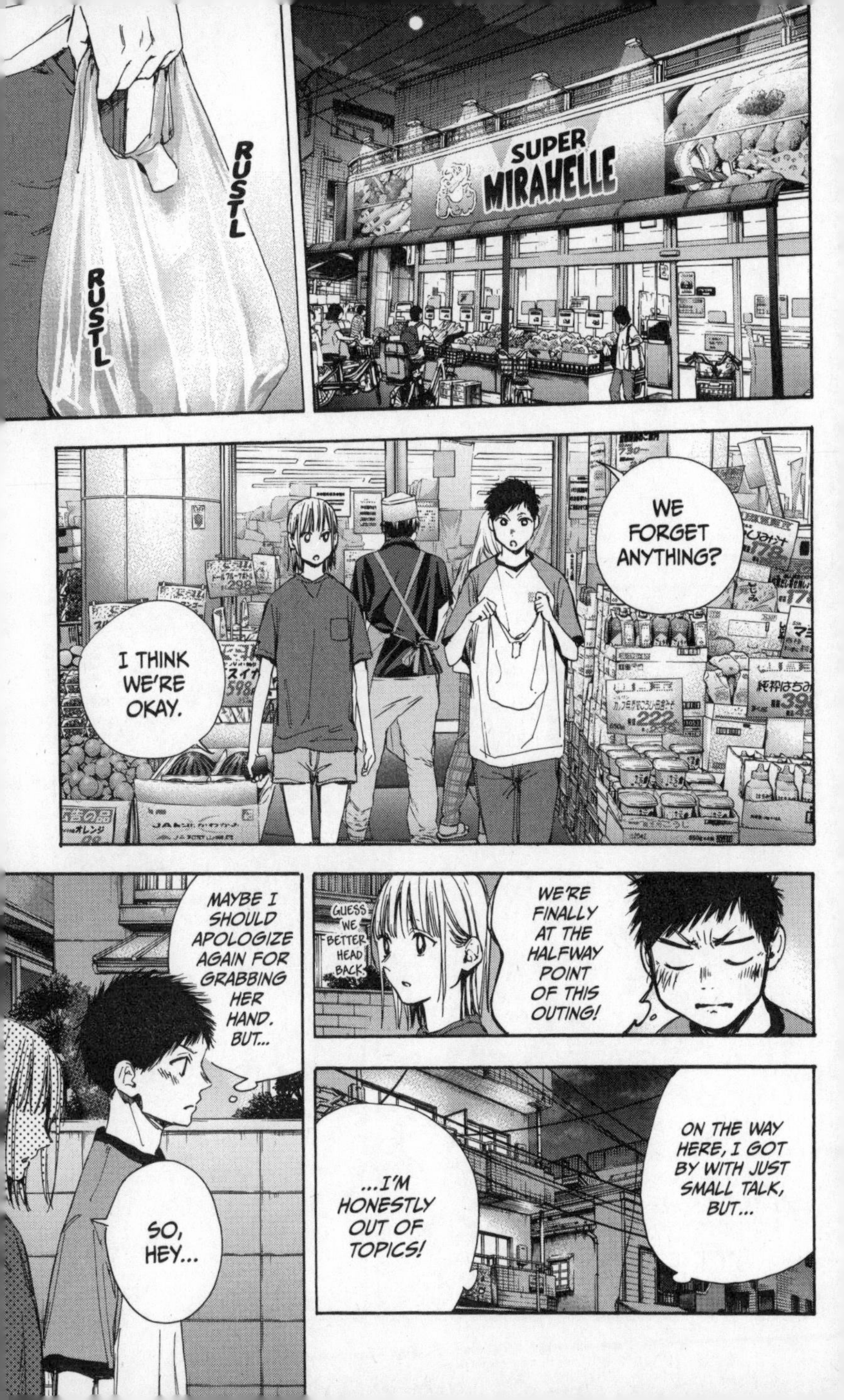
SUPER MIRAHELLE
RUSTL
RUSTL
WE FORGET ANYTHING?
I THINK WE'RE OKAY.
WE'RE FINALLY AT THE HALFWAY POINT OF THIS OUTING!
GUESS WE BETTER HEAD BACK.
MAYBE I SHOULD APOLOGIZE AGAIN FOR GRABBING HER HAND. BUT...
ON THE WAY HERE, I GOT BY WITH JUST SMALL TALK, BUT...
...I'M HONESTLY OUT OF TOPICS!
SO, HEY...

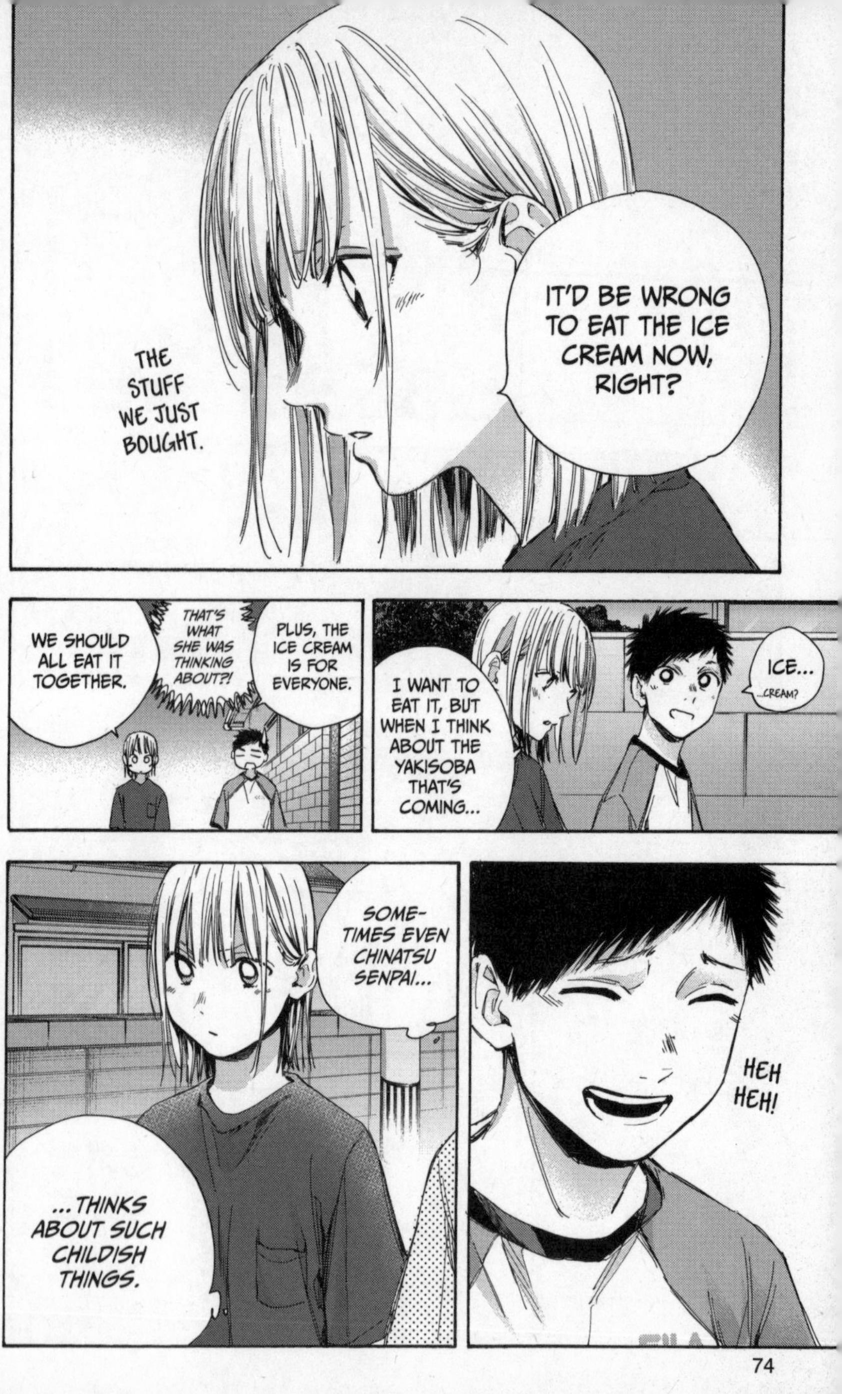
IT'D BE WRONG TO EAT THE ICE CREAM NOW, RIGHT?
THE STUFF WE JUST BOUGHT.
ICE...
...CREAM?
I WANT TO EAT IT, BUT WHEN I THINK ABOUT THE YAKISOBA THAT'S COMING...
PLUS, THE ICE CREAM IS FOR EVERYONE.
THAT'S WHAT SHE WAS THINKING ABOUT?!
WE SHOULD ALL EAT IT TOGETHER.
HEH HEH!
SOME-TIMES EVEN CHINATSU SENPAI...
...THINKS ABOUT SUCH CHILDISH THINGS.

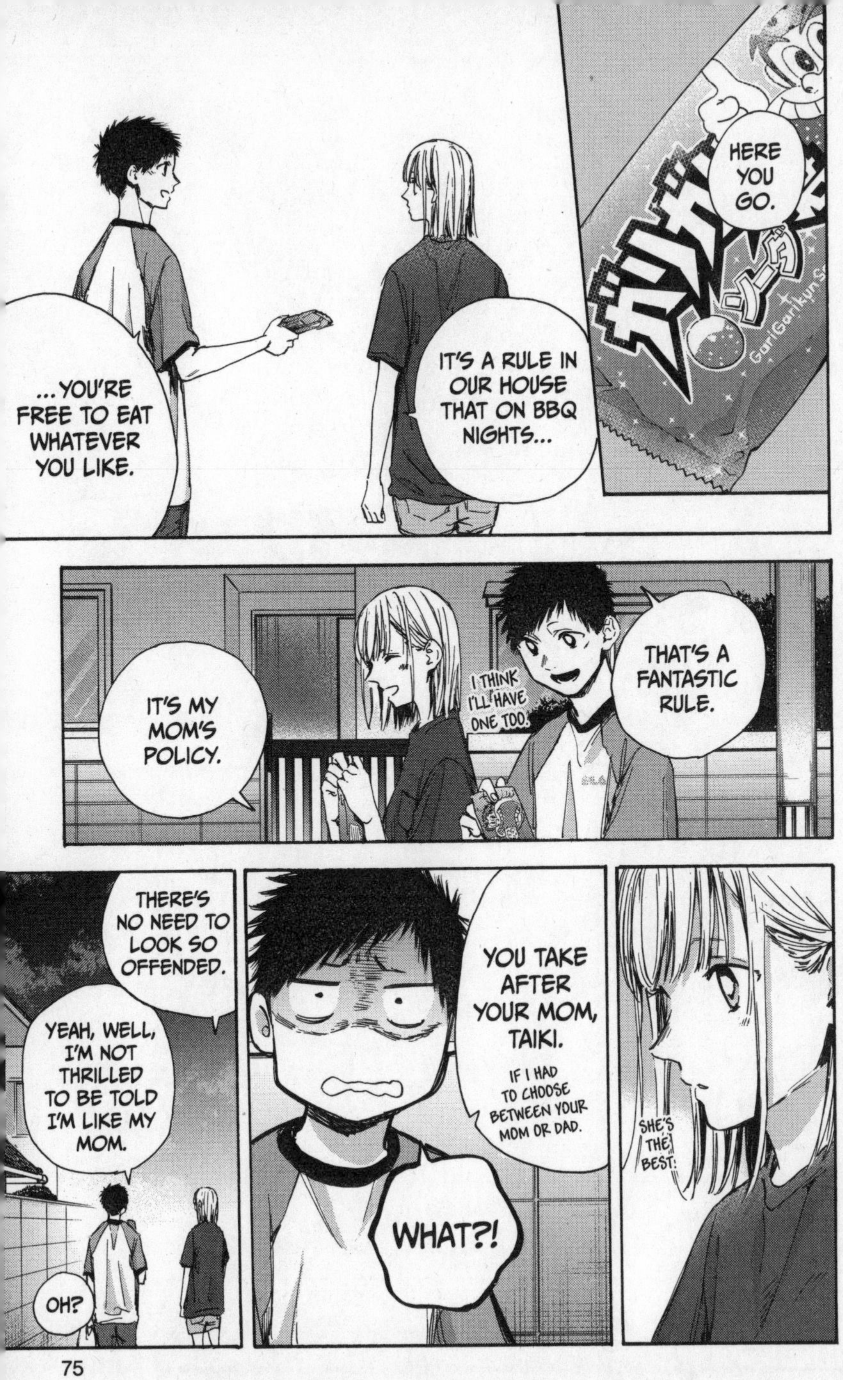
HERE YOU GO.
IT'S A RULE IN OUR HOUSE THAT ON BBQ NIGHTS...
...YOU'RE FREE TO EAT WHATEVER YOU LIKE.
THAT'S A FANTASTIC RULE.
I THINK I'LL HAVE ONE TOO.
IT'S MY MOM'S POLICY.
SHE'S THE BEST.
YOU TAKE AFTER YOUR MOM, TAIKI.
IF I HAD TO CHOOSE BETWEEN YOUR MOM OR DAD.
WHAT?!
THERE'S NO NEED TO LOOK SO OFFENDED.
YEAH, WELL, I'M NOT THRILLED TO BE TOLD I'M LIKE MY MOM.
OH?

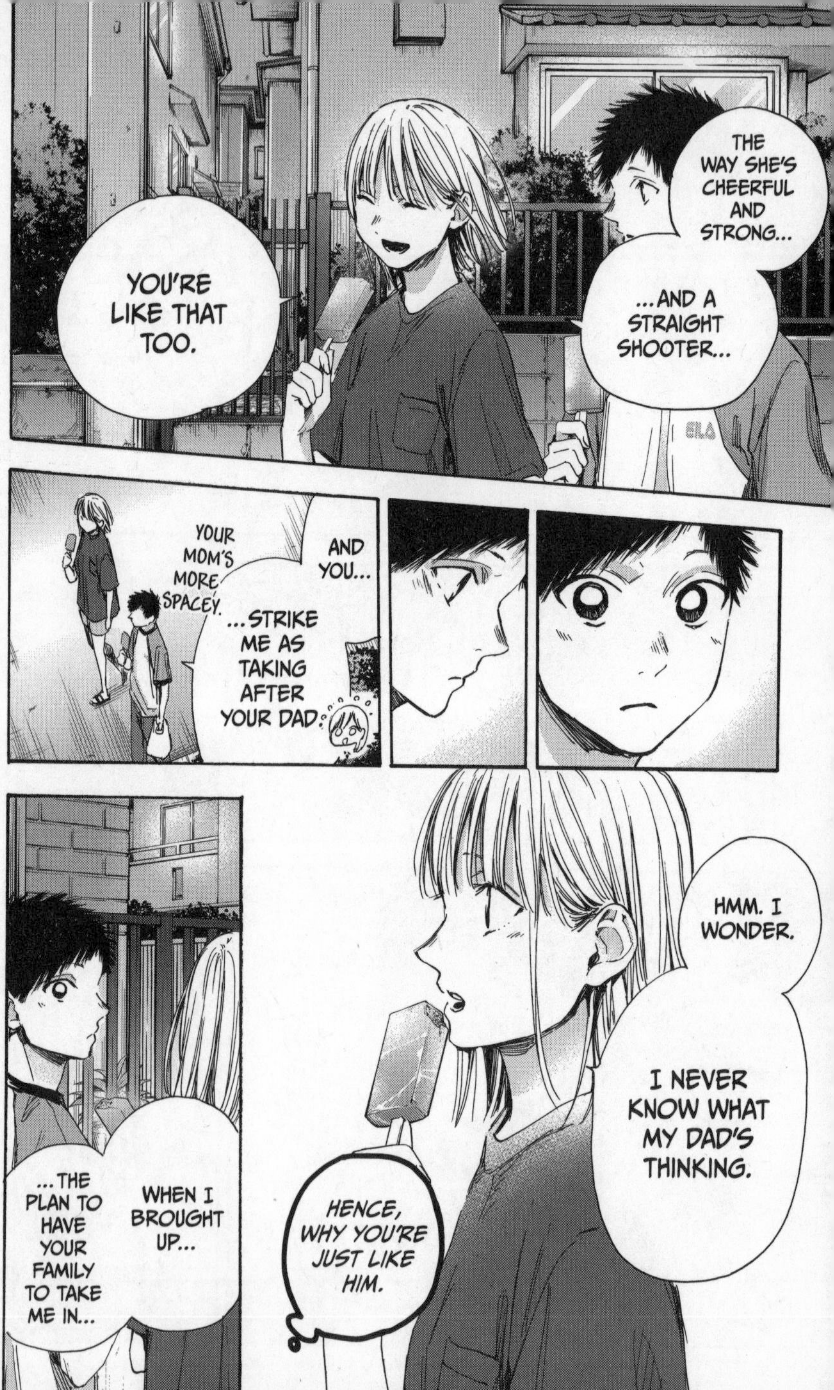

THE WAY SHE'S CHEERFUL AND STRONG...
...AND A STRAIGHT SHOOTER...
YOU'RE LIKE THAT TOO.
YOUR MOM'S MORE SPACEY.
AND YOU...
...STRIKE ME AS TAKING AFTER YOUR DAD.
HMM. I WONDER.
I NEVER KNOW WHAT MY DAD'S THINKING.
HENCE, WHY YOU'RE JUST LIKE HIM.
WHEN I BROUGHT UP...
...THE PLAN TO HAVE YOUR FAMILY TO TAKE ME IN...

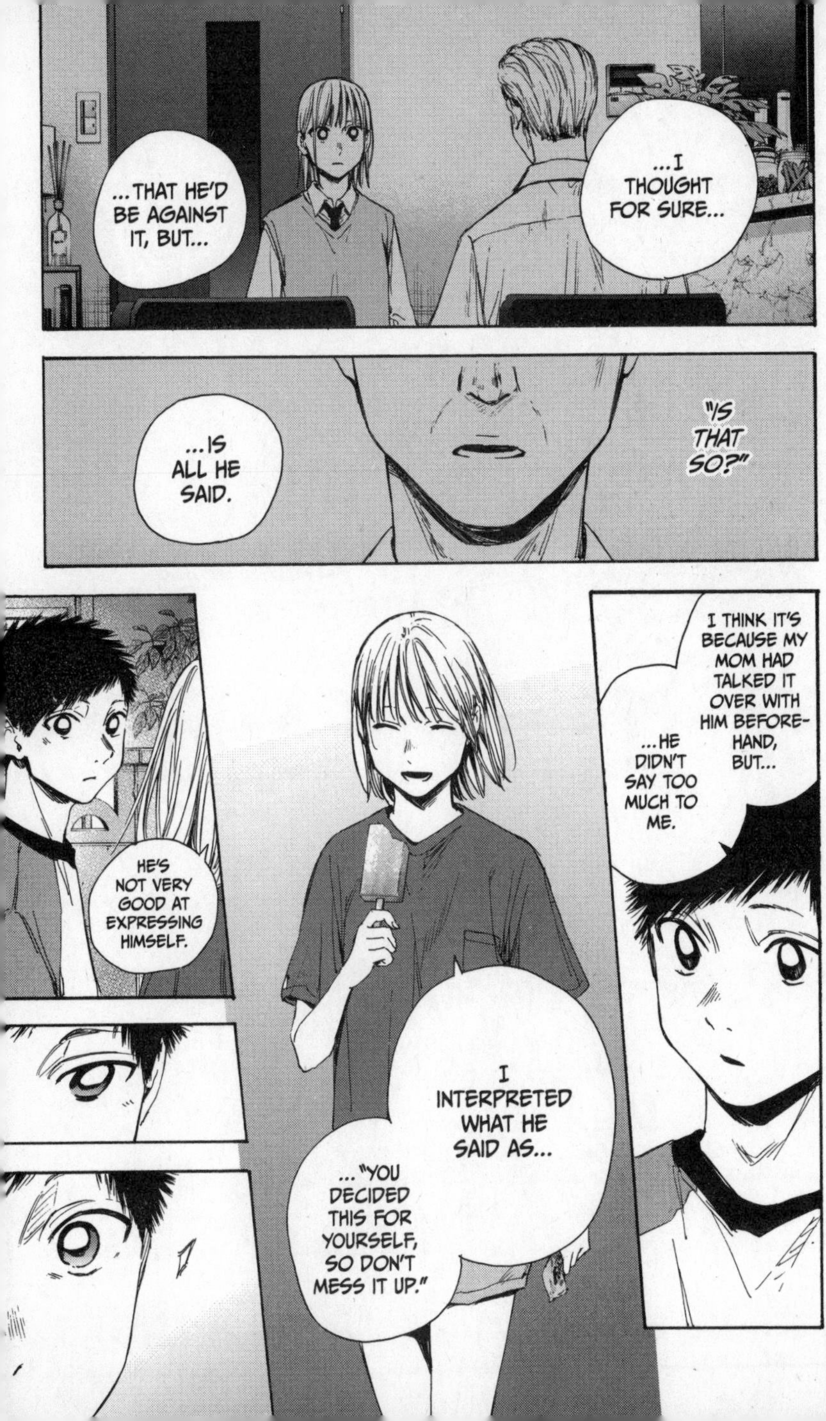
...I THOUGHT FOR SURE...
...THAT HE'D BE AGAINST IT, BUT...
"IS THAT SO?"
...IS ALL HE SAID.
I THINK IT'S BECAUSE MY MOM HAD TALKED IT OVER WITH HIM BEFOREHAND, BUT...
...HE DIDN'T SAY TOO MUCH TO ME.
HE'S NOT VERY GOOD AT EXPRESSING HIMSELF.
I INTERPRETED WHAT HE SAID AS...
..."YOU DECIDED THIS FOR YOURSELF, SO DON'T MESS IT UP."

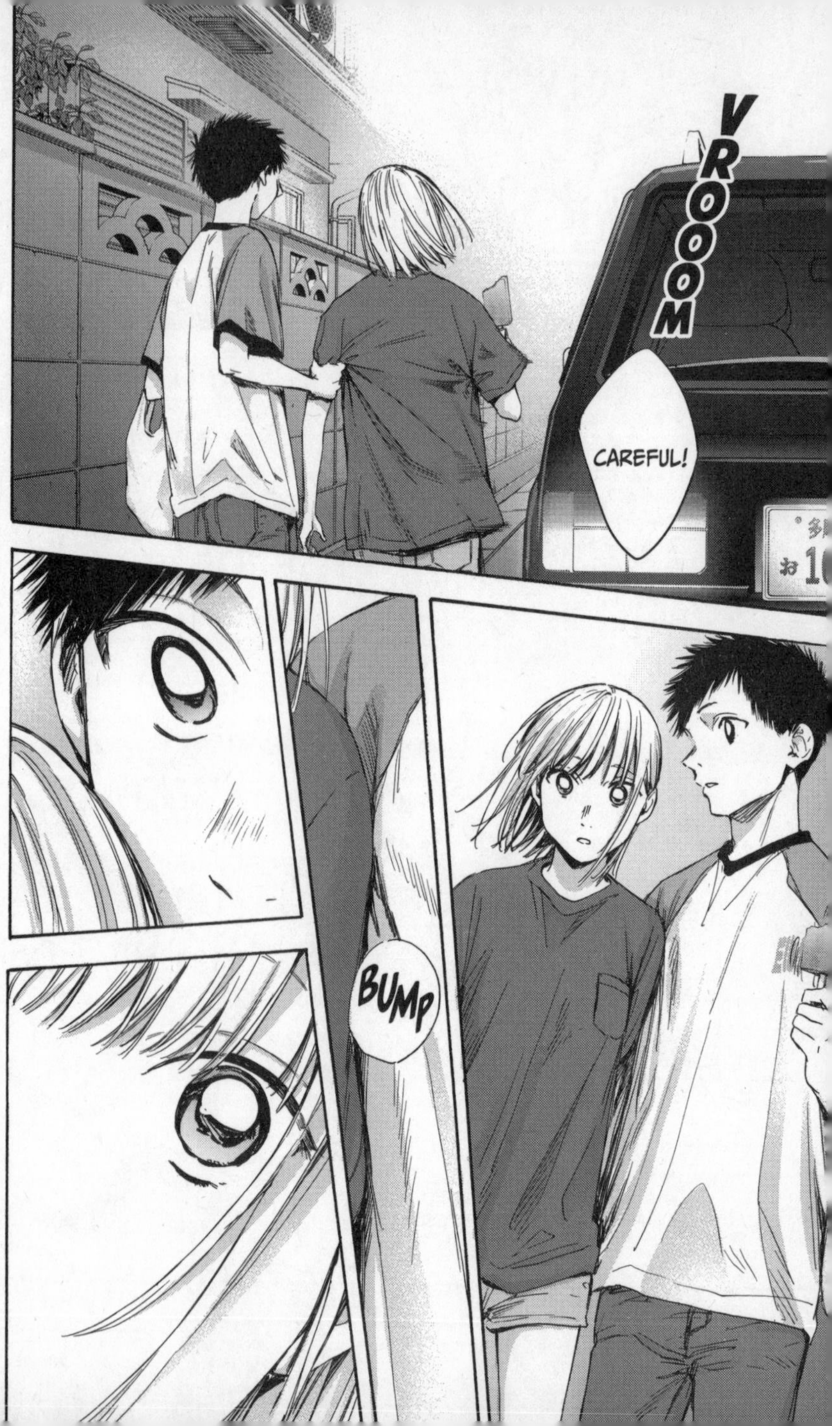
VROOOM
CAREFUL!
BUMP

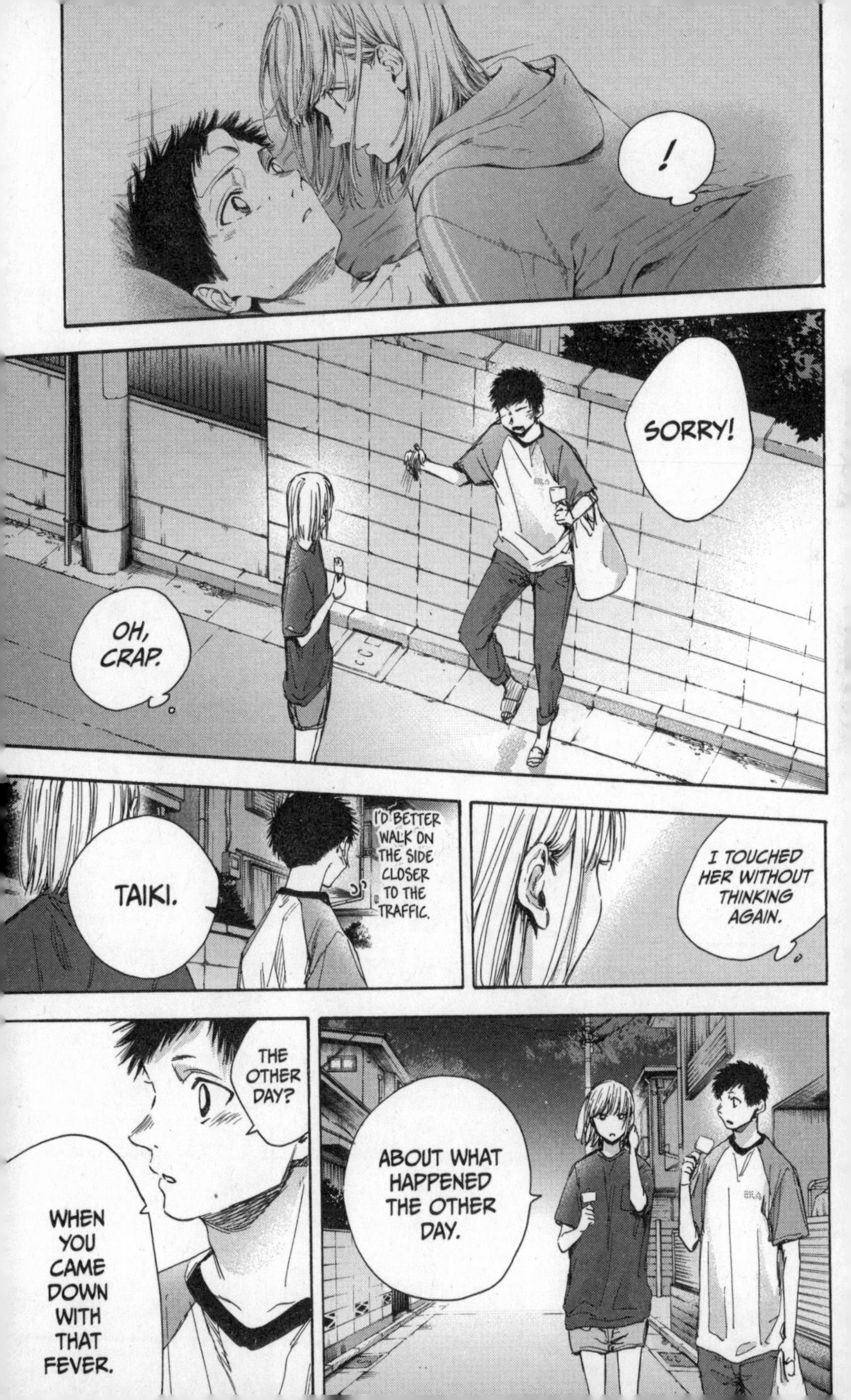
!
SORRY!
OH, CRAP.
I TOUCHED HER WITHOUT THINKING AGAIN.
I'D BETTER WALK ON THE SIDE CLOSER TO THE TRAFFIC.
TAIKI.
ABOUT WHAT HAPPENED THE OTHER DAY.
THE OTHER DAY?
WHEN YOU CAME DOWN WITH THAT FEVER.

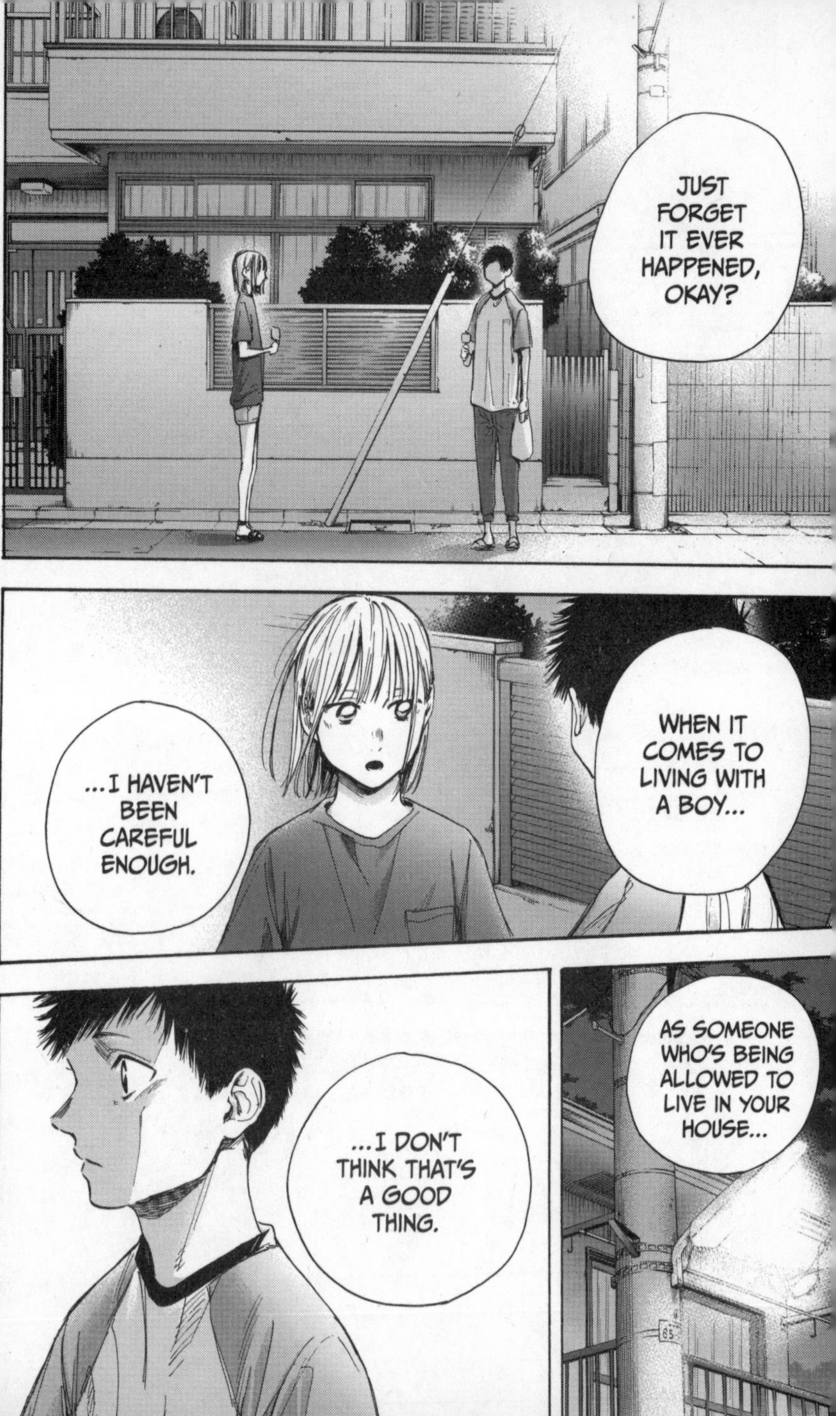
JUST FORGET IT EVER HAPPENED, OKAY?
WHEN IT COMES TO LIVING WITH A BOY...
...I HAVEN'T BEEN CAREFUL ENOUGH.
AS SOMEONE WHO'S BEING ALLOWED TO LIVE IN YOUR HOUSE...
...I DON'T THINK THAT'S A GOOD THING.

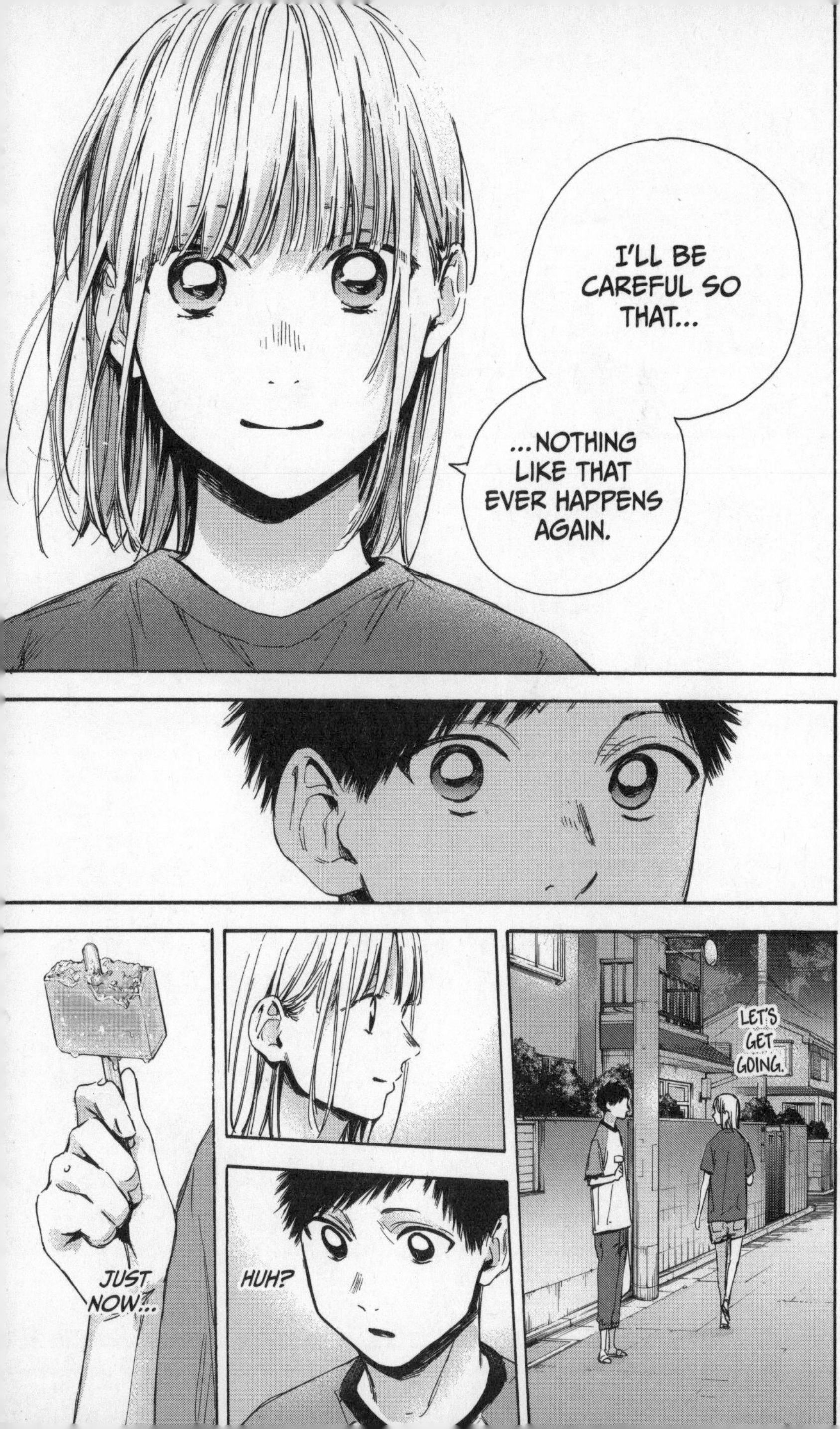
I'LL BE CAREFUL SO THAT...
...NOTHING LIKE THAT EVER HAPPENS AGAIN.
LET'S GET GOING.
HUH?
JUST NOW...

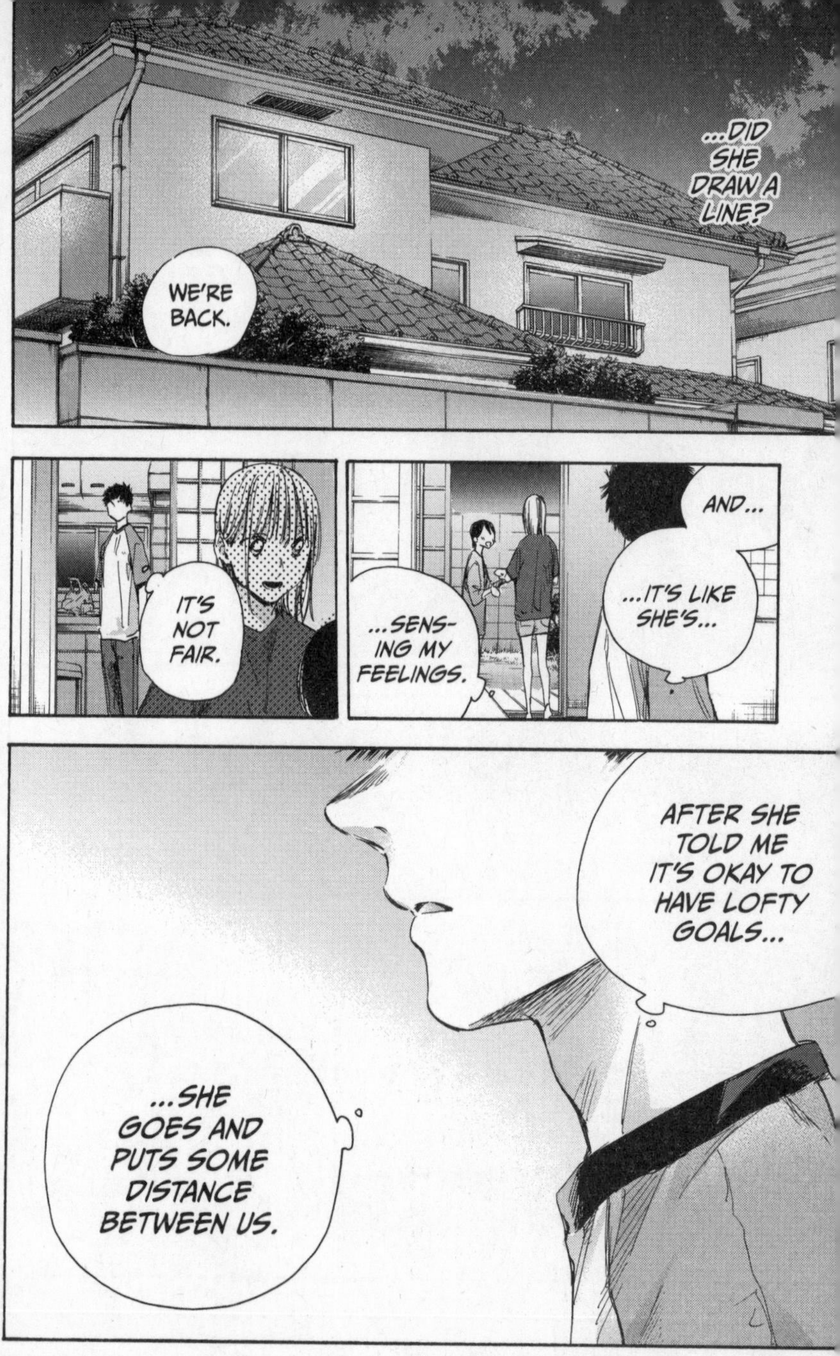
...DID SHE DRAW A LINE?
WE'RE BACK.
AND...
...IT'S LIKE SHE'S...
...SENS-ING MY FEELINGS.
IT'S NOT FAIR.
AFTER SHE TOLD ME IT'S OKAY TO HAVE LOFTY GOALS...
...SHE GOES AND PUTS SOME DISTANCE BETWEEN US.

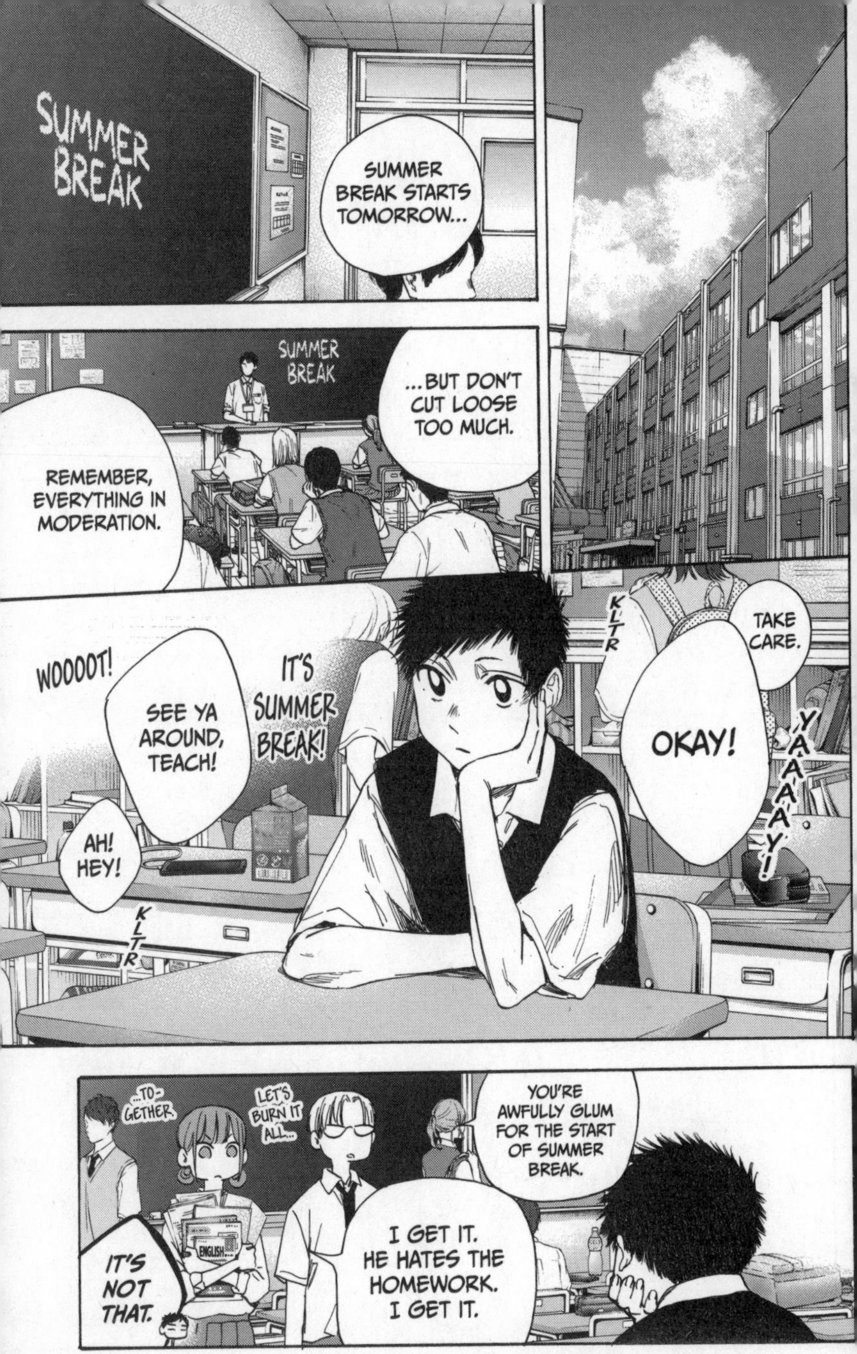
SUMMER BREAK
SUMMER BREAK STARTS TOMORROW...
SUMMER BREAK
...BUT DON'T CUT LOOSE TOO MUCH.
REMEMBER, EVERYTHING IN MODERATION.
TAKE CARE.
KLTR
OKAY!
YAAAAAY!
IT'S SUMMER BREAK!
SEE YA AROUND, TEACH!
WOOOOT!
AH! HEY!
KLTR
YOU'RE AWFULLY GLUM FOR THE START OF SUMMER BREAK.
LET'S BURN IT ALL...
...TO- GETHER.
ENGLISH
I GET IT. HE HATES THE HOMEWORK. I GET IT.
IT'S NOT THAT.

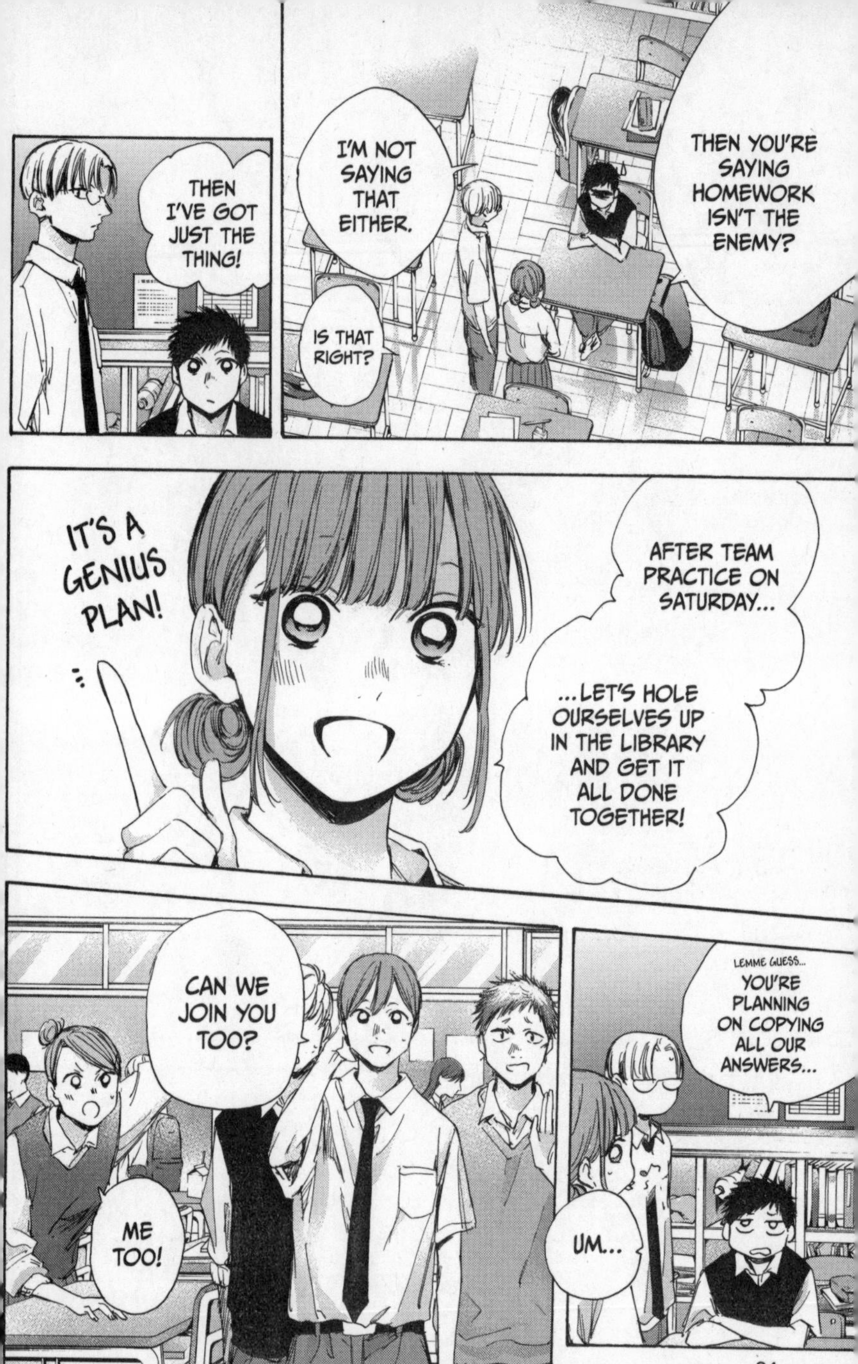
THEN YOU'RE SAYING HOMEWORK ISN'T THE ENEMY?
I'M NOT SAYING THAT EITHER.
IS THAT RIGHT?
THEN I'VE GOT JUST THE THING!
AFTER TEAM PRACTICE ON SATURDAY...
...LET'S HOLE OURSELVES UP IN THE LIBRARY AND GET IT ALL DONE TOGETHER!
IT'S A GENIUS PLAN!
LEMME GUESS... YOU'RE PLANNING ON COPYING ALL OUR ANSWERS...
UM...
CAN WE JOIN YOU TOO?
ME TOO!

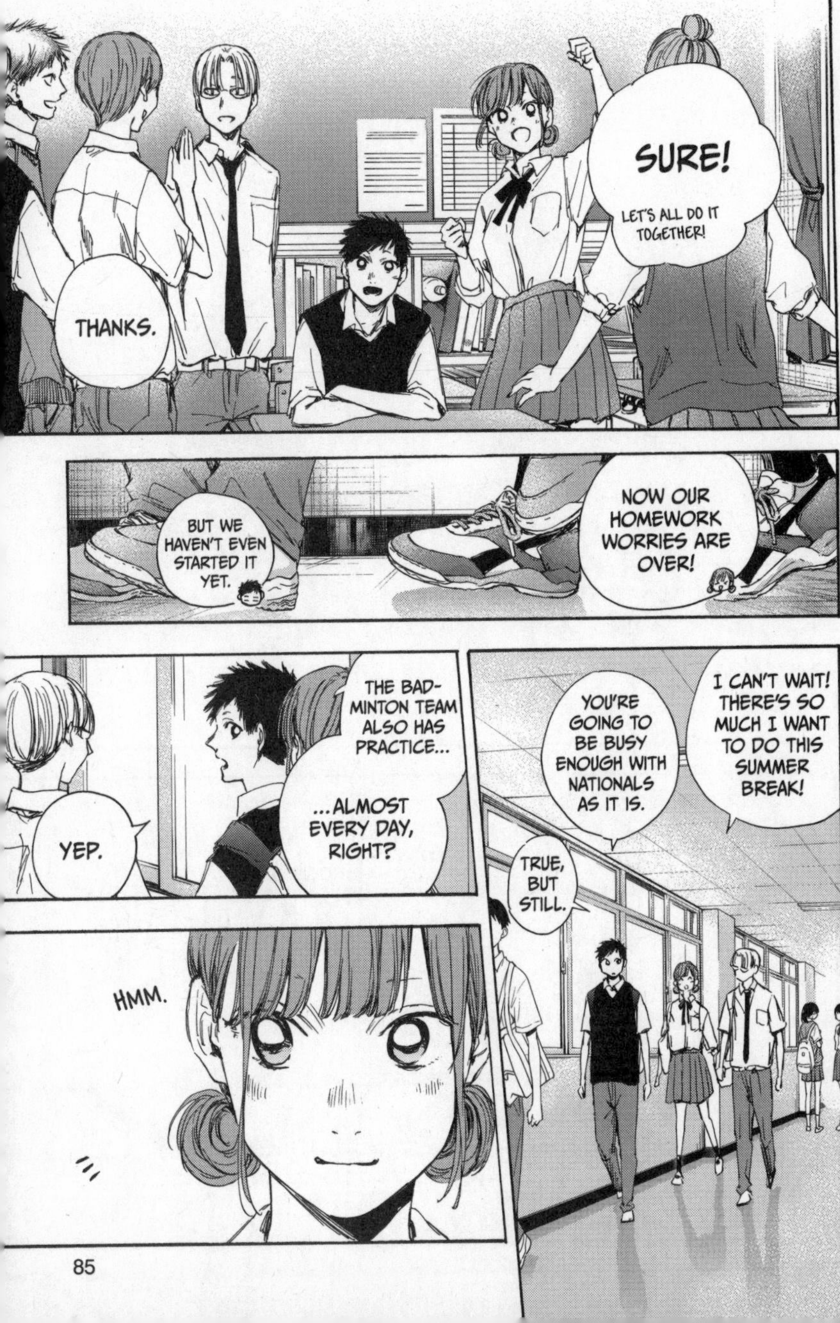
SURE!
LET'S ALL DO IT TOGETHER!
THANKS.
NOW OUR HOMEWORK WORRIES ARE OVER!
BUT WE HAVEN'T EVEN STARTED IT YET.
I CAN'T WAIT! THERE'S SO MUCH I WANT TO DO THIS SUMMER BREAK!
YOU'RE GOING TO BE BUSY ENOUGH WITH NATIONALS AS IT IS.
TRUE, BUT STILL.
THE BAD-MINTON TEAM ALSO HAS PRACTICE...
...ALMOST EVERY DAY, RIGHT?
YEP.
HMM.

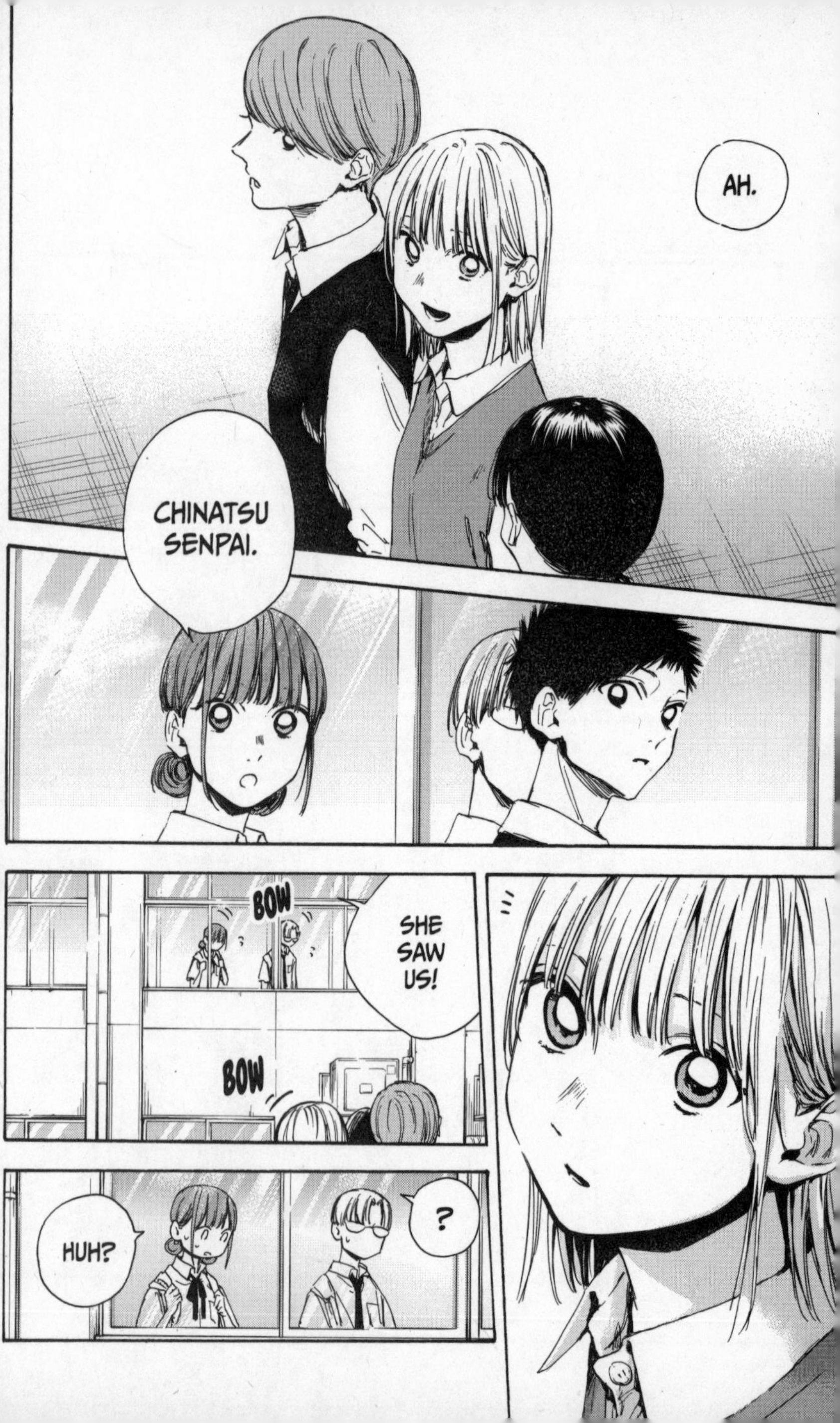
AH.
CHINATSU SENPAI.
SHE SAW US!
BOW
BOW
?
HUH?

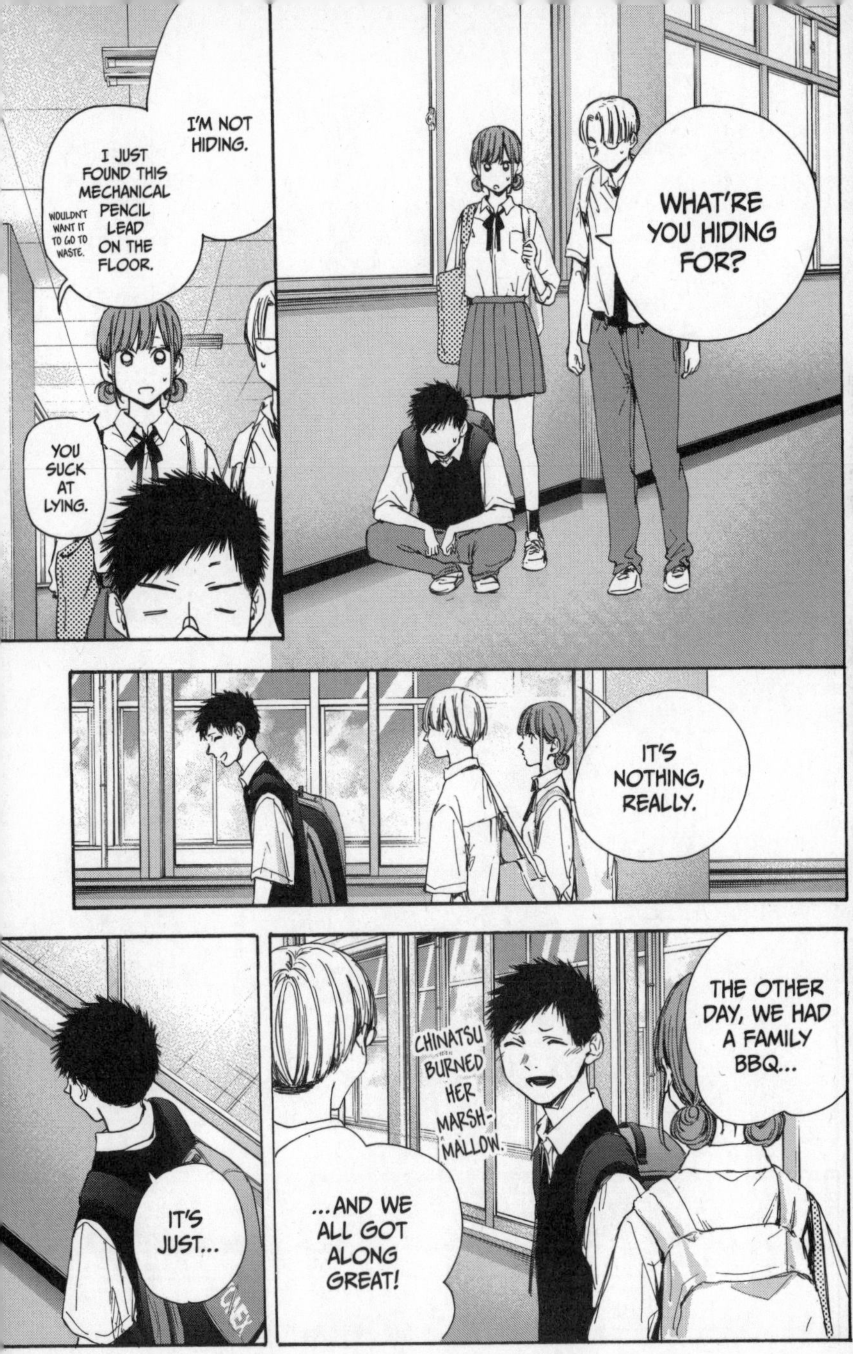
WHAT'RE YOU HIDING FOR?
I'M NOT HIDING.
I JUST FOUND THIS MECHANICAL PENCIL LEAD ON THE FLOOR.
WOULDN'T WANT IT TO GO TO WASTE.
YOU SUCK AT LYING.
IT'S NOTHING, REALLY.
THE OTHER DAY, WE HAD A FAMILY BBQ...
CHINATSU BURNED HER MARSH-MALLOW.
...AND WE ALL GOT ALONG GREAT!
IT'S JUST...

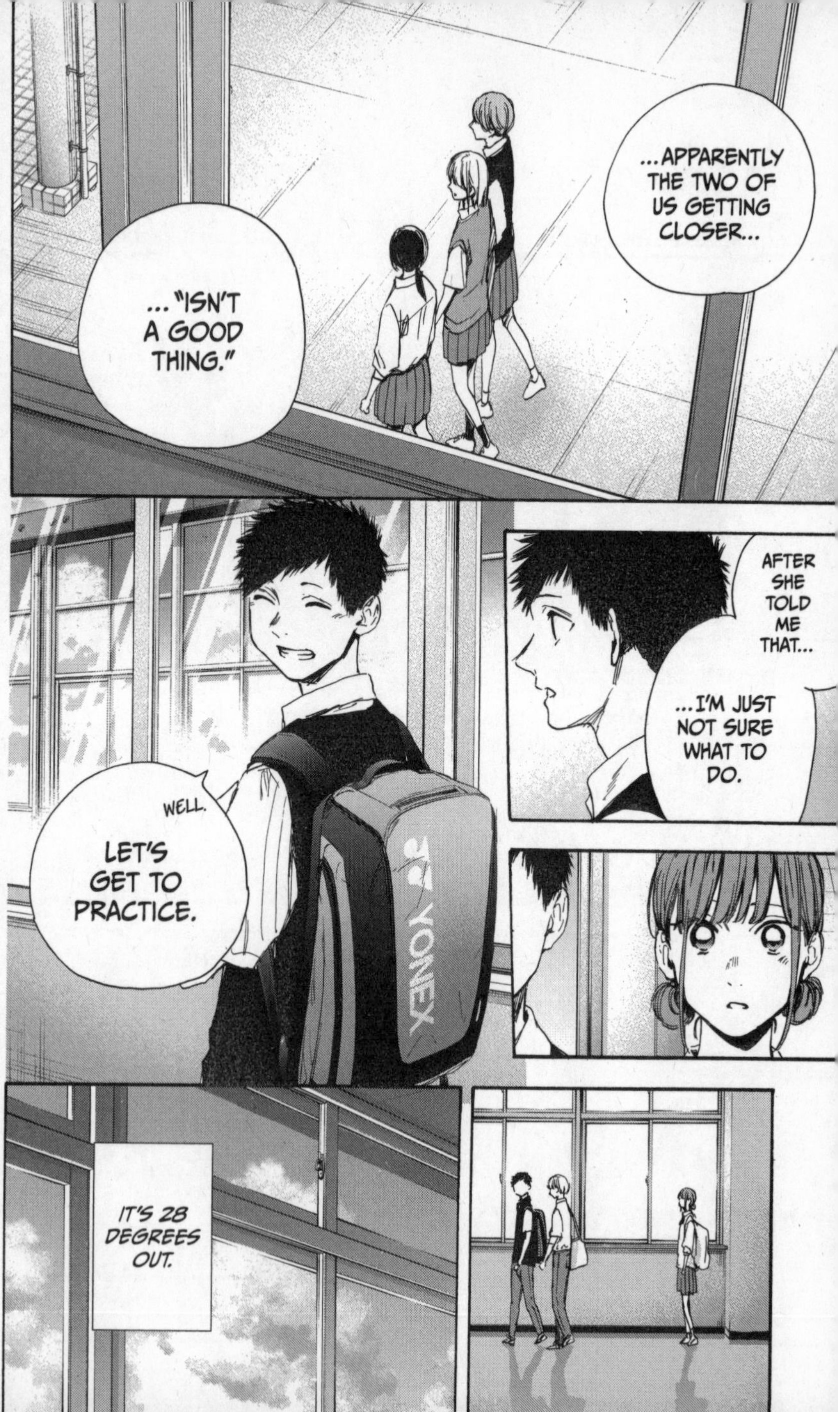
...APPARENTLY THE TWO OF US GETTING CLOSER...
..."ISN'T A GOOD THING."
AFTER SHE TOLD ME THAT...
...I'M JUST NOT SURE WHAT TO DO.
WELL.
LET'S GET TO PRACTICE.
YONEX
IT'S 28 DEGREES OUT.

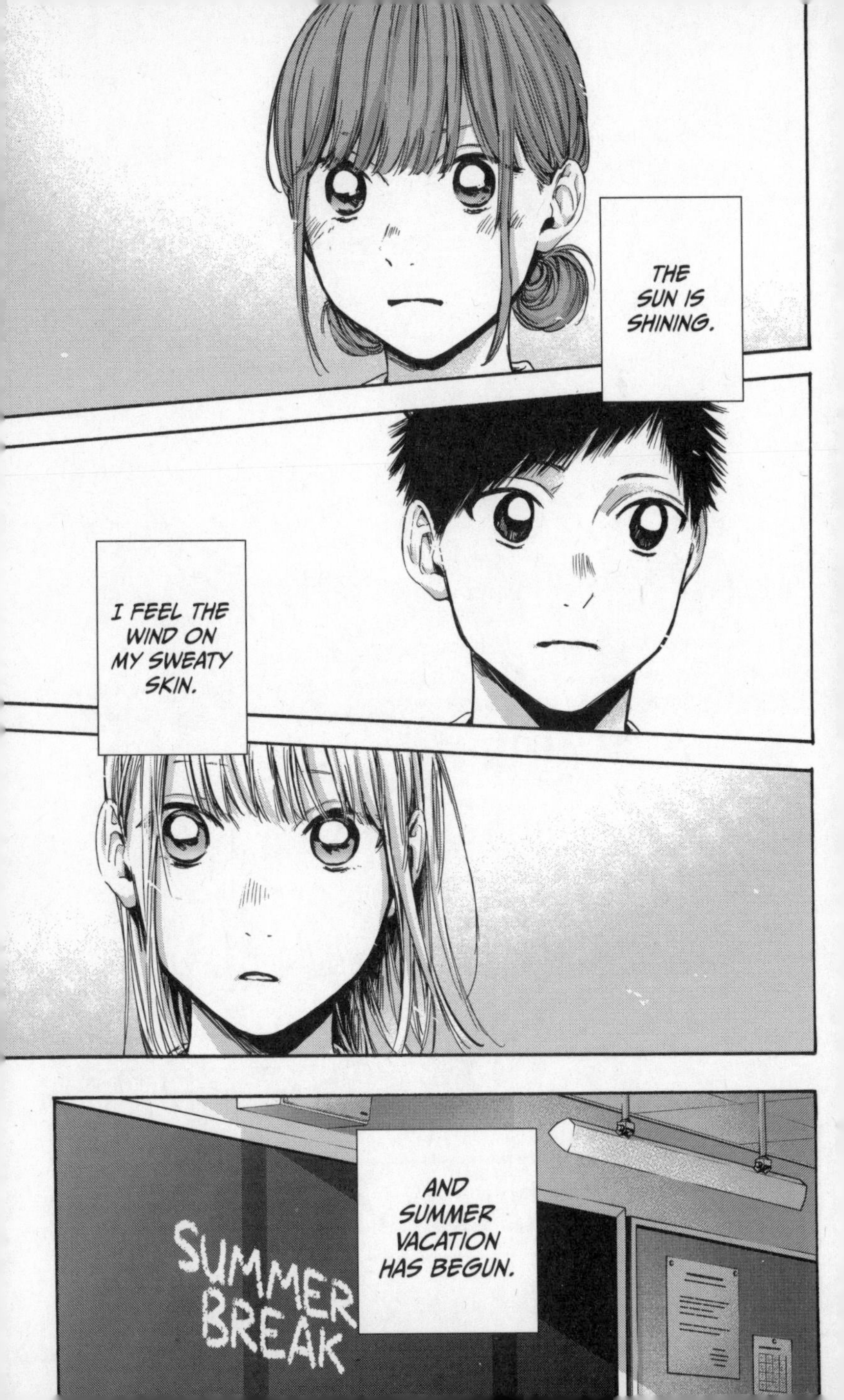
THE SUN IS SHINING.
I FEEL THE WIND ON MY SWEATY SKIN.
AND SUMMER VACATION HAS BEGUN.
SUMMER BREAK

CHII BURNS HER MARSHMALLOW

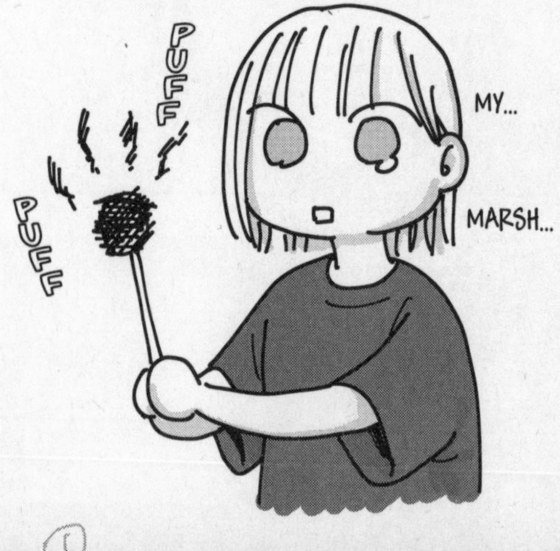
PUFF
PUFF
MY...
MARSH...

#30 Getting Closer

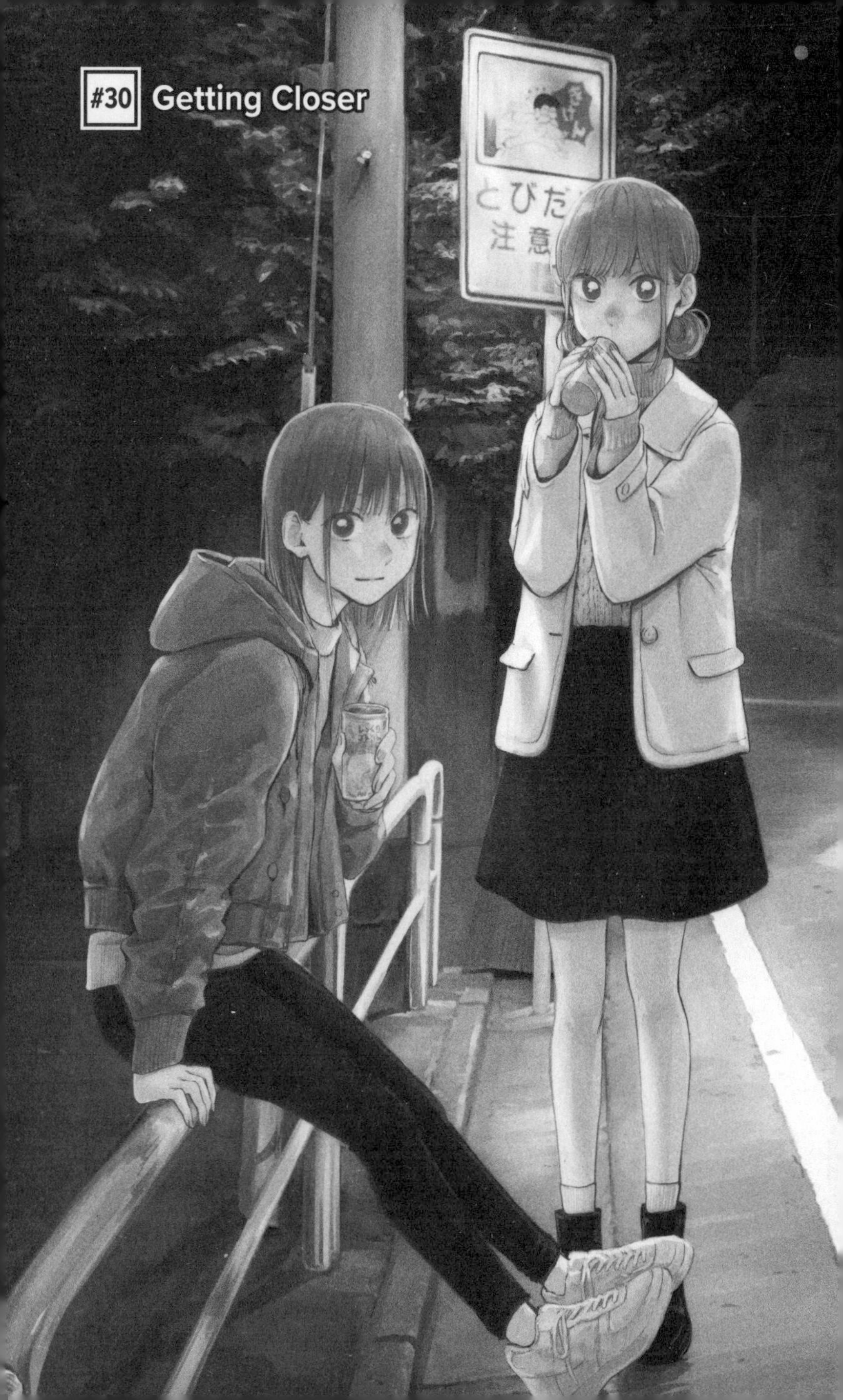
とびだ
注意

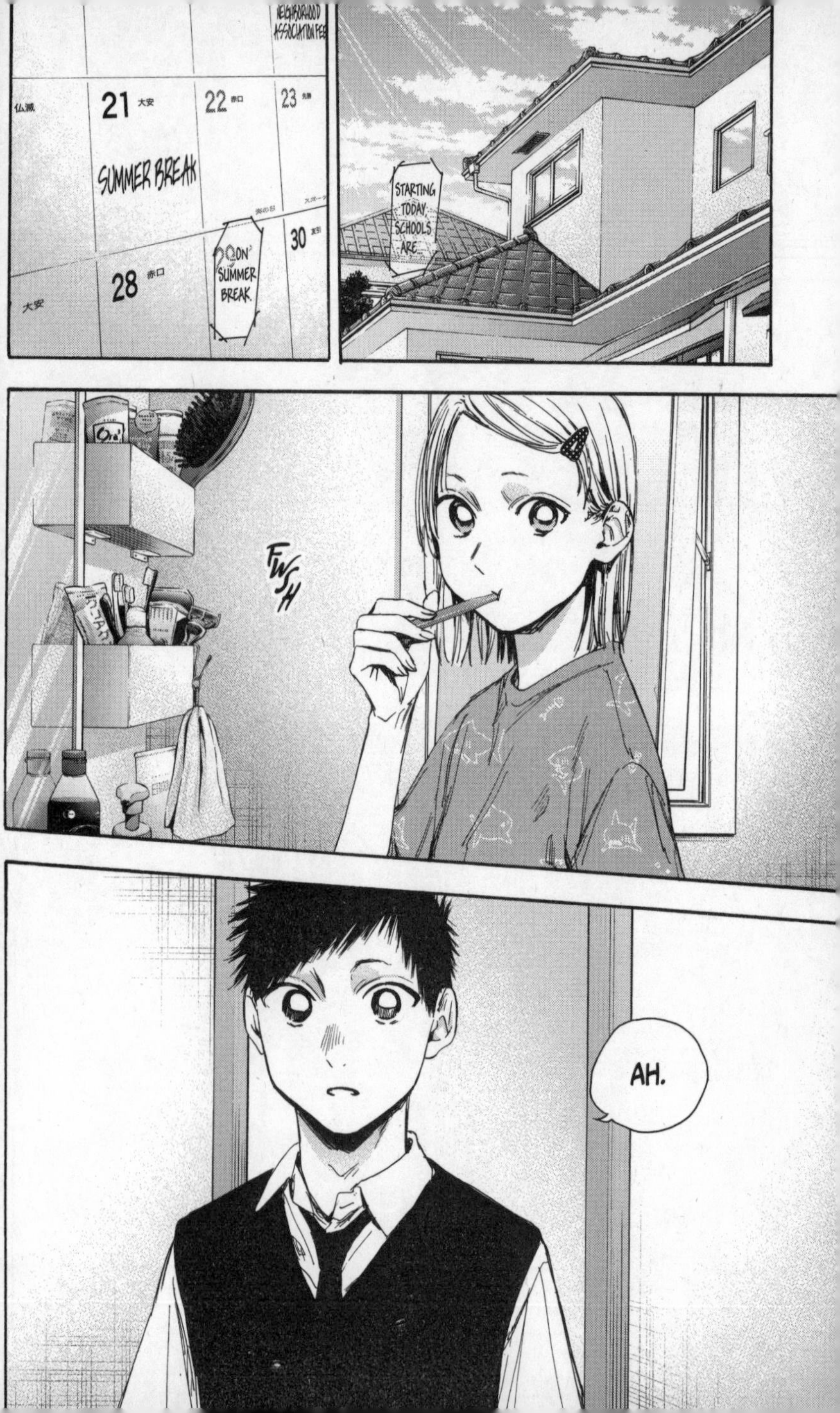

STARTING TODAY, SCHOOLS ARE...
NEIGHBORHOOD ASSOCIATION FEE
21 大安
22 赤口
仏滅
SUMMER BREAK
28 赤口
大安
30
...ON SUMMER BREAK.
FWSH
AH.

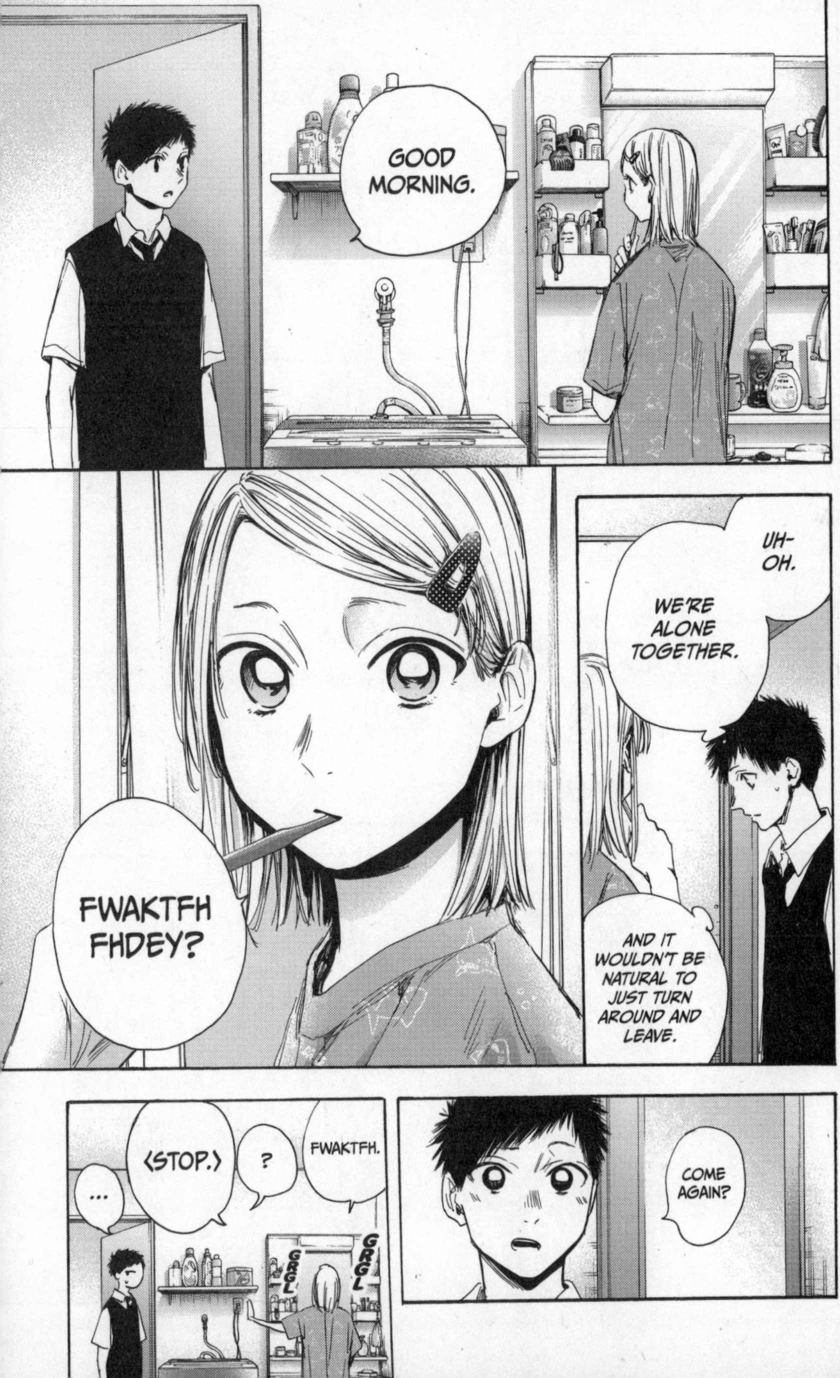
GOOD MORNING.
UH-OH.
WE'RE ALONE TOGETHER.
AND IT WOULDN'T BE NATURAL TO JUST TURN AROUND AND LEAVE.
FWAKTFH FHDEY?
COME AGAIN?
FWAKTFH.
?
〈STOP.〉
...
GRGL
GRGL

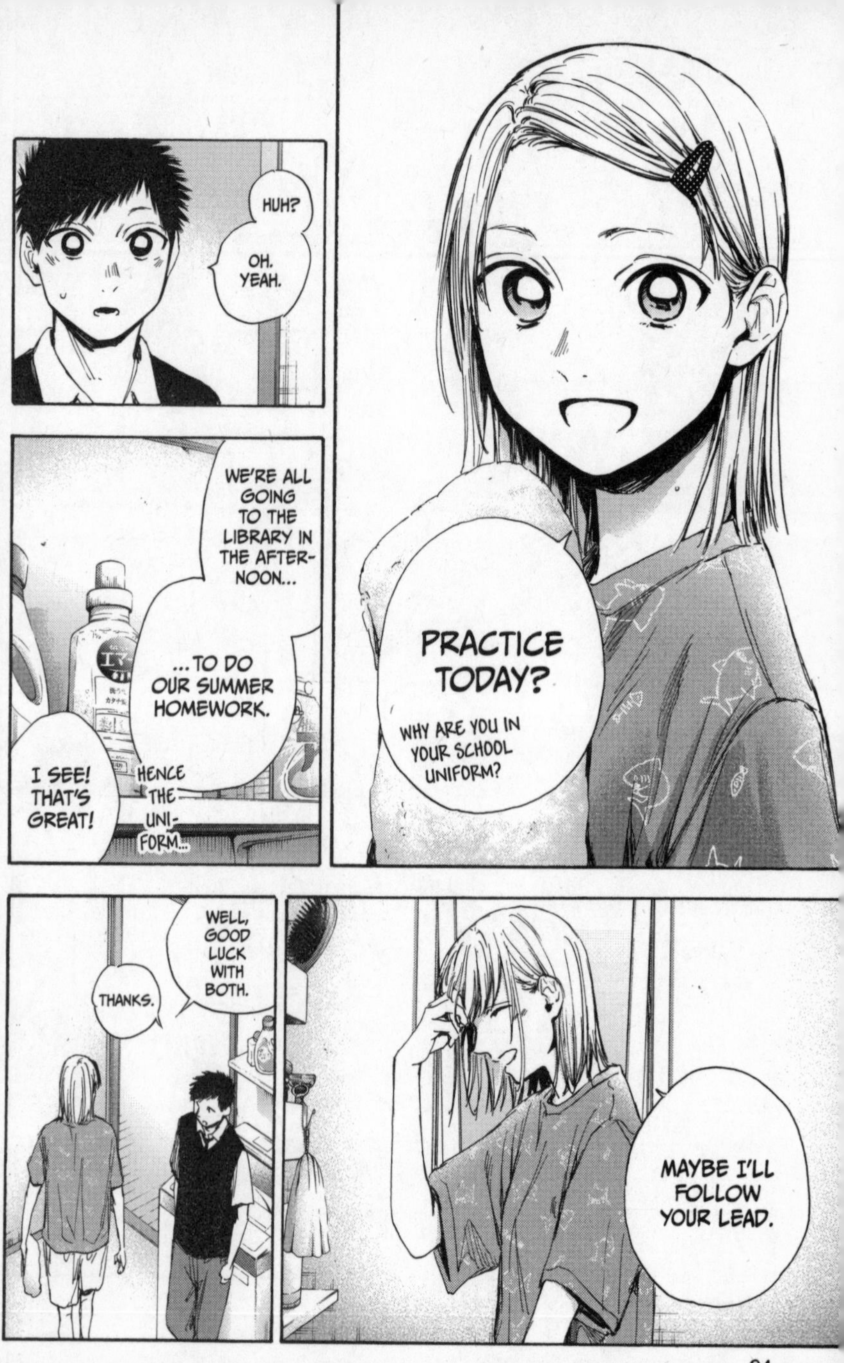
PRACTICE TODAY?
WHY ARE YOU IN YOUR SCHOOL UNIFORM?
HUH?
OH. YEAH.
WE'RE ALL GOING TO THE LIBRARY IN THE AFTER-NOON...
...TO DO OUR SUMMER HOMEWORK.
HENCE THE UNI-FORM...
I SEE! THAT'S GREAT!
MAYBE I'LL FOLLOW YOUR LEAD.
WELL, GOOD LUCK WITH BOTH.
THANKS.

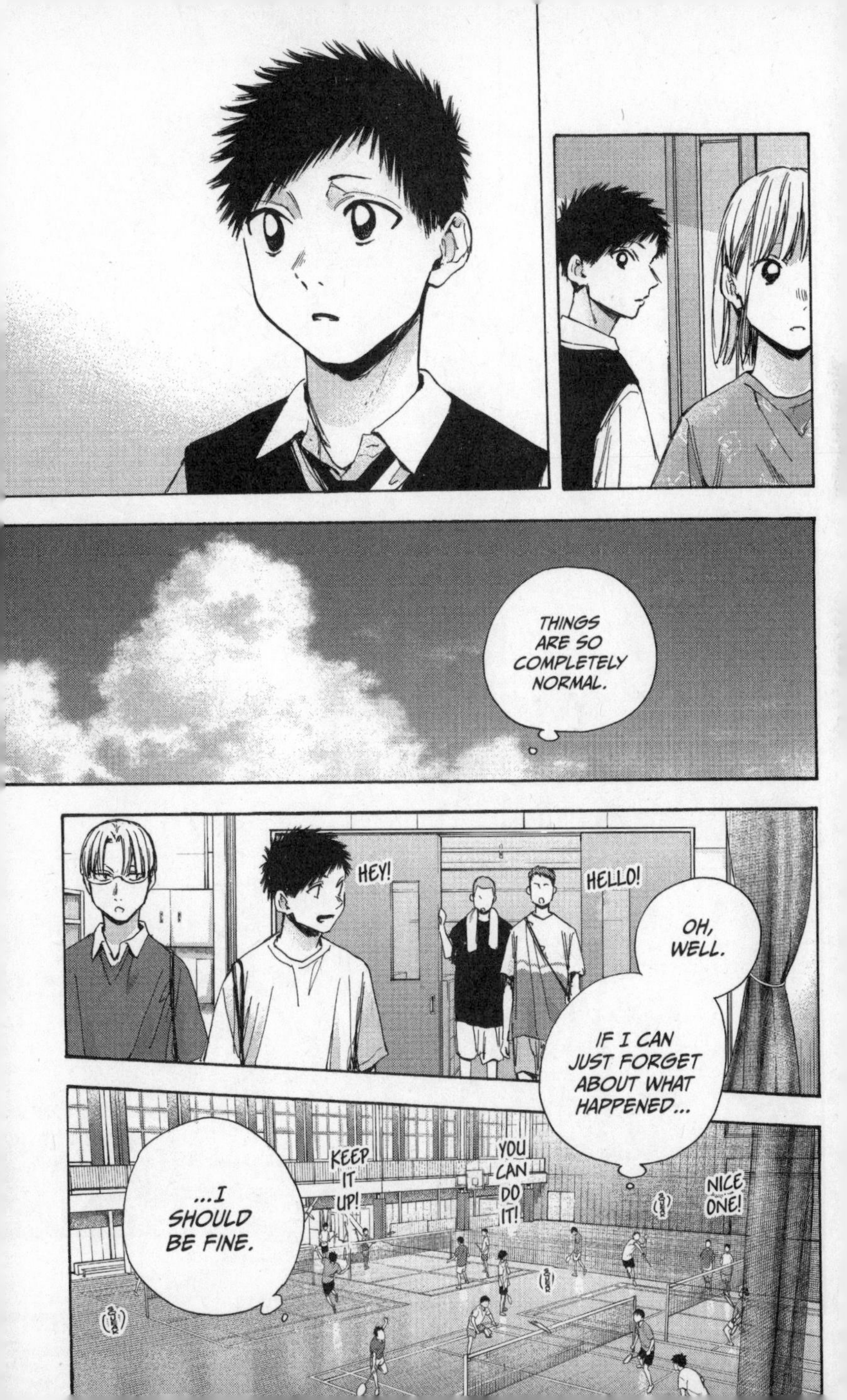
THINGS ARE SO COMPLETELY NORMAL.
OH, WELL.
HELLO!
HEY!
IF I CAN JUST FORGET ABOUT WHAT HAPPENED...
NICE ONE!
YOU CAN DO IT!
KEEP IT UP!
...I SHOULD BE FINE.

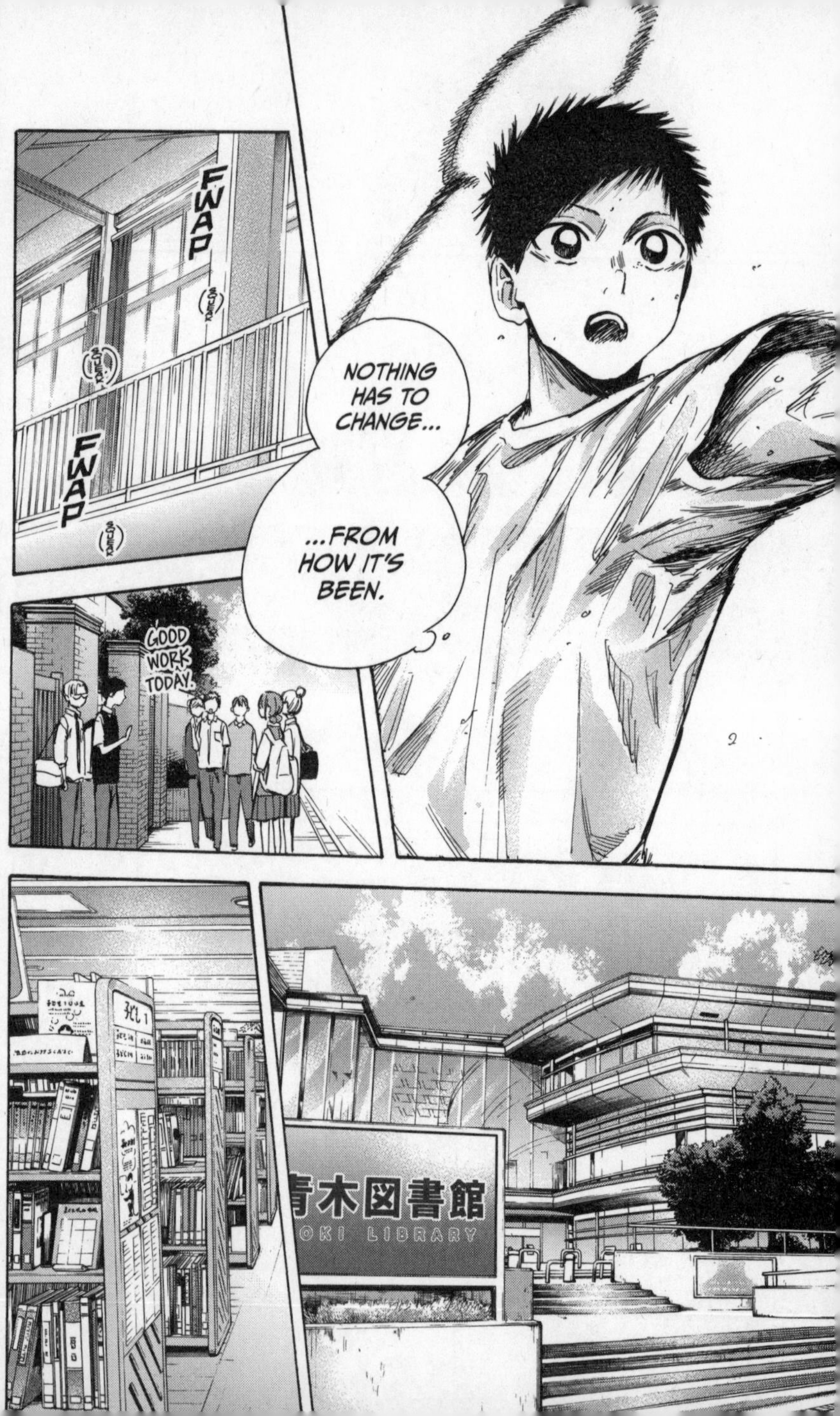
NOTHING HAS TO CHANGE...
...FROM HOW IT'S BEEN.
FWAP
(SQUEAK)
(SQUEAK)
FWAP
(SQUEAK)
GOOD WORK TODAY.
青木図書館
OKI LIBRARY

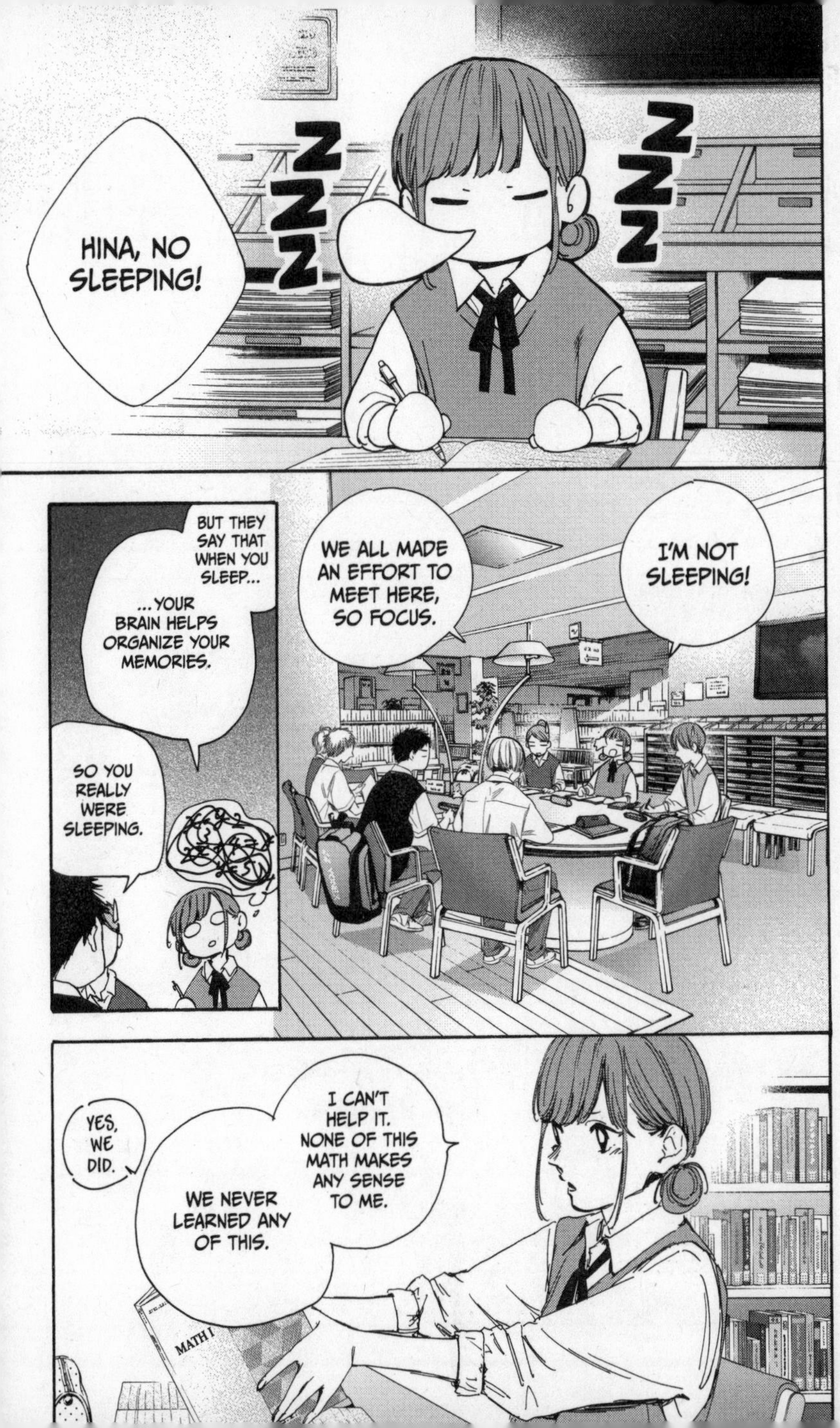
ZZZ
ZZZ
HINA, NO SLEEPING!
I'M NOT SLEEPING!
WE ALL MADE AN EFFORT TO MEET HERE, SO FOCUS.
BUT THEY SAY THAT WHEN YOU SLEEP...
...YOUR BRAIN HELPS ORGANIZE YOUR MEMORIES.
SO YOU REALLY WERE SLEEPING.
I CAN'T HELP IT. NONE OF THIS MATH MAKES ANY SENSE TO ME.
WE NEVER LEARNED ANY OF THIS.
YES, WE DID.
MATH I

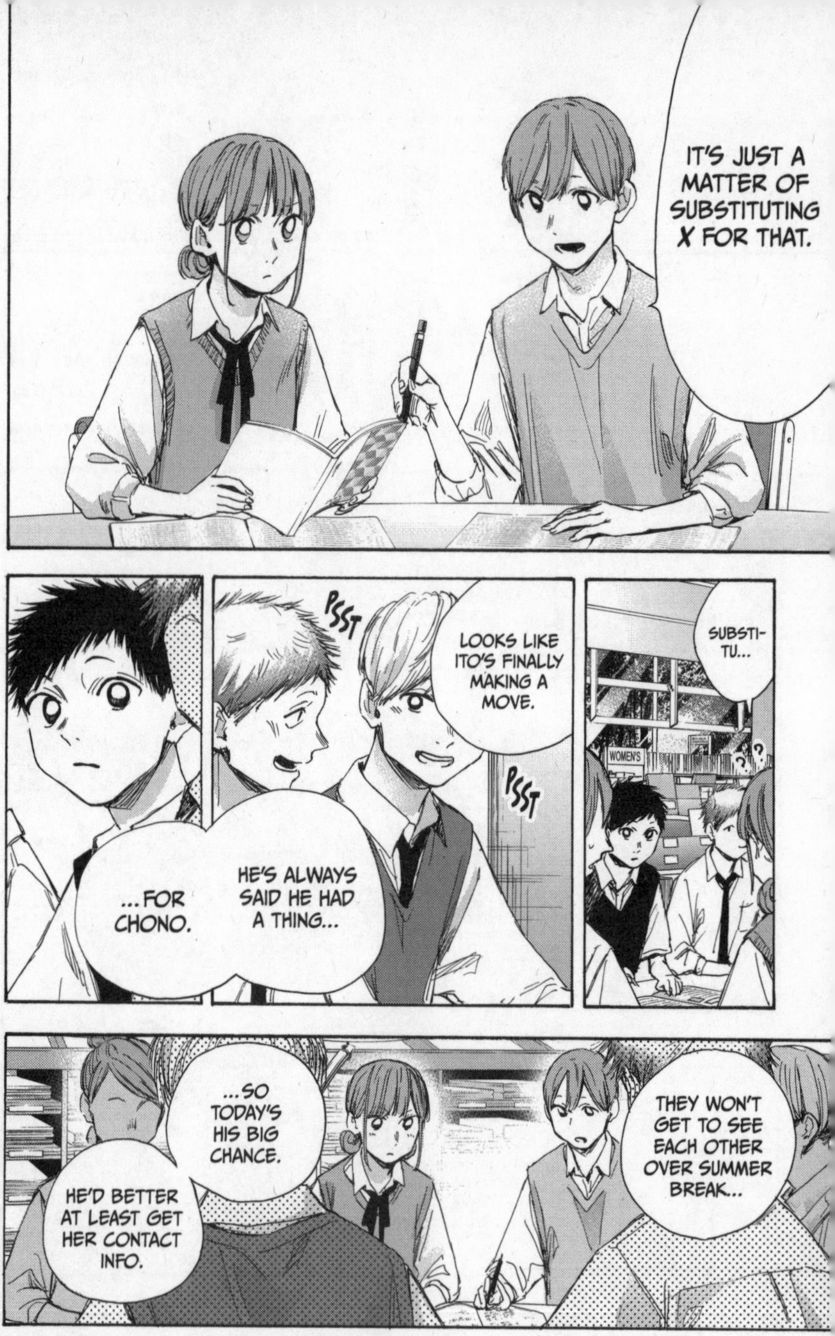
IT'S JUST A MATTER OF SUBSTITUTING X FOR THAT.
SUBSTI-TU...
WOMEN'S
PSST
LOOKS LIKE ITO'S FINALLY MAKING A MOVE.
PSST
HE'S ALWAYS SAID HE HAD A THING...
...FOR CHONO.
THEY WON'T GET TO SEE EACH OTHER OVER SUMMER BREAK...
...SO TODAY'S HIS BIG CHANCE.
HE'D BETTER AT LEAST GET HER CONTACT INFO.

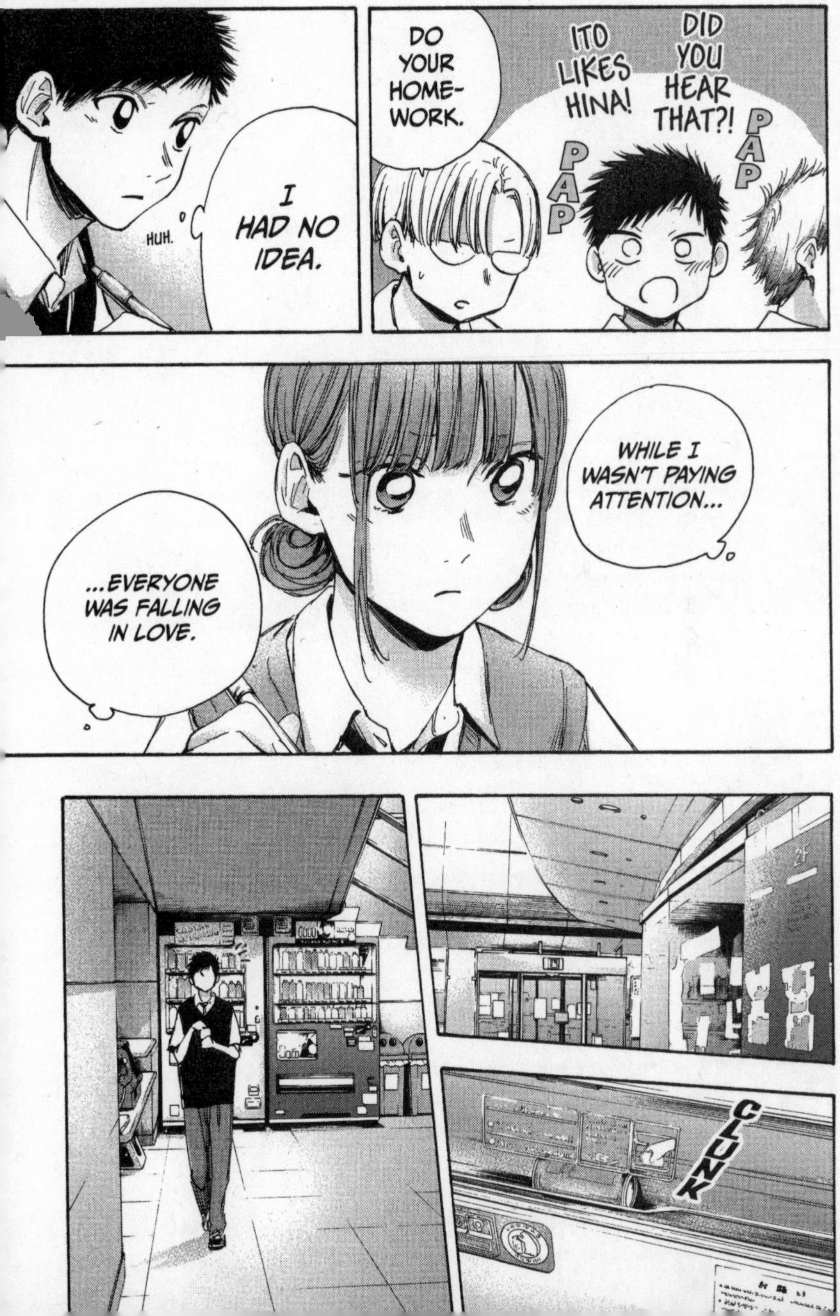
DID YOU HEAR THAT?!
ITO LIKES HINA!
PAP
PAP
DO YOUR HOME-WORK.
HUH.
I HAD NO IDEA.
WHILE I WASN'T PAYING ATTENTION...
...EVERYONE WAS FALLING IN LOVE.
CLUNK

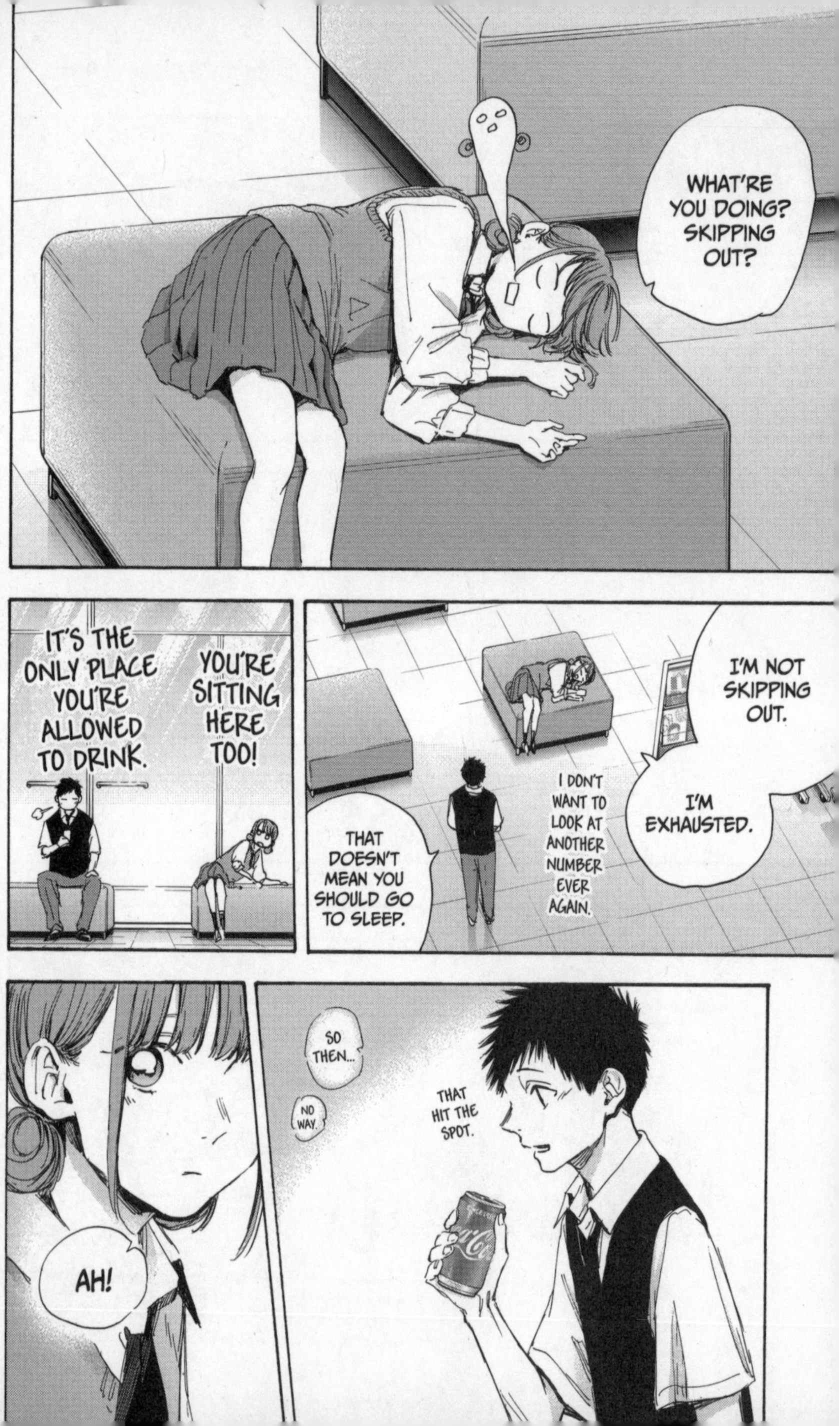
WHAT'RE YOU DOING? SKIPPING OUT?
I'M NOT SKIPPING OUT.
I'M EXHAUSTED.
I DON'T WANT TO LOOK AT ANOTHER NUMBER EVER AGAIN.
THAT DOESN'T MEAN YOU SHOULD GO TO SLEEP.
YOU'RE SITTING HERE TOO!
IT'S THE ONLY PLACE YOU'RE ALLOWED TO DRINK.
THAT HIT THE SPOT.
SO THEN...
NO WAY.
AH!

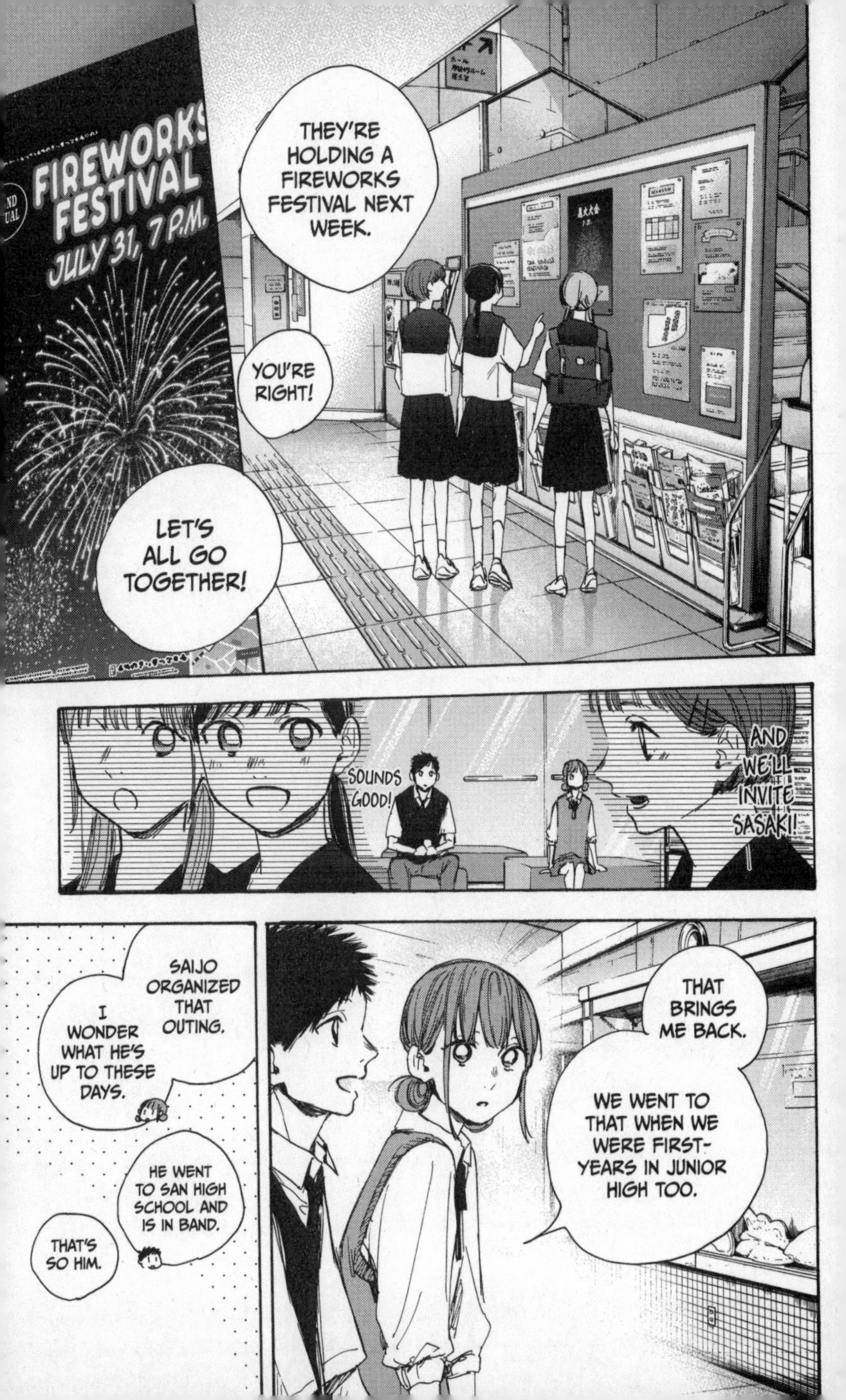
FIREWORKS FESTIVAL
JULY 31, 7 P.M.
THEY'RE HOLDING A FIREWORKS FESTIVAL NEXT WEEK.
YOU'RE RIGHT!
LET'S ALL GO TOGETHER!
AND WE'LL INVITE SASAKI!
SOUNDS GOOD!
THAT BRINGS ME BACK.
WE WENT TO THAT WHEN WE WERE FIRST-YEARS IN JUNIOR HIGH TOO.
SAIJO ORGANIZED THAT OUTING.
I WONDER WHAT HE'S UP TO THESE DAYS.
HE WENT TO SAN HIGH SCHOOL AND IS IN BAND.
THAT'S SO HIM.

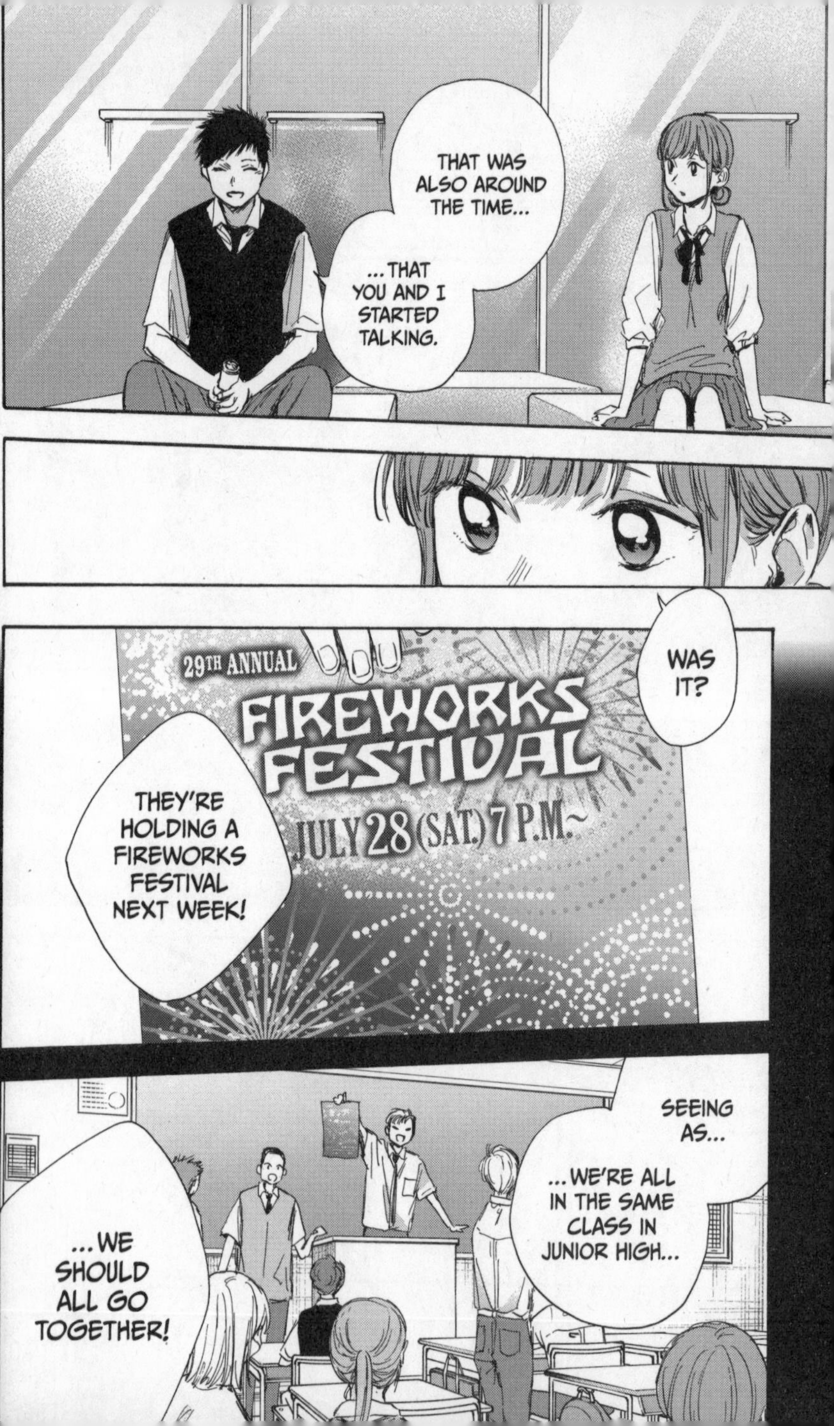
THAT WAS ALSO AROUND THE TIME...
...THAT YOU AND I STARTED TALKING.
WAS IT?
29TH ANNUAL
FIREWORKS FESTIVAL
JULY 28 (SAT.) 7 P.M.~
THEY'RE HOLDING A FIREWORKS FESTIVAL NEXT WEEK!
SEEING AS...
...WE'RE ALL IN THE SAME CLASS IN JUNIOR HIGH...
...WE SHOULD ALL GO TOGETHER!

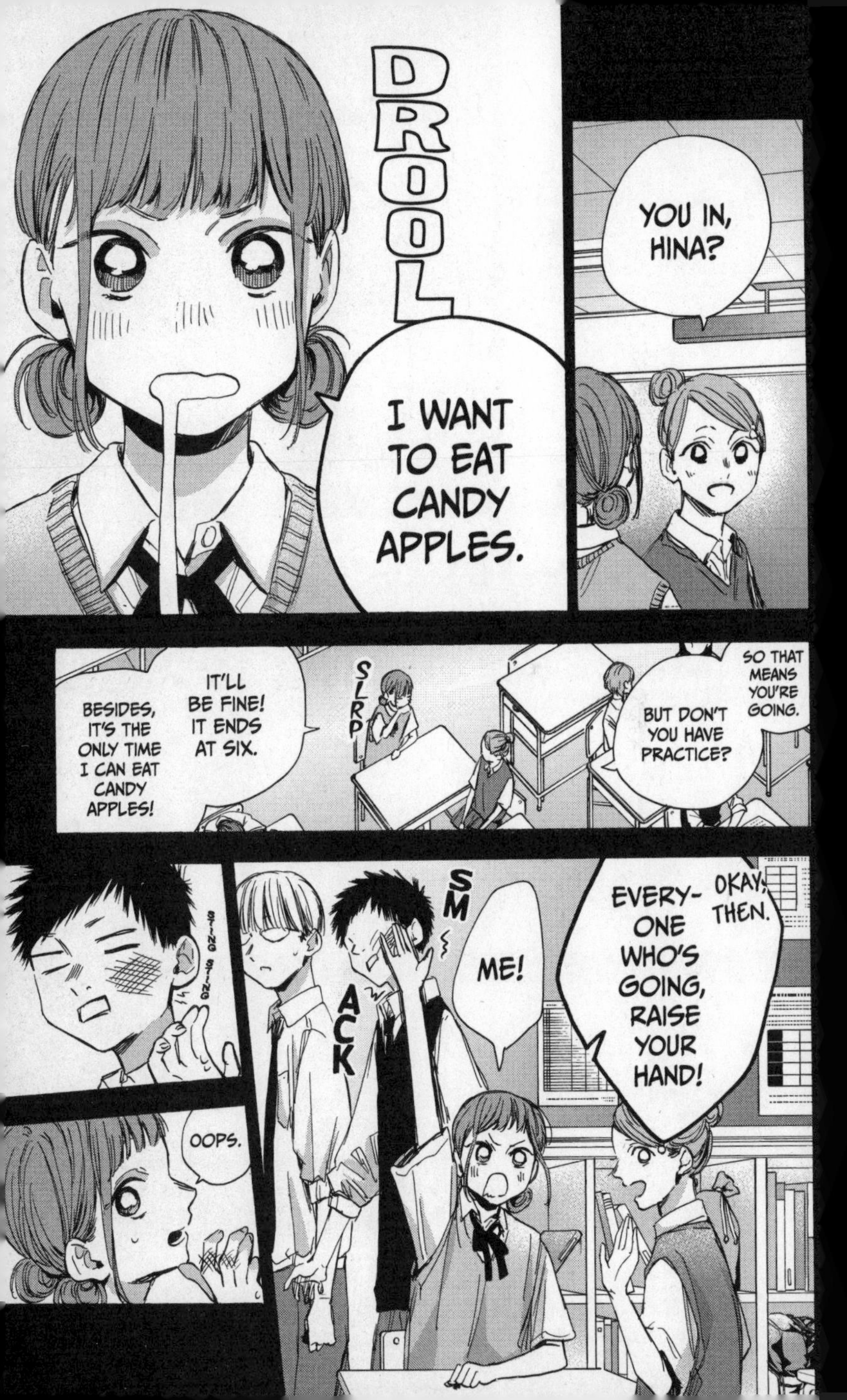
YOU IN, HINA?
DROOL
I WANT TO EAT CANDY APPLES.
SO THAT MEANS YOU'RE GOING.
BUT DON'T YOU HAVE PRACTICE?
SLRP
IT'LL BE FINE! IT ENDS AT SIX.
BESIDES, IT'S THE ONLY TIME I CAN EAT CANDY APPLES!
OKAY, THEN.
EVERYONE WHO'S GOING, RAISE YOUR HAND!
ME!
SM
ACK
STING STING
OOPS.

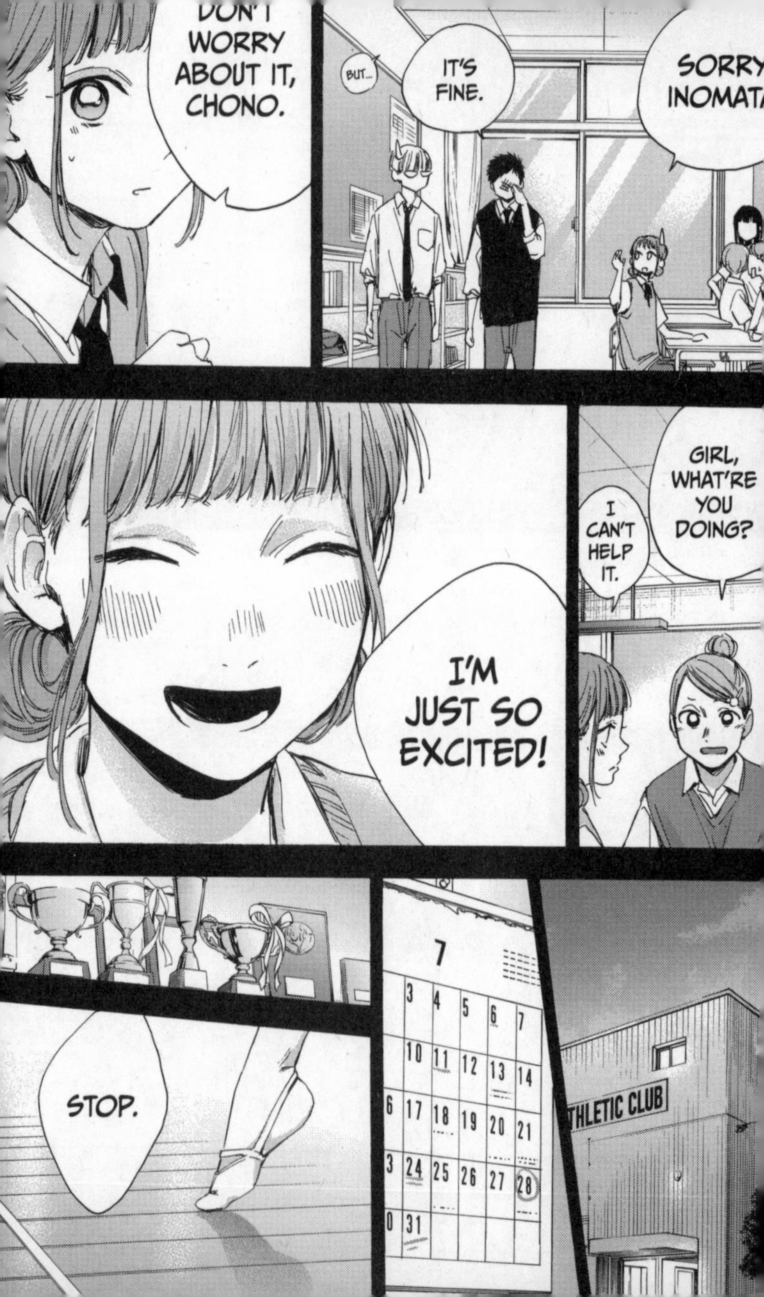
SORRY INOMAT
IT'S FINE.
BUT...
WORRY ABOUT IT, CHONO.
GIRL, WHAT'RE YOU DOING?
I CAN'T HELP IT.
I'M JUST SO EXCITED!
THLETIC CLUB
STOP.

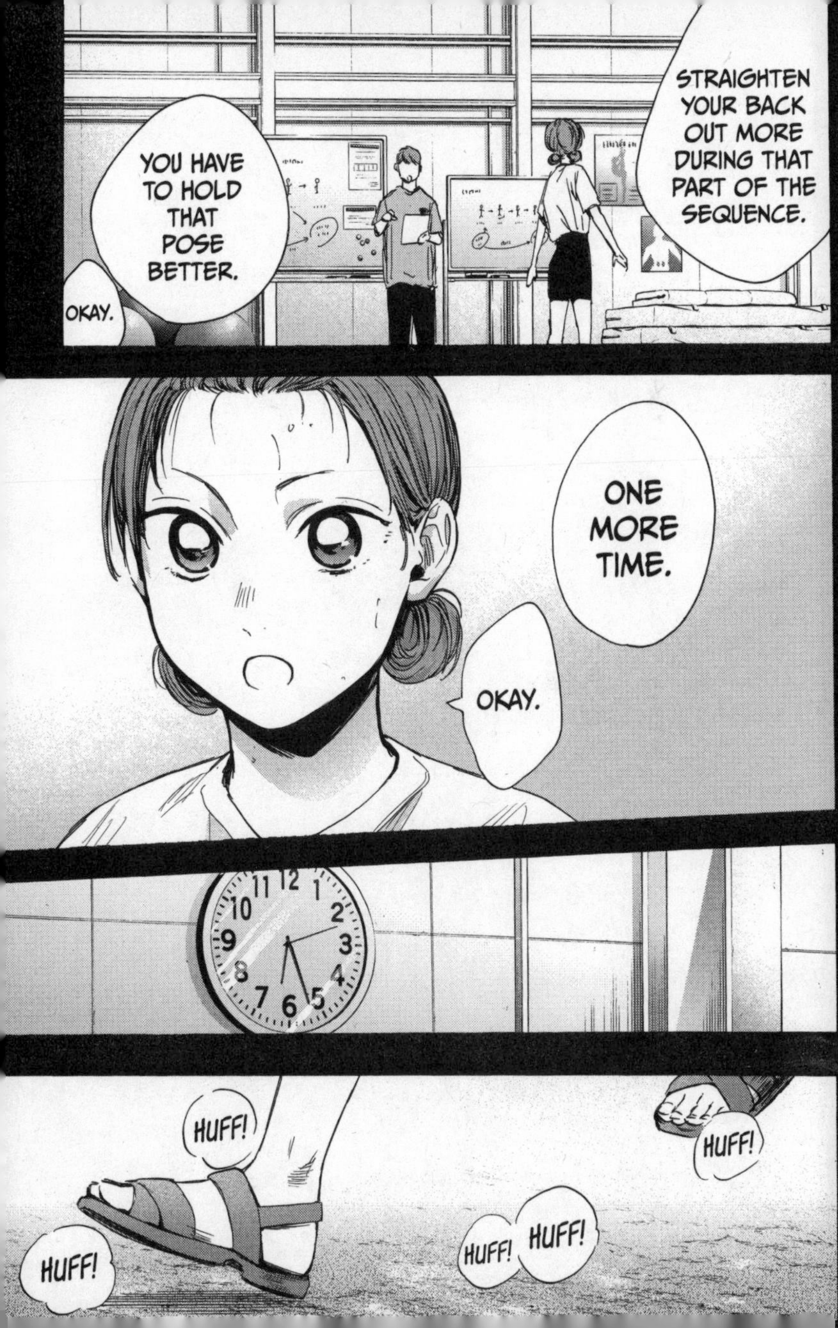
STRAIGHTEN YOUR BACK OUT MORE DURING THAT PART OF THE SEQUENCE.
YOU HAVE TO HOLD THAT POSE BETTER.
OKAY.
ONE MORE TIME.
OKAY.
HUFF!
HUFF!
HUFF!
HUFF!
HUFF!

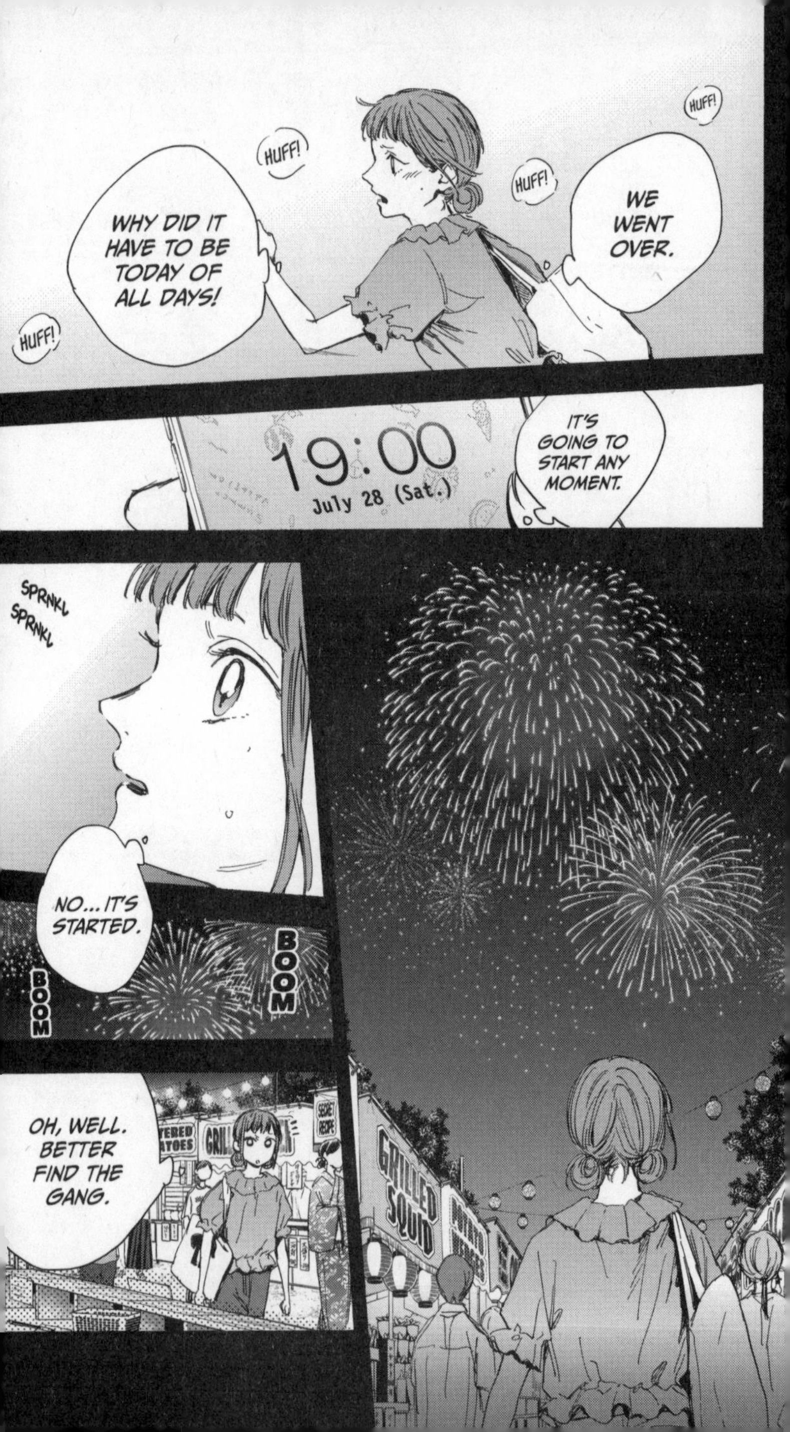

HUFF!
WE WENT OVER.
HUFF!
HUFF!
WHY DID IT HAVE TO BE TODAY OF ALL DAYS!
HUFF!
IT'S GOING TO START ANY MOMENT.
19:00
July 28 (Sat.)
SPRNKL
SPRNKL
NO... IT'S STARTED.
BOOM
BOOM
GRILLED SQUID
SECRET RECIPE
OH, WELL. BETTER FIND THE GANG.

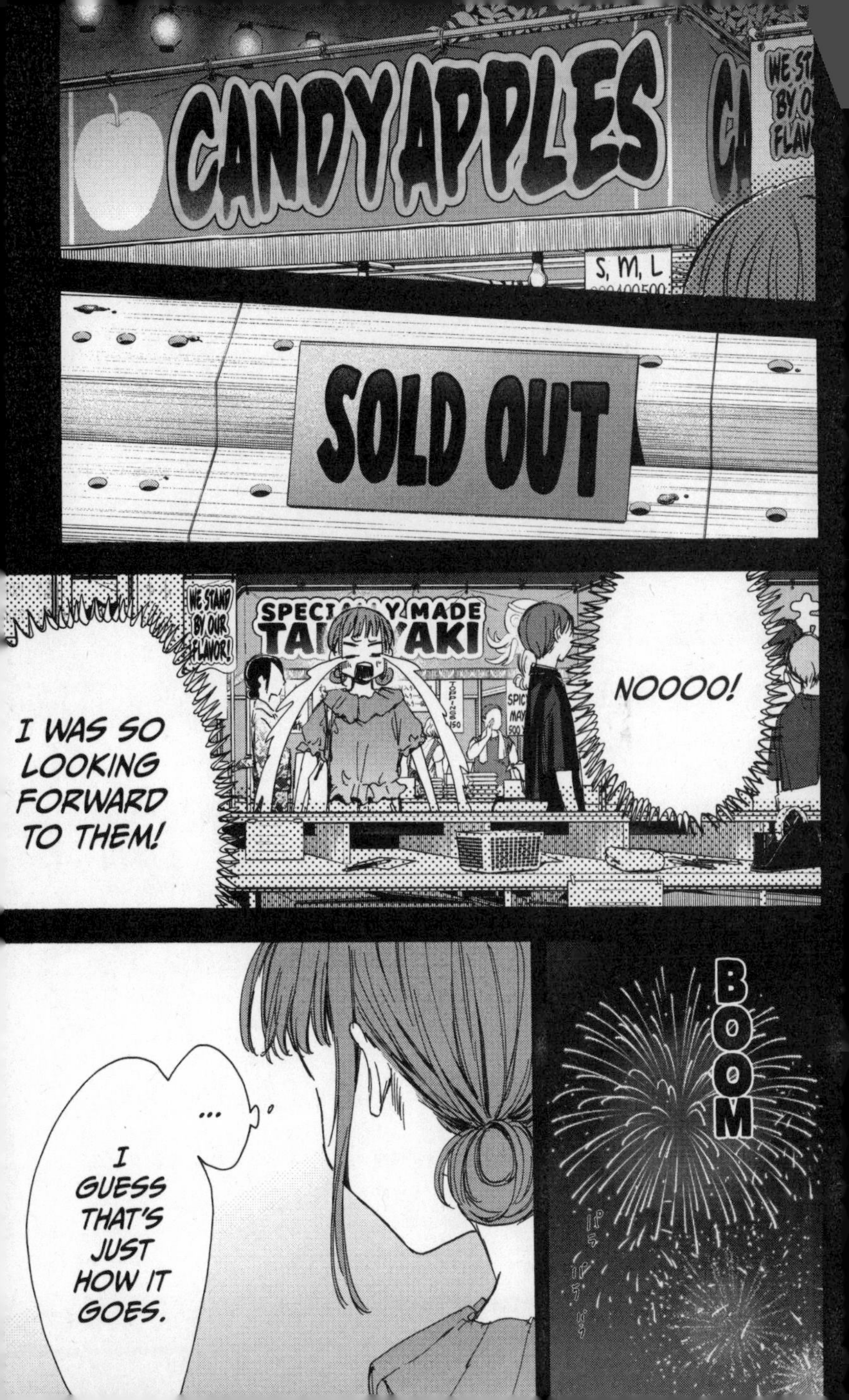

CANDY APPLES
S, M, L
SOLD OUT
WE STAND BY OUR FLAVOR!
NOOOO!
I WAS SO LOOKING FORWARD TO THEM!
BOOM
パラ パラ
...
I GUESS THAT'S JUST HOW IT GOES.

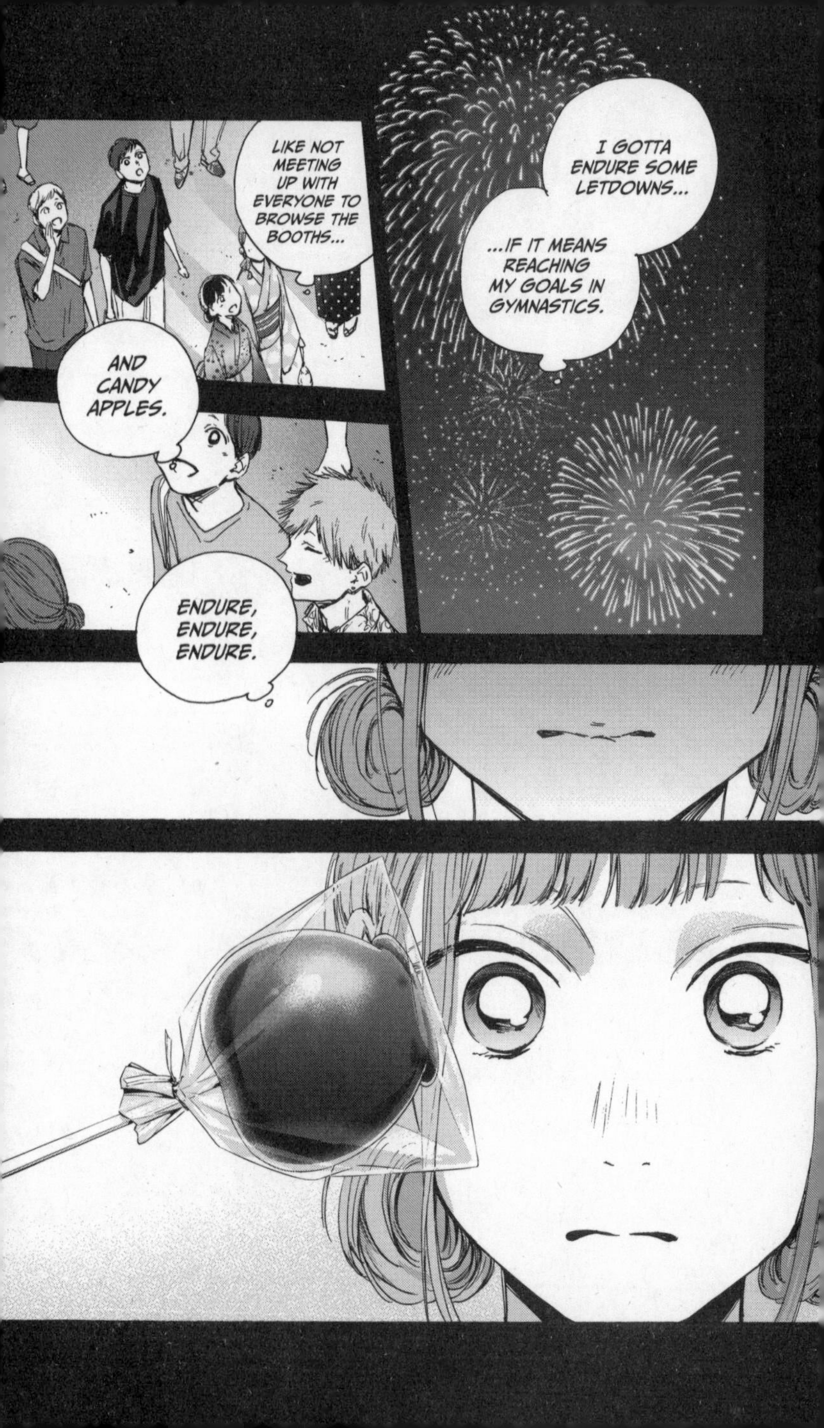
I GOTTA ENDURE SOME LETDOWNS...
...IF IT MEANS REACHING MY GOALS IN GYMNASTICS.
LIKE NOT MEETING UP WITH EVERYONE TO BROWSE THE BOOTHS...
AND CANDY APPLES.
ENDURE, ENDURE, ENDURE.

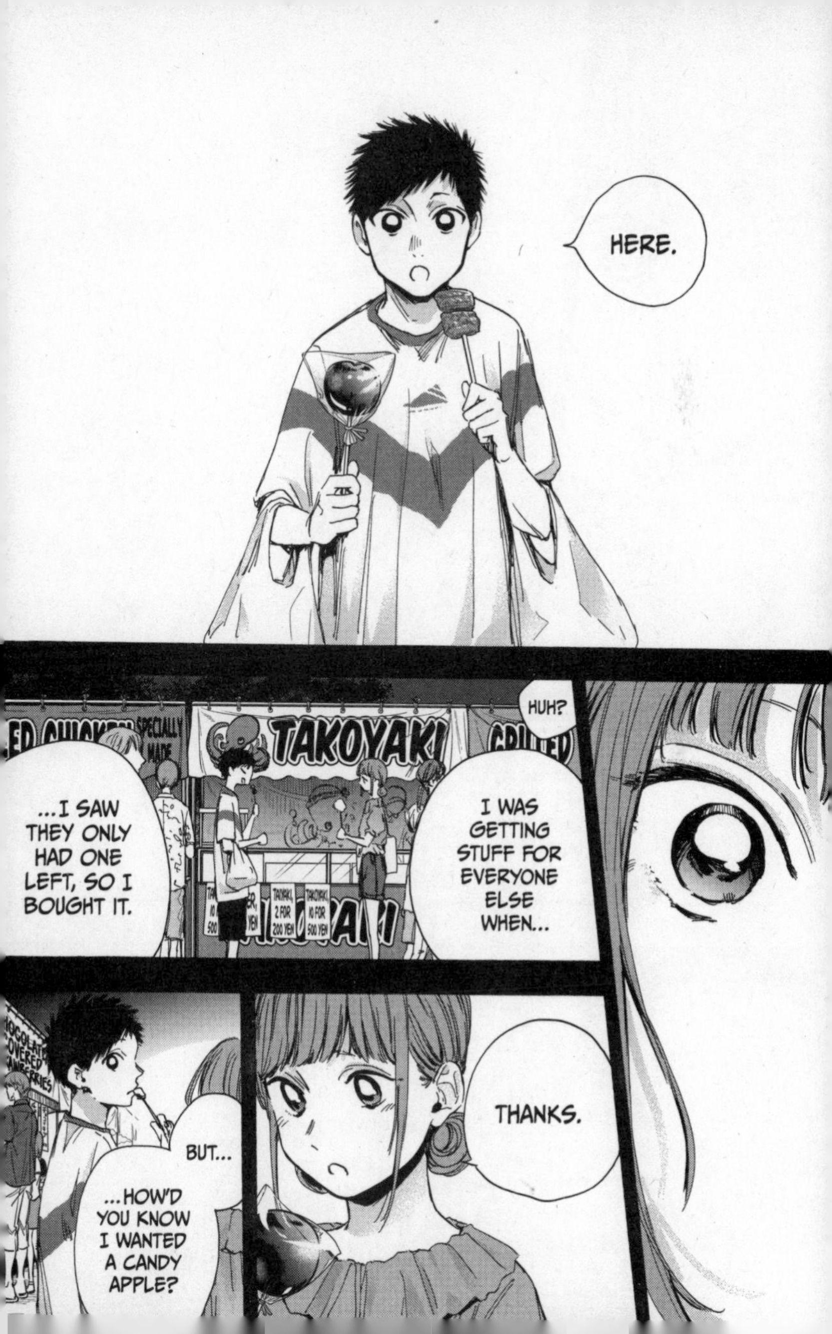
HERE.
HUH?
TAKOYAKI
SPECIALLY MADE
I WAS GETTING STUFF FOR EVERYONE ELSE WHEN...
...I SAW THEY ONLY HAD ONE LEFT, SO I BOUGHT IT.
THANKS.
BUT...
...HOW'D YOU KNOW I WANTED A CANDY APPLE?

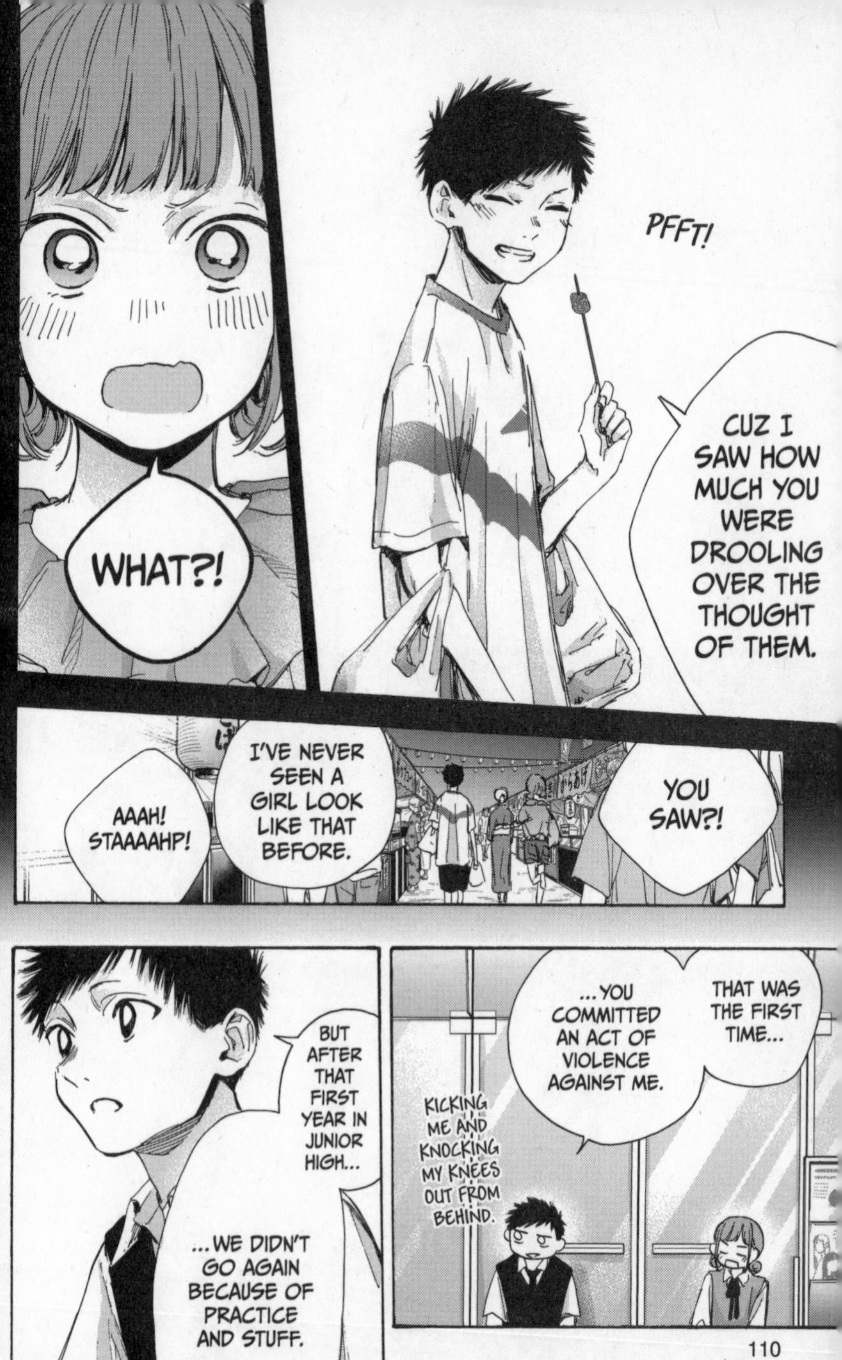
PFFT!
CUZ I SAW HOW MUCH YOU WERE DROOLING OVER THE THOUGHT OF THEM.
WHAT?!
YOU SAW?!
I'VE NEVER SEEN A GIRL LOOK LIKE THAT BEFORE.
AAAH! STAAAAHP!
THAT WAS THE FIRST TIME...
...YOU COMMITTED AN ACT OF VIOLENCE AGAINST ME.
KICKING ME AND KNOCKING MY KNEES OUT FROM BEHIND.
BUT AFTER THAT FIRST YEAR IN JUNIOR HIGH...
...WE DIDN'T GO AGAIN BECAUSE OF PRACTICE AND STUFF.

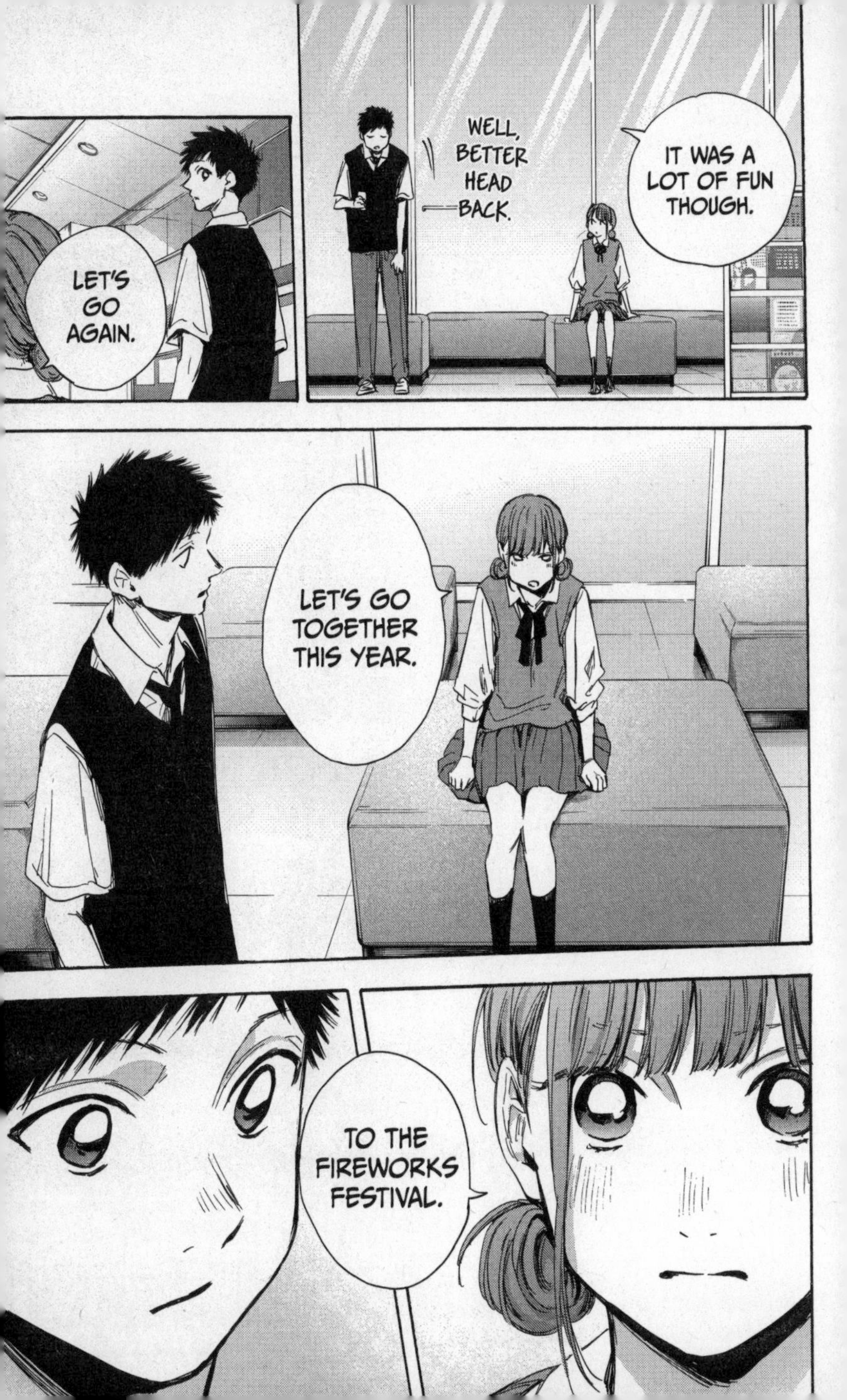
IT WAS A LOT OF FUN THOUGH.
WELL, BETTER HEAD BACK.
LET'S GO AGAIN.
LET'S GO TOGETHER THIS YEAR.
TO THE FIREWORKS FESTIVAL.

DID I CUT MY
BANGS TOO SHORT?
NAH, THIS SHOULD
BE OKAY.

THIS
IS...
FINE!

HINA IN
JUNIOR
HIGH

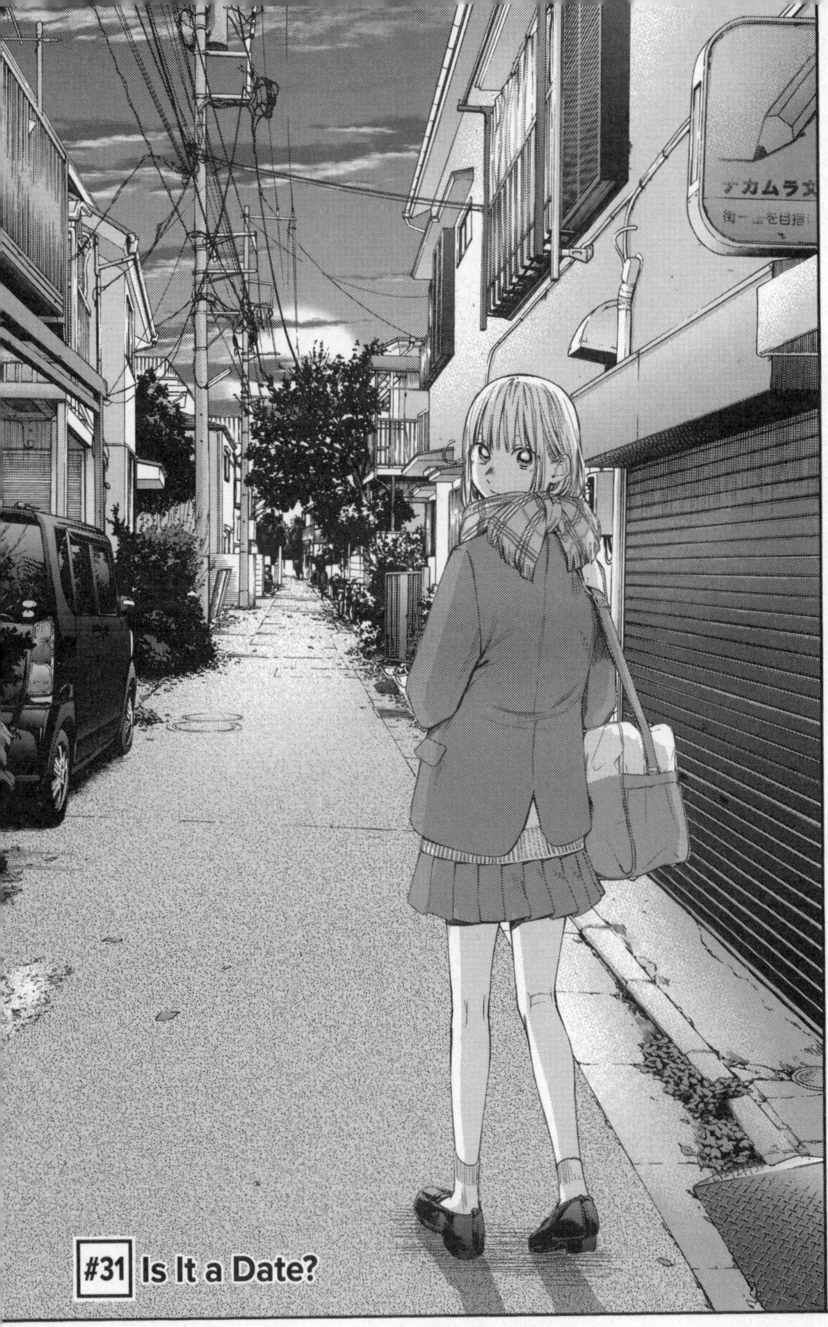

#31 Is It a Date?

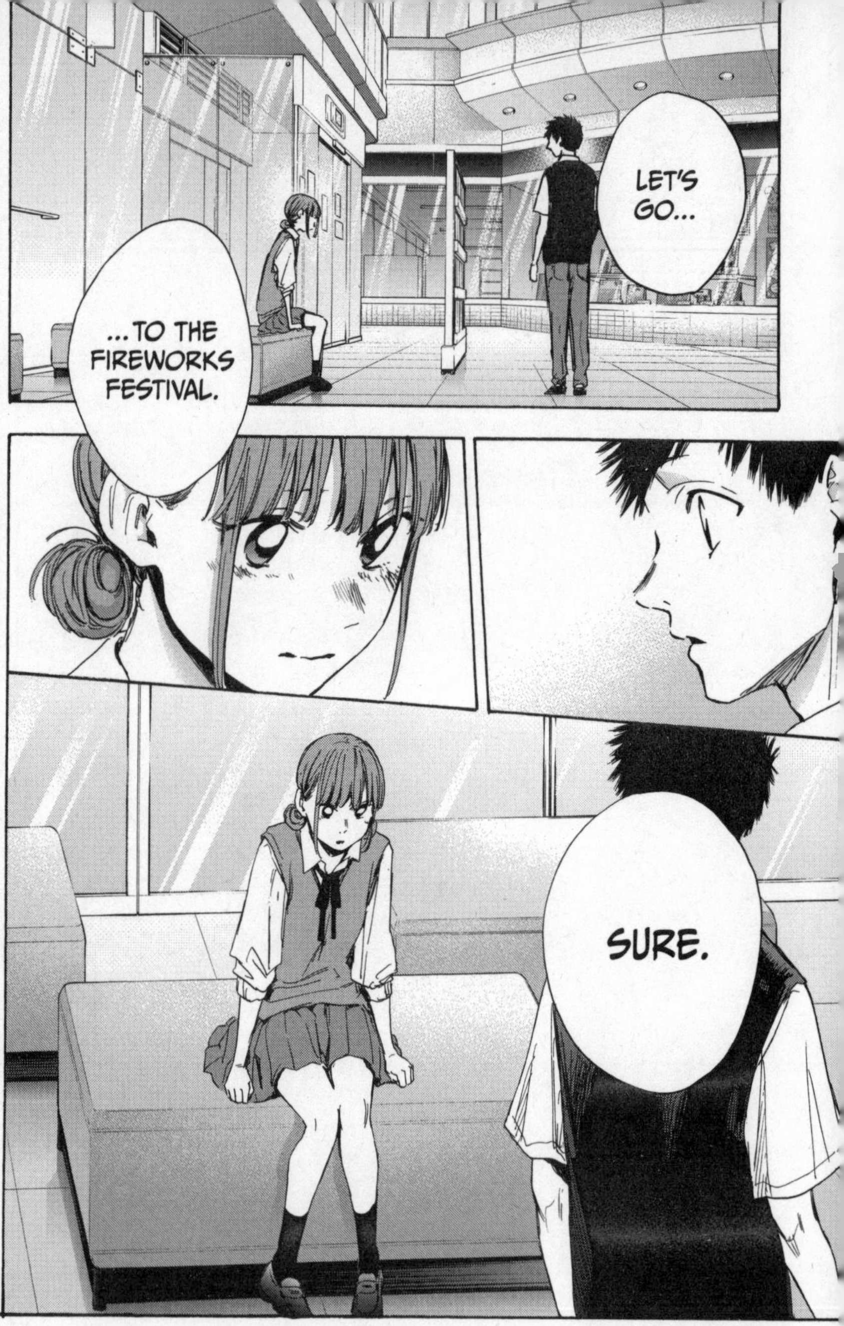
LET'S GO...
...TO THE FIREWORKS FESTIVAL.
SURE.

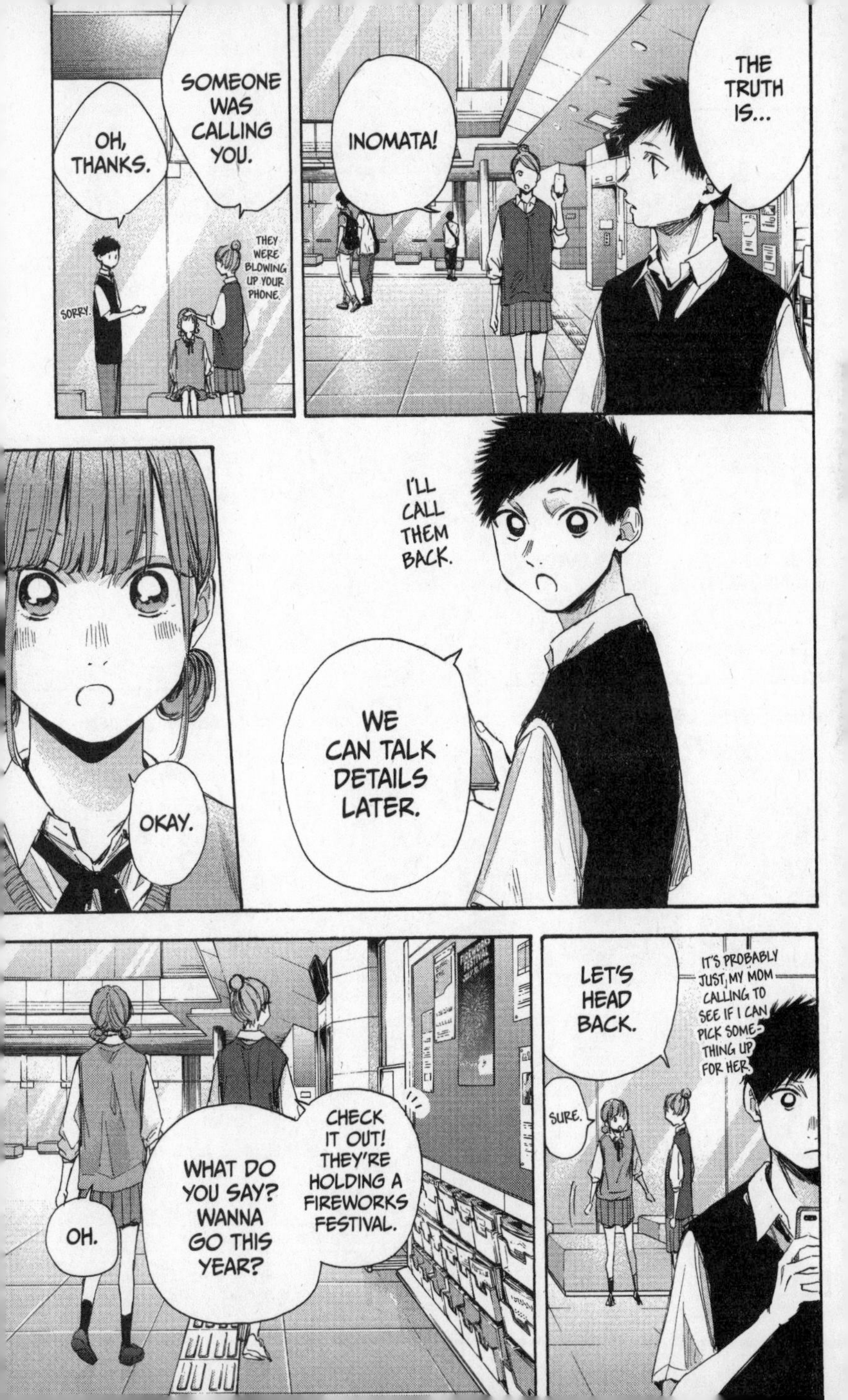
THE TRUTH IS...
INOMATA!
SOMEONE WAS CALLING YOU.
THEY WERE BLOWING UP YOUR PHONE.
OH, THANKS.
SORRY.
I'LL CALL THEM BACK.
WE CAN TALK DETAILS LATER.
OKAY.
IT'S PROBABLY JUST MY MOM CALLING TO SEE IF I CAN PICK SOME-THING UP FOR HER.
LET'S HEAD BACK.
SURE.
CHECK IT OUT! THEY'RE HOLDING A FIREWORKS FESTIVAL.
WHAT DO YOU SAY? WANNA GO THIS YEAR?
OH.

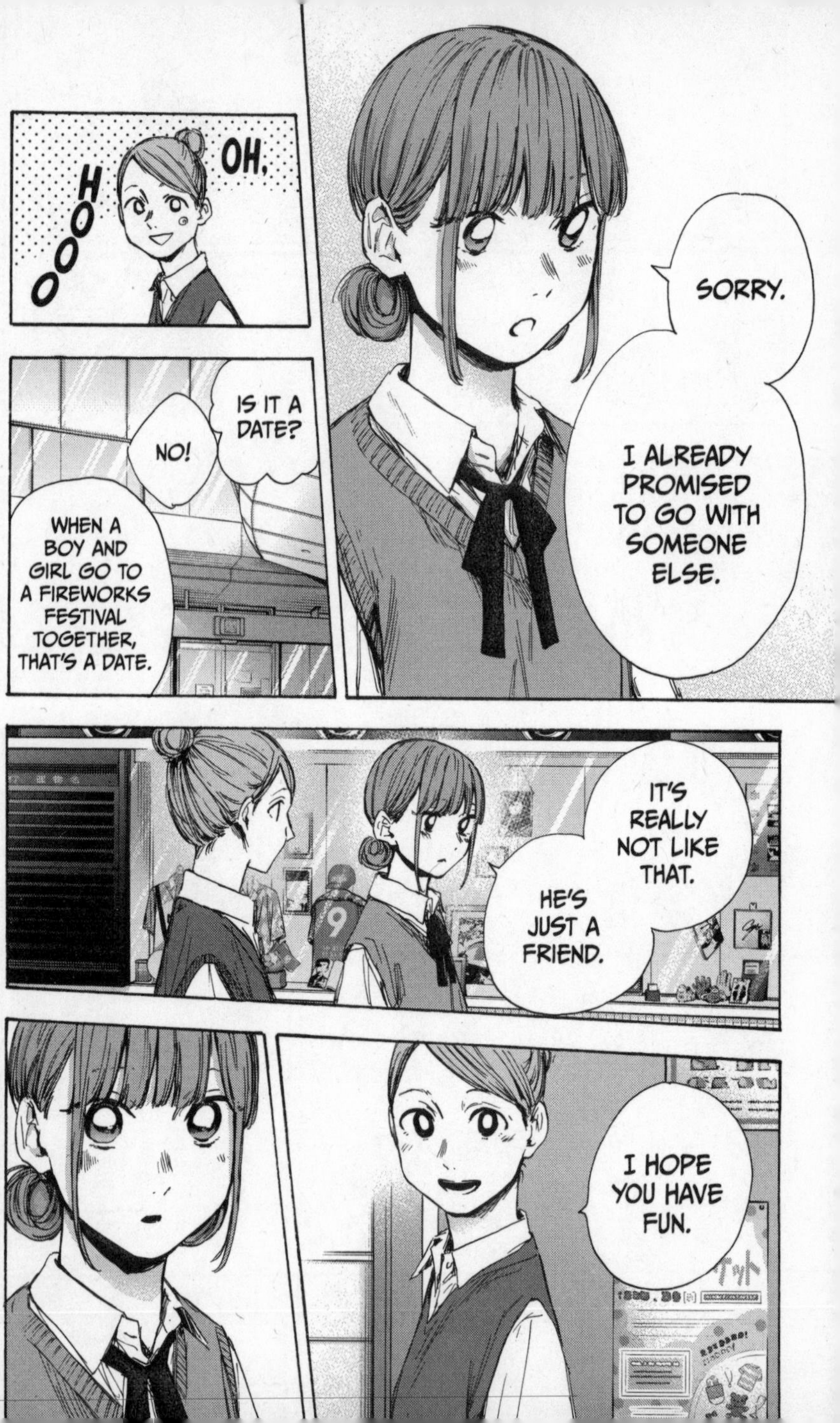
SORRY.
I ALREADY PROMISED TO GO WITH SOMEONE ELSE.
OH, HOOOOO
IS IT A DATE?
NO!
WHEN A BOY AND GIRL GO TO A FIREWORKS FESTIVAL TOGETHER, THAT'S A DATE.
IT'S REALLY NOT LIKE THAT.
HE'S JUST A FRIEND.
I HOPE YOU HAVE FUN.

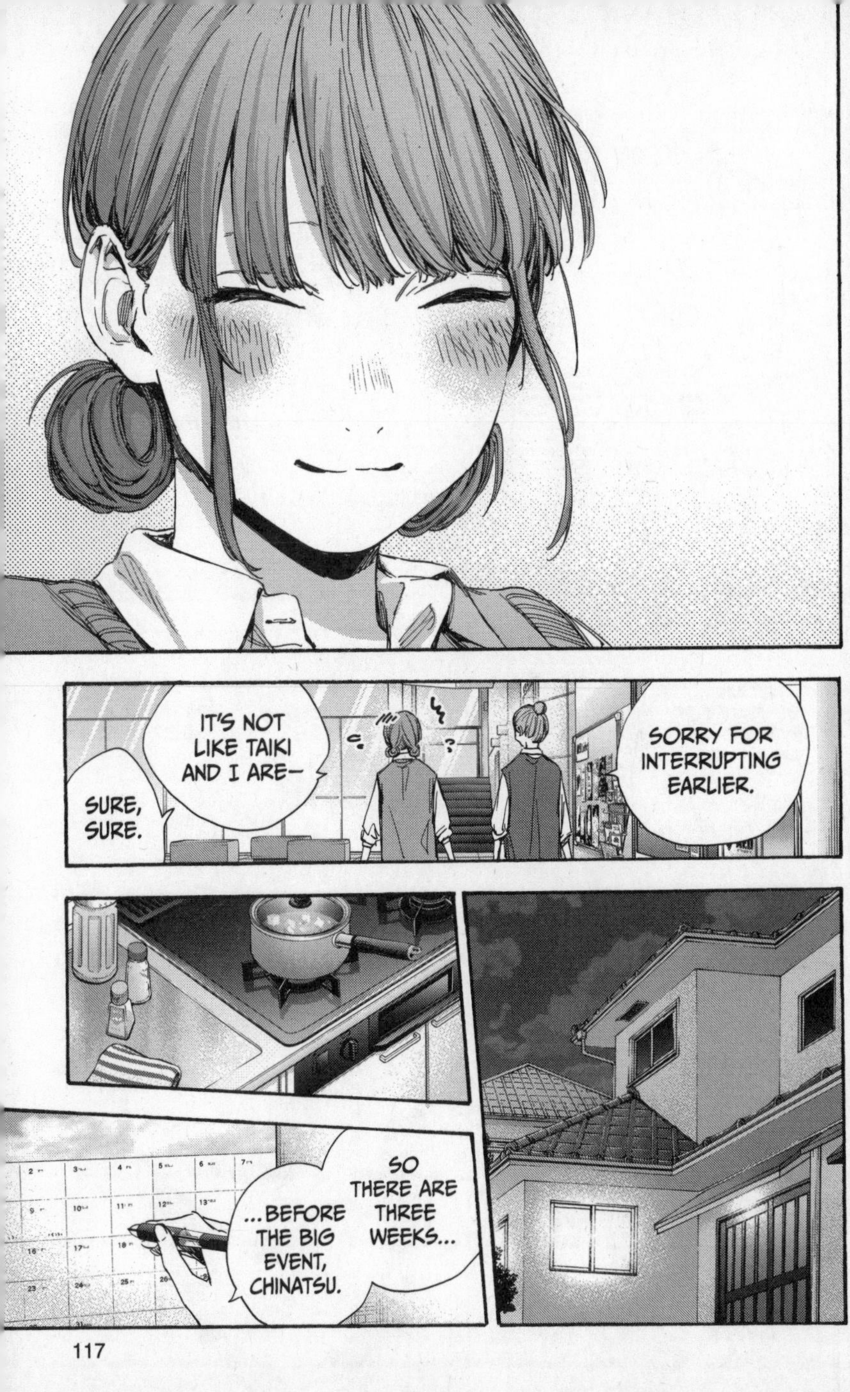
SORRY FOR INTERRUPTING EARLIER.
IT'S NOT LIKE TAIKI AND I ARE—
SURE, SURE.
SO THERE ARE THREE WEEKS...
...BEFORE THE BIG EVENT, CHINATSU.

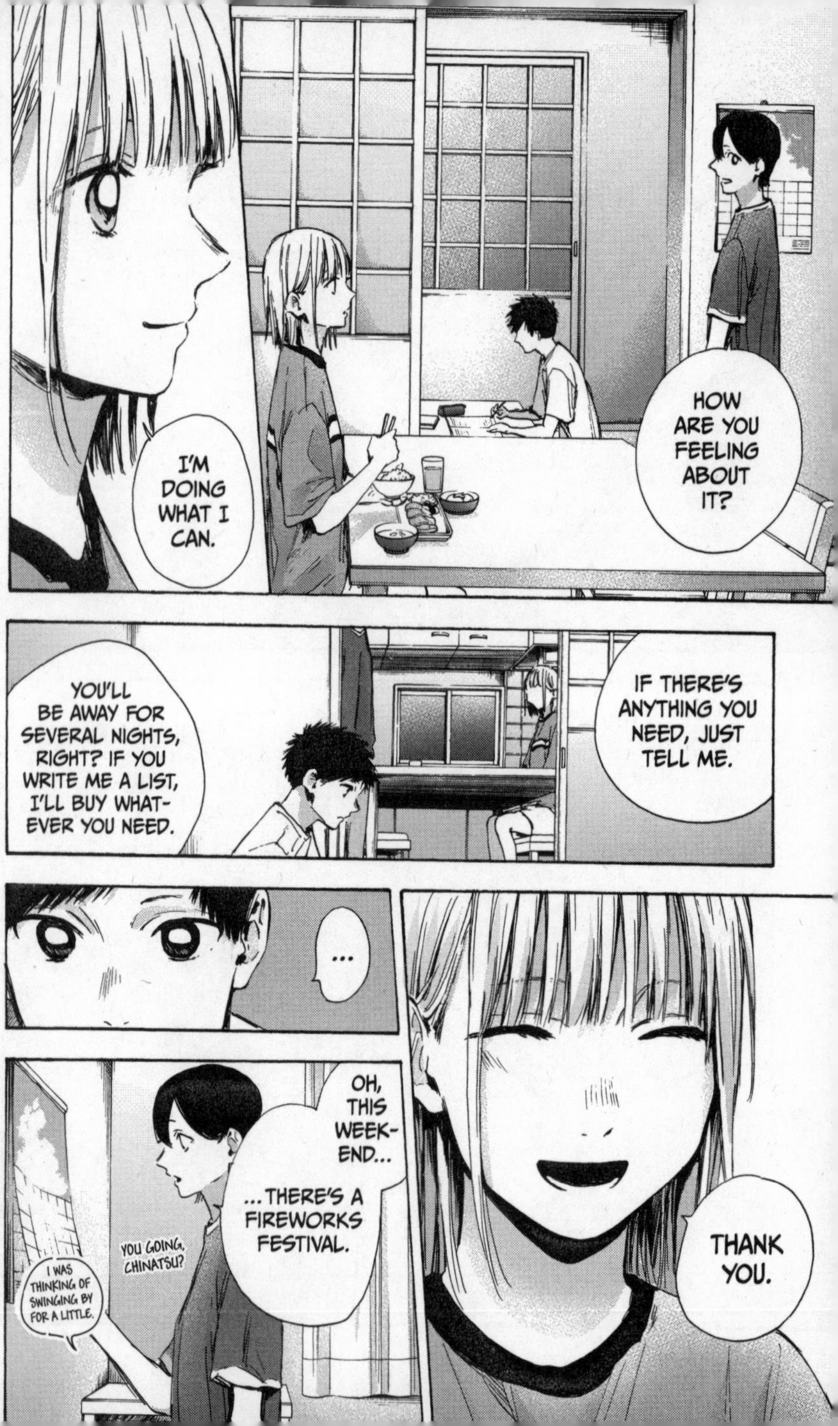
HOW ARE YOU FEELING ABOUT IT?
I'M DOING WHAT I CAN.
IF THERE'S ANYTHING YOU NEED, JUST TELL ME.
YOU'LL BE AWAY FOR SEVERAL NIGHTS, RIGHT? IF YOU WRITE ME A LIST, I'LL BUY WHAT-EVER YOU NEED.
THANK YOU.
...
OH, THIS WEEK-END...
...THERE'S A FIREWORKS FESTIVAL.
YOU GOING, CHINATSU?
I WAS THINKING OF SWINGING BY FOR A LITTLE.

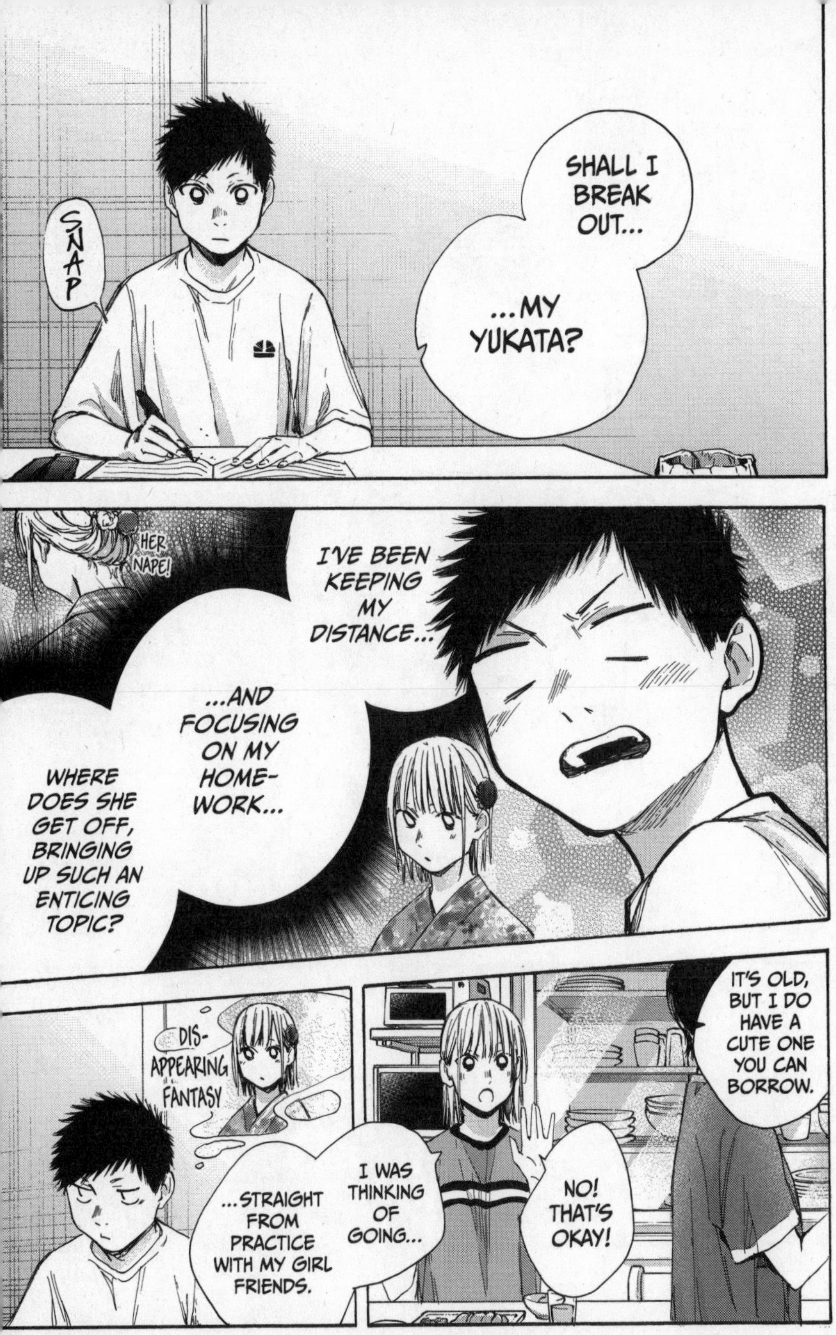

SHALL I BREAK OUT...
...MY YUKATA?
SNAP
I'VE BEEN KEEPING MY DISTANCE...
...AND FOCUSING ON MY HOME-WORK...
WHERE DOES SHE GET OFF, BRINGING UP SUCH AN ENTICING TOPIC?
HER NAPE!
IT'S OLD, BUT I DO HAVE A CUTE ONE YOU CAN BORROW.
NO! THAT'S OKAY!
I WAS THINKING OF GOING...
...STRAIGHT FROM PRACTICE WITH MY GIRL FRIENDS.
DIS-APPEARING FANTASY

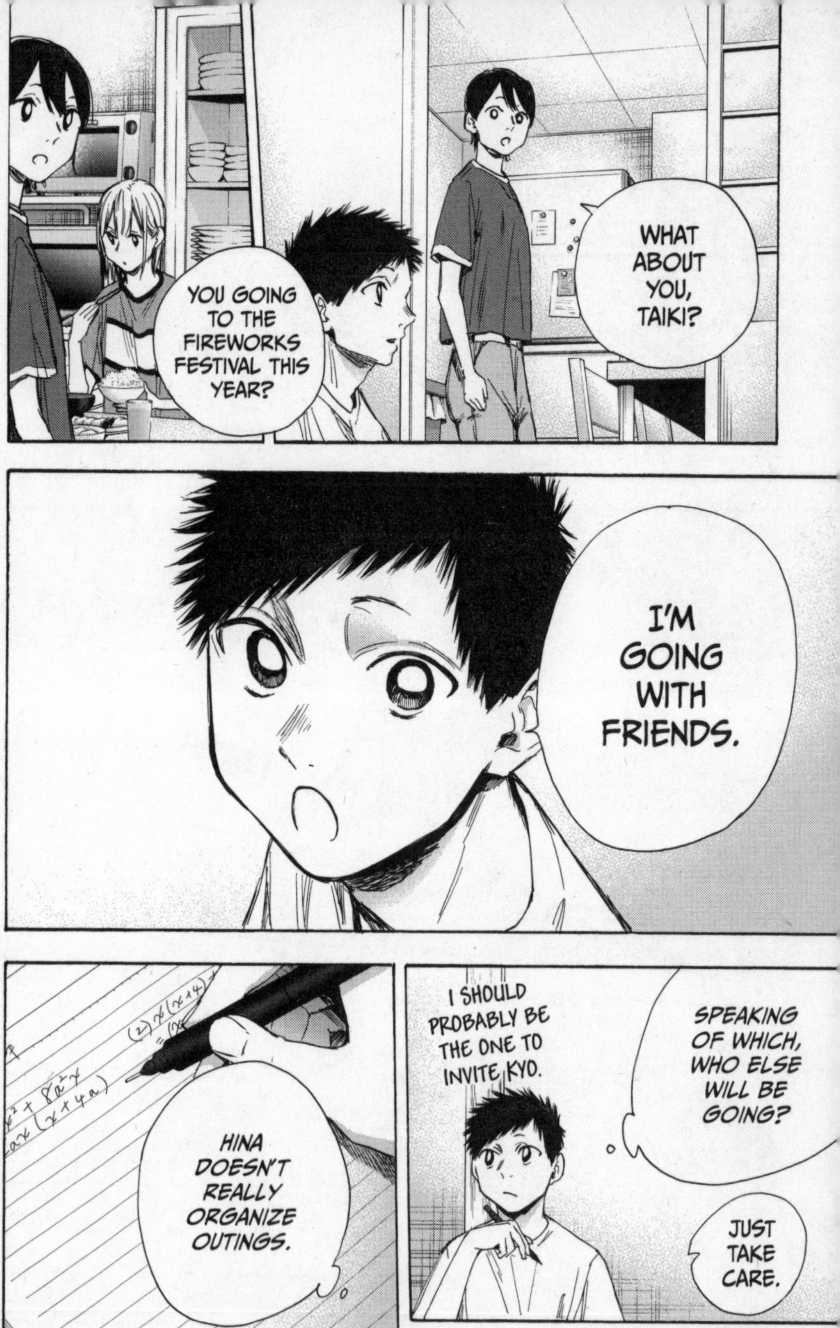
WHAT ABOUT YOU, TAIKI?
YOU GOING TO THE FIREWORKS FESTIVAL THIS YEAR?
I'M GOING WITH FRIENDS.
SPEAKING OF WHICH, WHO ELSE WILL BE GOING?
I SHOULD PROBABLY BE THE ONE TO INVITE KYO.
JUST TAKE CARE.
HINA DOESN'T REALLY ORGANIZE OUTINGS.

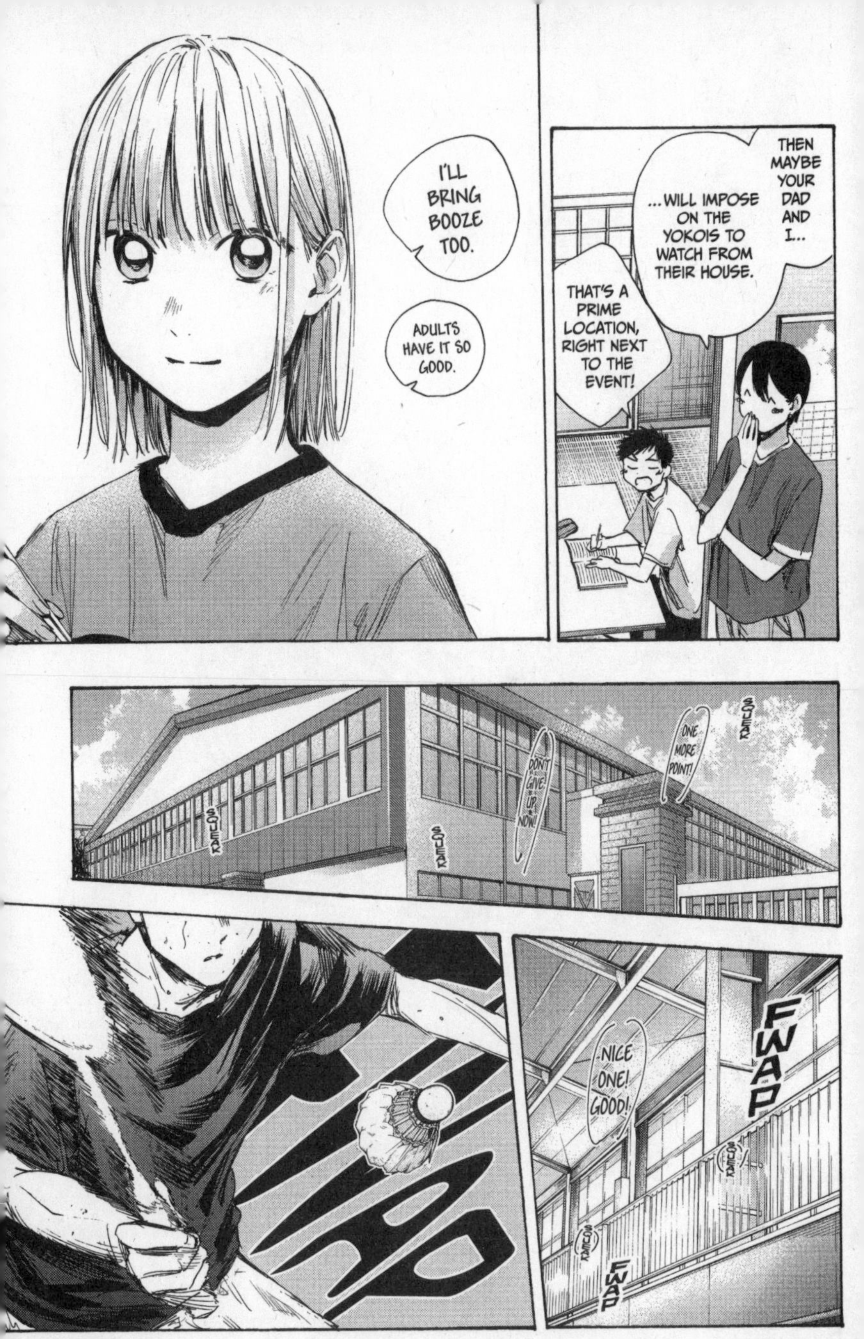
THEN MAYBE YOUR DAD AND I...
...WILL IMPOSE ON THE YOKOIS TO WATCH FROM THEIR HOUSE.
THAT'S A PRIME LOCATION, RIGHT NEXT TO THE EVENT!
I'LL BRING BOOZE TOO.
ADULTS HAVE IT SO GOOD.
SQUEAK
ONE MORE POINT!
DON'T GIVE UP NOW!
SQUEAK
SQUEAK
FWAP
SQUEAK
NICE ONE! GOOD!
SQUEAK
FWAP

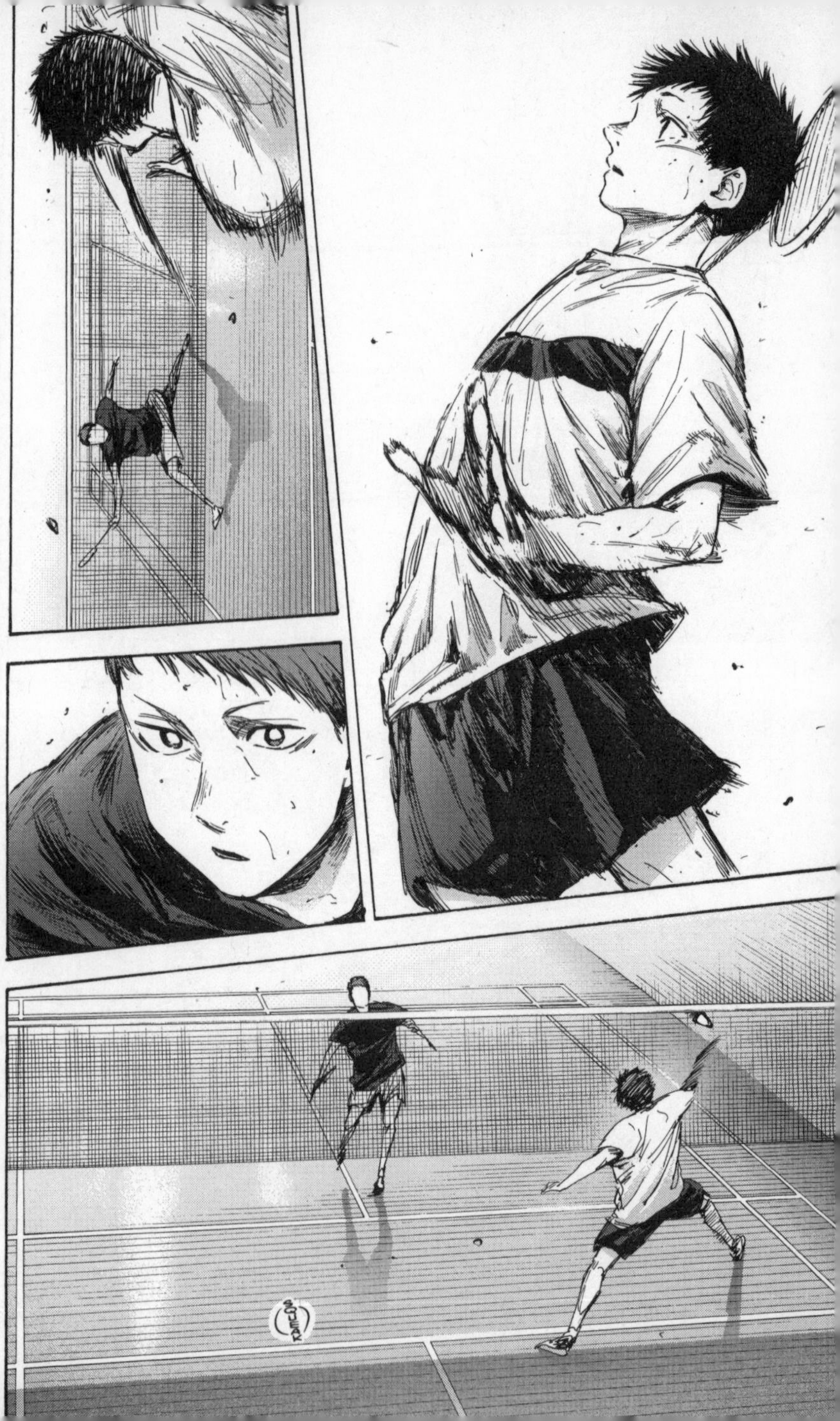
SQUEAK

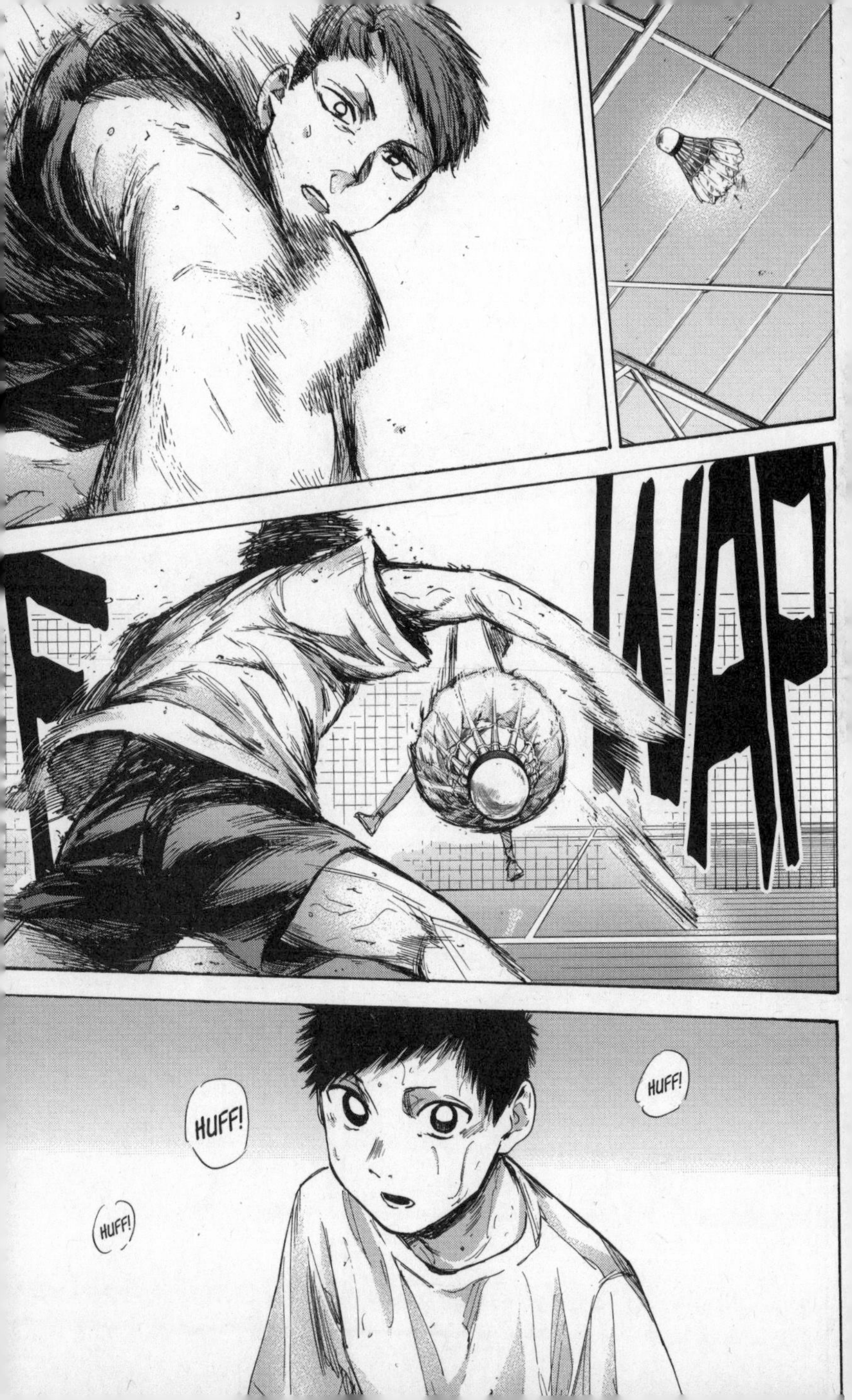

WAP
HUFF!
HUFF!
HUFF!

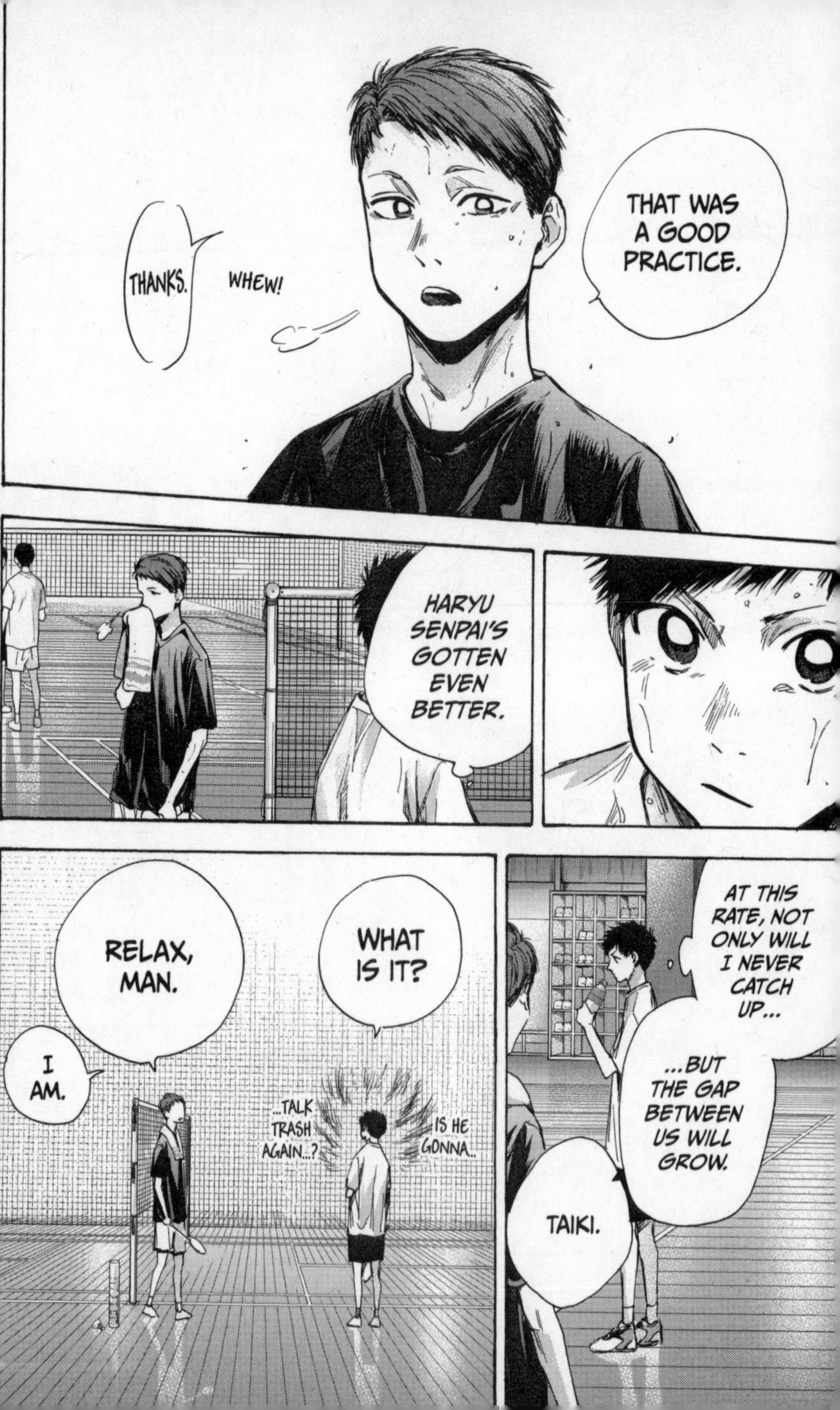
THAT WAS A GOOD PRACTICE.
WHEW!
THANKS.
HARYU SENPAI'S GOTTEN EVEN BETTER.
AT THIS RATE, NOT ONLY WILL I NEVER CATCH UP...
...BUT THE GAP BETWEEN US WILL GROW.
TAIKI.
WHAT IS IT?
IS HE GONNA...
...TALK TRASH AGAIN...?
RELAX, MAN.
I AM.

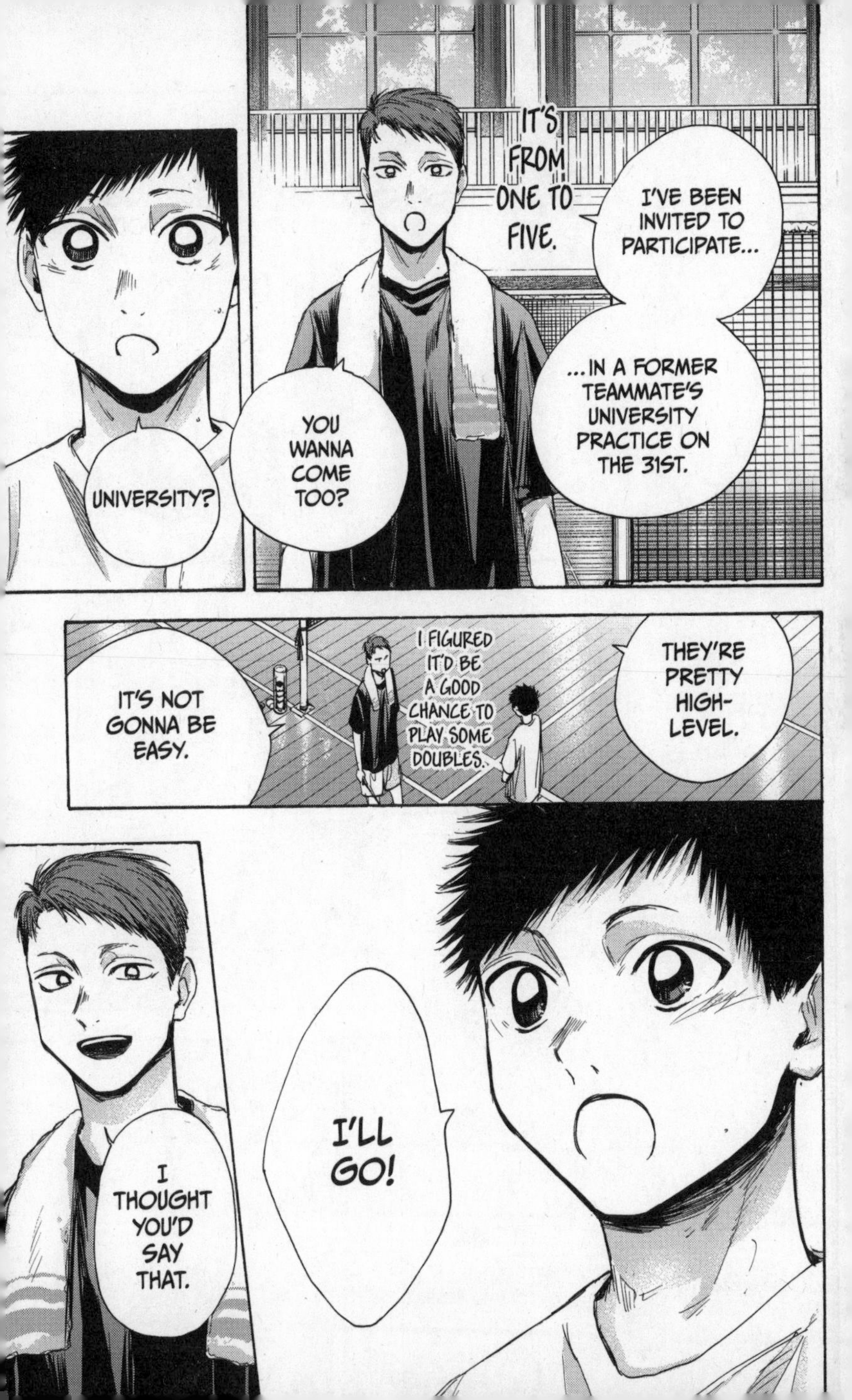
IT'S FROM ONE TO FIVE.
I'VE BEEN INVITED TO PARTICIPATE...
...IN A FORMER TEAMMATE'S UNIVERSITY PRACTICE ON THE 31ST.
YOU WANNA COME TOO?
UNIVERSITY?
THEY'RE PRETTY HIGH-LEVEL.
I FIGURED IT'D BE A GOOD CHANCE TO PLAY SOME DOUBLES.
IT'S NOT GONNA BE EASY.
I'LL GO!
I THOUGHT YOU'D SAY THAT.

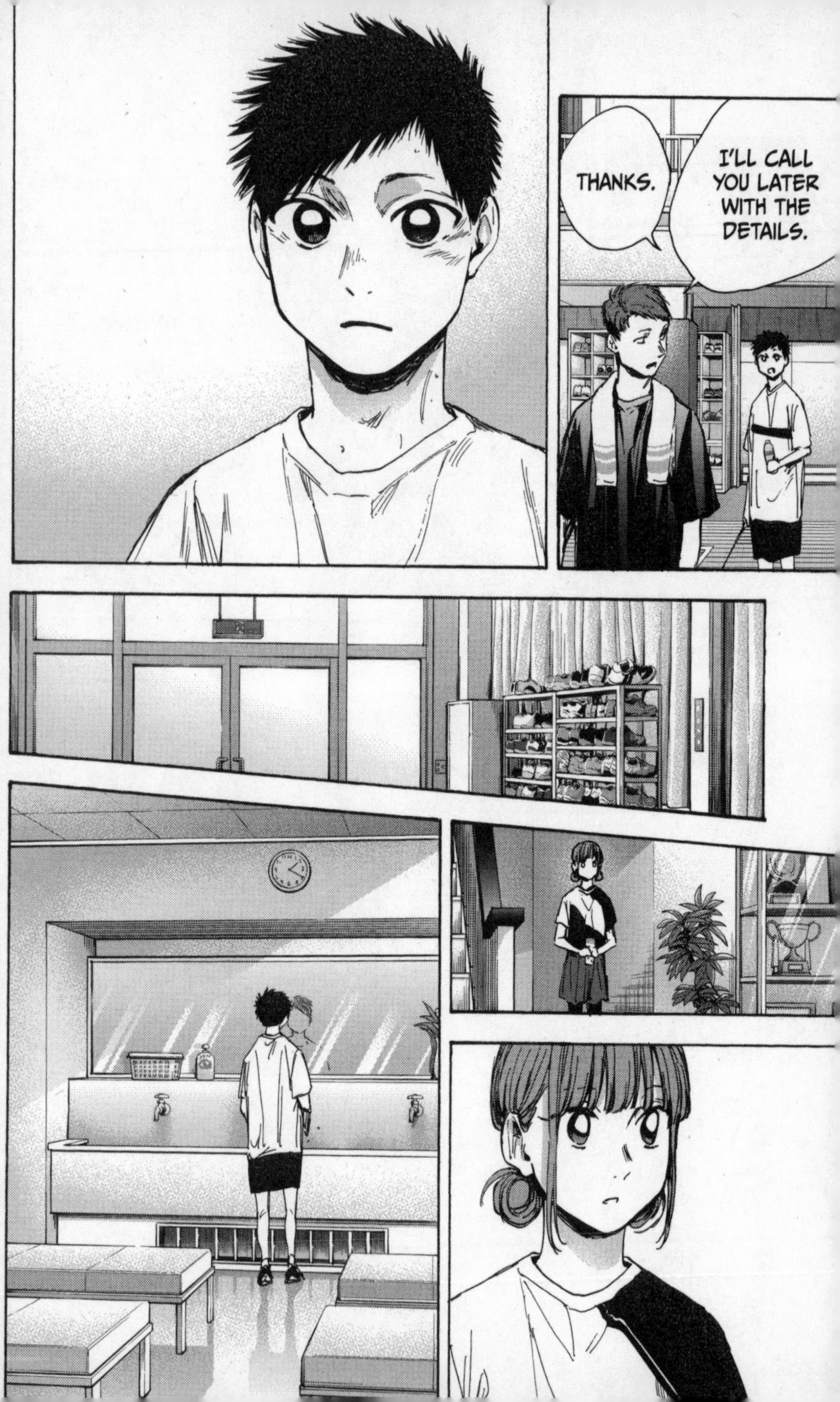
I'LL CALL YOU LATER WITH THE DETAILS.
THANKS.

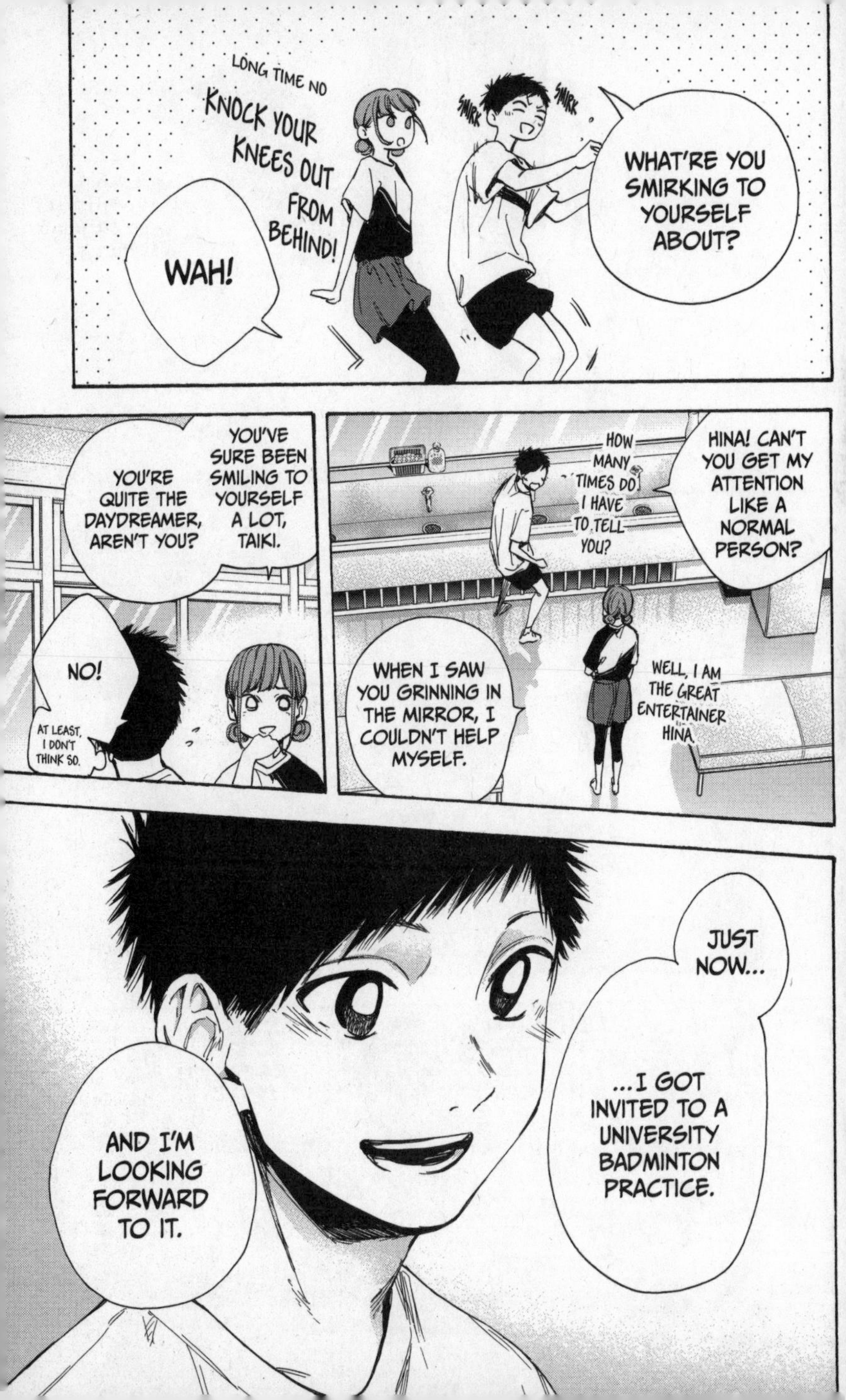
WHAT'RE YOU SMIRKING TO YOURSELF ABOUT?
SMIRK
SMIRK
LONG TIME NO KNOCK YOUR KNEES OUT FROM BEHIND!
WAH!
HINA! CAN'T YOU GET MY ATTENTION LIKE A NORMAL PERSON?
HOW MANY TIMES DO I HAVE TO TELL YOU?
WELL, I AM THE GREAT ENTERTAINER HINA.
WHEN I SAW YOU GRINNING IN THE MIRROR, I COULDN'T HELP MYSELF.
YOU'VE SURE BEEN SMILING TO YOURSELF A LOT, TAIKI.
YOU'RE QUITE THE DAYDREAMER, AREN'T YOU?
NO!
AT LEAST, I DON'T THINK SO.
JUST NOW...
...I GOT INVITED TO A UNIVERSITY BADMINTON PRACTICE.
AND I'M LOOKING FORWARD TO IT.

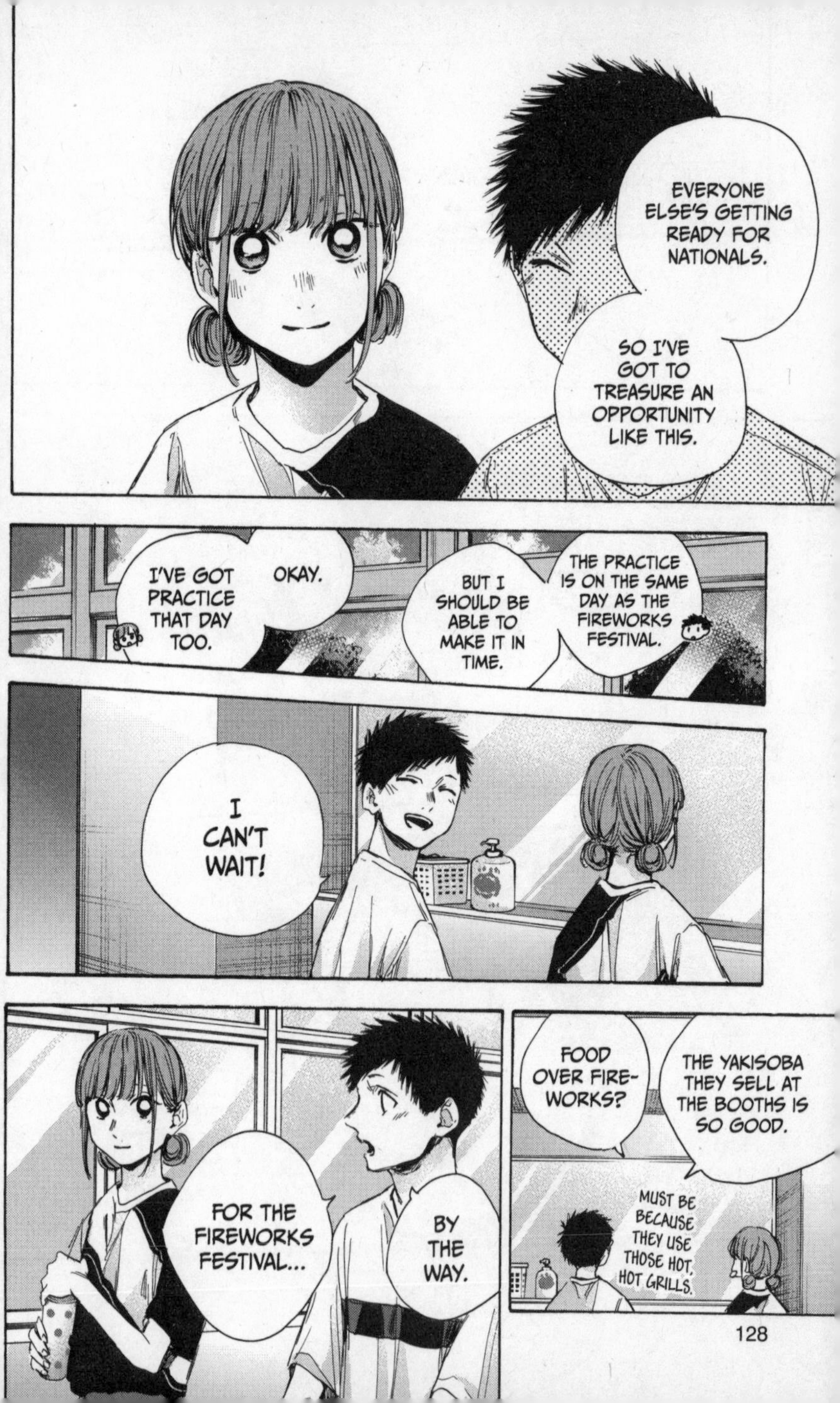
EVERYONE ELSE'S GETTING READY FOR NATIONALS.
SO I'VE GOT TO TREASURE AN OPPORTUNITY LIKE THIS.
THE PRACTICE IS ON THE SAME DAY AS THE FIREWORKS FESTIVAL.
BUT I SHOULD BE ABLE TO MAKE IT IN TIME.
OKAY.
I'VE GOT PRACTICE THAT DAY TOO.
I CAN'T WAIT!
THE YAKISOBA THEY SELL AT THE BOOTHS IS SO GOOD.
FOOD OVER FIRE-WORKS?
MUST BE BECAUSE THEY USE THOSE HOT, HOT GRILLS.
BY THE WAY.
FOR THE FIREWORKS FESTIVAL...

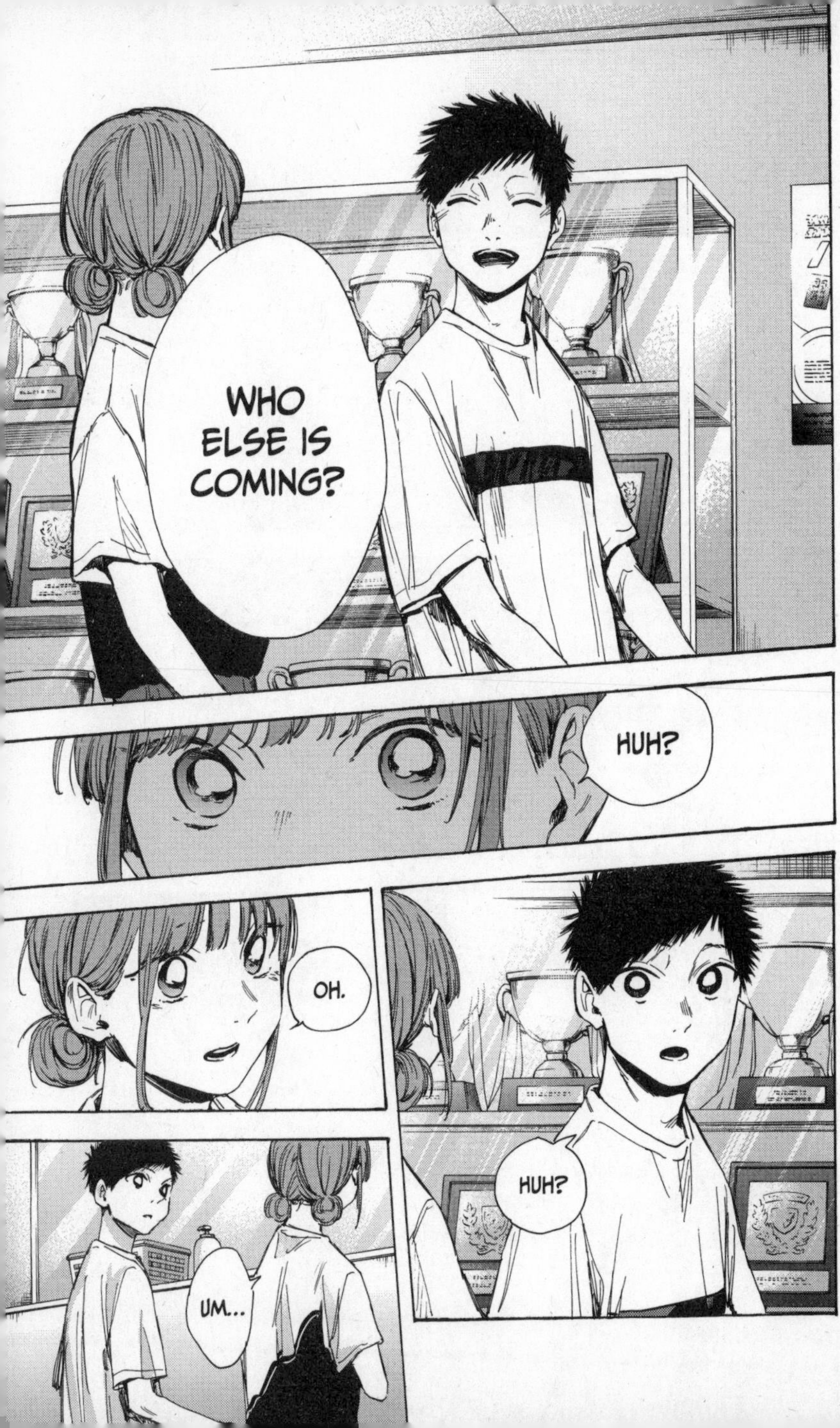
WHO ELSE IS COMING?
HUH?
OH.
HUH?
UM...

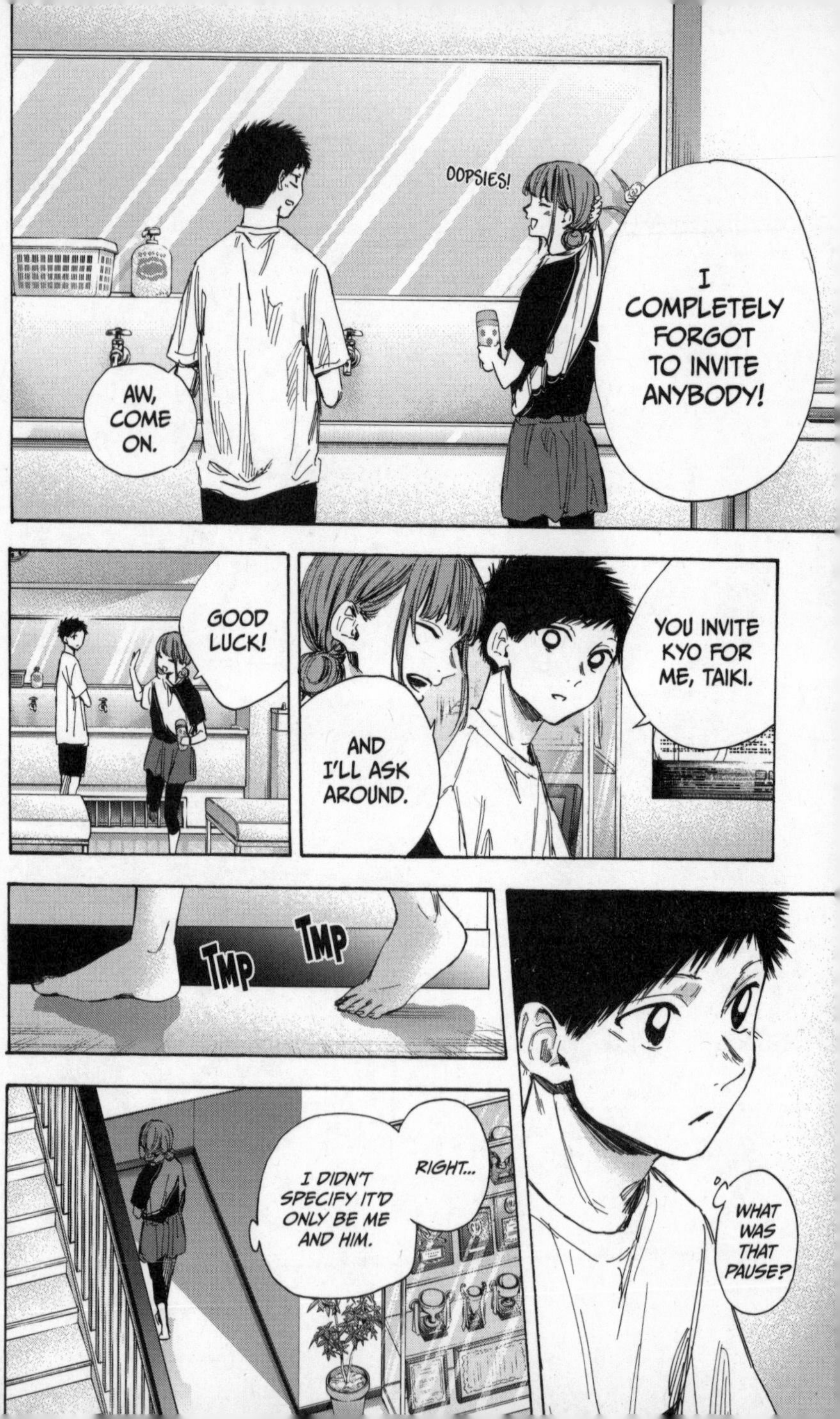
I COMPLETELY FORGOT TO INVITE ANYBODY!
OOPSIES!
AW, COME ON.
YOU INVITE KYO FOR ME, TAIKI.
AND I'LL ASK AROUND.
GOOD LUCK!
TMP
TMP
WHAT WAS THAT PAUSE?
RIGHT...
I DIDN'T SPECIFY IT'D ONLY BE ME AND HIM.

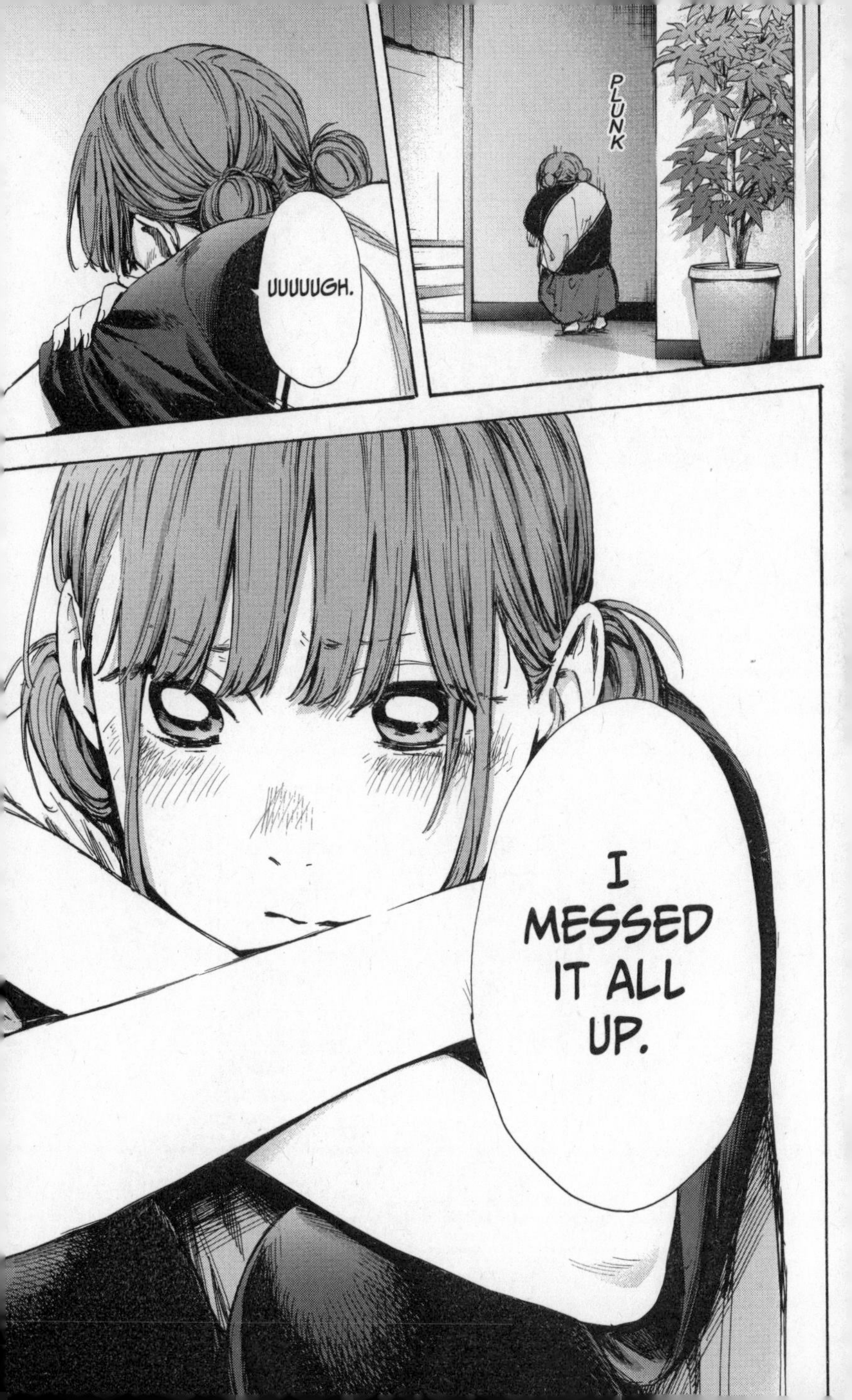
PLUNK
UUUUUGH.
I MESSED IT ALL UP.

Blue Box

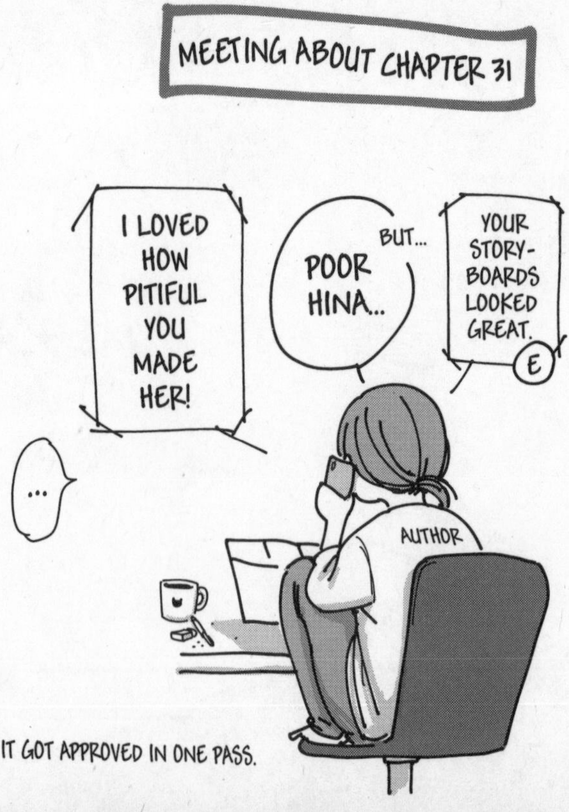
MEETING ABOUT CHAPTER 31
YOUR STORY-BOARDS LOOKED GREAT.
E
POOR HINA... BUT...
I LOVED HOW PITIFUL YOU MADE HER!
...
AUTHOR
IT GOT APPROVED IN ONE PASS.

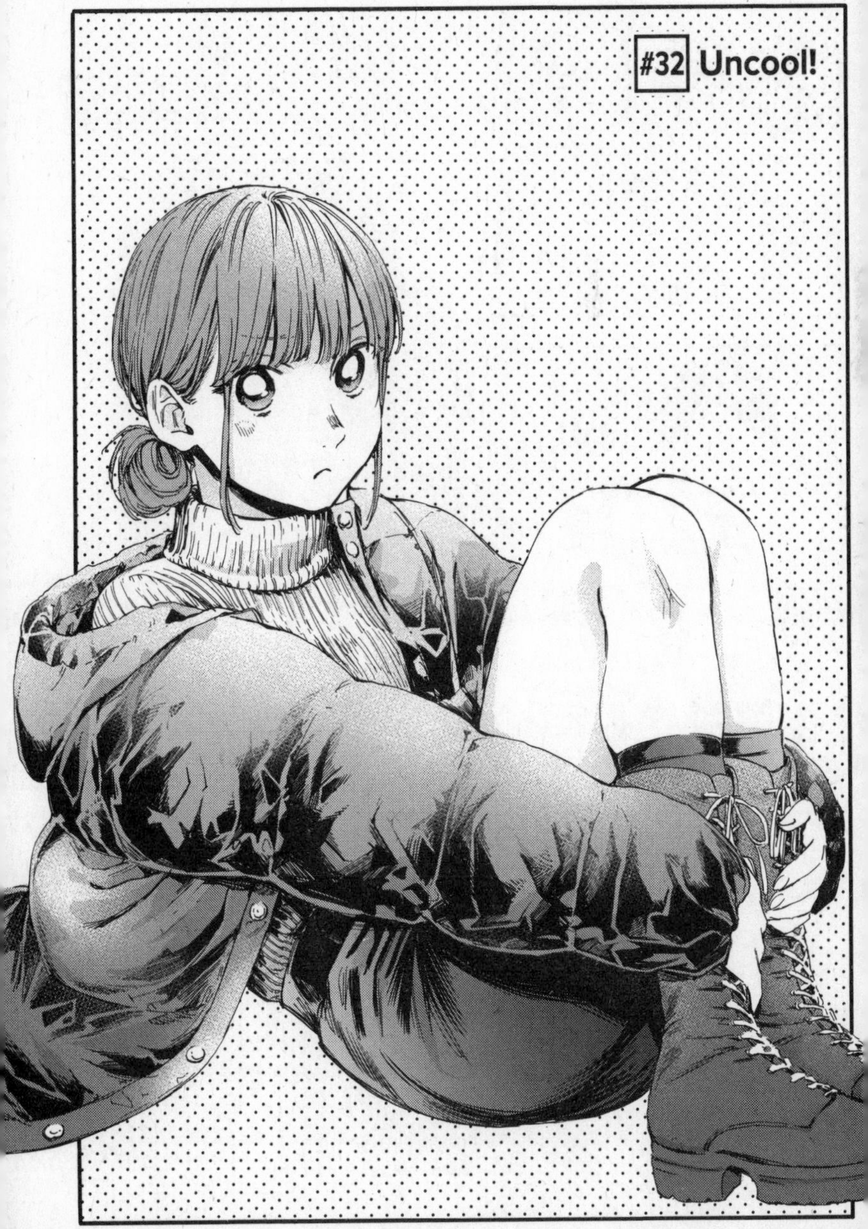
#32 Uncool!

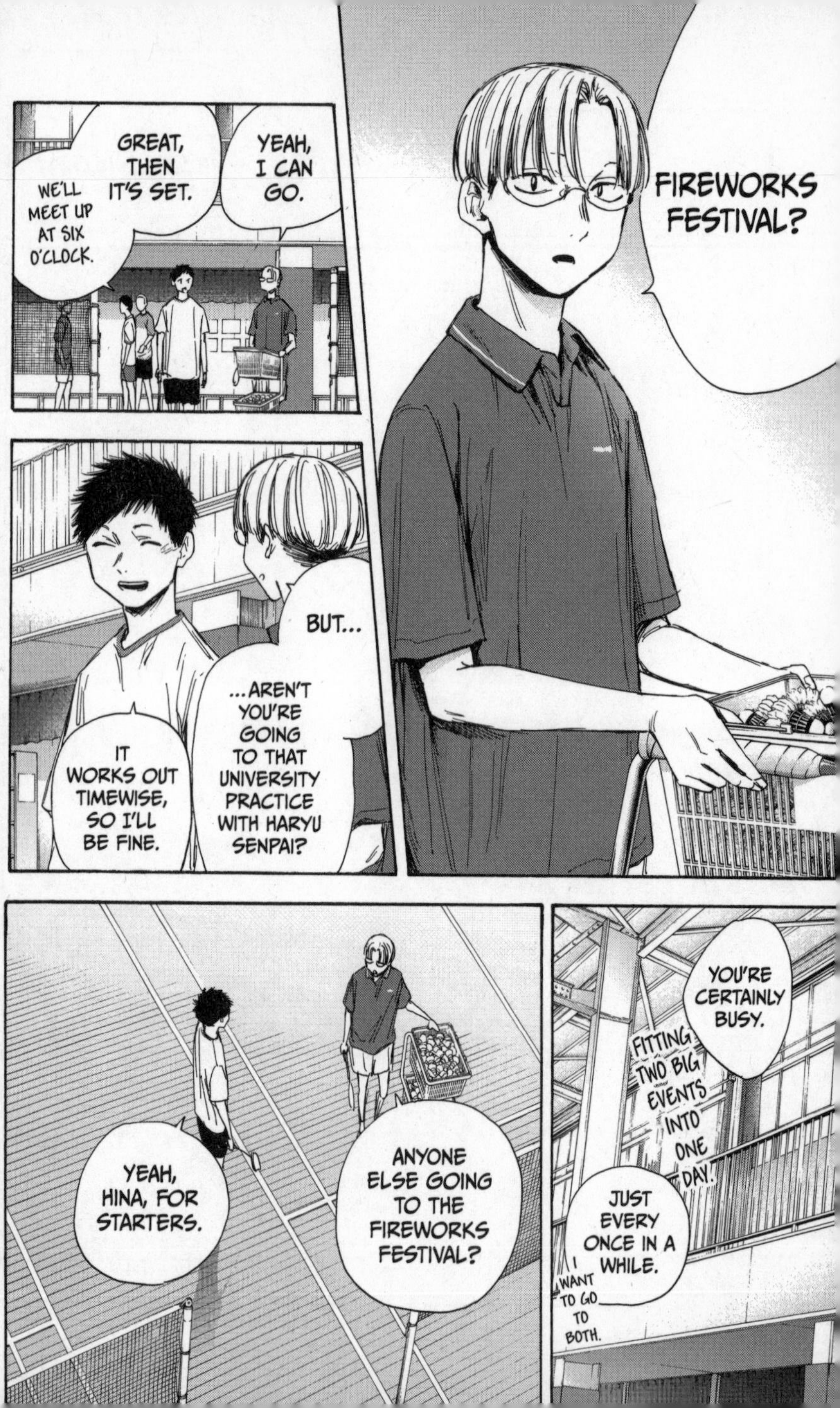
FIREWORKS FESTIVAL?
YEAH, I CAN GO.
GREAT, THEN IT'S SET.
WE'LL MEET UP AT SIX O'CLOCK.
BUT...
...AREN'T YOU'RE GOING TO THAT UNIVERSITY PRACTICE WITH HARYU SENPAI?
IT WORKS OUT TIMEWISE, SO I'LL BE FINE.
YOU'RE CERTAINLY BUSY.
FITTING TWO BIG EVENTS INTO ONE DAY.
JUST EVERY ONCE IN A WHILE.
I WANT TO GO TO BOTH.
ANYONE ELSE GOING TO THE FIREWORKS FESTIVAL?
YEAH, HINA, FOR STARTERS.

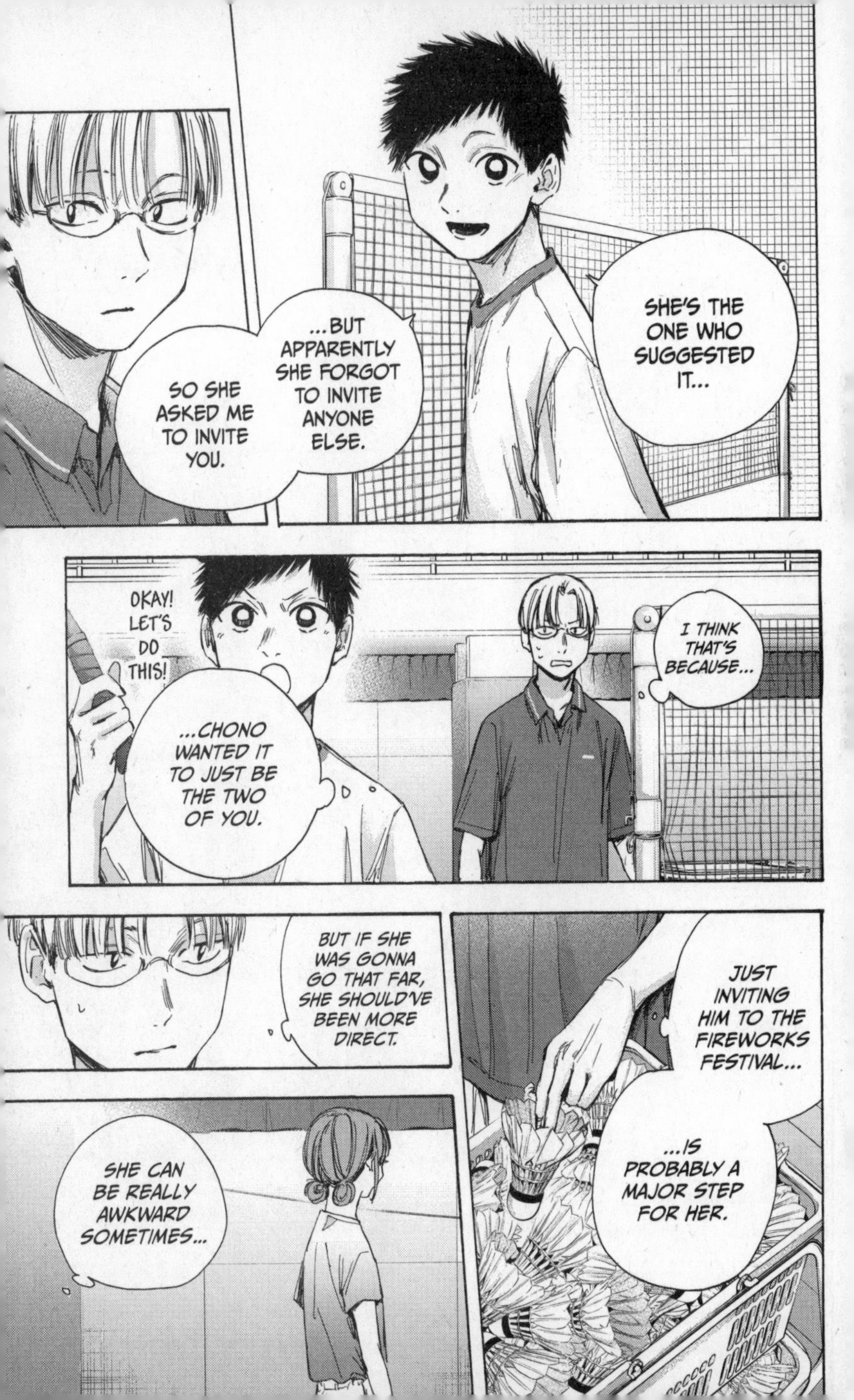
SHE'S THE ONE WHO SUGGESTED IT...
...BUT APPARENTLY SHE FORGOT TO INVITE ANYONE ELSE.
SO SHE ASKED ME TO INVITE YOU.
I THINK THAT'S BECAUSE...
OKAY! LET'S DO THIS!
...CHONO WANTED IT TO JUST BE THE TWO OF YOU.
JUST INVITING HIM TO THE FIREWORKS FESTIVAL...
...IS PROBABLY A MAJOR STEP FOR HER.
BUT IF SHE WAS GONNA GO THAT FAR, SHE SHOULD'VE BEEN MORE DIRECT.
SHE CAN BE REALLY AWKWARD SOMETIMES...

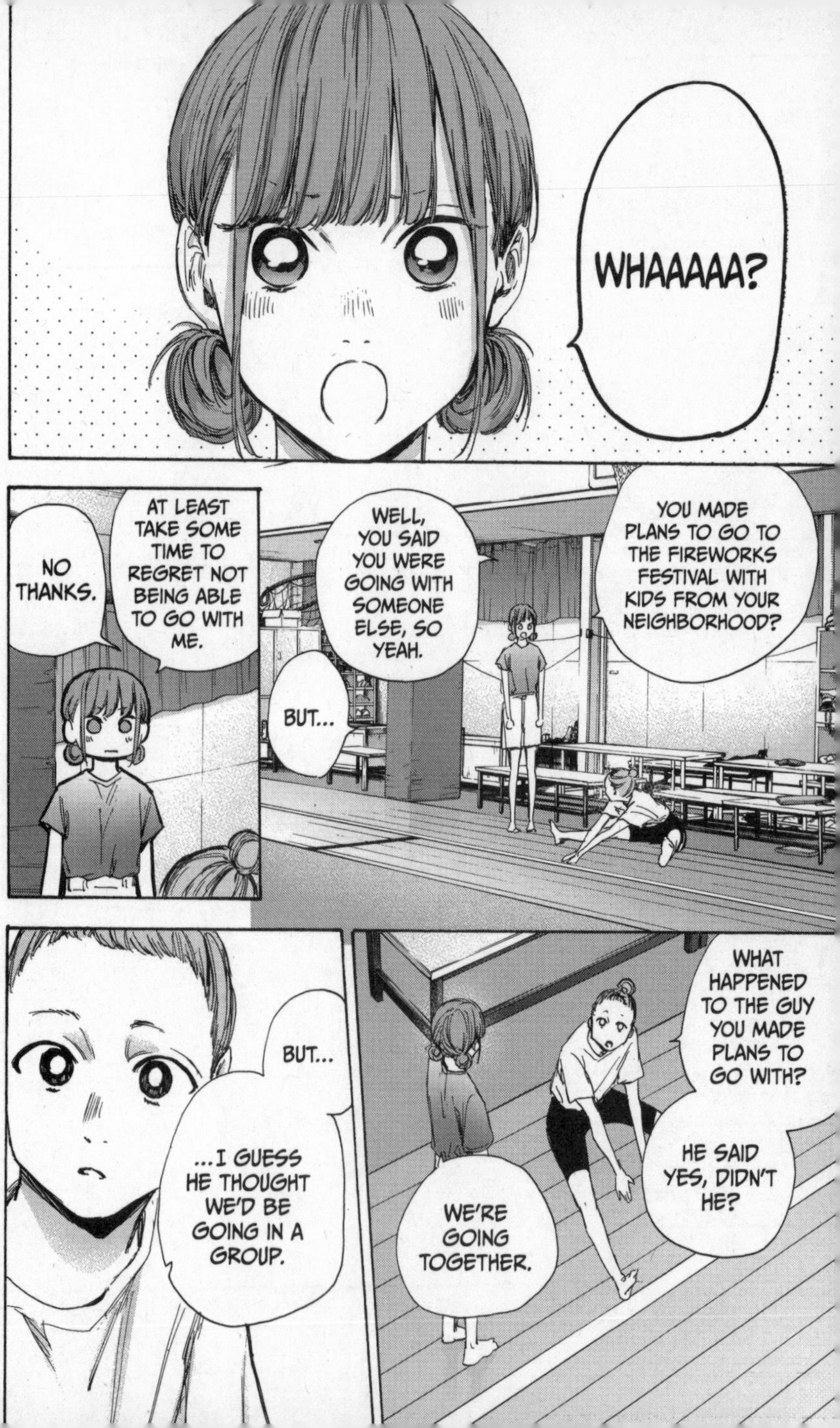
WHAAAAA?
YOU MADE PLANS TO GO TO THE FIREWORKS FESTIVAL WITH KIDS FROM YOUR NEIGHBORHOOD?
WELL, YOU SAID YOU WERE GOING WITH SOMEONE ELSE, SO YEAH.
BUT...
AT LEAST TAKE SOME TIME TO REGRET NOT BEING ABLE TO GO WITH ME.
NO THANKS.
WHAT HAPPENED TO THE GUY YOU MADE PLANS TO GO WITH?
HE SAID YES, DIDN'T HE?
WE'RE GOING TOGETHER.
BUT...
...I GUESS HE THOUGHT WE'D BE GOING IN A GROUP.

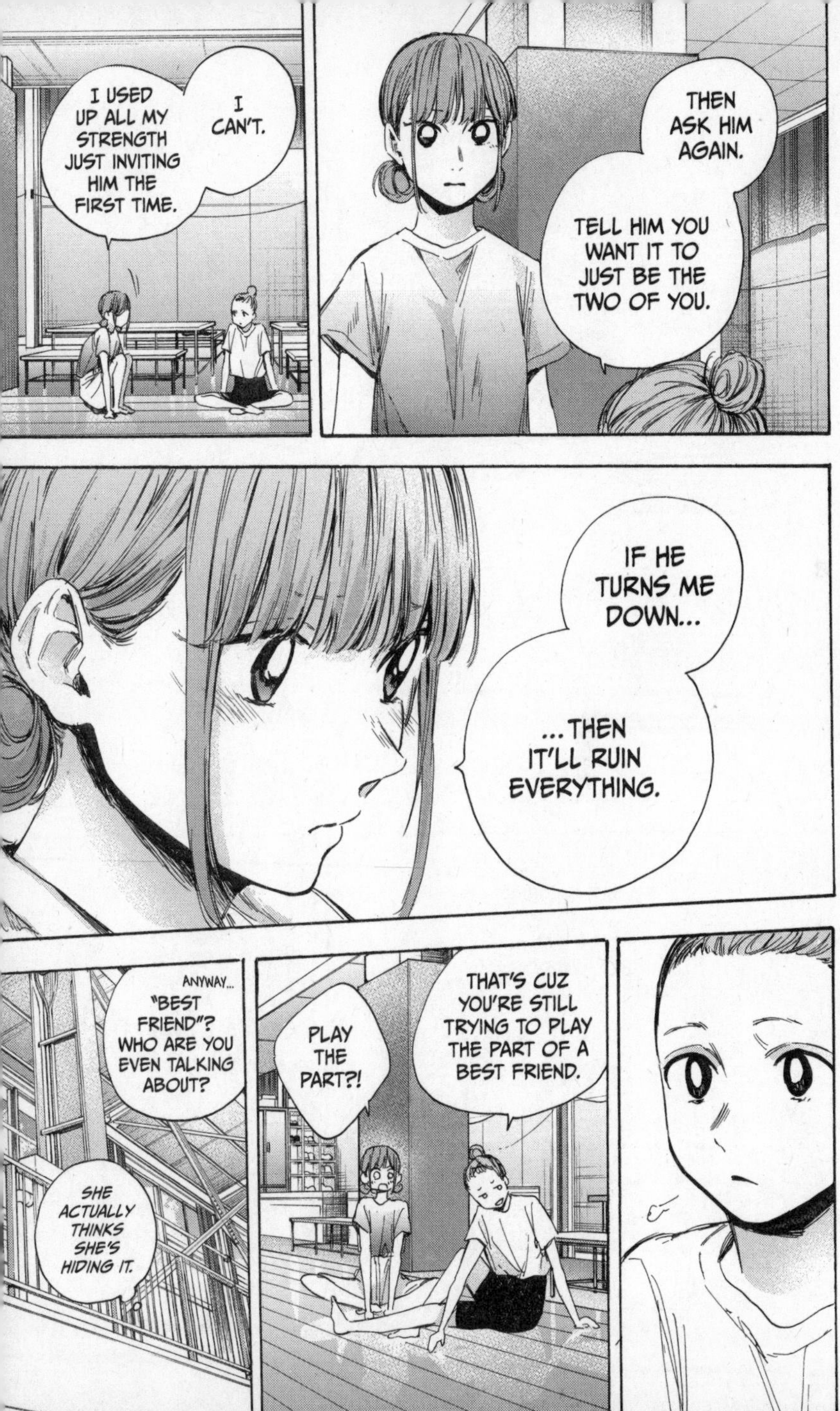
THEN ASK HIM AGAIN.
TELL HIM YOU WANT IT TO JUST BE THE TWO OF YOU.
I CAN'T.
I USED UP ALL MY STRENGTH JUST INVITING HIM THE FIRST TIME.
IF HE TURNS ME DOWN...
...THEN IT'LL RUIN EVERYTHING.
THAT'S CUZ YOU'RE STILL TRYING TO PLAY THE PART OF A BEST FRIEND.
PLAY THE PART?!
ANYWAY... "BEST FRIEND"? WHO ARE YOU EVEN TALKING ABOUT?
SHE ACTUALLY THINKS SHE'S HIDING IT.

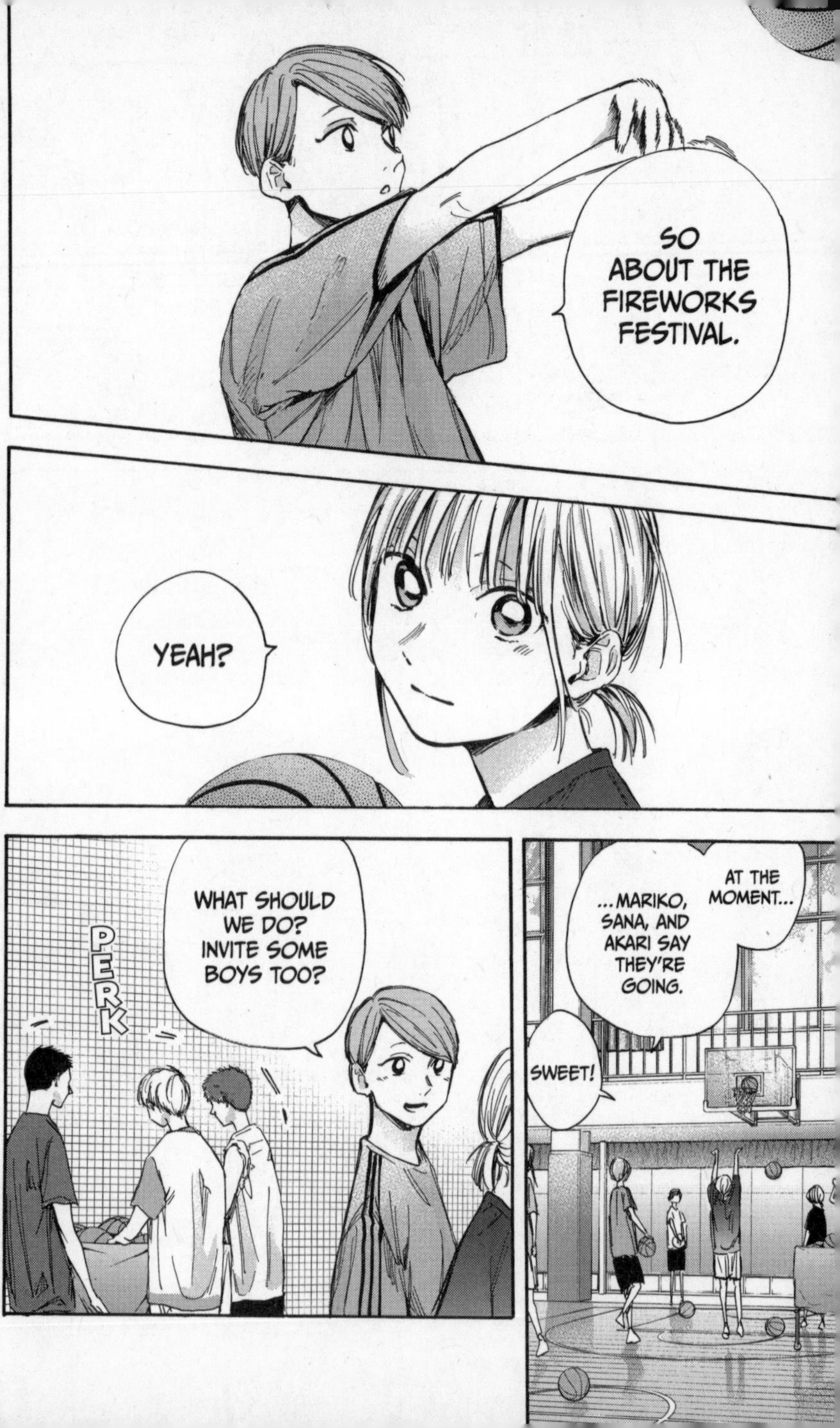
SO ABOUT THE FIREWORKS FESTIVAL.
YEAH?
AT THE MOMENT...
...MARIKO, SANA, AND AKARI SAY THEY'RE GOING.
SWEET!
WHAT SHOULD WE DO? INVITE SOME BOYS TOO?
PERK

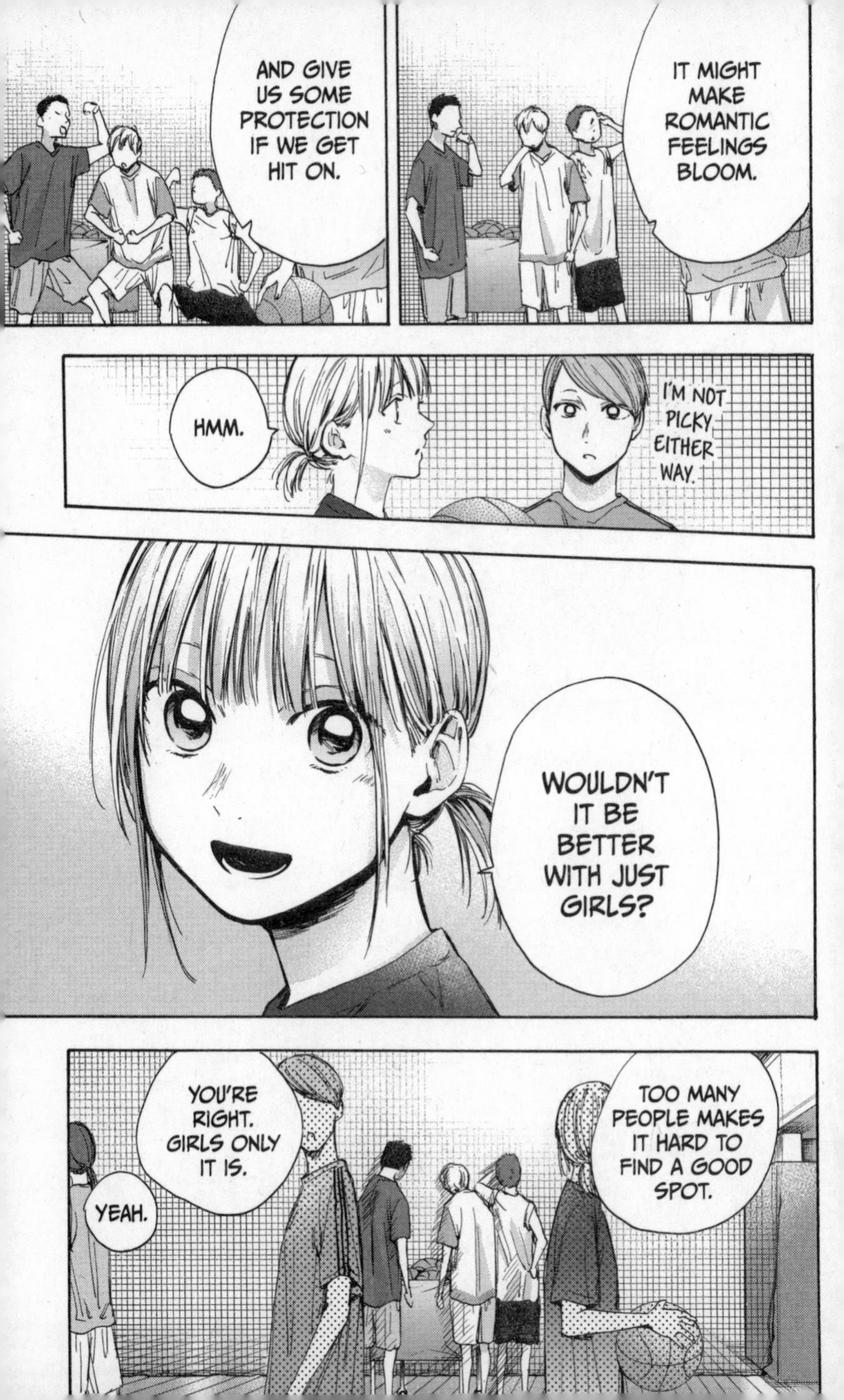
IT MIGHT MAKE ROMANTIC FEELINGS BLOOM.
AND GIVE US SOME PROTECTION IF WE GET HIT ON.
I'M NOT PICKY EITHER WAY.
HMM.
WOULDN'T IT BE BETTER WITH JUST GIRLS?
TOO MANY PEOPLE MAKES IT HARD TO FIND A GOOD SPOT.
YOU'RE RIGHT. GIRLS ONLY IT IS.
YEAH.

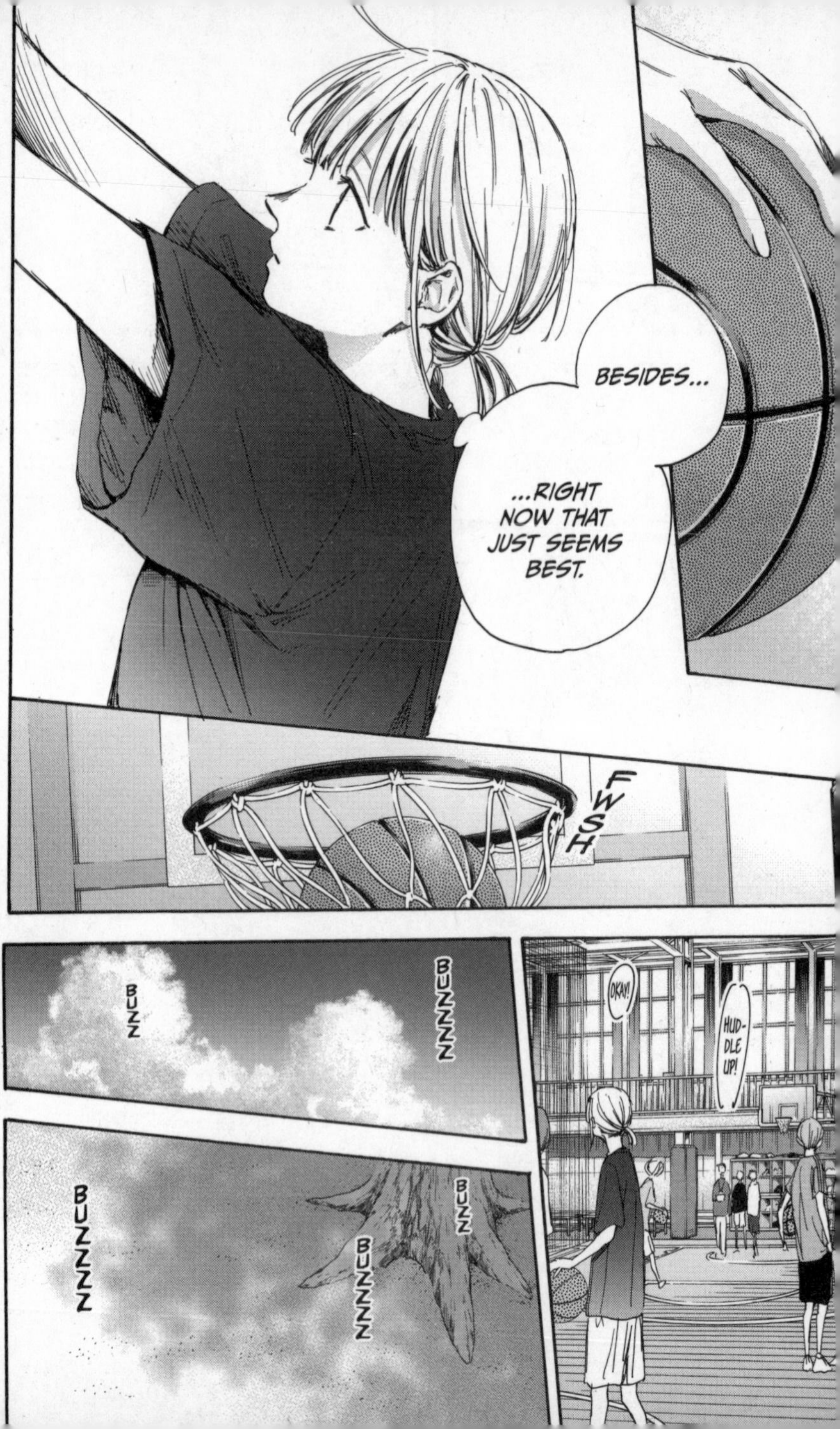
BESIDES...
...RIGHT NOW THAT JUST SEEMS BEST.
FWSH
HUD-DLE UP!
OKAY!
BUZZZZ
BUZZ
BUZZ
BUZZZZ
BUZZZZ

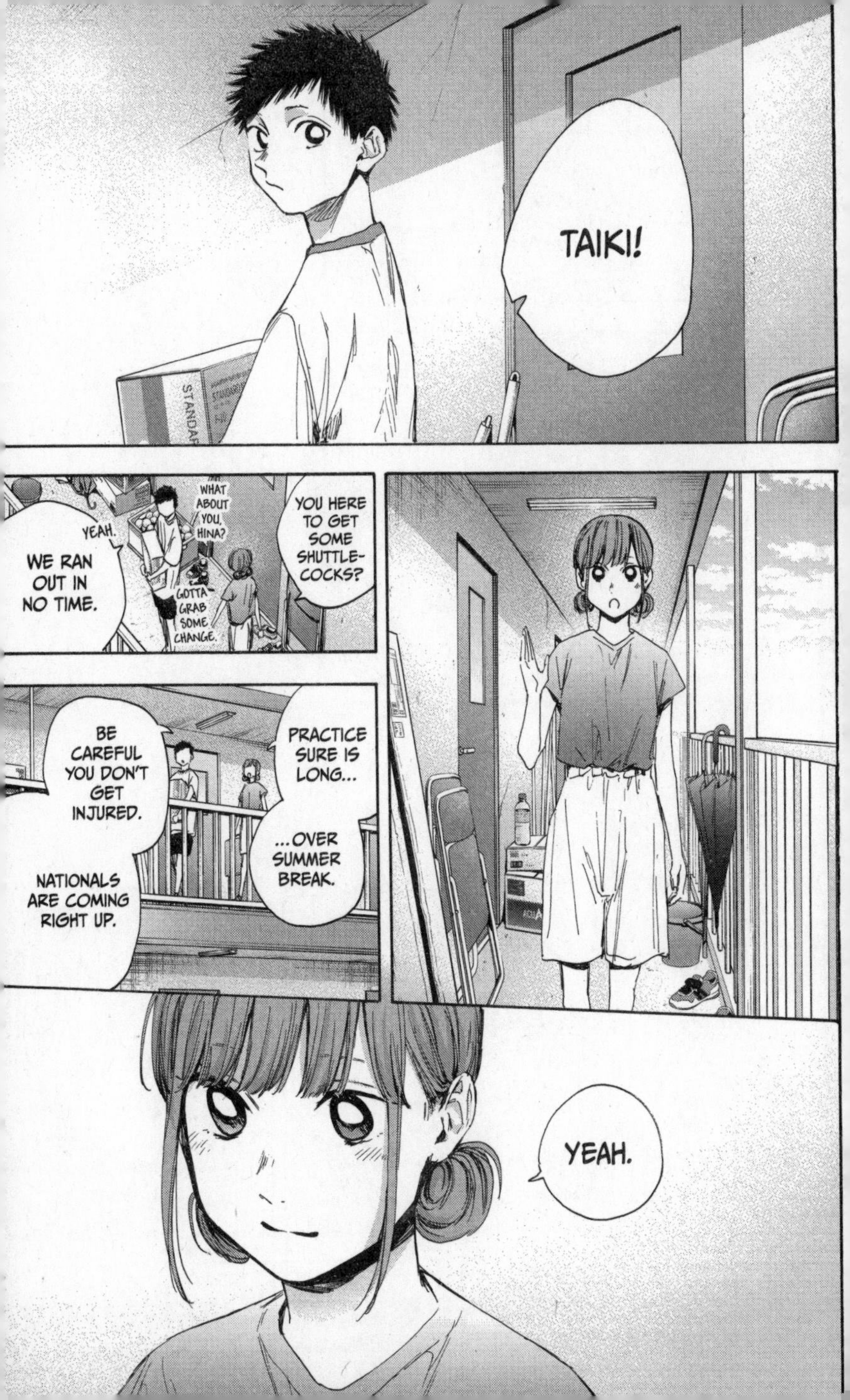
TAIKI!
YOU HERE TO GET SOME SHUTTLE-COCKS?
YEAH.
WE RAN OUT IN NO TIME.
WHAT ABOUT YOU, HINA?
GOTTA GRAB SOME CHANGE.
PRACTICE SURE IS LONG...
...OVER SUMMER BREAK.
BE CAREFUL YOU DON'T GET INJURED.
NATIONALS ARE COMING RIGHT UP.
YEAH.

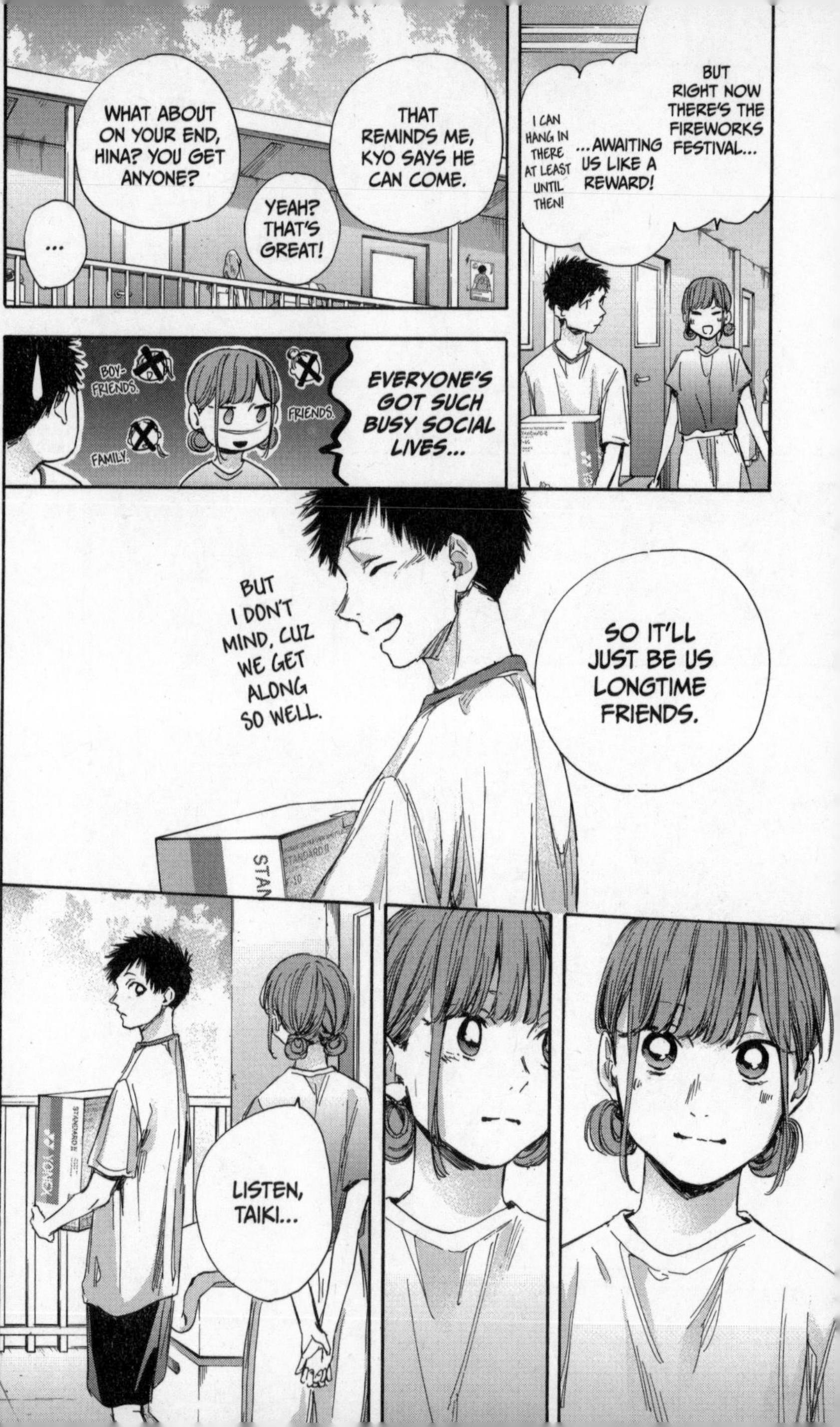
BUT RIGHT NOW THERE'S THE FIREWORKS FESTIVAL...
...AWAITING US LIKE A REWARD!
I CAN HANG IN THERE AT LEAST UNTIL THEN!
THAT REMINDS ME, KYO SAYS HE CAN COME.
YEAH? THAT'S GREAT!
WHAT ABOUT ON YOUR END, HINA? YOU GET ANYONE?
...
EVERYONE'S GOT SUCH BUSY SOCIAL LIVES...
FRIENDS.
BOY-FRIENDS.
FAMILY.
SO IT'LL JUST BE US LONGTIME FRIENDS.
BUT I DON'T MIND, CUZ WE GET ALONG SO WELL.
LISTEN, TAIKI...

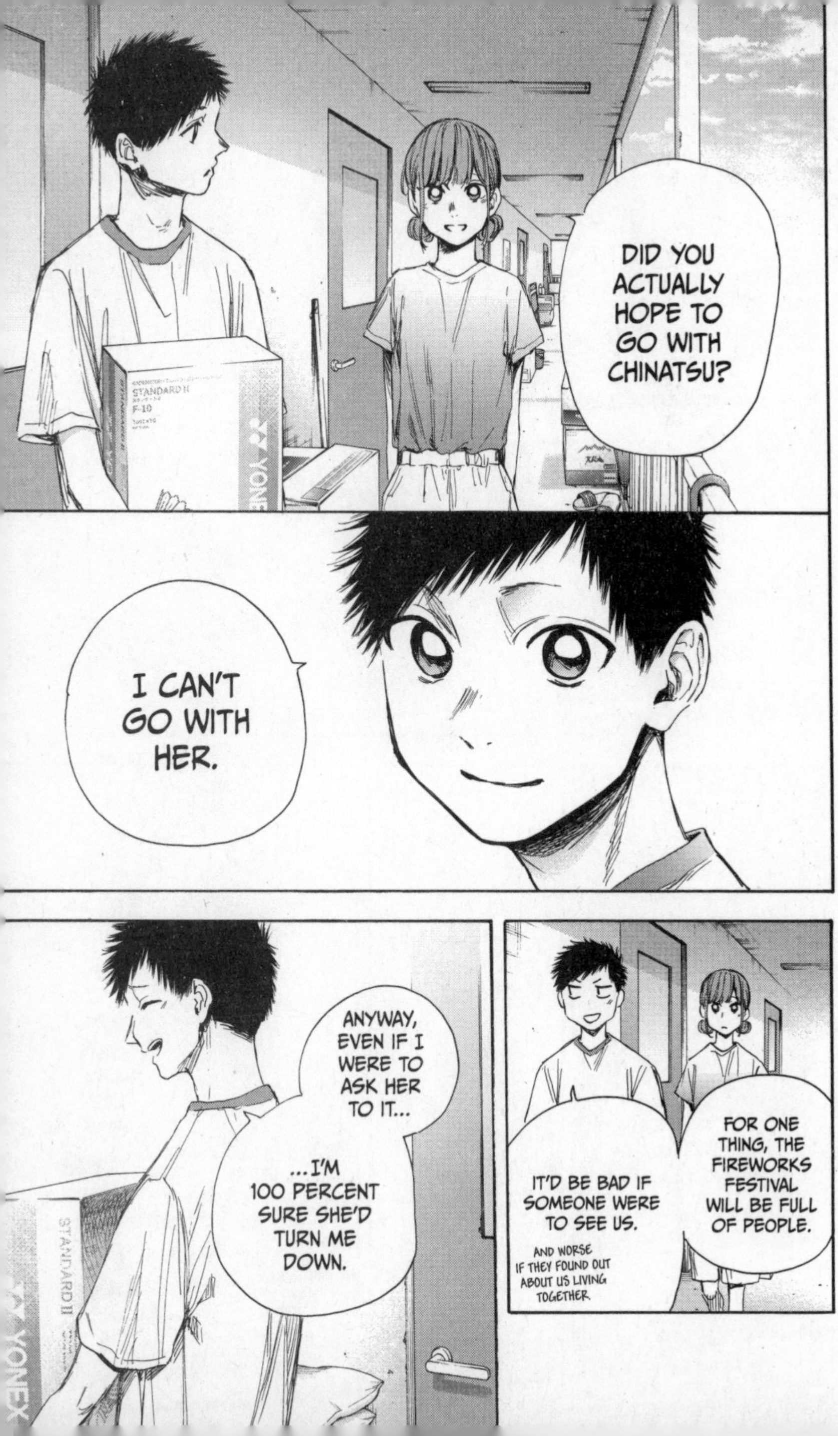
DID YOU ACTUALLY HOPE TO GO WITH CHINATSU?
I CAN'T GO WITH HER.
FOR ONE THING, THE FIREWORKS FESTIVAL WILL BE FULL OF PEOPLE.
IT'D BE BAD IF SOMEONE WERE TO SEE US.
AND WORSE IF THEY FOUND OUT ABOUT US LIVING TOGETHER.
ANYWAY, EVEN IF I WERE TO ASK HER TO IT...
...I'M 100 PERCENT SURE SHE'D TURN ME DOWN.

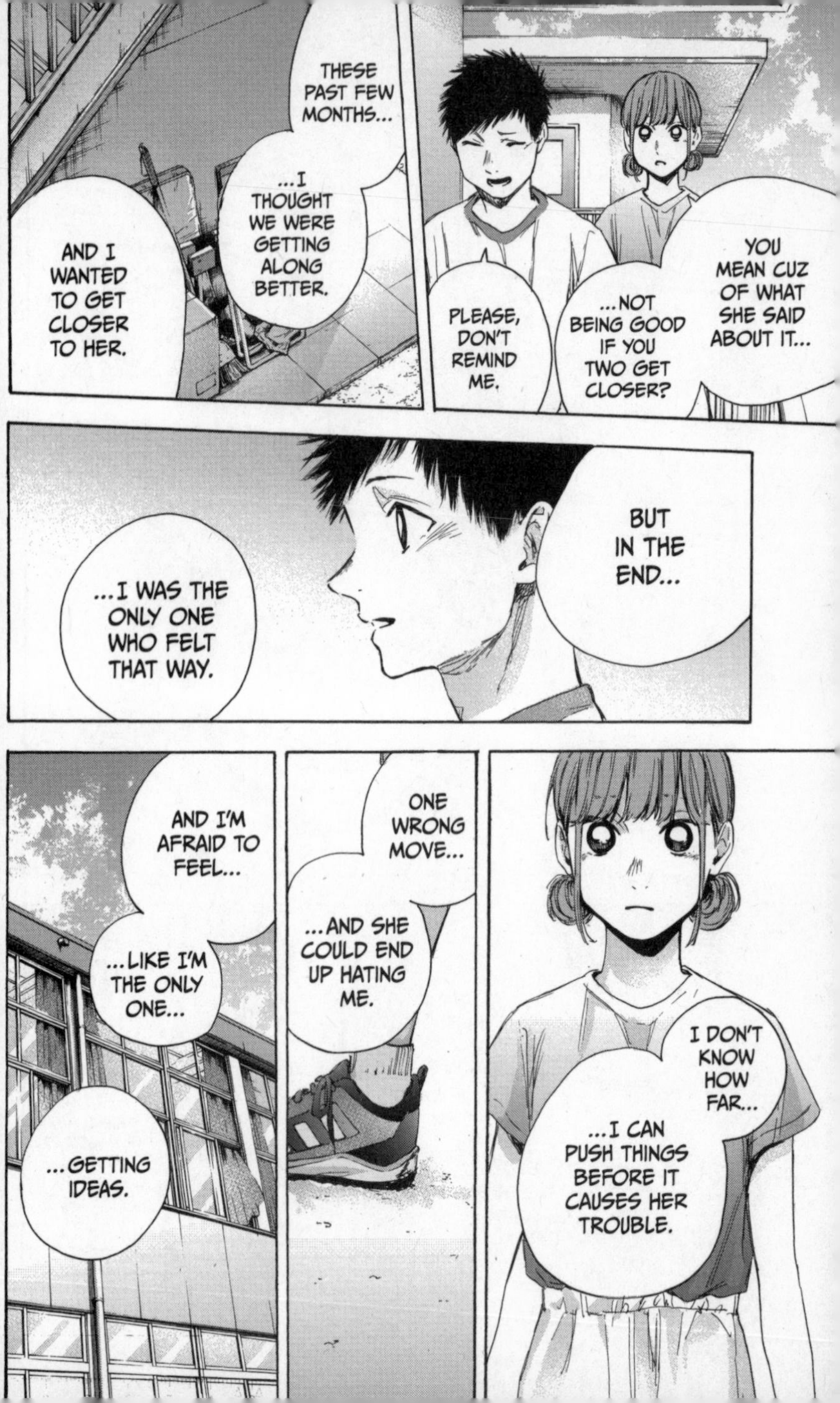
YOU MEAN CUZ OF WHAT SHE SAID ABOUT IT...
...NOT BEING GOOD IF YOU TWO GET CLOSER?
PLEASE, DON'T REMIND ME.
THESE PAST FEW MONTHS...
...I THOUGHT WE WERE GETTING ALONG BETTER.
AND I WANTED TO GET CLOSER TO HER.
BUT IN THE END...
...I WAS THE ONLY ONE WHO FELT THAT WAY.
I DON'T KNOW HOW FAR...
...I CAN PUSH THINGS BEFORE IT CAUSES HER TROUBLE.
ONE WRONG MOVE...
...AND SHE COULD END UP HATING ME.
AND I'M AFRAID TO FEEL...
...LIKE I'M THE ONLY ONE...
...GETTING IDEAS.

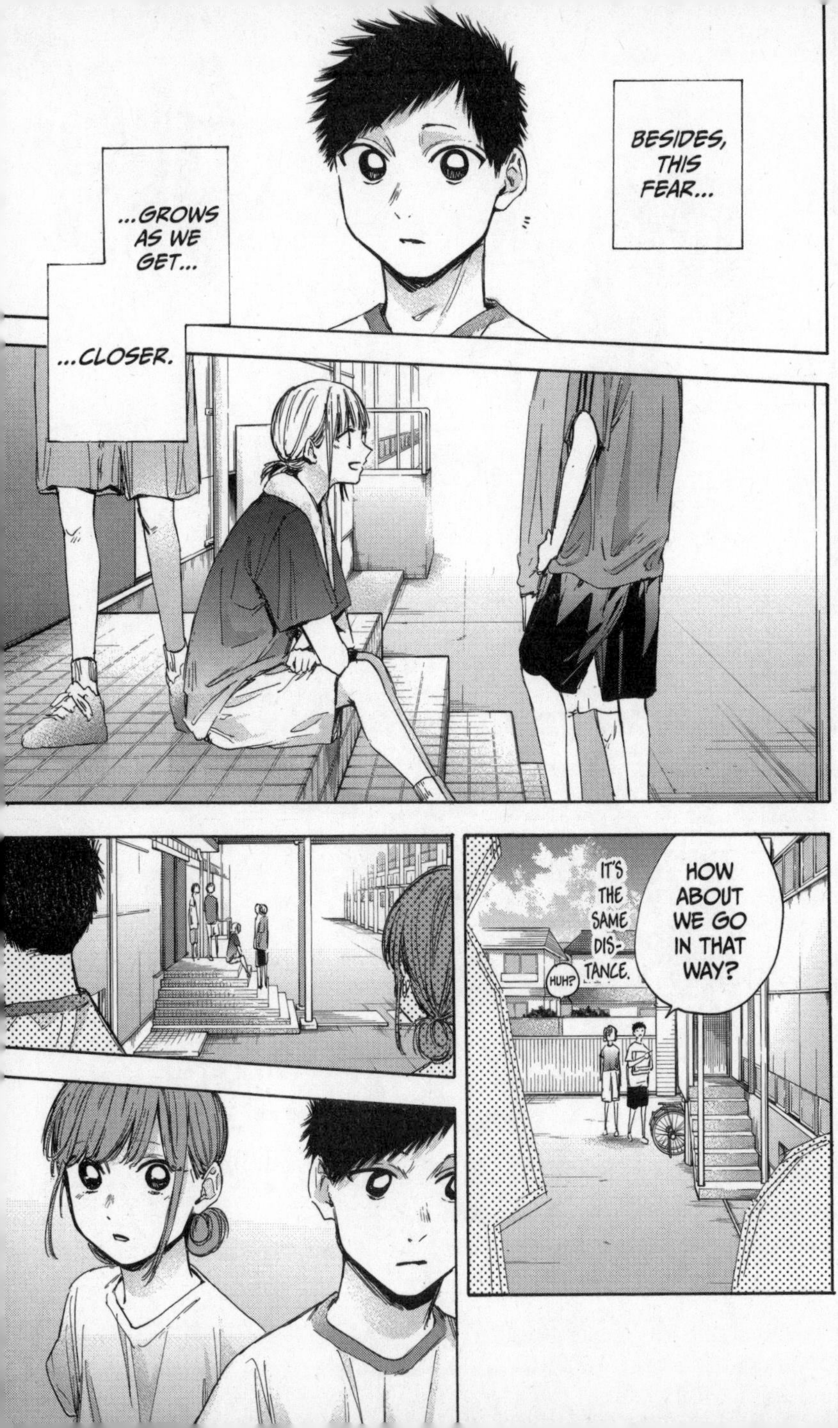
BESIDES, THIS FEAR...
...GROWS AS WE GET...
...CLOSER.
HOW ABOUT WE GO IN THAT WAY?
IT'S THE SAME DIS-TANCE.
HUH?

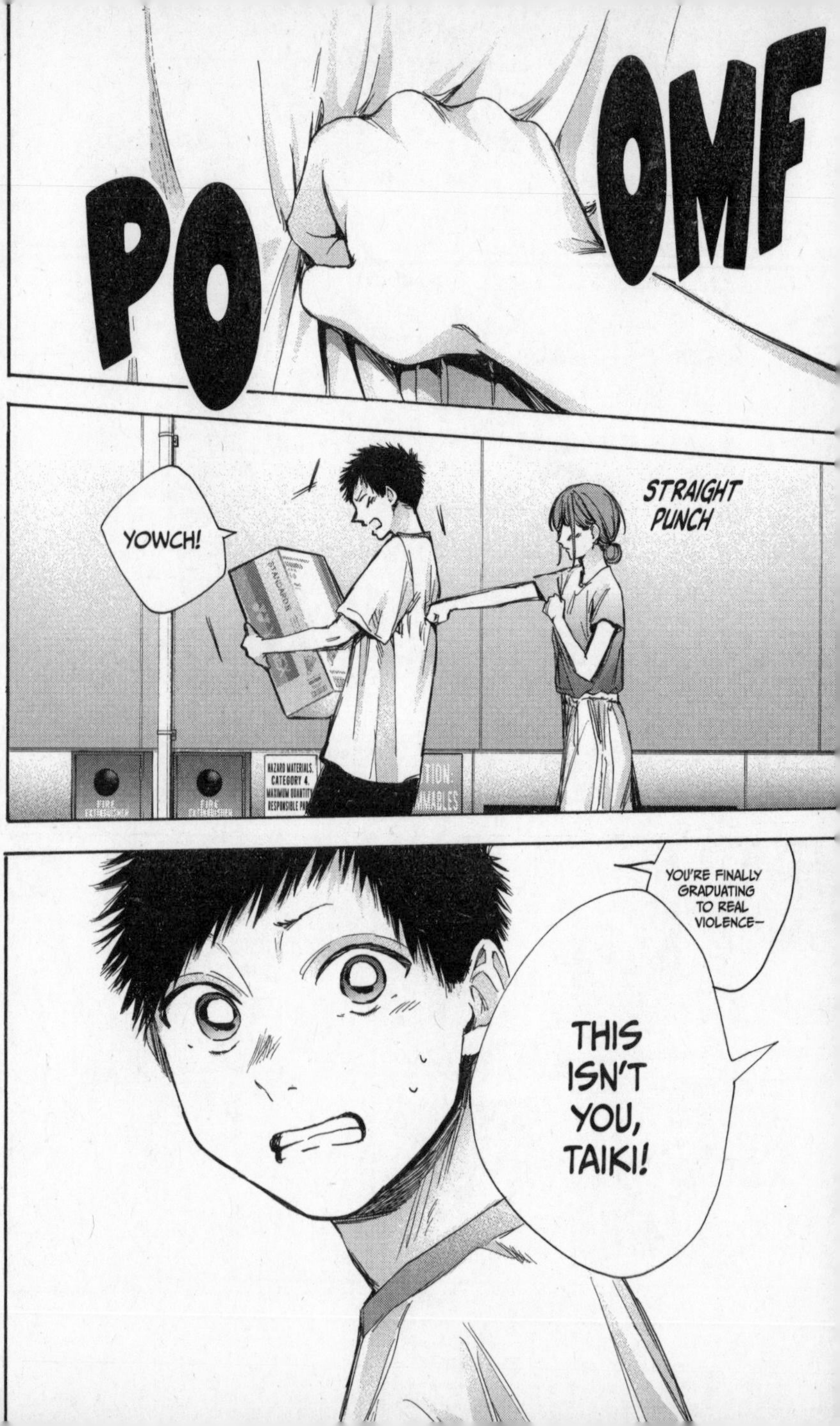
POOMF
STRAIGHT PUNCH
YOWCH!
HAZARD MATERIALS. CATEGORY 4.
YOU'RE FINALLY GRADUATING TO REAL VIOLENCE—
THIS ISN'T YOU, TAIKI!

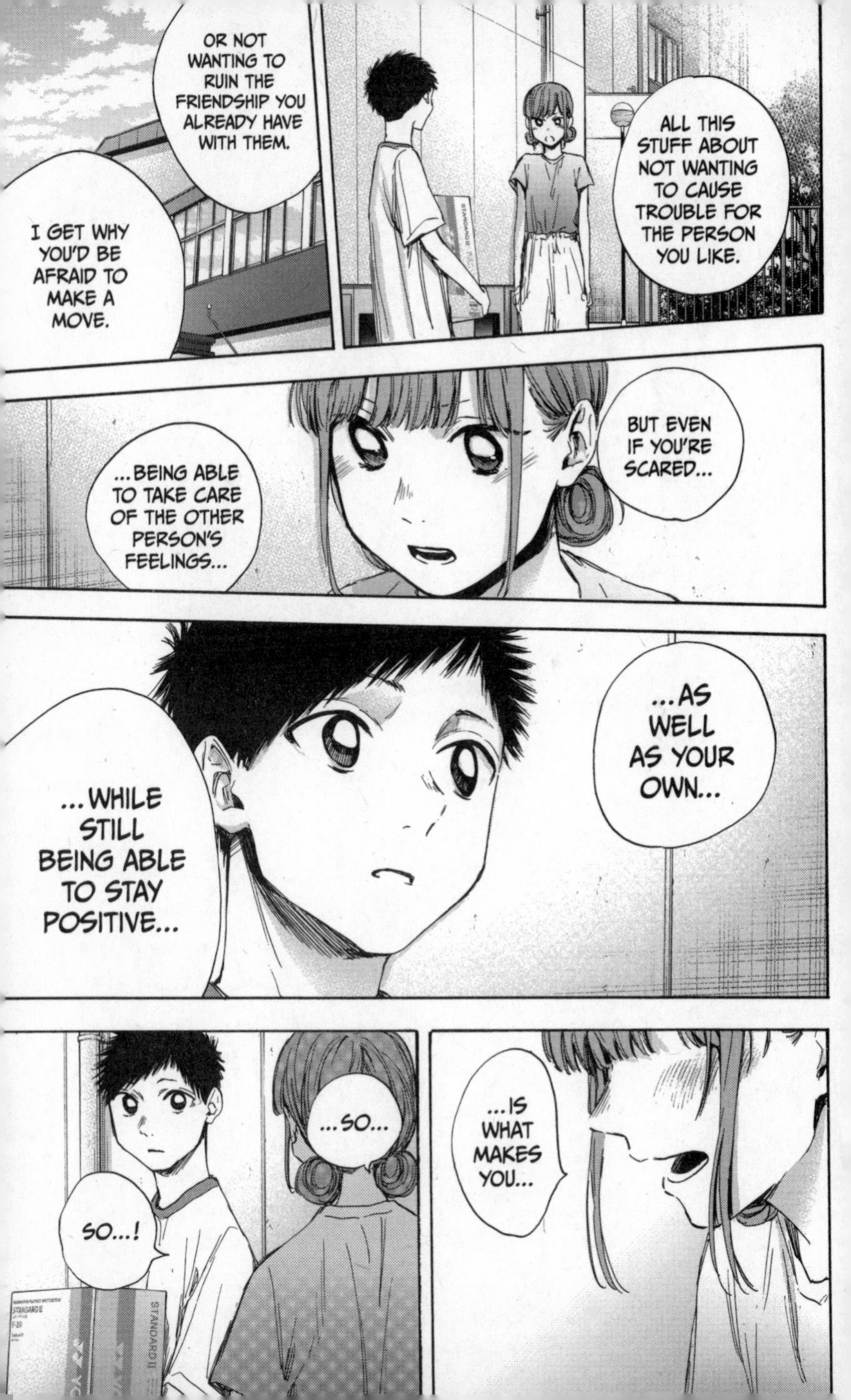
ALL THIS STUFF ABOUT NOT WANTING TO CAUSE TROUBLE FOR THE PERSON YOU LIKE.
OR NOT WANTING TO RUIN THE FRIENDSHIP YOU ALREADY HAVE WITH THEM.
I GET WHY YOU'D BE AFRAID TO MAKE A MOVE.
BUT EVEN IF YOU'RE SCARED...
...BEING ABLE TO TAKE CARE OF THE OTHER PERSON'S FEELINGS...
...AS WELL AS YOUR OWN...
...WHILE STILL BEING ABLE TO STAY POSITIVE...
...IS WHAT MAKES YOU...
...SO...
SO...!

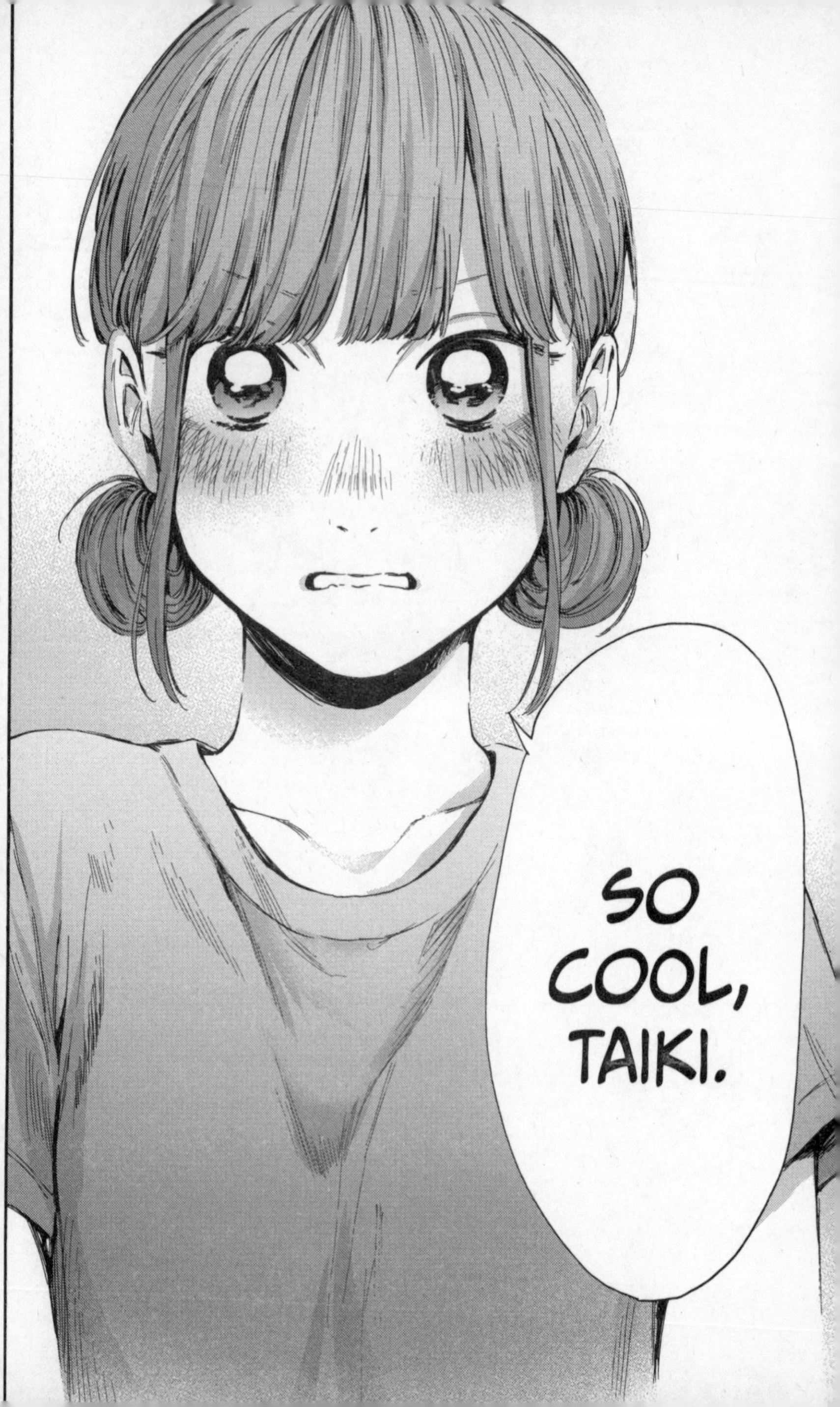
SO COOL, TAIKI.

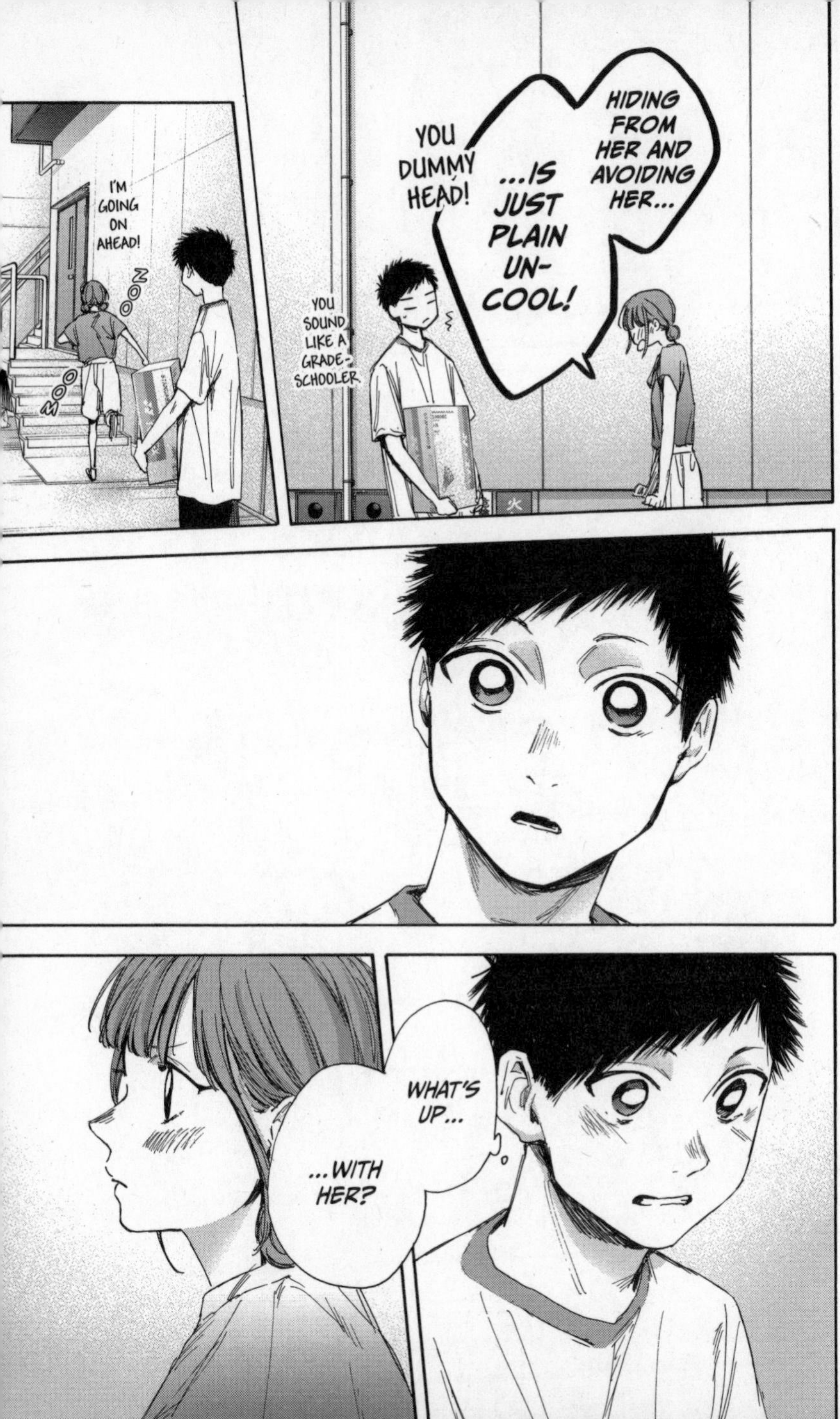
HIDING FROM HER AND AVOIDING HER...
...IS JUST PLAIN UN-COOL!
YOU DUMMY HEAD!
YOU SOUND LIKE A GRADE-SCHOOLER.
I'M GOING ON AHEAD!
ZOOM
ZOOM
WHAT'S UP...
...WITH HER?

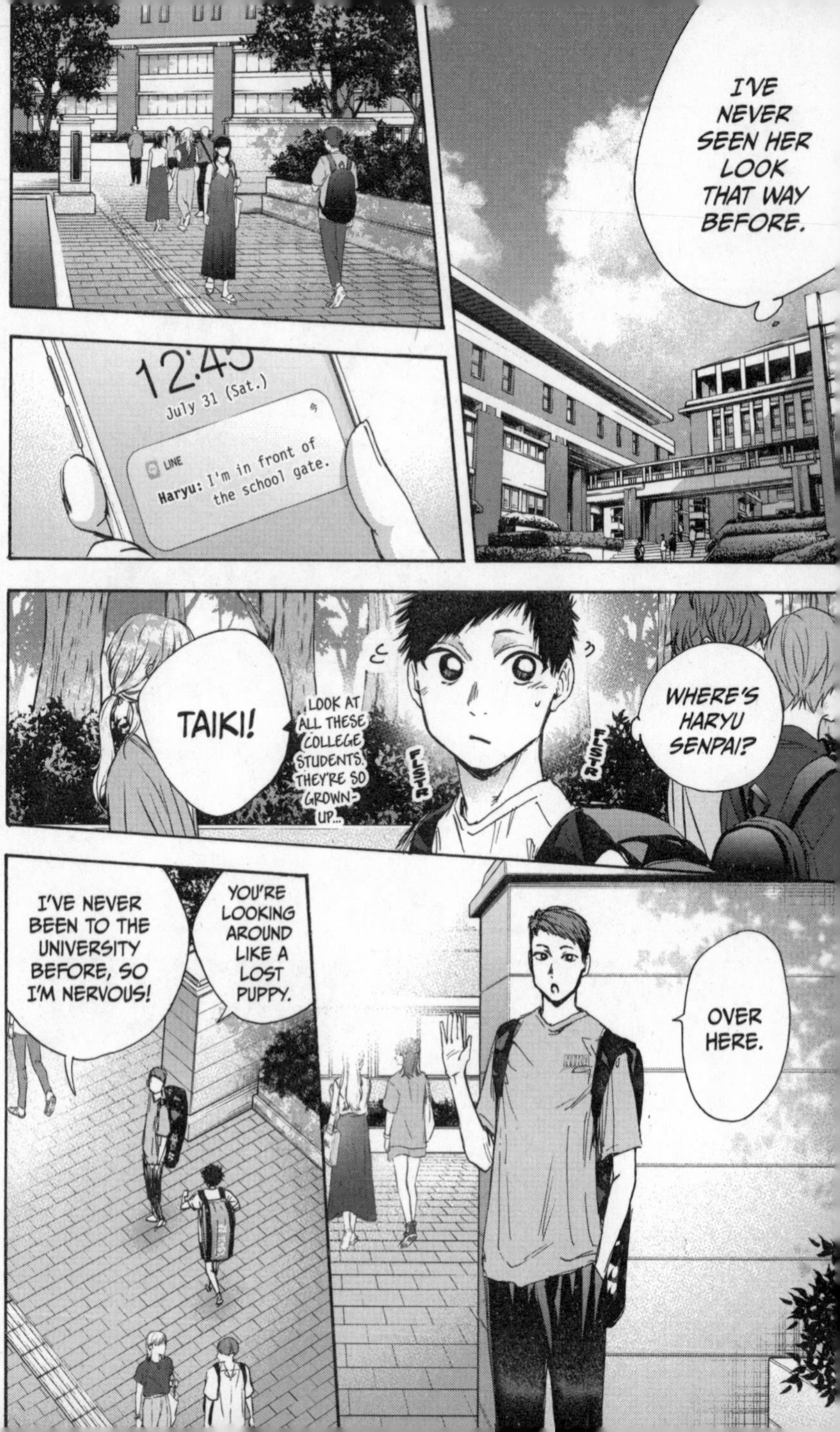
I'VE NEVER SEEN HER LOOK THAT WAY BEFORE.
12:45
July 31 (Sat.)
LINE
Haryu: I'm in front of the school gate.
WHERE'S HARYU SENPAI?
FLSTR
FLSTR
LOOK AT ALL THESE COLLEGE STUDENTS. THEY'RE SO GROWN-UP...
TAIKI!
OVER HERE.
YOU'RE LOOKING AROUND LIKE A LOST PUPPY.
I'VE NEVER BEEN TO THE UNIVERSITY BEFORE, SO I'M NERVOUS!

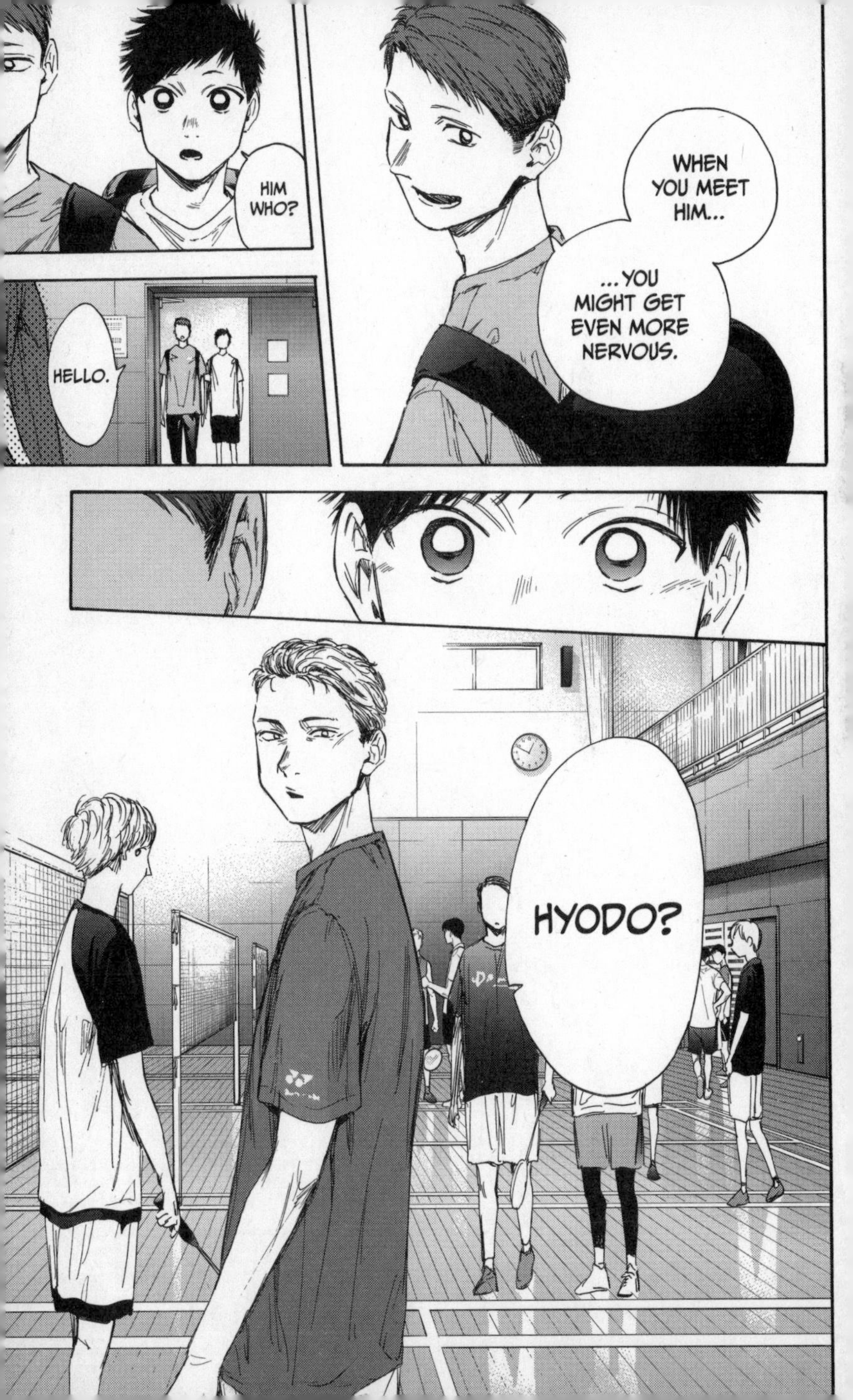
WHEN YOU MEET HIM...
...YOU MIGHT GET EVEN MORE NERVOUS.
HIM WHO?
HELLO.
HYODO?

BLUE·BOX

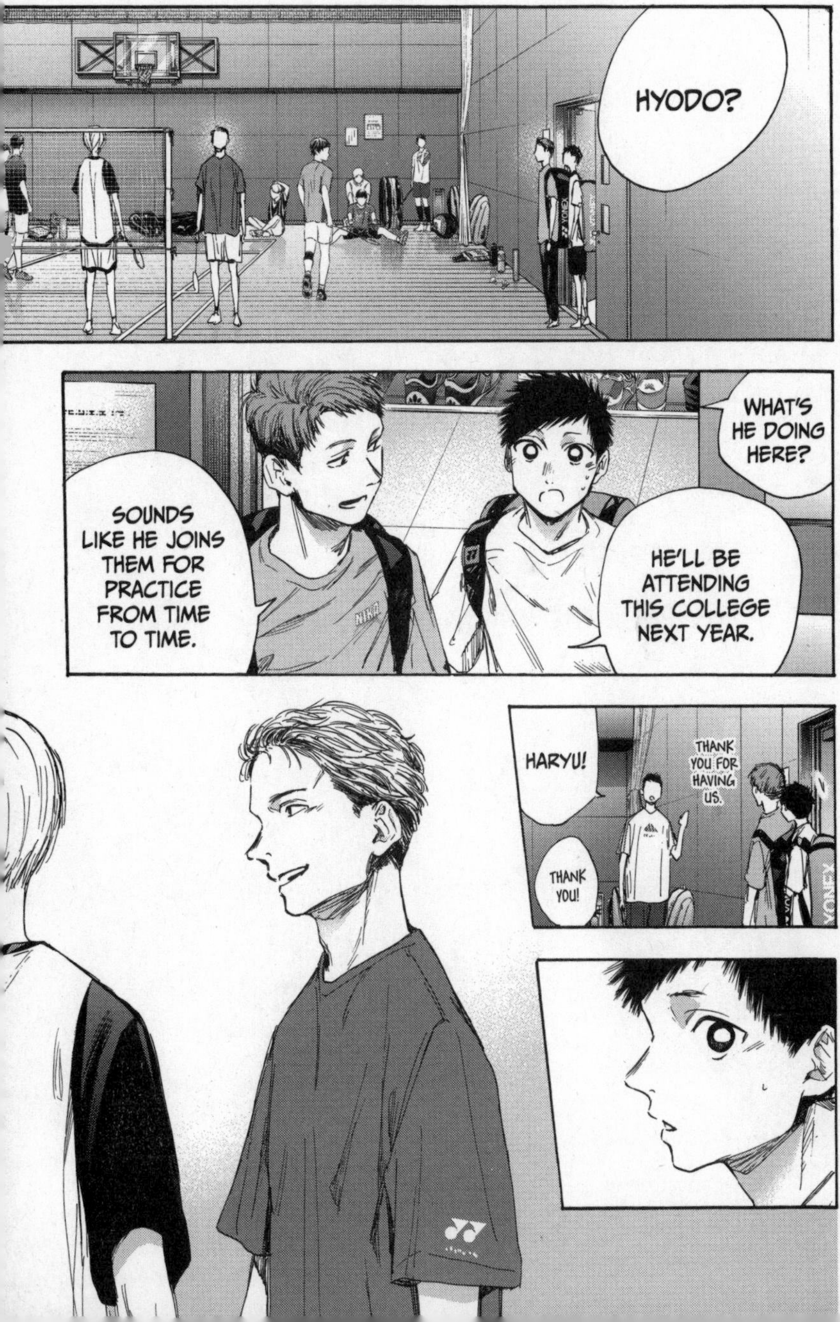
HYODO?
WHAT'S HE DOING HERE?
HE'LL BE ATTENDING THIS COLLEGE NEXT YEAR.
SOUNDS LIKE HE JOINS THEM FOR PRACTICE FROM TIME TO TIME.
THANK YOU FOR HAVING US.
HARYU!
THANK YOU!

#33 When the Underdog Wins

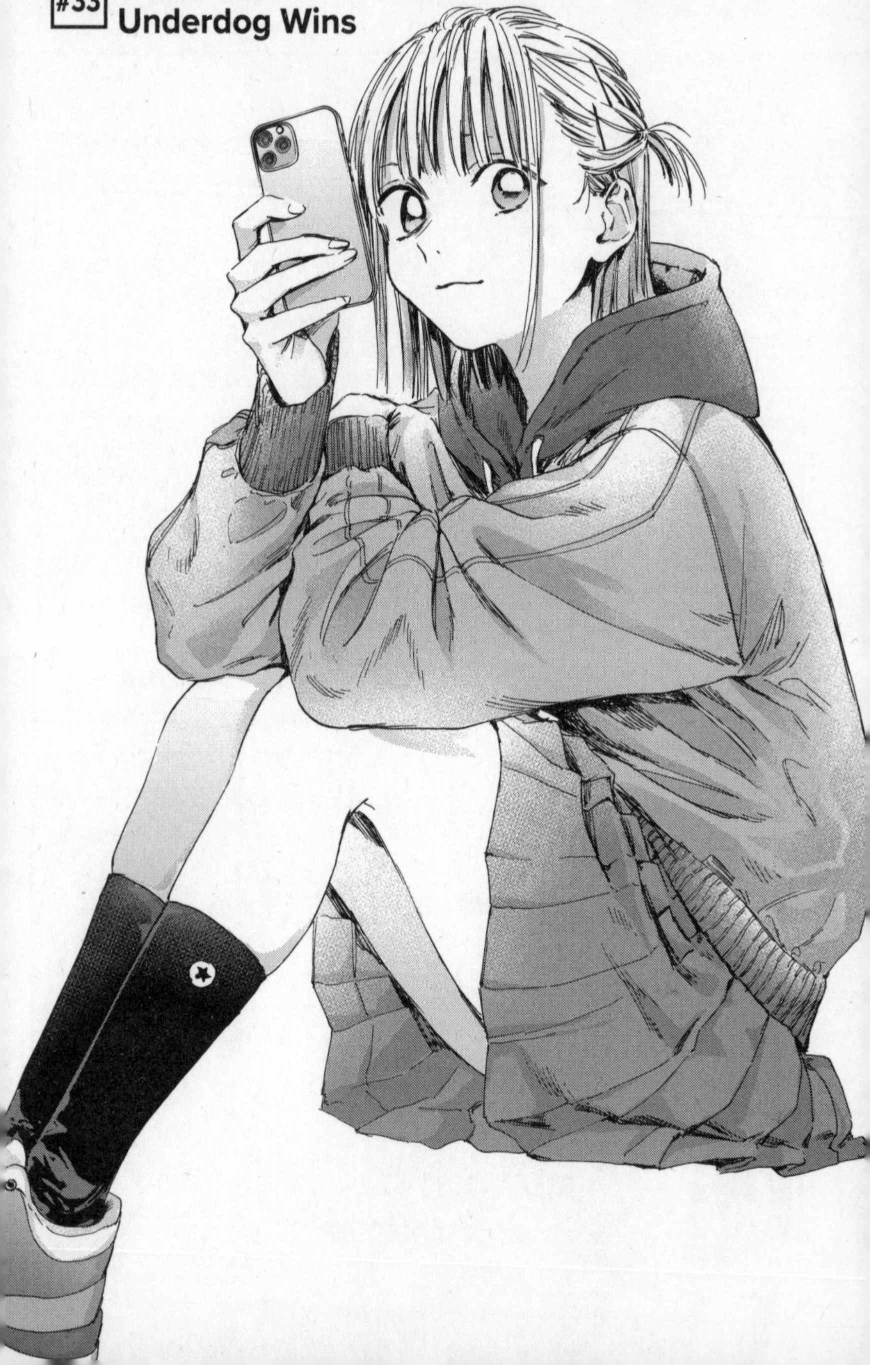

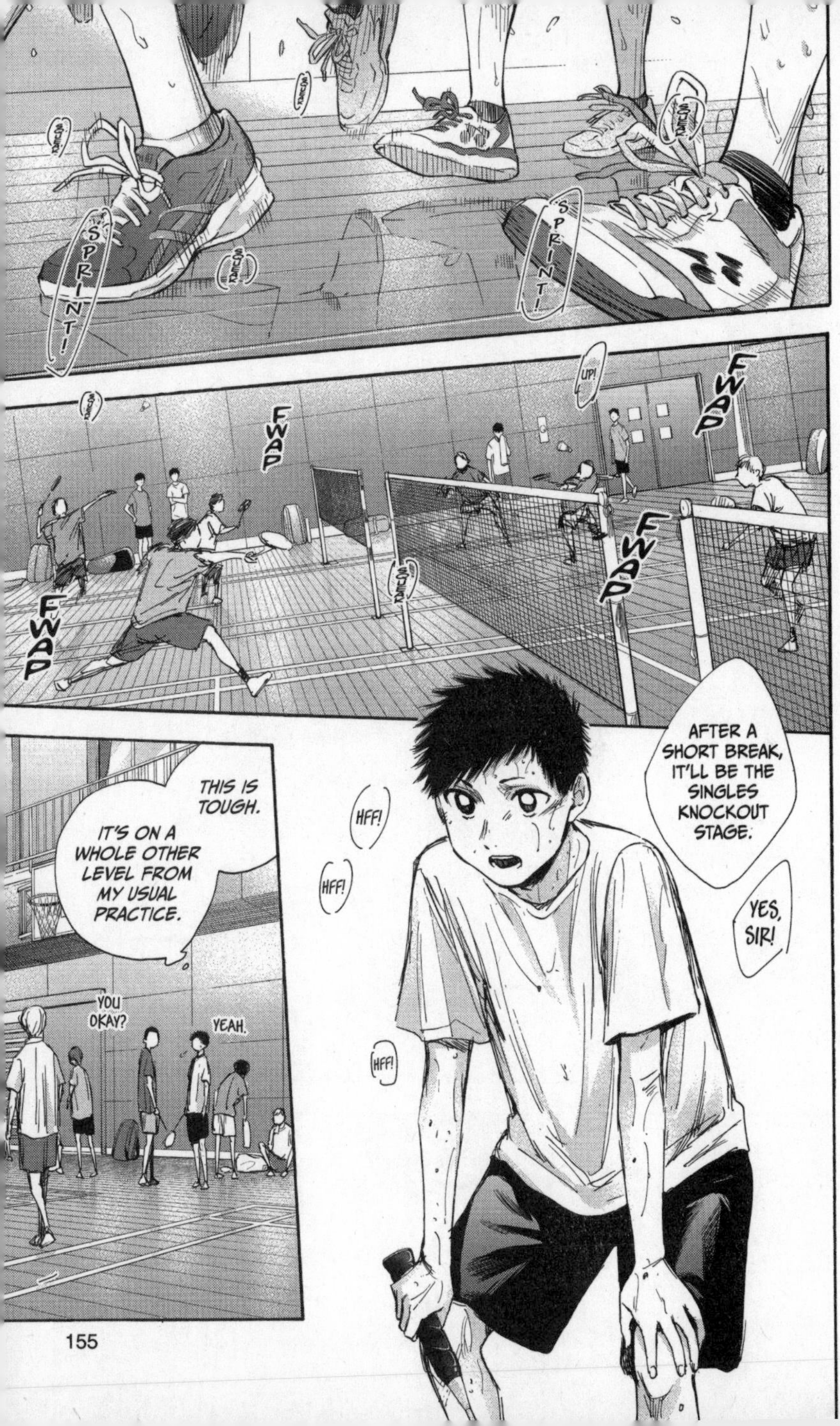
SQUEAK
SQUEAK
SQUEAK
SPRINT!
SQUEAK
SPRINT!
UP!
FWAP
FWAP
SQUEAK
FWAP
SQUEAK
FWAP
AFTER A SHORT BREAK, IT'LL BE THE SINGLES KNOCKOUT STAGE.
YES, SIR!
HFF!
HFF!
HFF!
THIS IS TOUGH.
IT'S ON A WHOLE OTHER LEVEL FROM MY USUAL PRACTICE.
YOU OKAY?
YEAH.

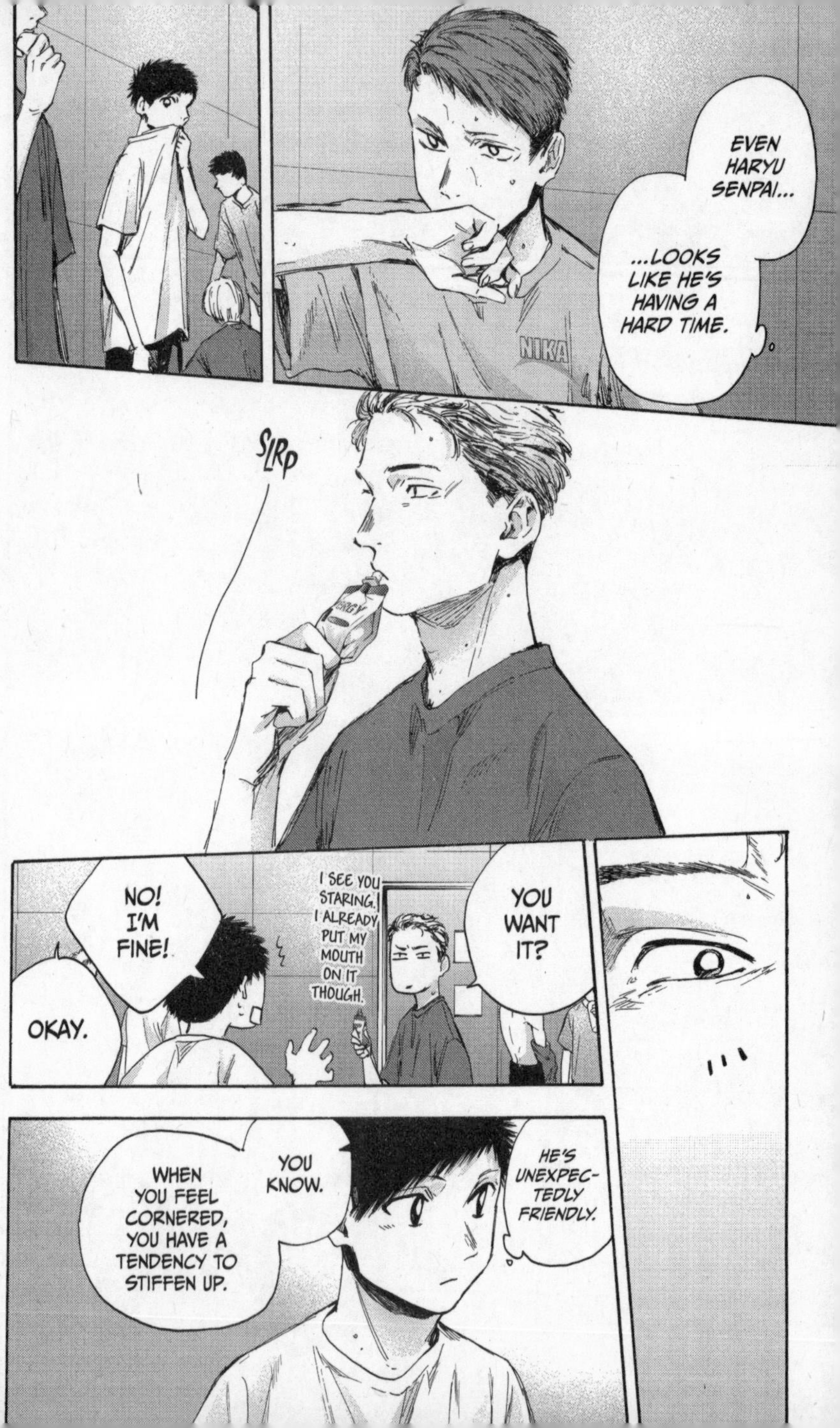
EVEN HARYU SENPAI...
...LOOKS LIKE HE'S HAVING A HARD TIME.
NIKA
SLRP
...
YOU WANT IT?
I SEE YOU STARING. I ALREADY PUT MY MOUTH ON IT THOUGH.
NO! I'M FINE!
OKAY.
HE'S UNEXPECTEDLY FRIENDLY.
YOU KNOW.
WHEN YOU FEEL CORNERED, YOU HAVE A TENDENCY TO STIFFEN UP.

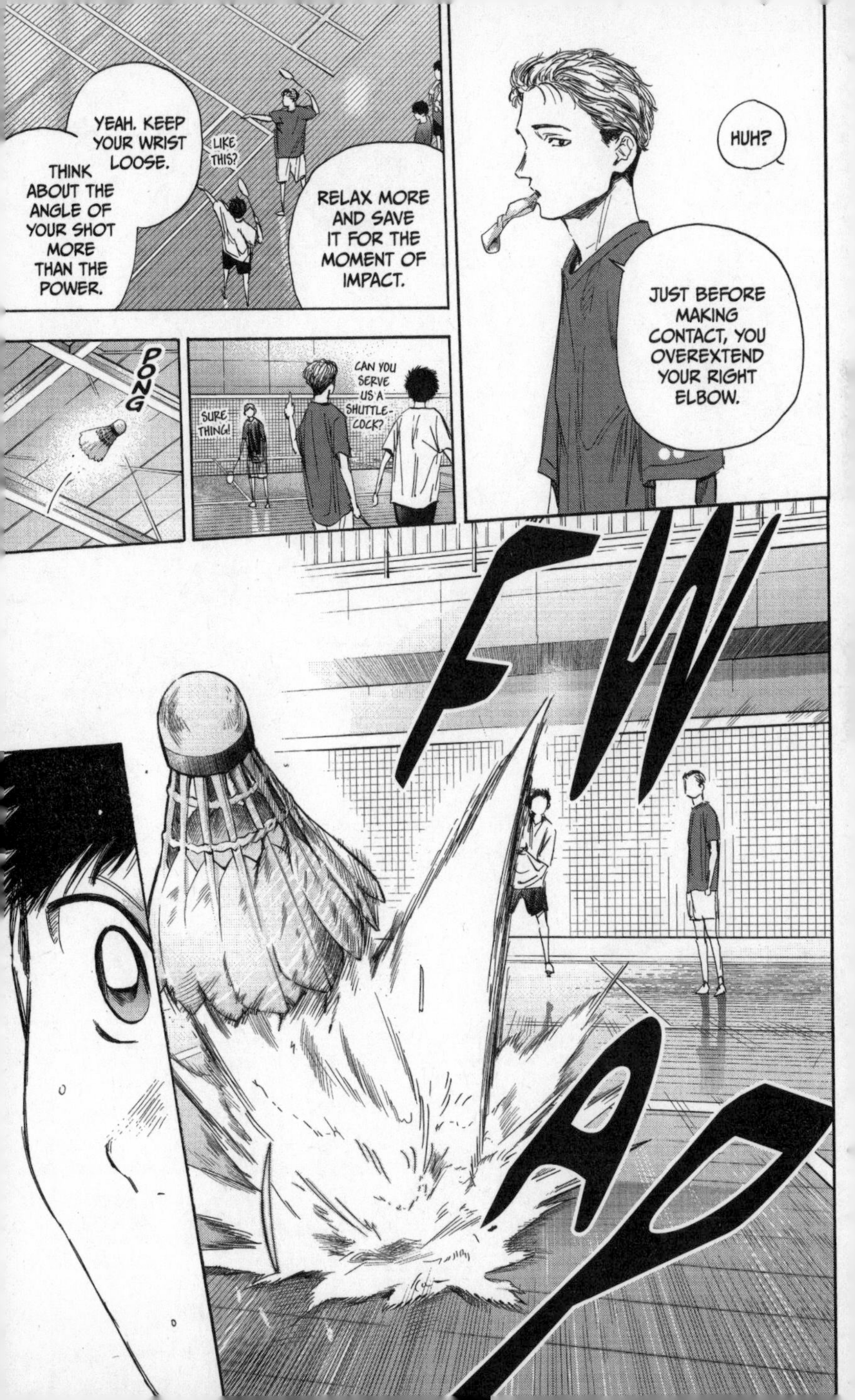
HUH?
JUST BEFORE MAKING CONTACT, YOU OVEREXTEND YOUR RIGHT ELBOW.
RELAX MORE AND SAVE IT FOR THE MOMENT OF IMPACT.
LIKE THIS?
YEAH. KEEP YOUR WRIST LOOSE.
THINK ABOUT THE ANGLE OF YOUR SHOT MORE THAN THE POWER.
CAN YOU SERVE US A SHUTTLECOCK?
SURE THING!
PONG
FWAP

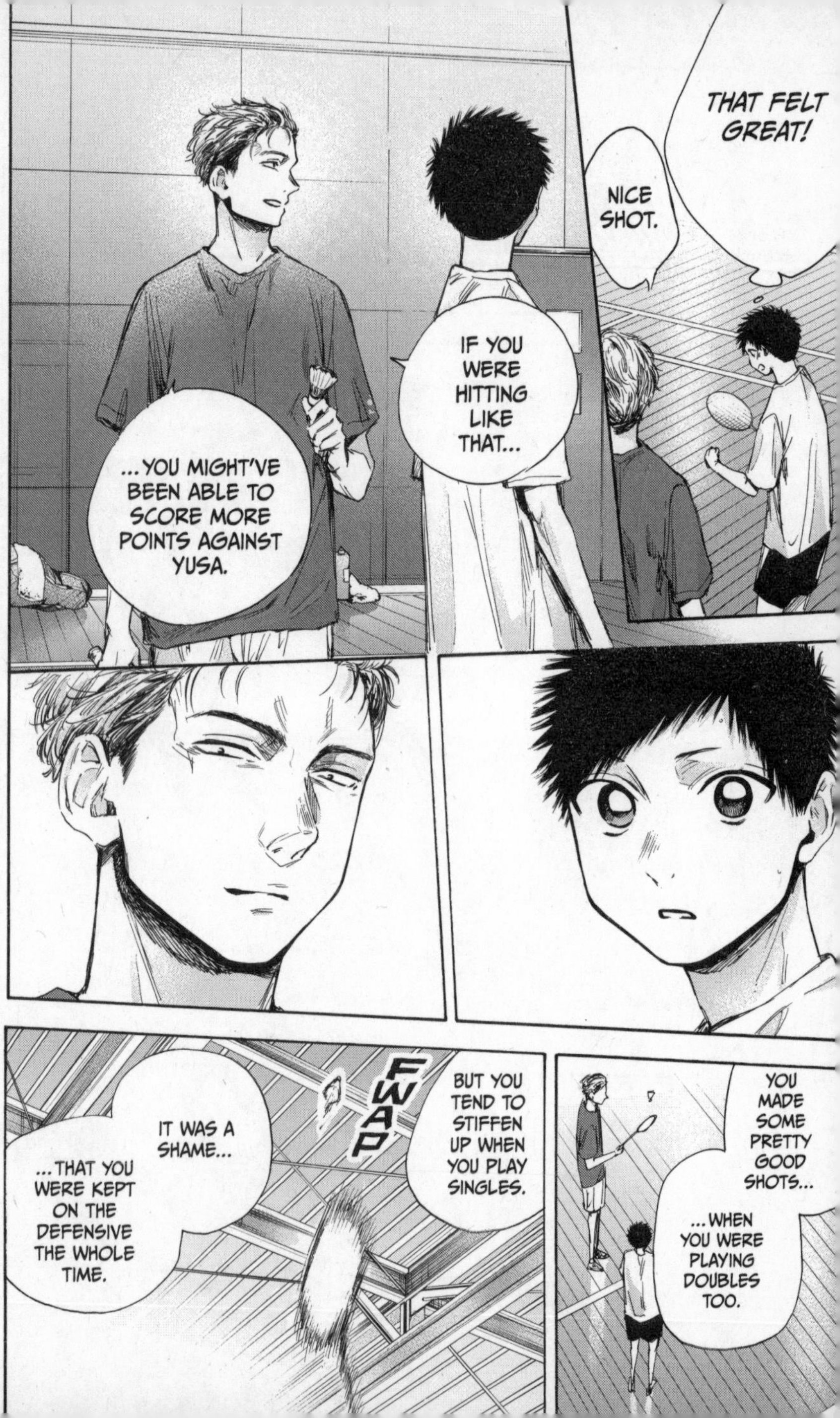
THAT FELT GREAT!
NICE SHOT.
IF YOU WERE HITTING LIKE THAT...
...YOU MIGHT'VE BEEN ABLE TO SCORE MORE POINTS AGAINST YUSA.
YOU MADE SOME PRETTY GOOD SHOTS...
...WHEN YOU WERE PLAYING DOUBLES TOO.
BUT YOU TEND TO STIFFEN UP WHEN YOU PLAY SINGLES.
FWAP
IT WAS A SHAME...
...THAT YOU WERE KEPT ON THE DEFENSIVE THE WHOLE TIME.

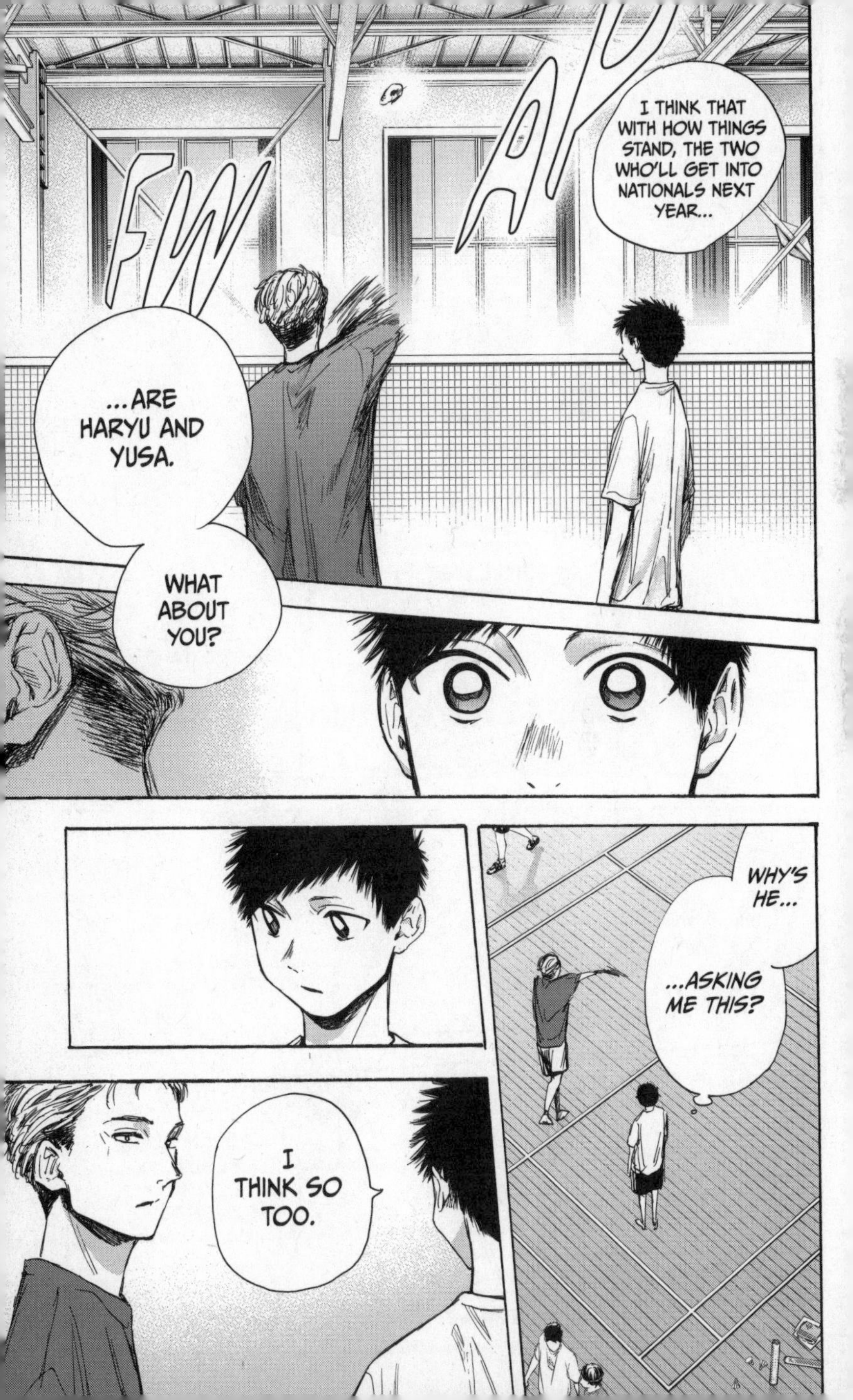
I THINK THAT WITH HOW THINGS STAND, THE TWO WHO'LL GET INTO NATIONALS NEXT YEAR...
FWAP
...ARE HARYU AND YUSA.
WHAT ABOUT YOU?
WHY'S HE...
...ASKING ME THIS?
I THINK SO TOO.

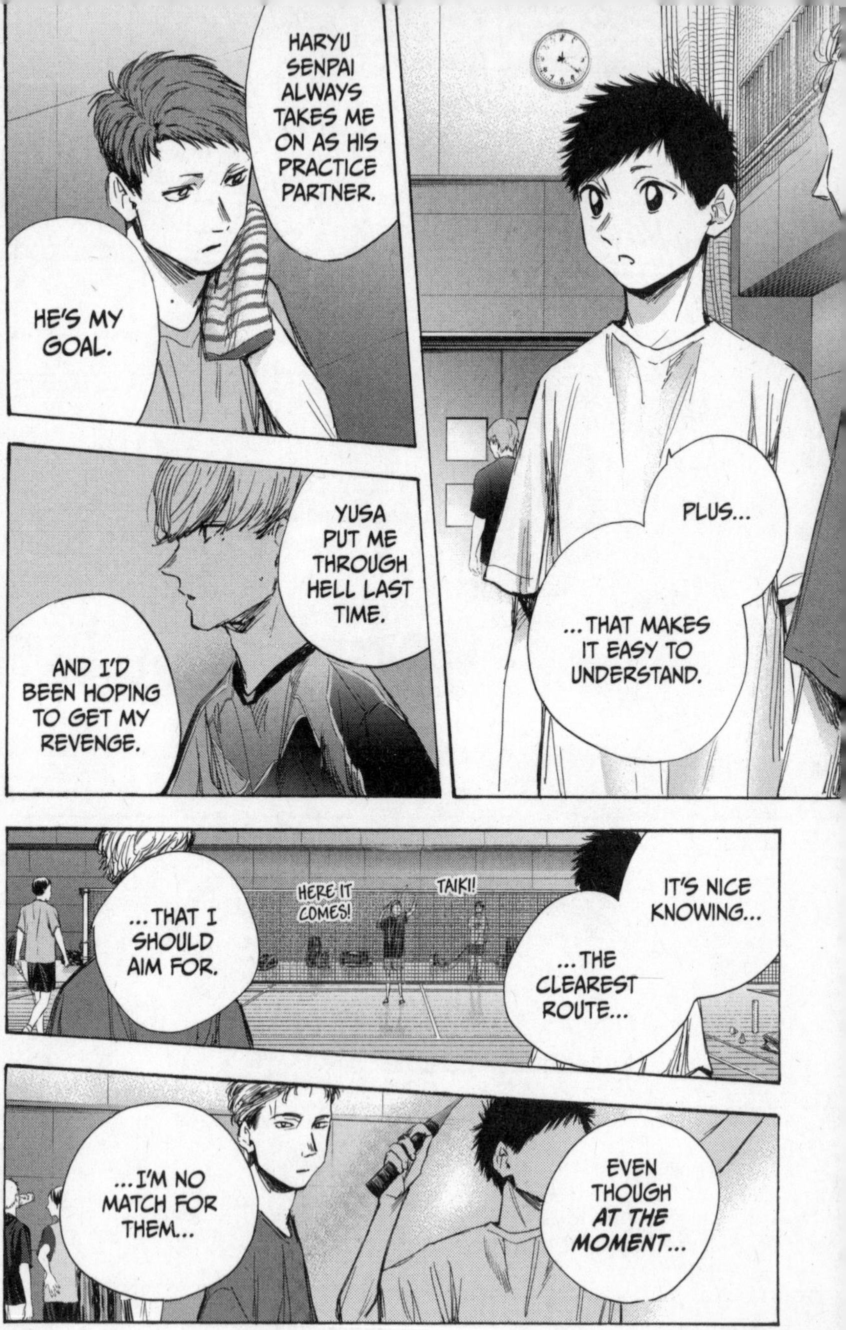
HARYU SENPAI ALWAYS TAKES ME ON AS HIS PRACTICE PARTNER.
HE'S MY GOAL.
YUSA PUT ME THROUGH HELL LAST TIME.
AND I'D BEEN HOPING TO GET MY REVENGE.
PLUS...
...THAT MAKES IT EASY TO UNDERSTAND.
IT'S NICE KNOWING...
...THE CLEAREST ROUTE...
TAIKI!
HERE IT COMES!
...THAT I SHOULD AIM FOR.
EVEN THOUGH AT THE MOMENT...
...I'M NO MATCH FOR THEM...

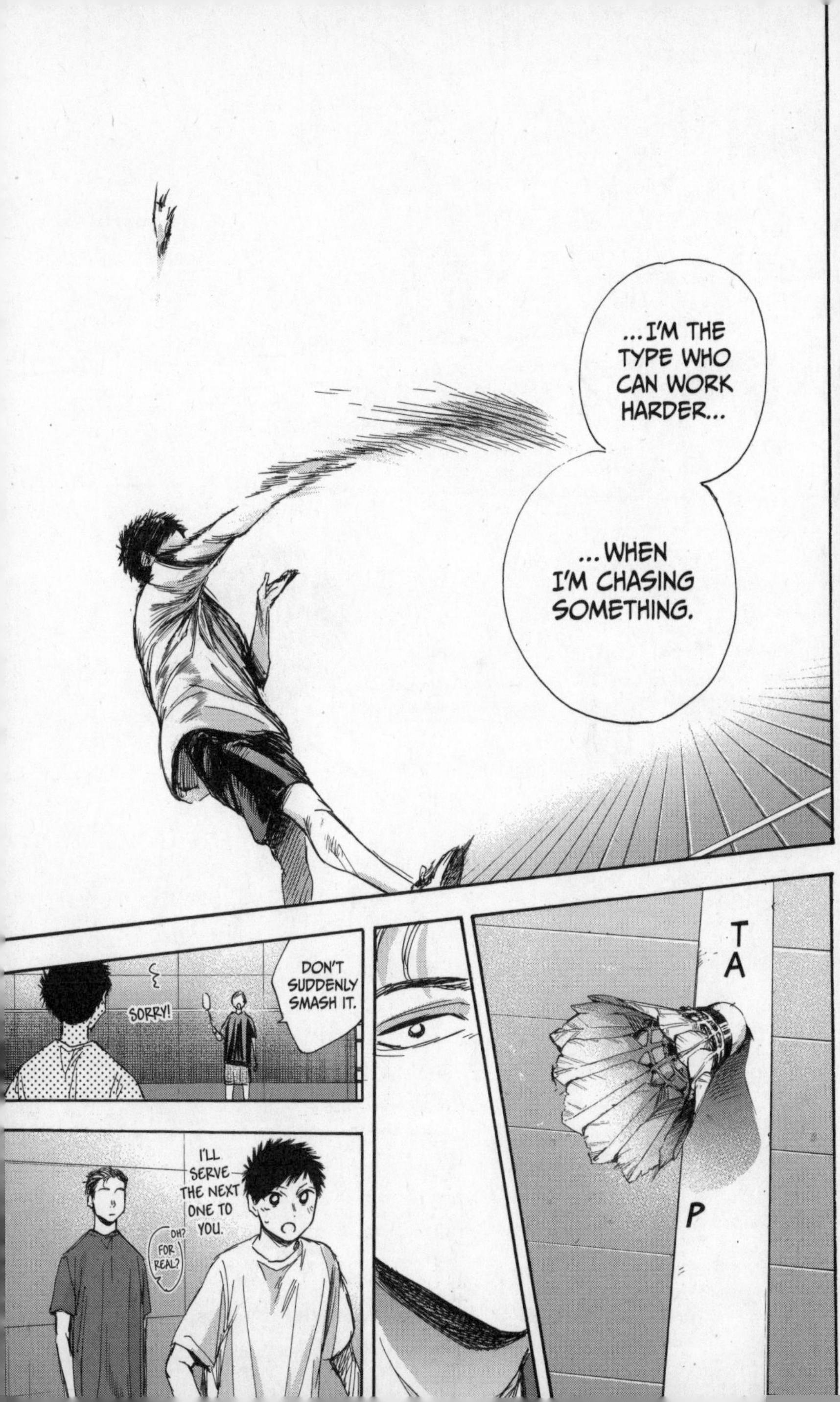
...I'M THE TYPE WHO CAN WORK HARDER...
...WHEN I'M CHASING SOMETHING.
TA
P
DON'T SUDDENLY SMASH IT.
SORRY!
I'LL SERVE THE NEXT ONE TO YOU.
OH? FOR REAL?

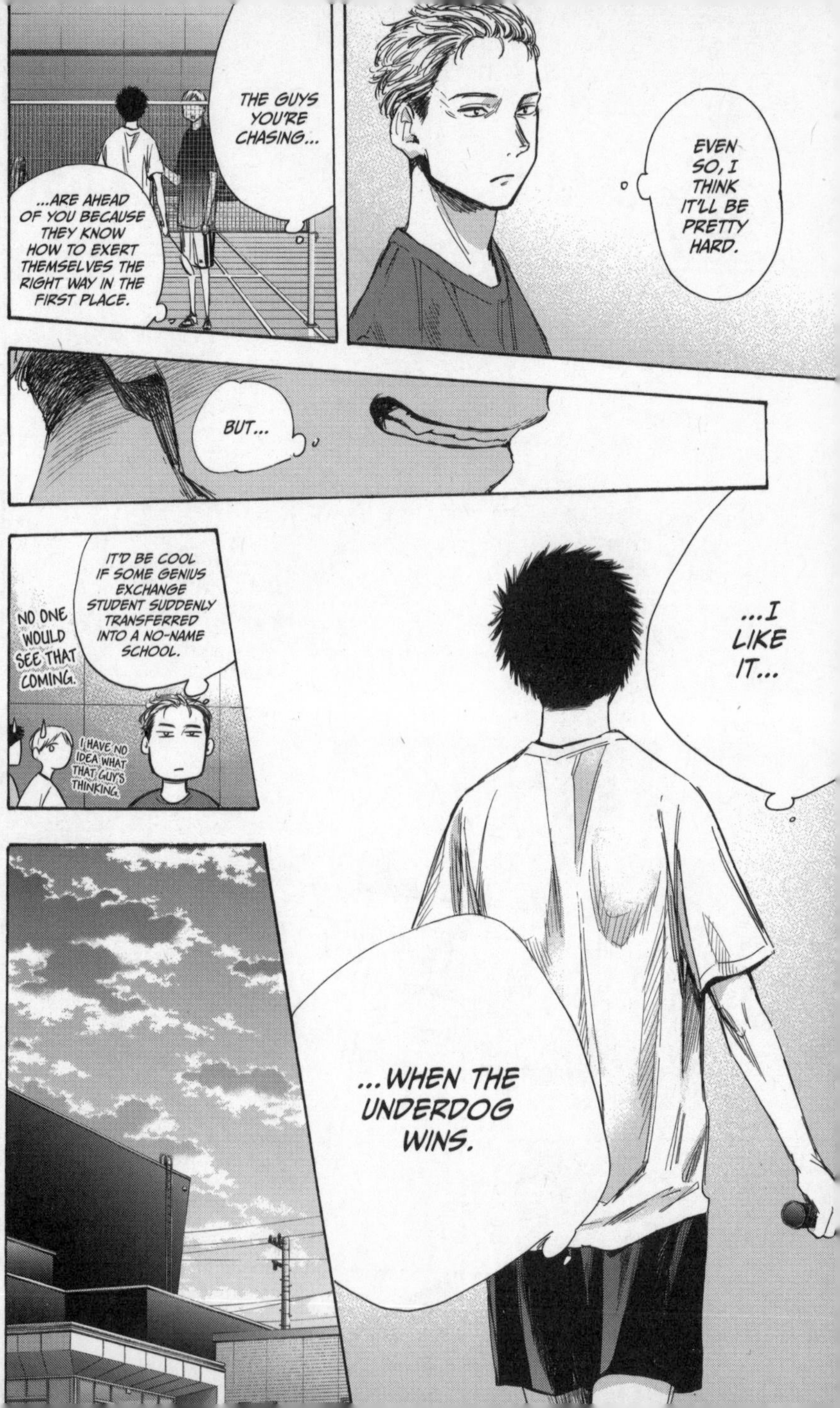
EVEN SO, I THINK IT'LL BE PRETTY HARD.
THE GUYS YOU'RE CHASING...
...ARE AHEAD OF YOU BECAUSE THEY KNOW HOW TO EXERT THEMSELVES THE RIGHT WAY IN THE FIRST PLACE.
BUT...
...I LIKE IT...
...WHEN THE UNDERDOG WINS.
IT'D BE COOL IF SOME GENIUS EXCHANGE STUDENT SUDDENLY TRANSFERRED INTO A NO-NAME SCHOOL.
NO ONE WOULD SEE THAT COMING.
I HAVE NO IDEA WHAT THAT GUY'S THINKING.

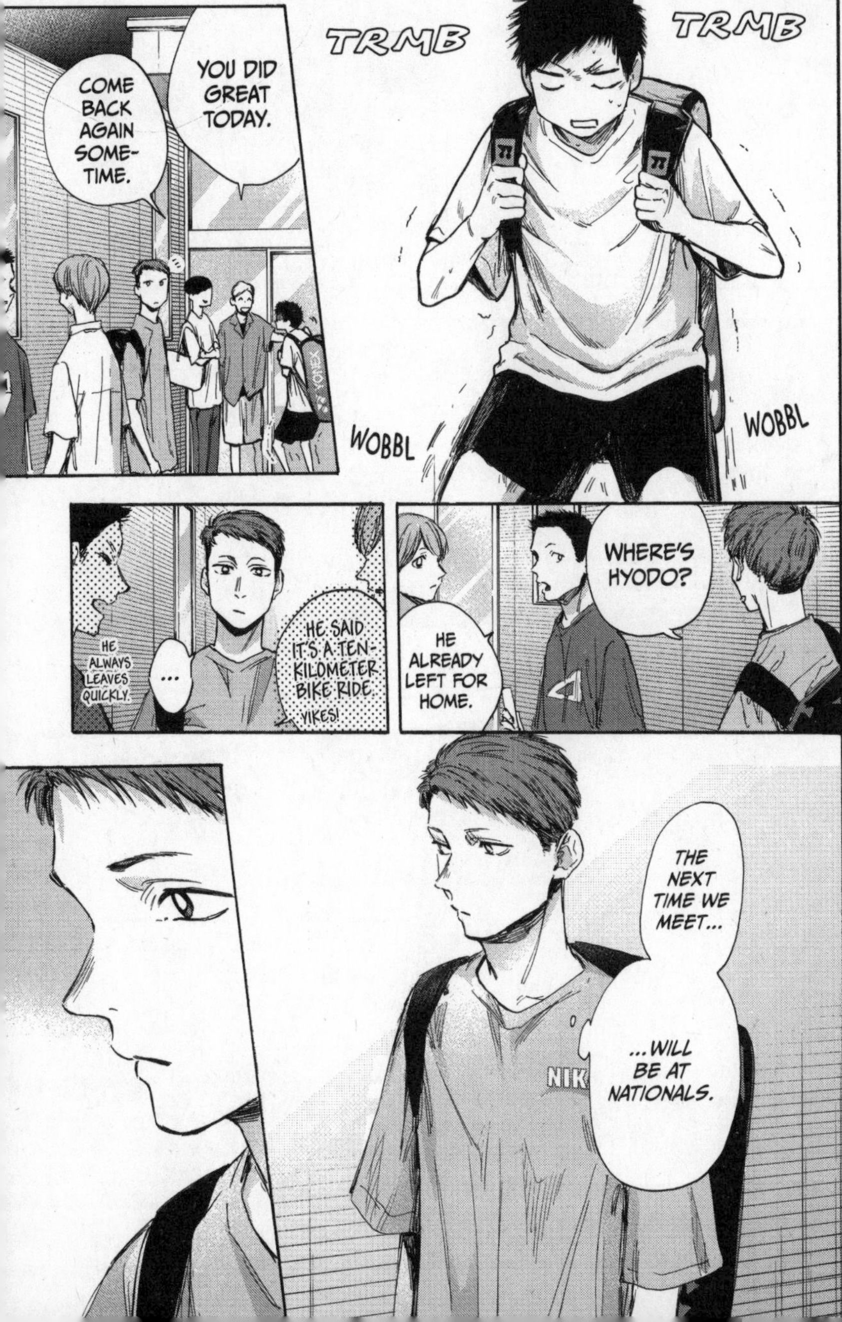
TRMB
TRMB
WOBBL
WOBBL
YOU DID GREAT TODAY.
COME BACK AGAIN SOME-TIME.
WHERE'S HYODO?
HE ALREADY LEFT FOR HOME.
HE SAID IT'S A TEN-KILOMETER BIKE RIDE.
YIKES!
...
HE ALWAYS LEAVES QUICKLY.
THE NEXT TIME WE MEET...
...WILL BE AT NATIONALS.

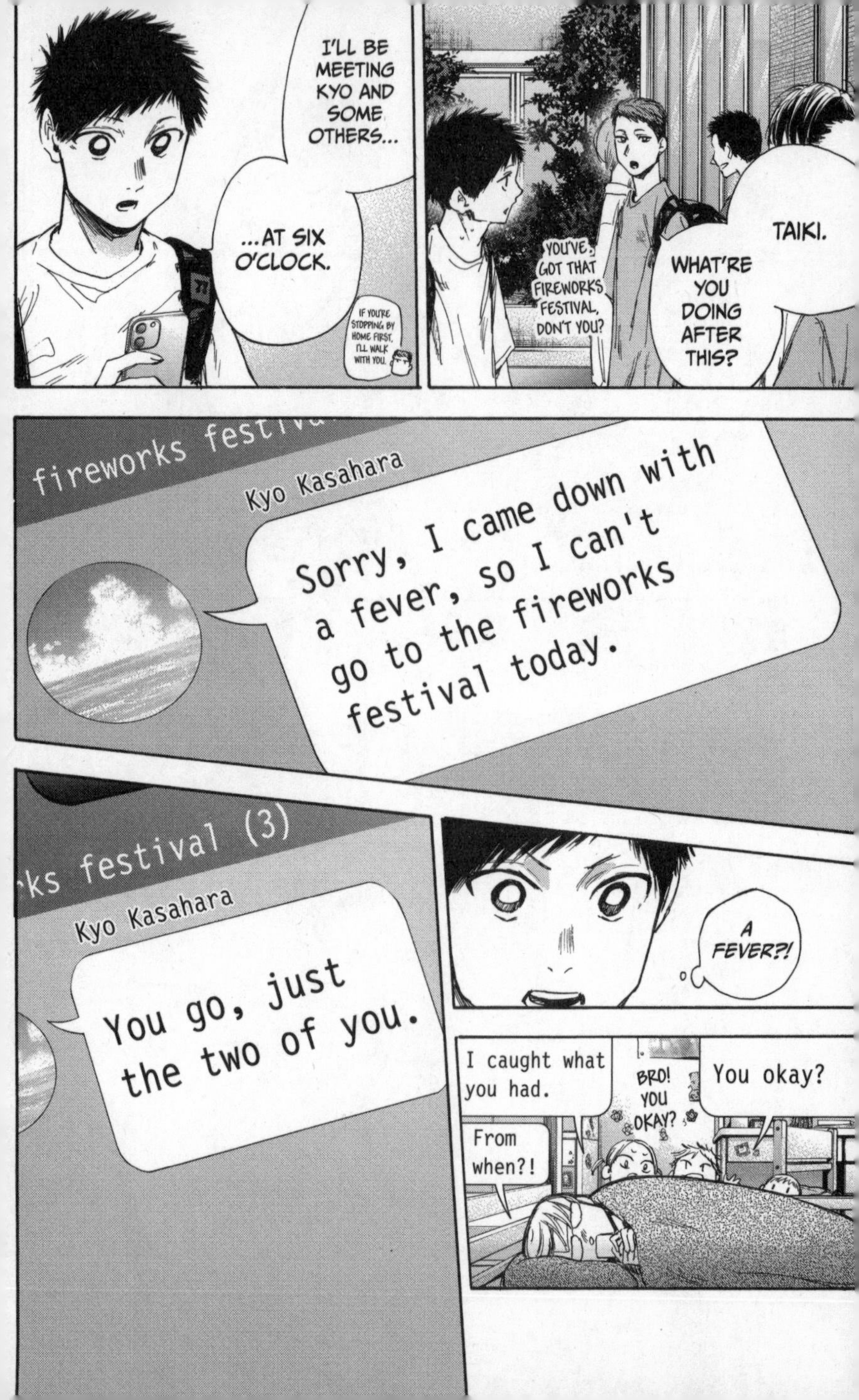
TAIKI.
WHAT'RE YOU DOING AFTER THIS?
YOU'VE GOT THAT FIREWORKS FESTIVAL, DON'T YOU?
IF YOU'RE STOPPING BY HOME FIRST, I'LL WALK WITH YOU.
I'LL BE MEETING KYO AND SOME OTHERS...
...AT SIX O'CLOCK.
fireworks festiva
Kyo Kasahara
Sorry, I came down with a fever, so I can't go to the fireworks festival today.
rks festival (3)
Kyo Kasahara
You go, just the two of you.
A FEVER?!
You okay?
BRO! YOU OKAY?
I caught what you had.
From when?!

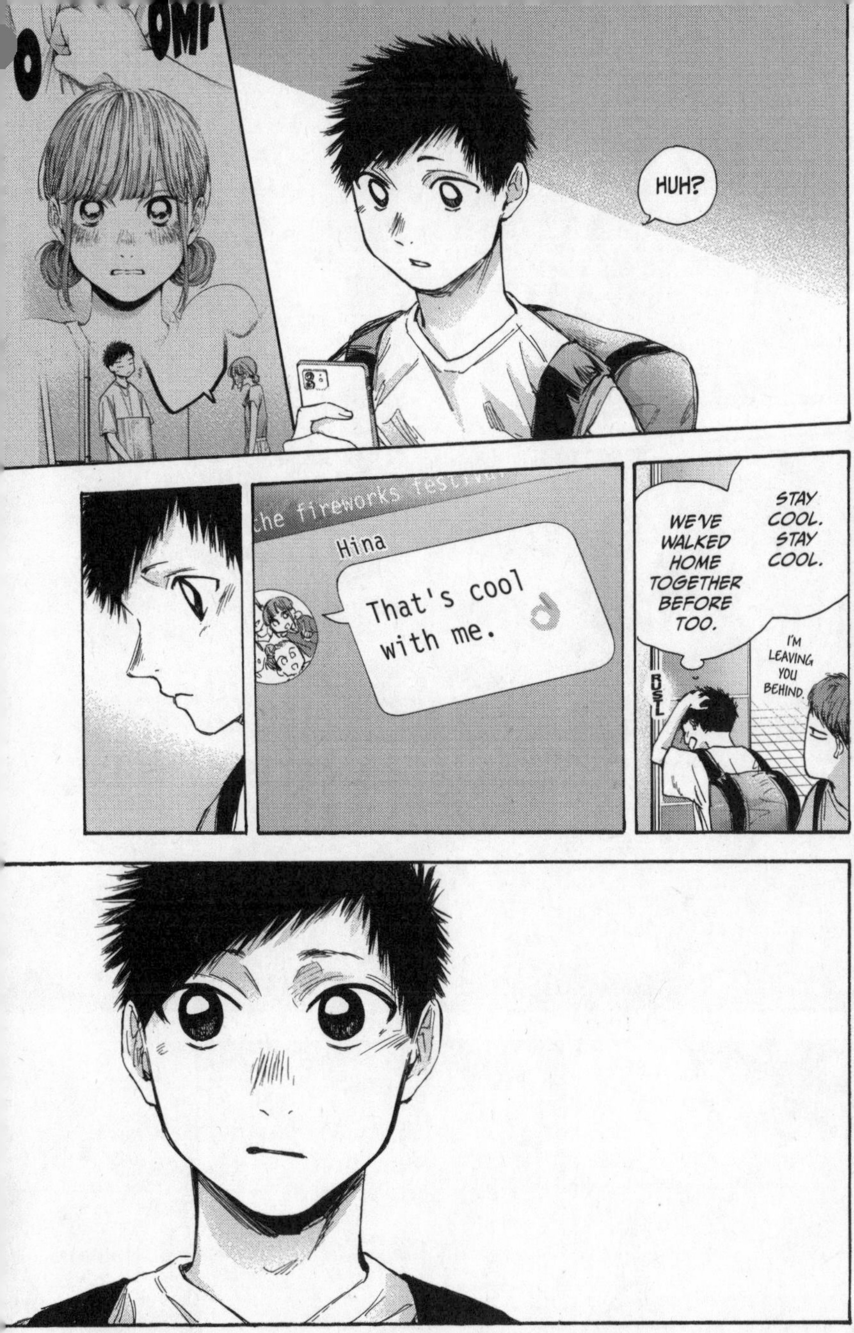
HUH?
STAY COOL. STAY COOL.
WE'VE WALKED HOME TOGETHER BEFORE TOO.
I'M LEAVING YOU BEHIND.
RUSTL
the fireworks festiv
Hina
That's cool with me.

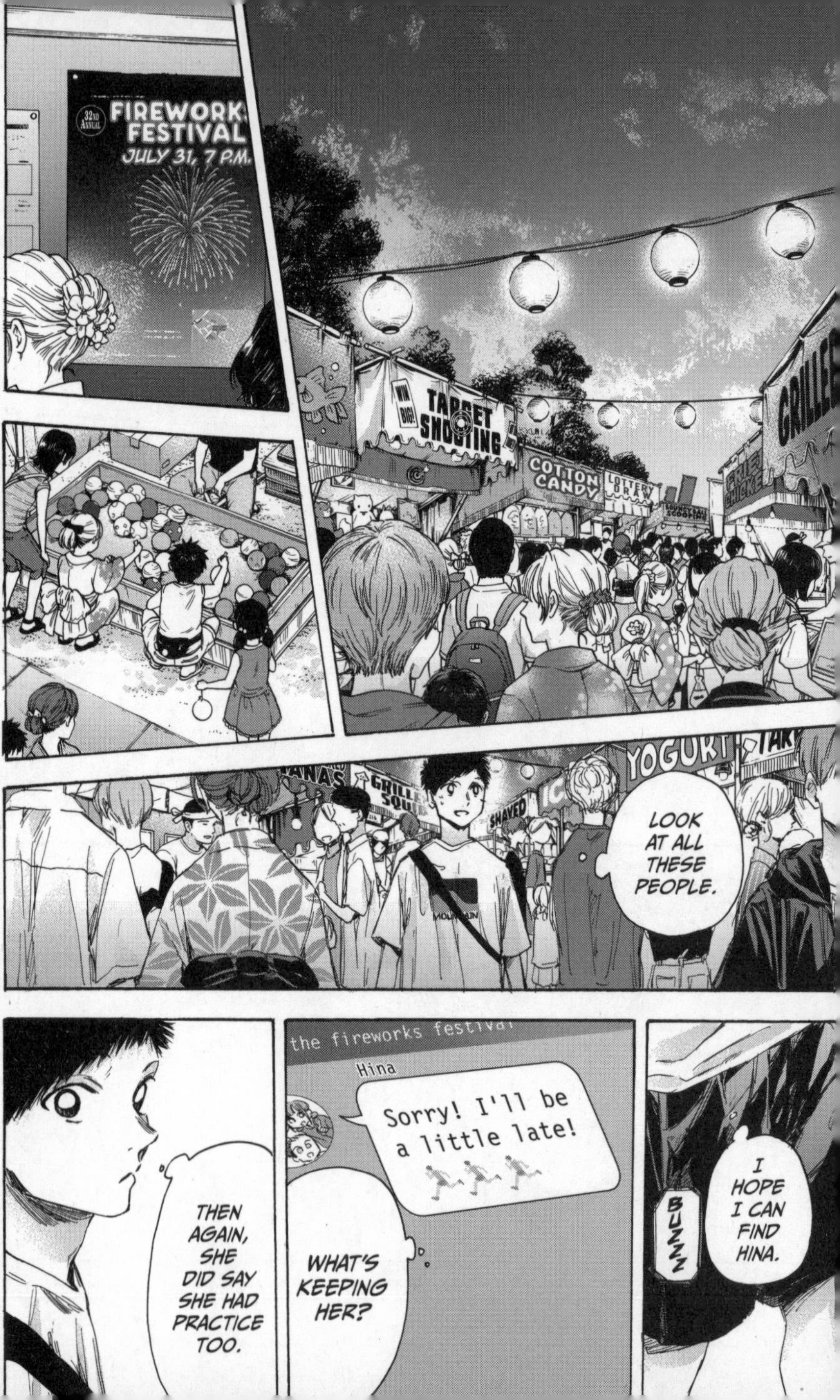
32ND ANNUAL
FIREWORKS FESTIVAL
JULY 31, 7 P.M.
WIN BIG!
TARGET SHOOTING
COTTON CANDY
LOTTERY DRAW
YOGURT
SHAVED
LOOK AT ALL THESE PEOPLE.
I HOPE I CAN FIND HINA.
BUZZ
Hina
Sorry! I'll be a little late!
WHAT'S KEEPING HER?
THEN AGAIN, SHE DID SAY SHE HAD PRACTICE TOO.

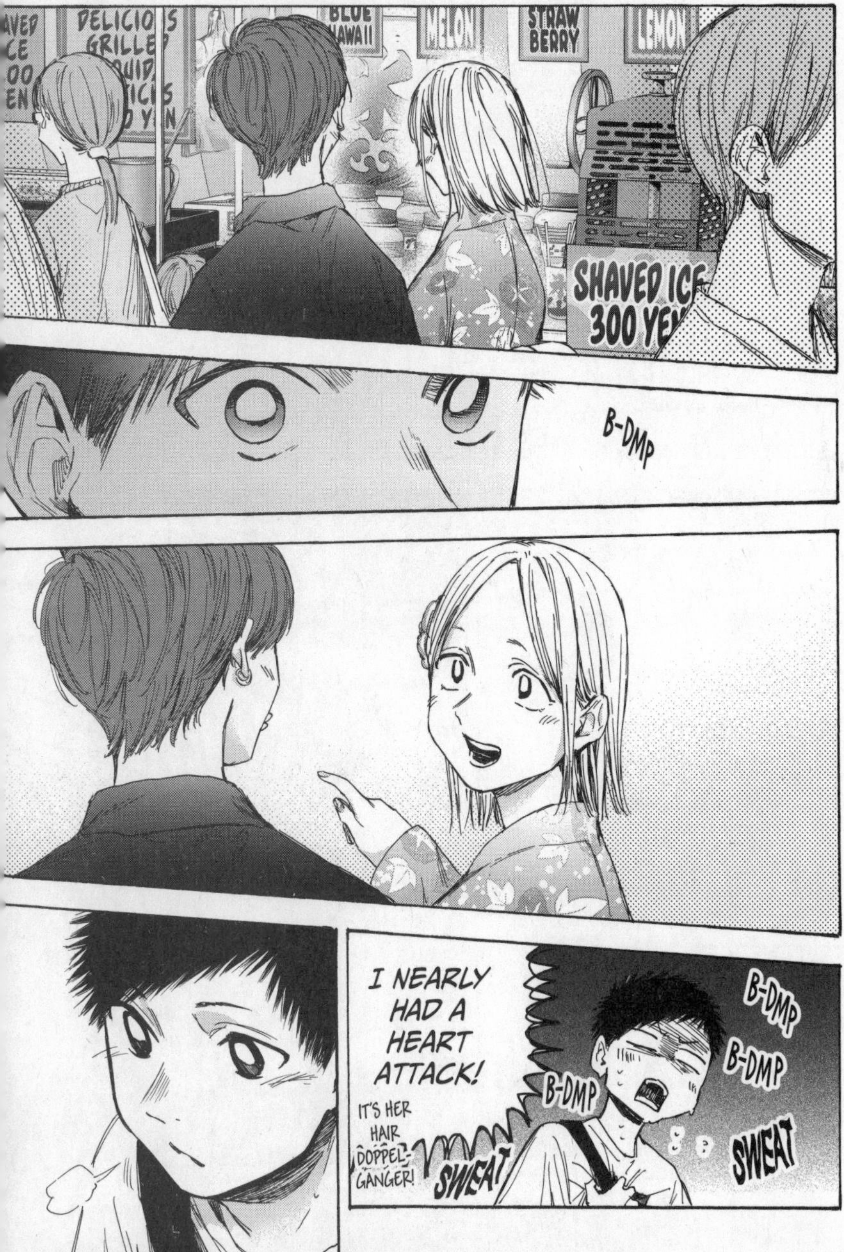
LEMON
STRAW BERRY
MELON
BLUE HAWAII
B-DMP
B-DMP
B-DMP
B-DMP
SWEAT
I NEARLY HAD A HEART ATTACK!
IT'S HER HAIR DOPPEL-GANGER!
SWEAT

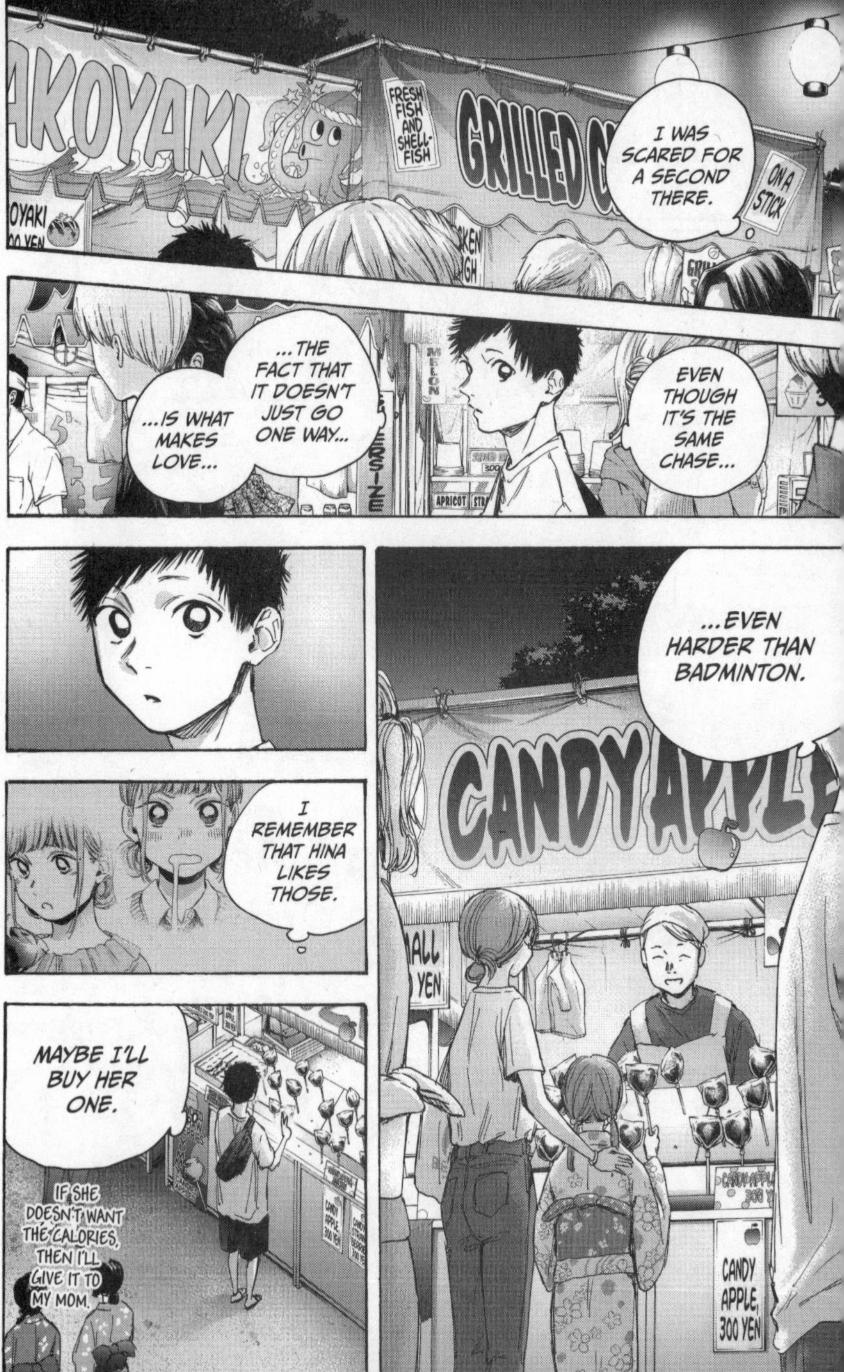
AKOYAKI
FRESH FISH AND SHELL-FISH
GRILLED C
ON A STICK
I WAS SCARED FOR A SECOND THERE.
MELON
EVEN THOUGH IT'S THE SAME CHASE...
...THE FACT THAT IT DOESN'T JUST GO ONE WAY...
...IS WHAT MAKES LOVE...
APRICOT
...EVEN HARDER THAN BADMINTON.
CANDY APPLE
CANDY APPLE, 300 YEN
I REMEMBER THAT HINA LIKES THOSE.
MAYBE I'LL BUY HER ONE.
IF SHE DOESN'T WANT THE CALORIES, THEN I'LL GIVE IT TO MY MOM.

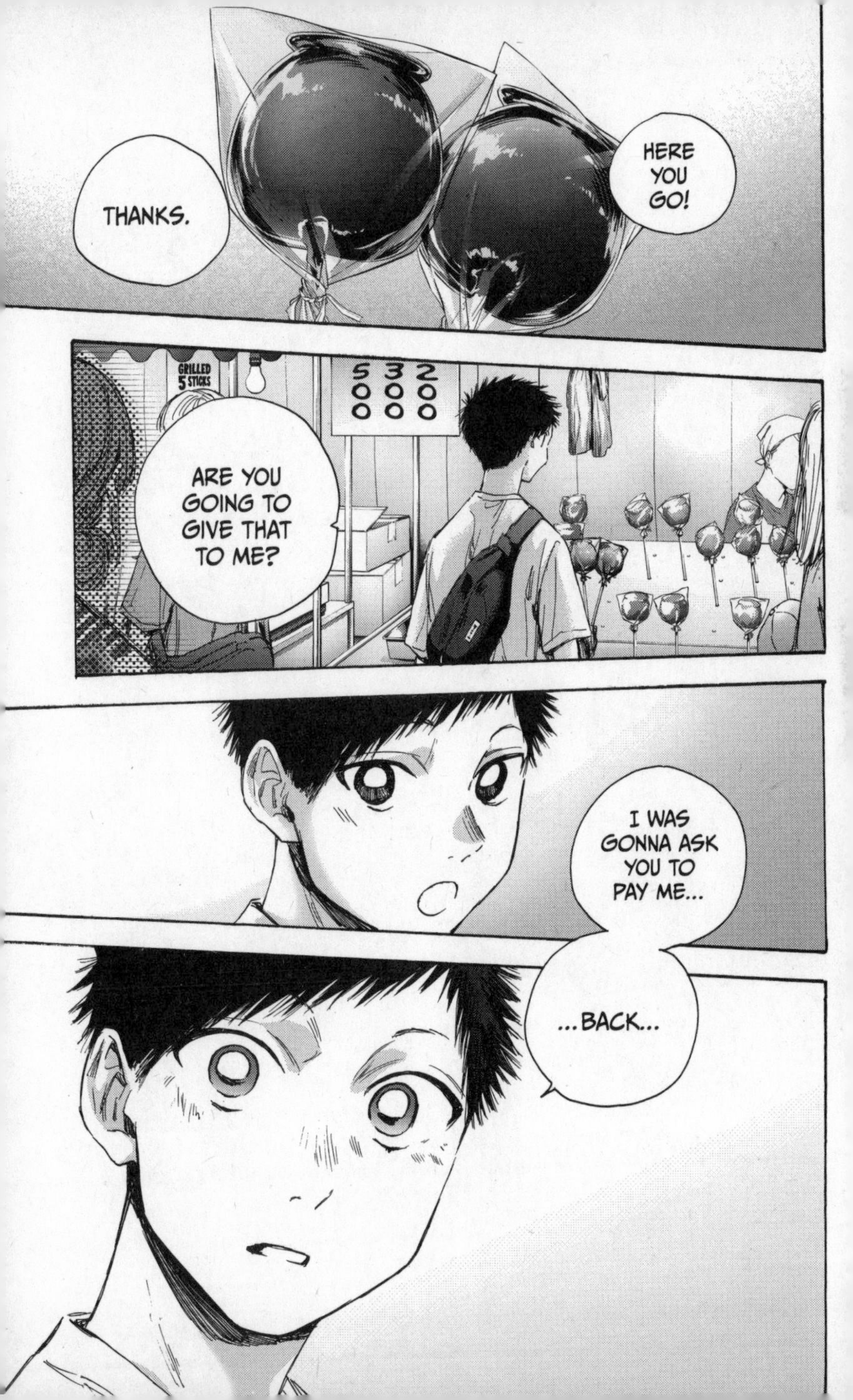
HERE YOU GO!
THANKS.
GRILLED 5 STICKS
5 3 2
0 0 0
0 0 0
ARE YOU GOING TO GIVE THAT TO ME?
I WAS GONNA ASK YOU TO PAY ME...
...BACK...

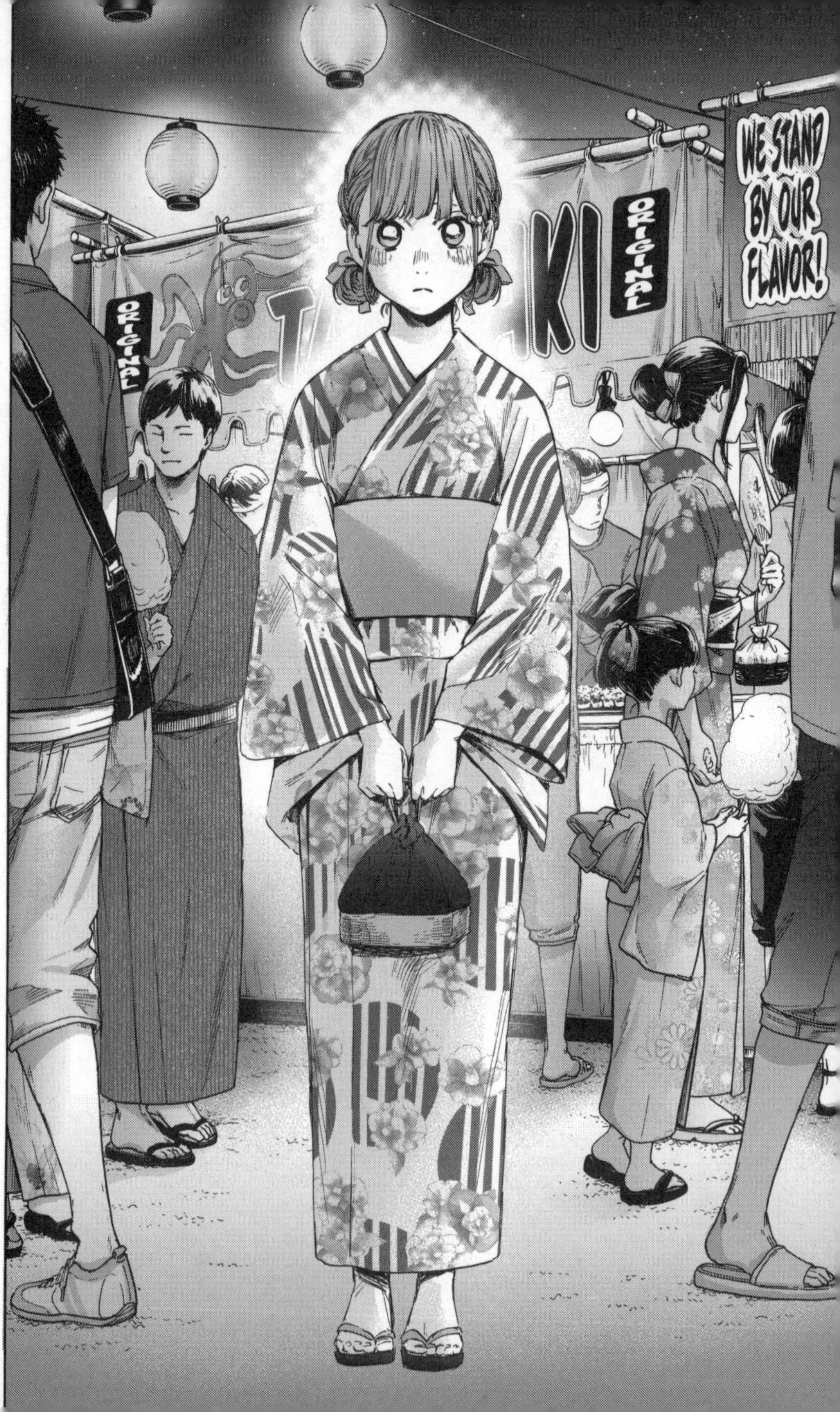
WE STAND BY OUR FLAVOR!
ORIGINAL
ORIGINAL

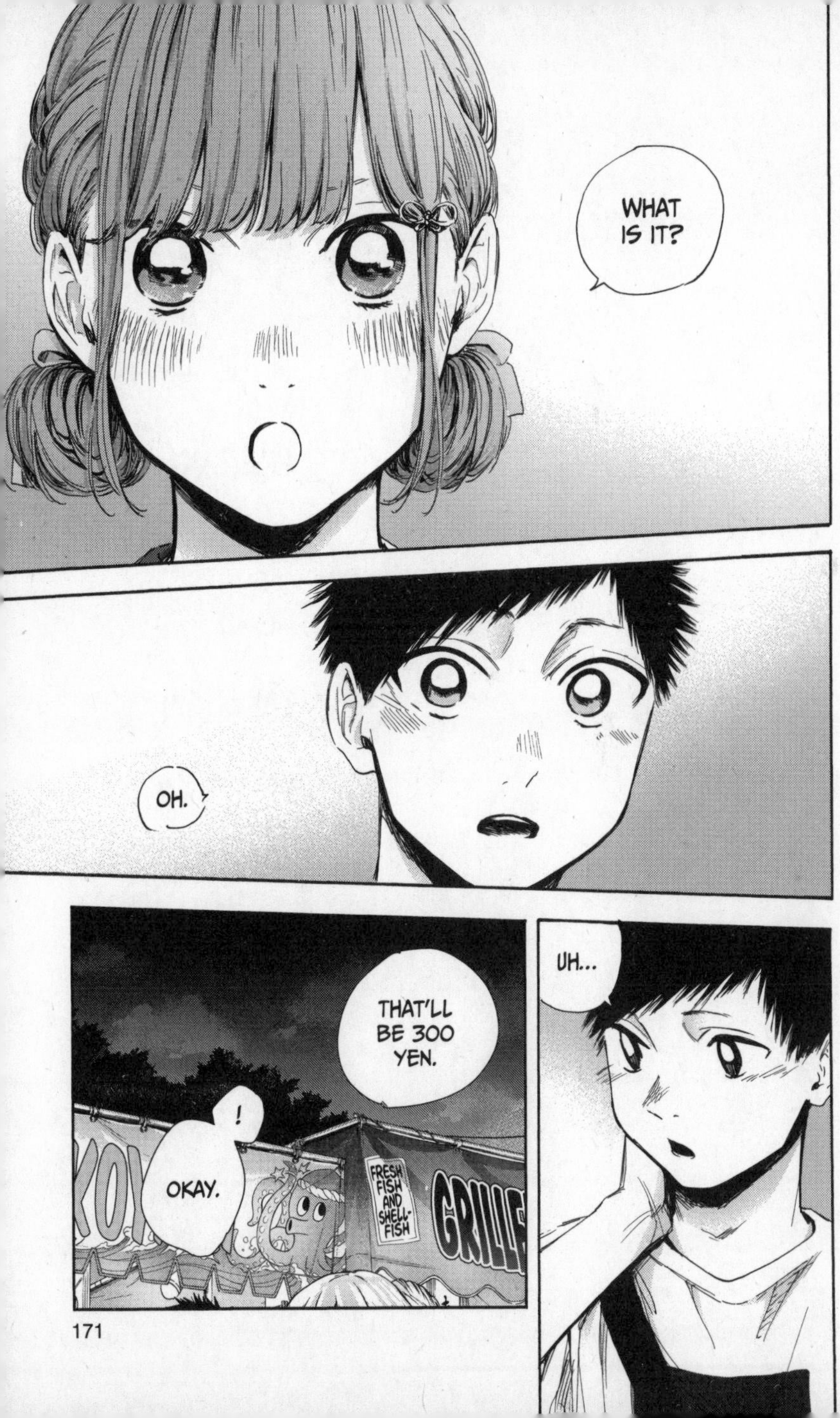
WHAT IS IT?
OH.
UH...
THAT'LL BE 300 YEN.
!
OKAY.
FRESH FISH AND SHELL-FISH

BLUE BOX ④
Special thanks

ARAGAKI

OKINO

KONO

TAKEUCHI

HINOHARA

TOBITA
(HELP)

MURAKOSHI

CHIBA

TSUJI

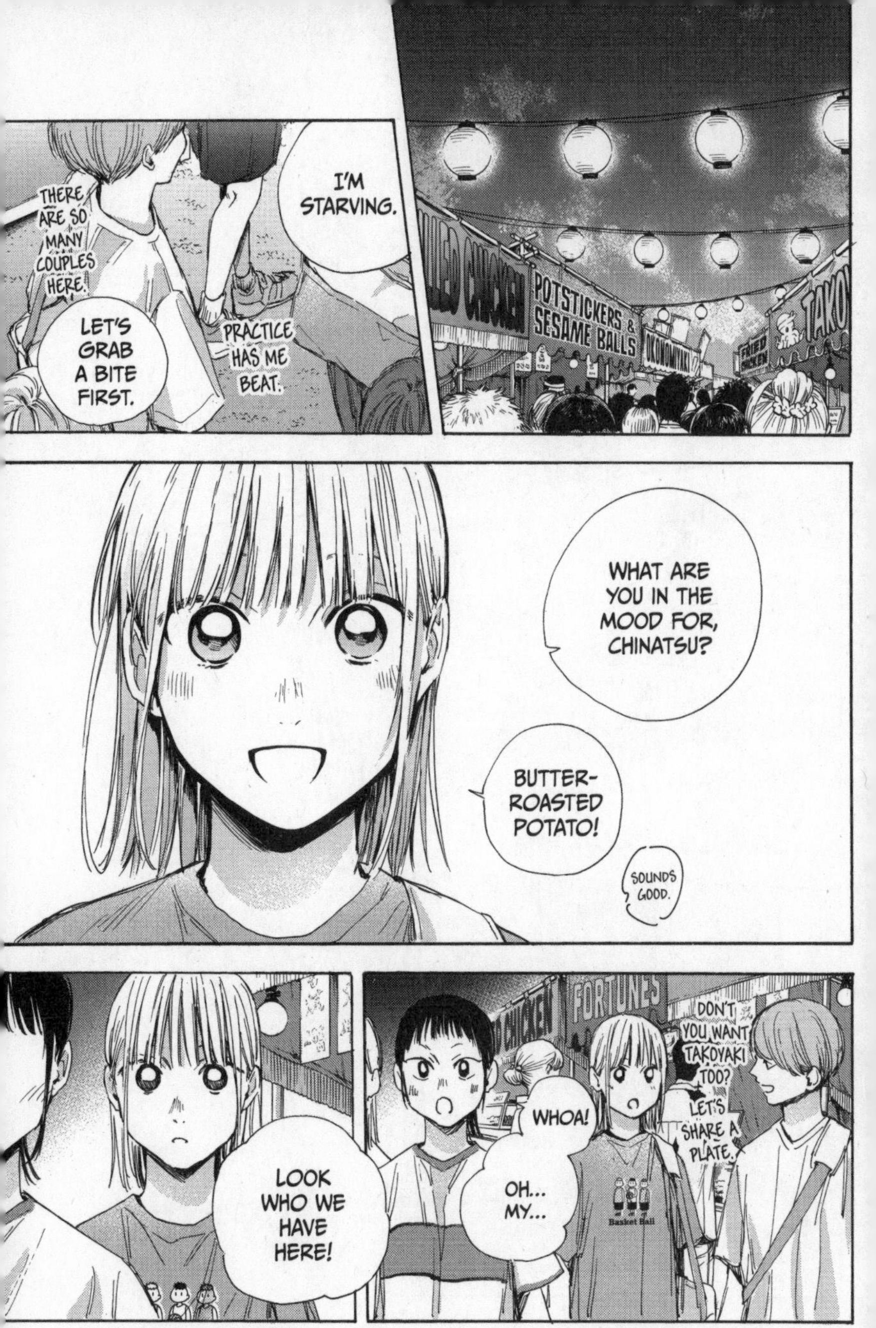
POTSTICKERS & SESAME BALLS
OKONOMIYAKI
FRIED CHICKEN
I'M STARVING.
PRACTICE HAS ME BEAT.
THERE ARE SO MANY COUPLES HERE.
LET'S GRAB A BITE FIRST.
WHAT ARE YOU IN THE MOOD FOR, CHINATSU?
BUTTER-ROASTED POTATO!
SOUNDS GOOD.
FORTUNES
DON'T YOU WANT TAKOYAKI TOO?
LET'S SHARE A PLATE.
WHOA!
OH... MY...
Basket Ball
LOOK WHO WE HAVE HERE!

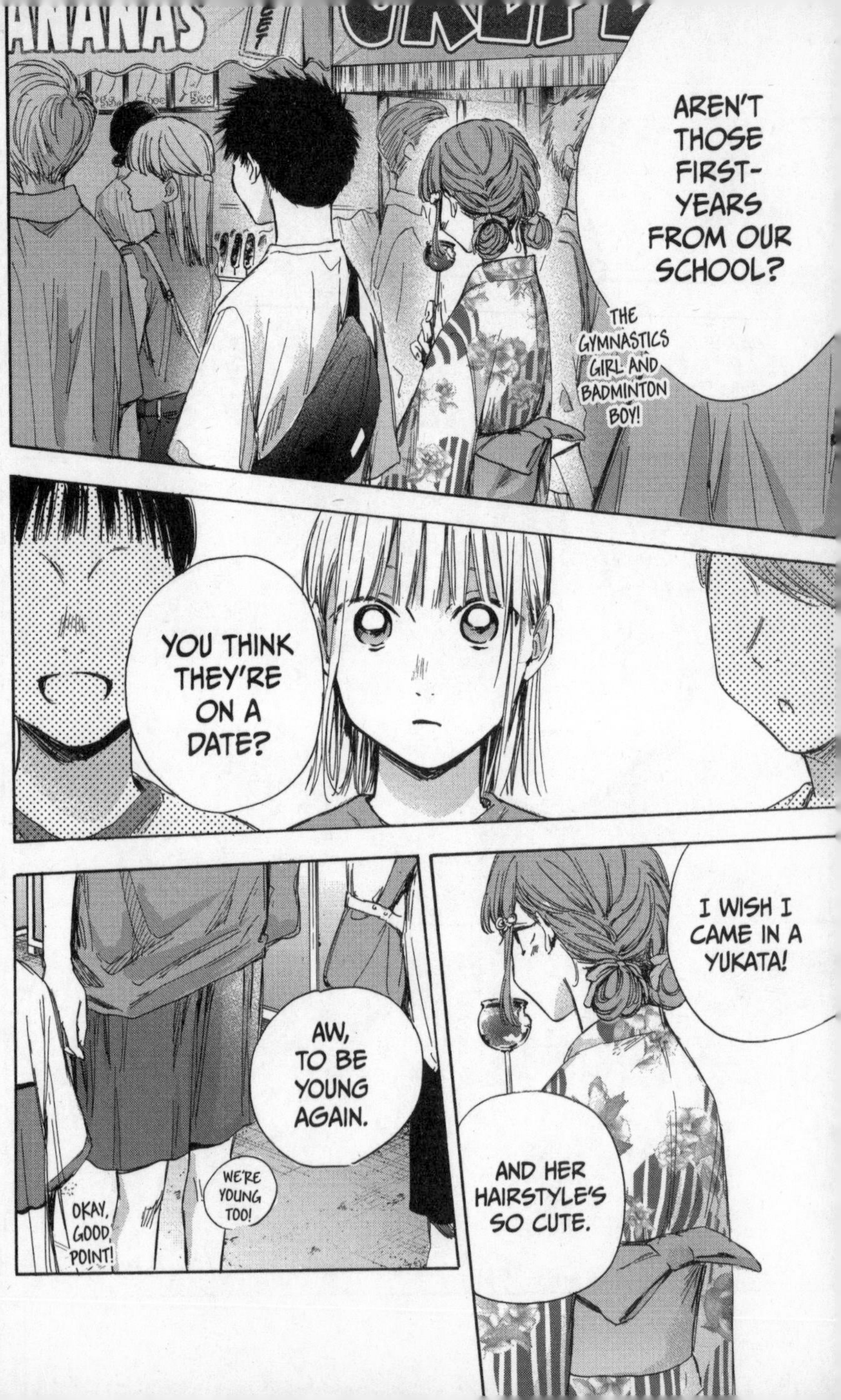
AREN'T THOSE FIRST-YEARS FROM OUR SCHOOL?
THE GYMNASTICS GIRL AND BADMINTON BOY!
YOU THINK THEY'RE ON A DATE?
I WISH I CAME IN A YUKATA!
AND HER HAIRSTYLE'S SO CUTE.
AW, TO BE YOUNG AGAIN.
WE'RE YOUNG TOO!
OKAY, GOOD POINT!

#34 Girls...

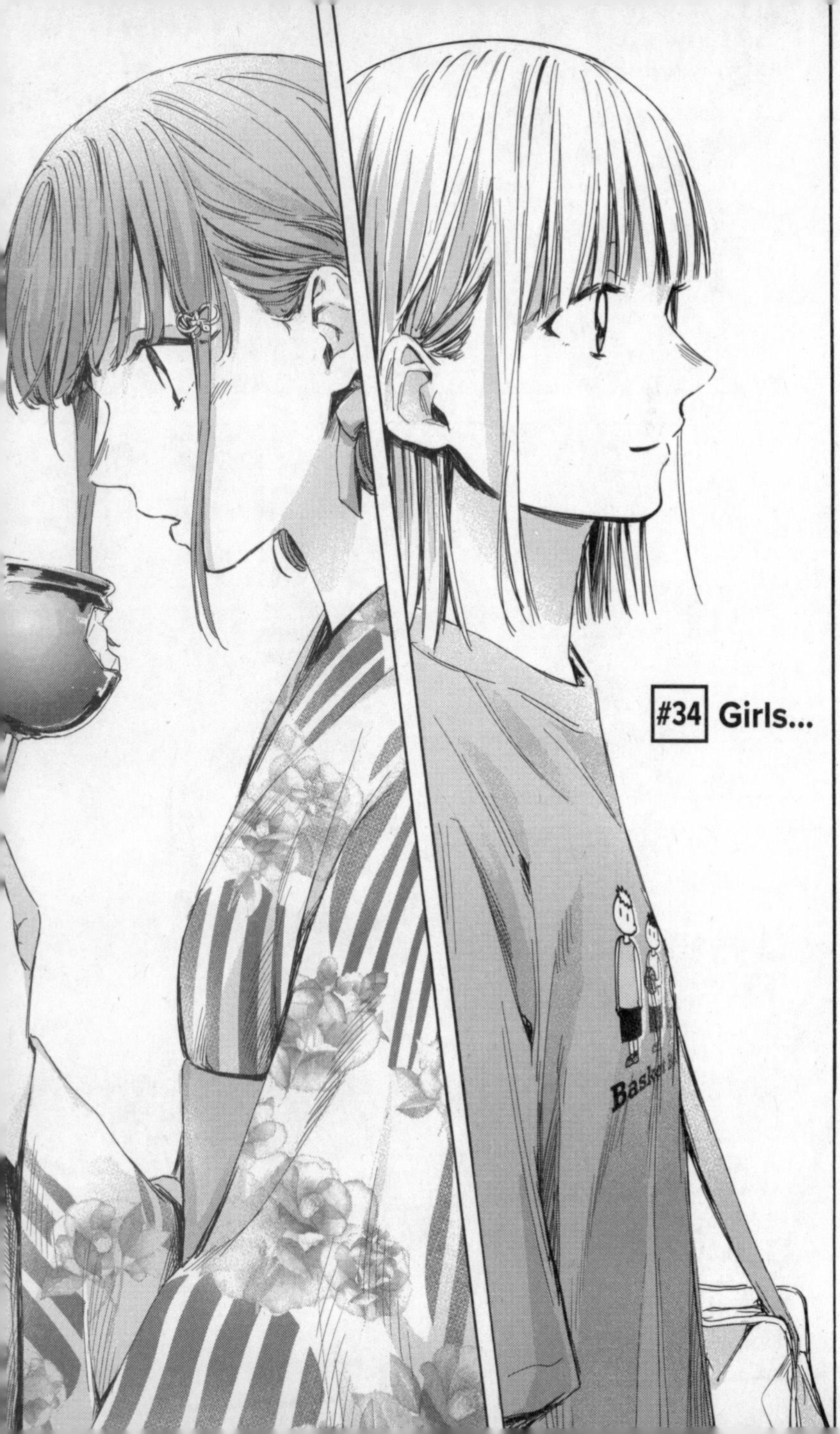

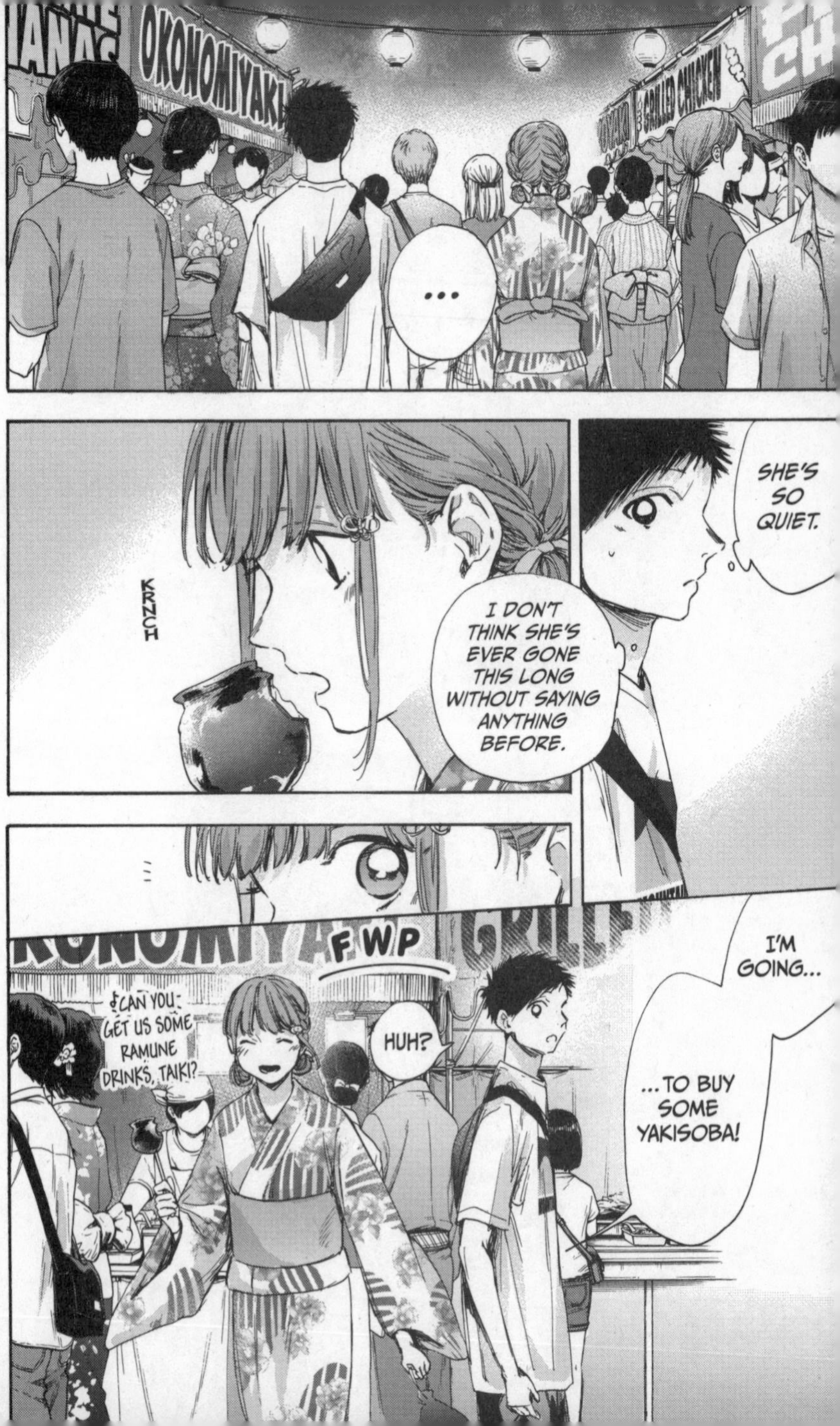

OKONOMIYAKI
GRILLED CHICKEN
...
SHE'S SO QUIET.
I DON'T THINK SHE'S EVER GONE THIS LONG WITHOUT SAYING ANYTHING BEFORE.
KRNCH
I'M GOING...
...TO BUY SOME YAKISOBA!
FWP
HUH?
CAN YOU GET US SOME RAMUNE DRINKS, TAIKI?

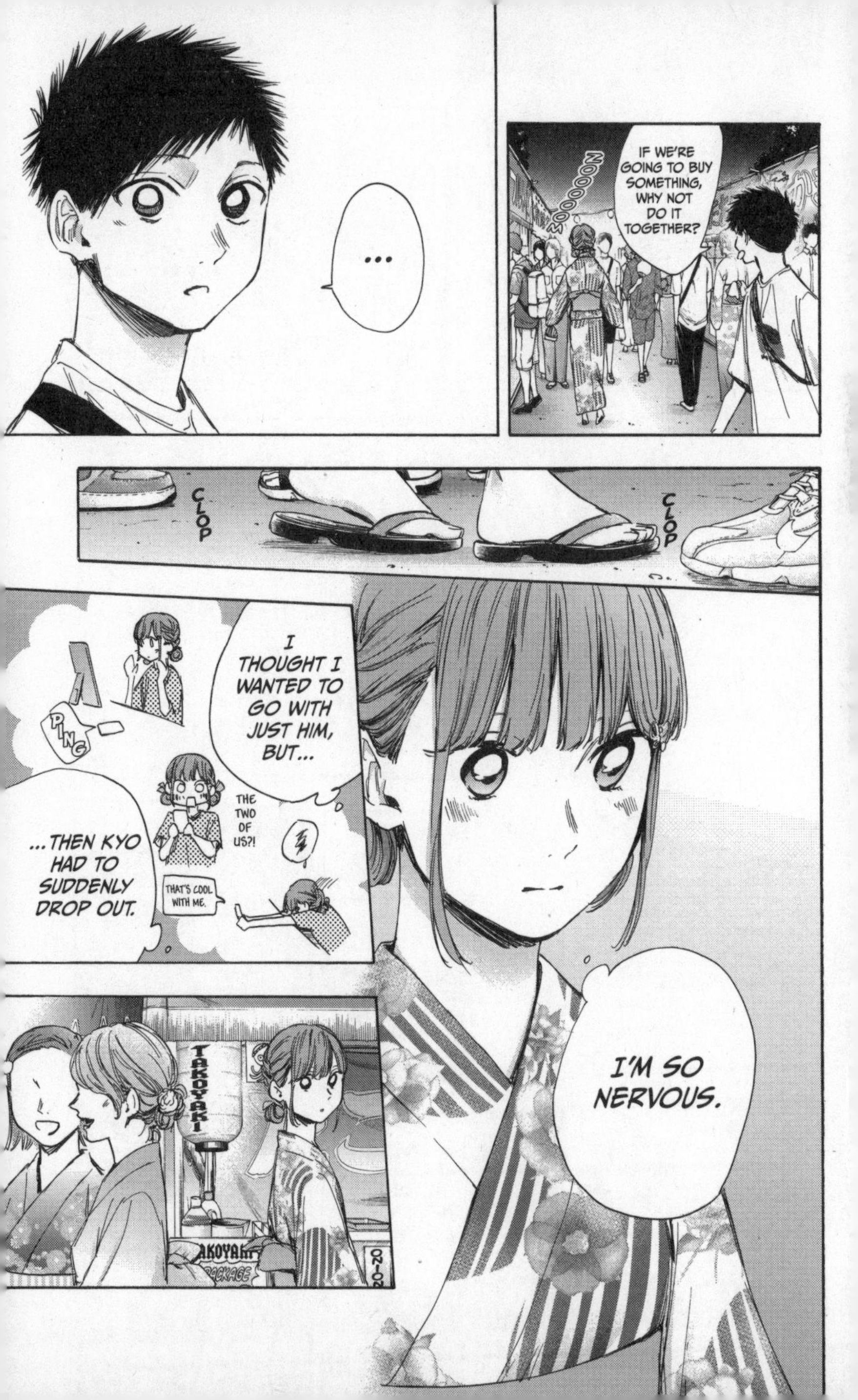
ZOOOOOOM
IF WE'RE GOING TO BUY SOMETHING, WHY NOT DO IT TOGETHER?
...
CLOP
CLOP
I THOUGHT I WANTED TO GO WITH JUST HIM, BUT...
PING
THE TWO OF US?!
THAT'S COOL WITH ME.
...THEN KYO HAD TO SUDDENLY DROP OUT.
I'M SO NERVOUS.
TAKOYAKI
PACKAGE
ONION

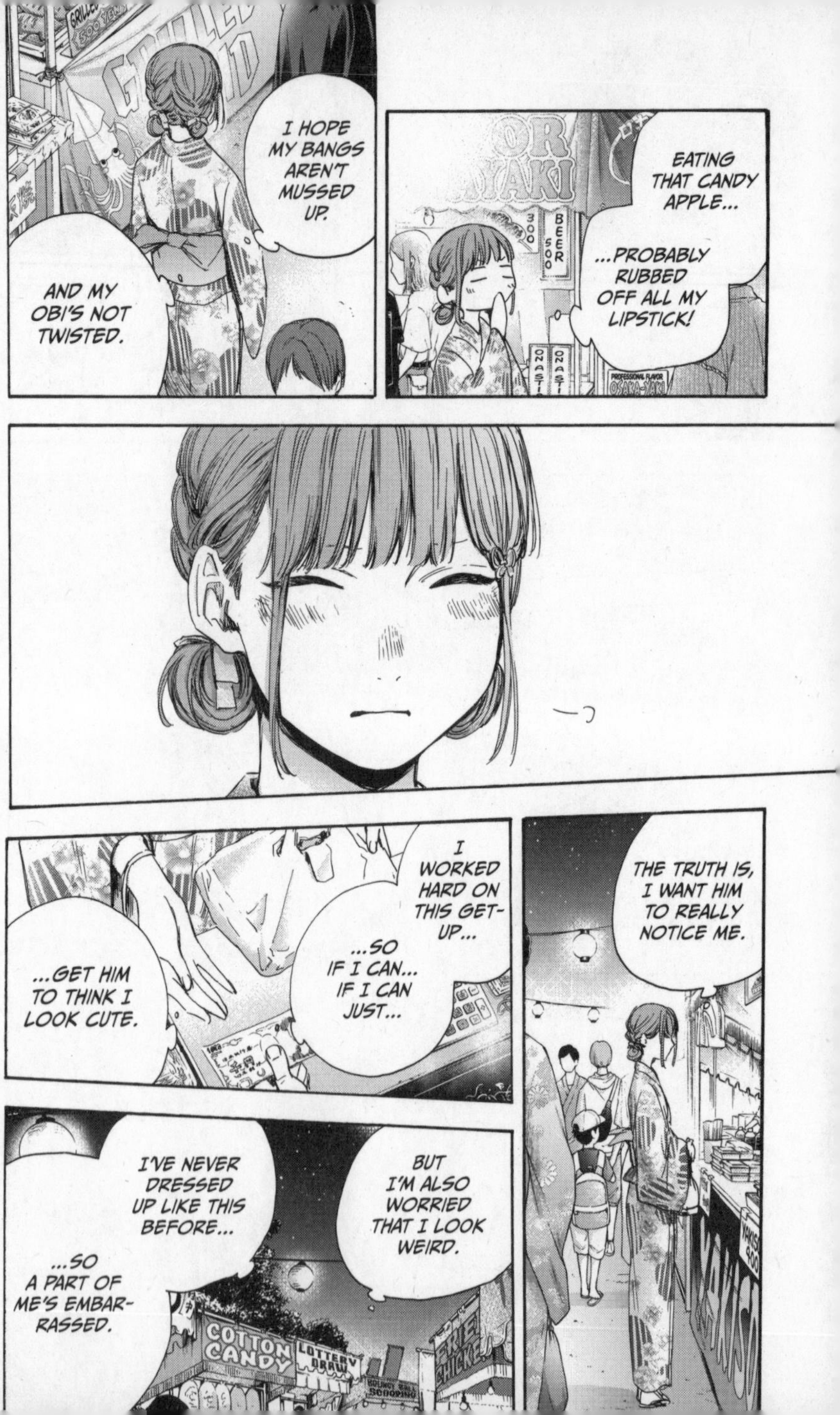
EATING THAT CANDY APPLE...
...PROBABLY RUBBED OFF ALL MY LIPSTICK!
BEER 500
300
PROFESSIONAL FLAVOR OSAKA-YAKI
I HOPE MY BANGS AREN'T MUSSED UP.
AND MY OBI'S NOT TWISTED.
THE TRUTH IS, I WANT HIM TO REALLY NOTICE ME.
I WORKED HARD ON THIS GET-UP...
...SO IF I CAN... IF I CAN JUST...
...GET HIM TO THINK I LOOK CUTE.
BUT I'M ALSO WORRIED THAT I LOOK WEIRD.
I'VE NEVER DRESSED UP LIKE THIS BEFORE...
...SO A PART OF ME'S EMBARRASSED.
COTTON CANDY
LOTTERY DRAW

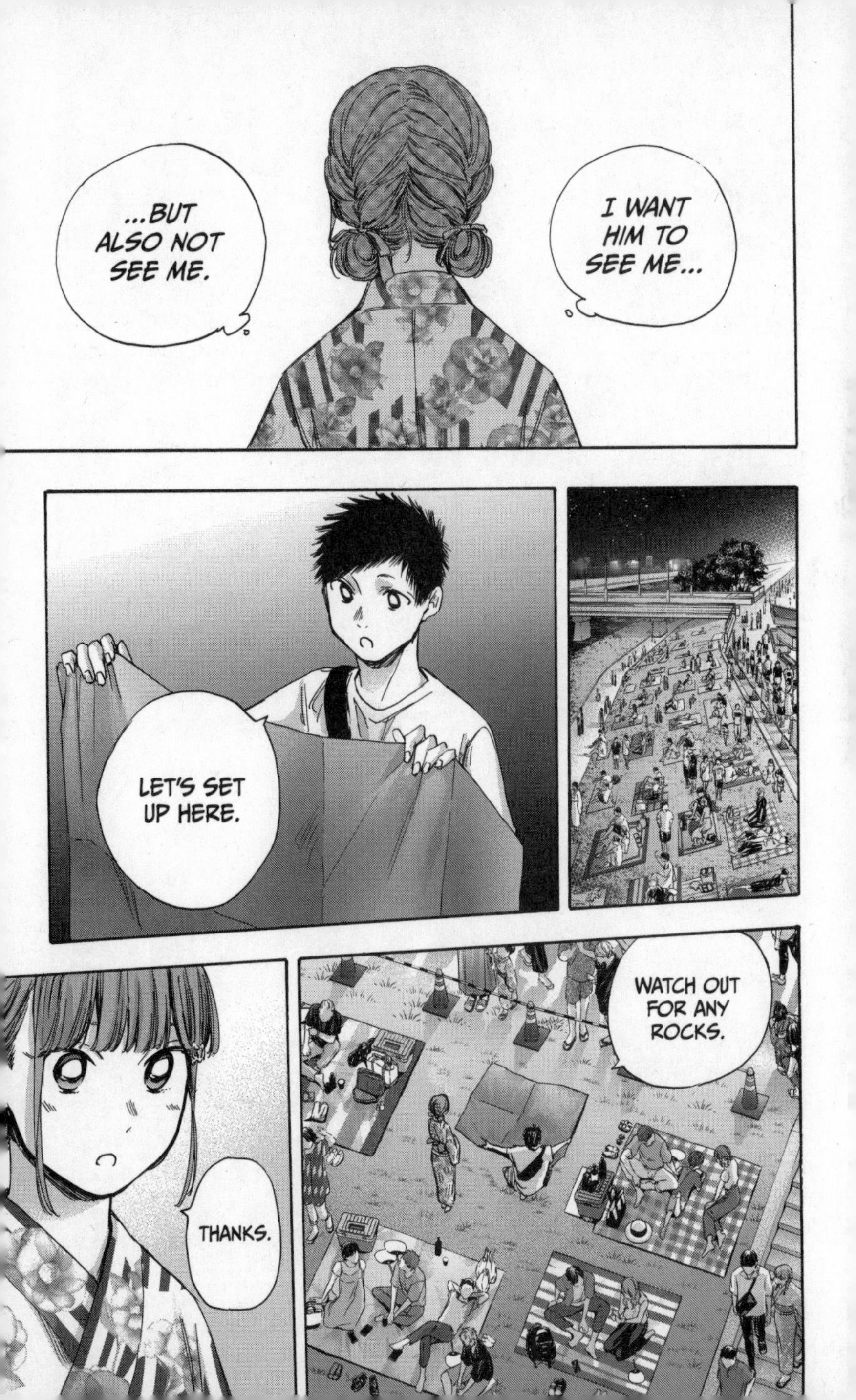
I WANT HIM TO SEE ME...
...BUT ALSO NOT SEE ME.
LET'S SET UP HERE.
WATCH OUT FOR ANY ROCKS.
THANKS.

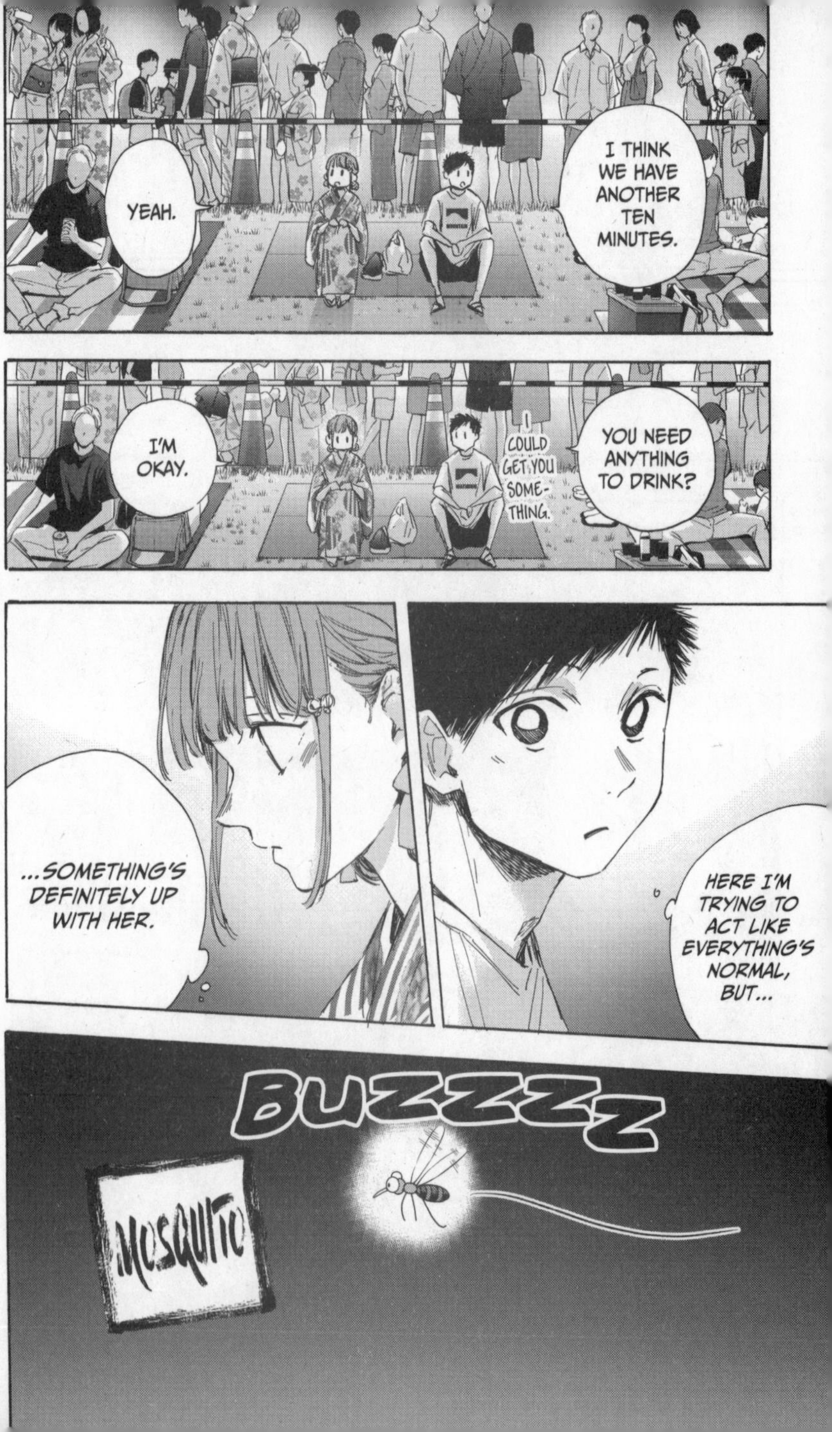
I THINK WE HAVE ANOTHER TEN MINUTES.
YEAH.
YOU NEED ANYTHING TO DRINK?
I COULD GET YOU SOMETHING.
I'M OKAY.
HERE I'M TRYING TO ACT LIKE EVERYTHING'S NORMAL, BUT...
...SOMETHING'S DEFINITELY UP WITH HER.
BUZZZZ
MOSQUITO

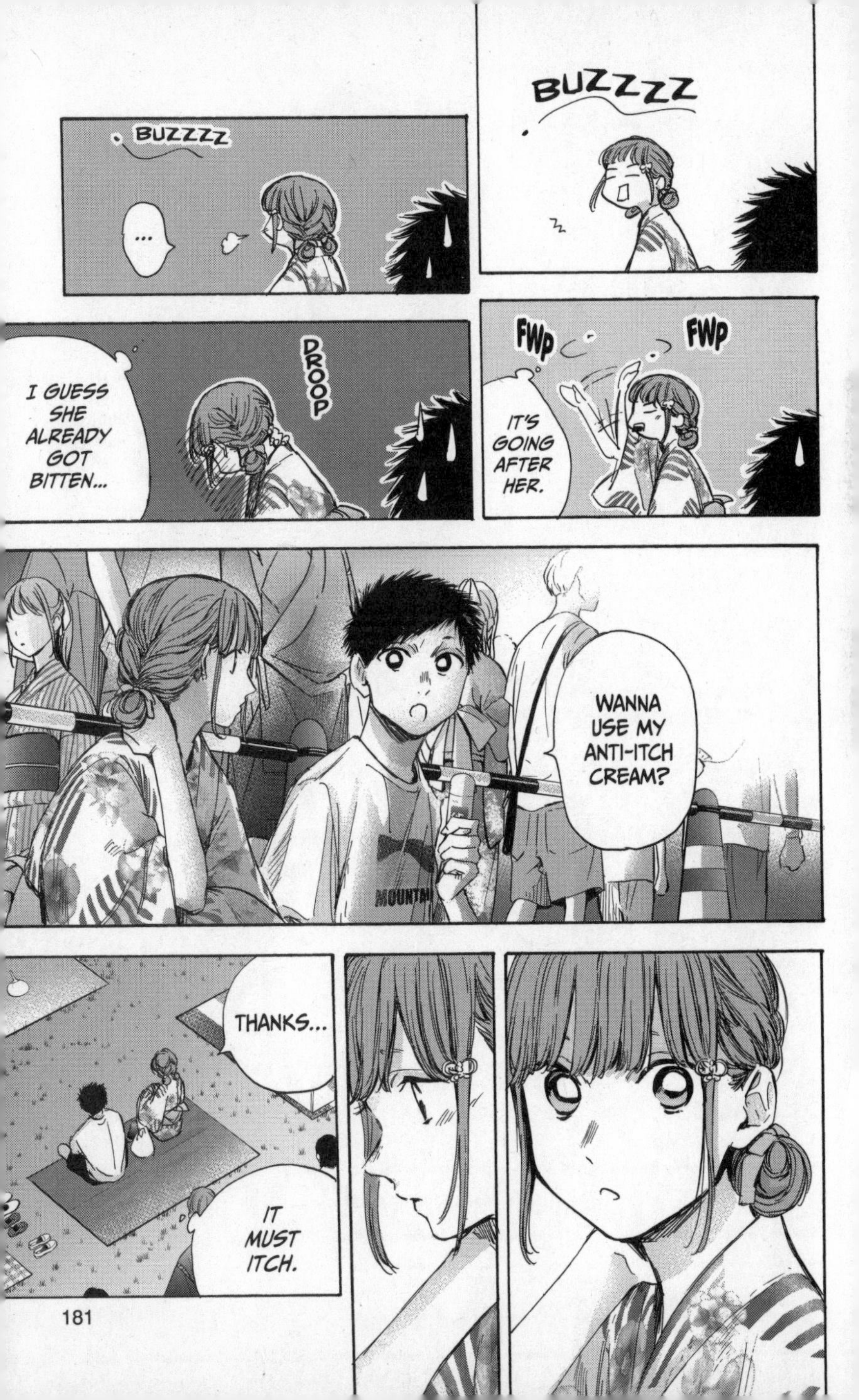
BUZZZZZ
BUZZZZ
...
FWP
FWP
IT'S GOING AFTER HER.
DROOP
I GUESS SHE ALREADY GOT BITTEN...
WANNA USE MY ANTI-ITCH CREAM?
MOUNTAI
THANKS...
IT MUST ITCH.

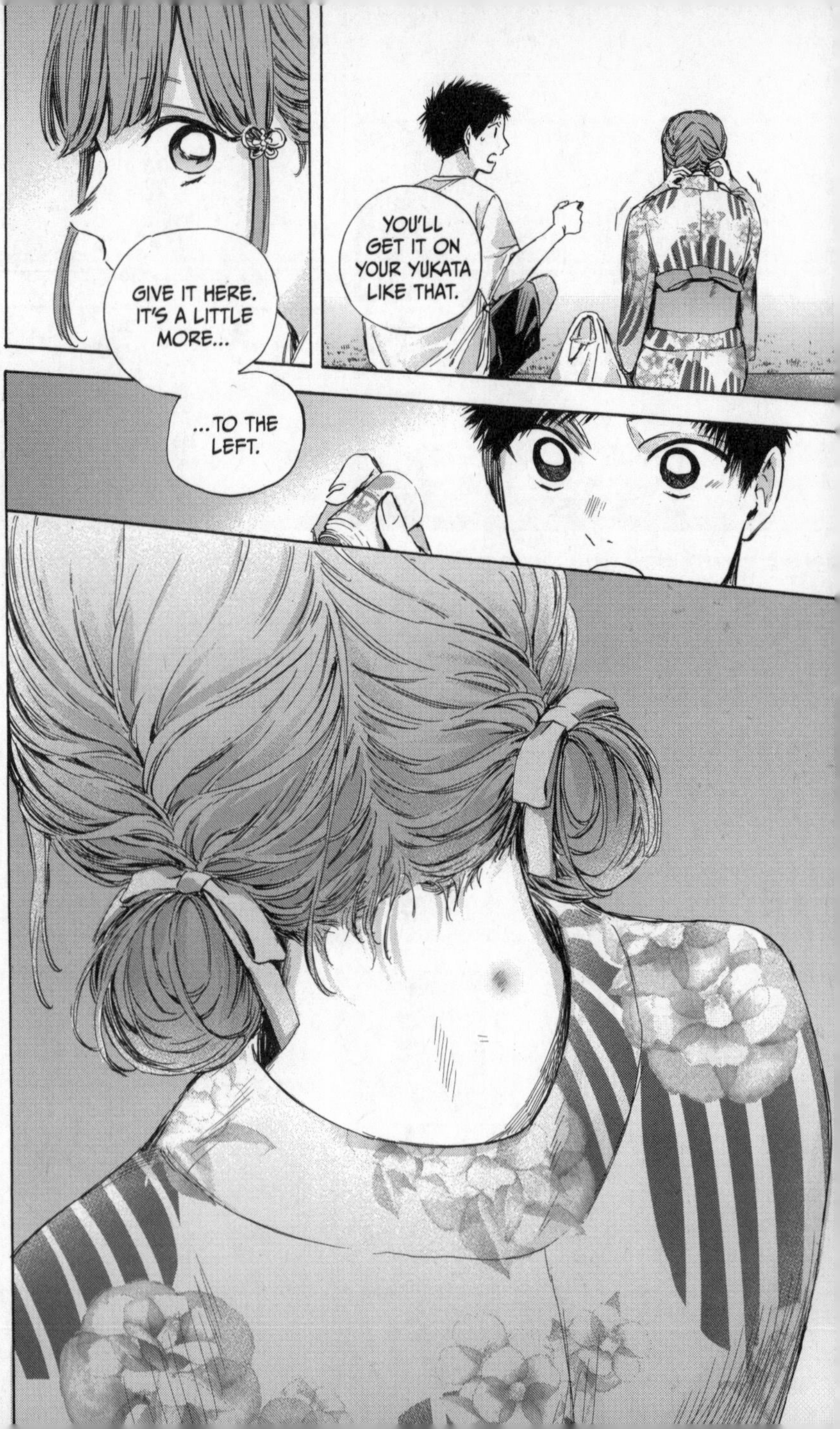
YOU'LL GET IT ON YOUR YUKATA LIKE THAT.
GIVE IT HERE. IT'S A LITTLE MORE...
...TO THE LEFT.

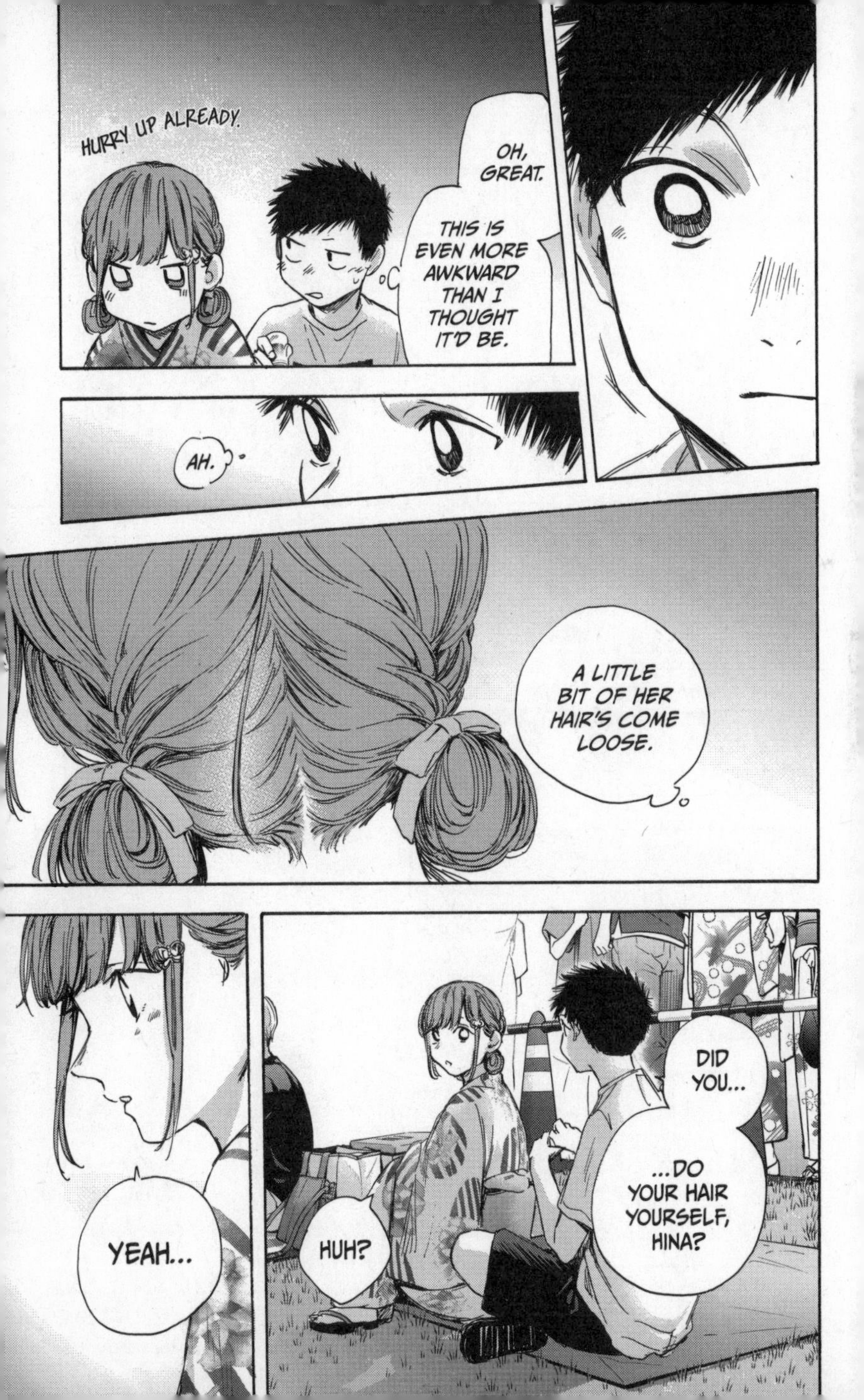
OH, GREAT.
THIS IS EVEN MORE AWKWARD THAN I THOUGHT IT'D BE.
HURRY UP ALREADY.
AH.
A LITTLE BIT OF HER HAIR'S COME LOOSE.
DID YOU...
...DO YOUR HAIR YOURSELF, HINA?
HUH?
YEAH...

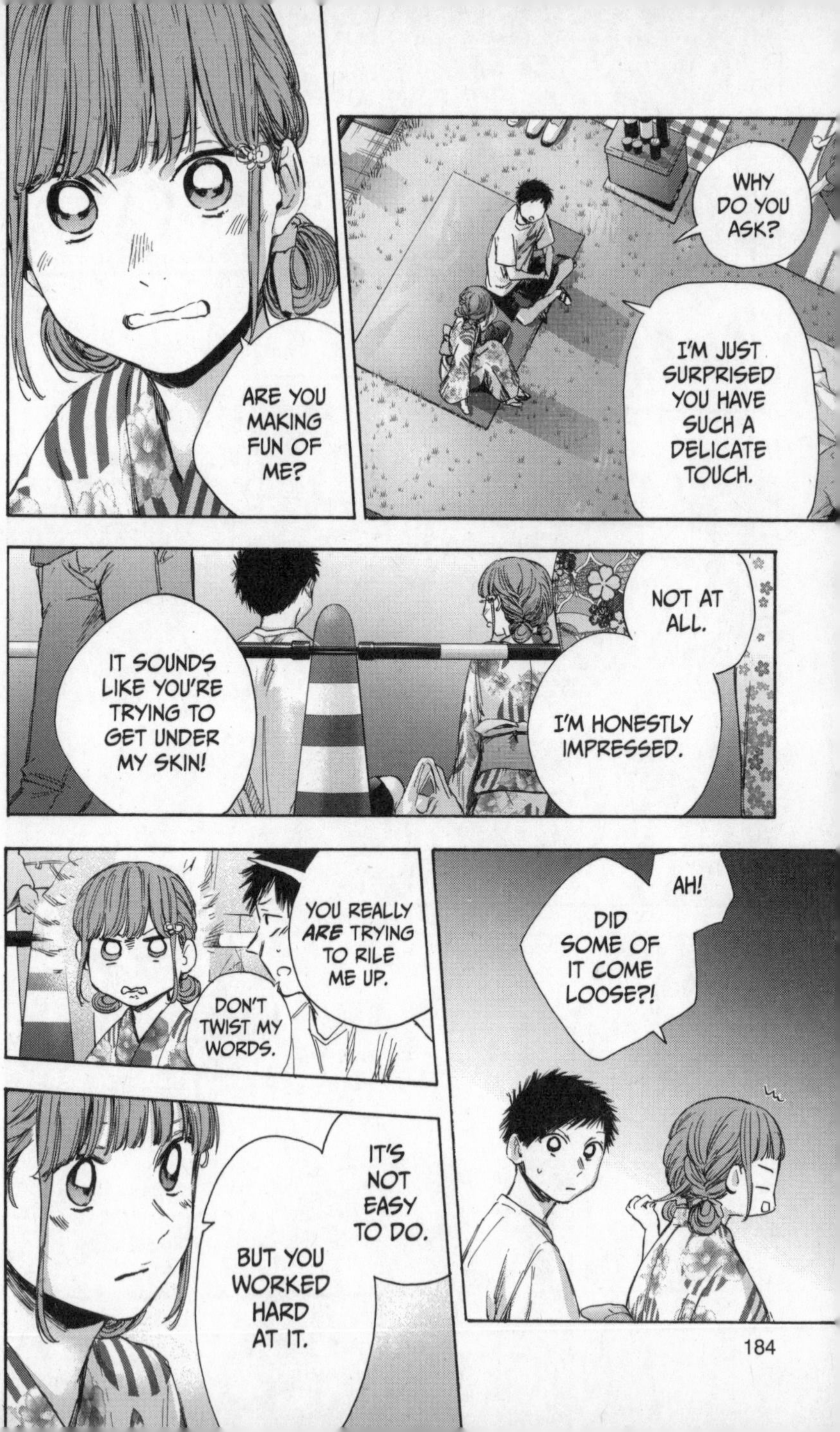
WHY DO YOU ASK?
I'M JUST SURPRISED YOU HAVE SUCH A DELICATE TOUCH.
ARE YOU MAKING FUN OF ME?
NOT AT ALL.
I'M HONESTLY IMPRESSED.
IT SOUNDS LIKE YOU'RE TRYING TO GET UNDER MY SKIN!
YOU REALLY *ARE* TRYING TO RILE ME UP.
DON'T TWIST MY WORDS.
IT'S NOT EASY TO DO.
BUT YOU WORKED HARD AT IT.
AH!
DID SOME OF IT COME LOOSE?!

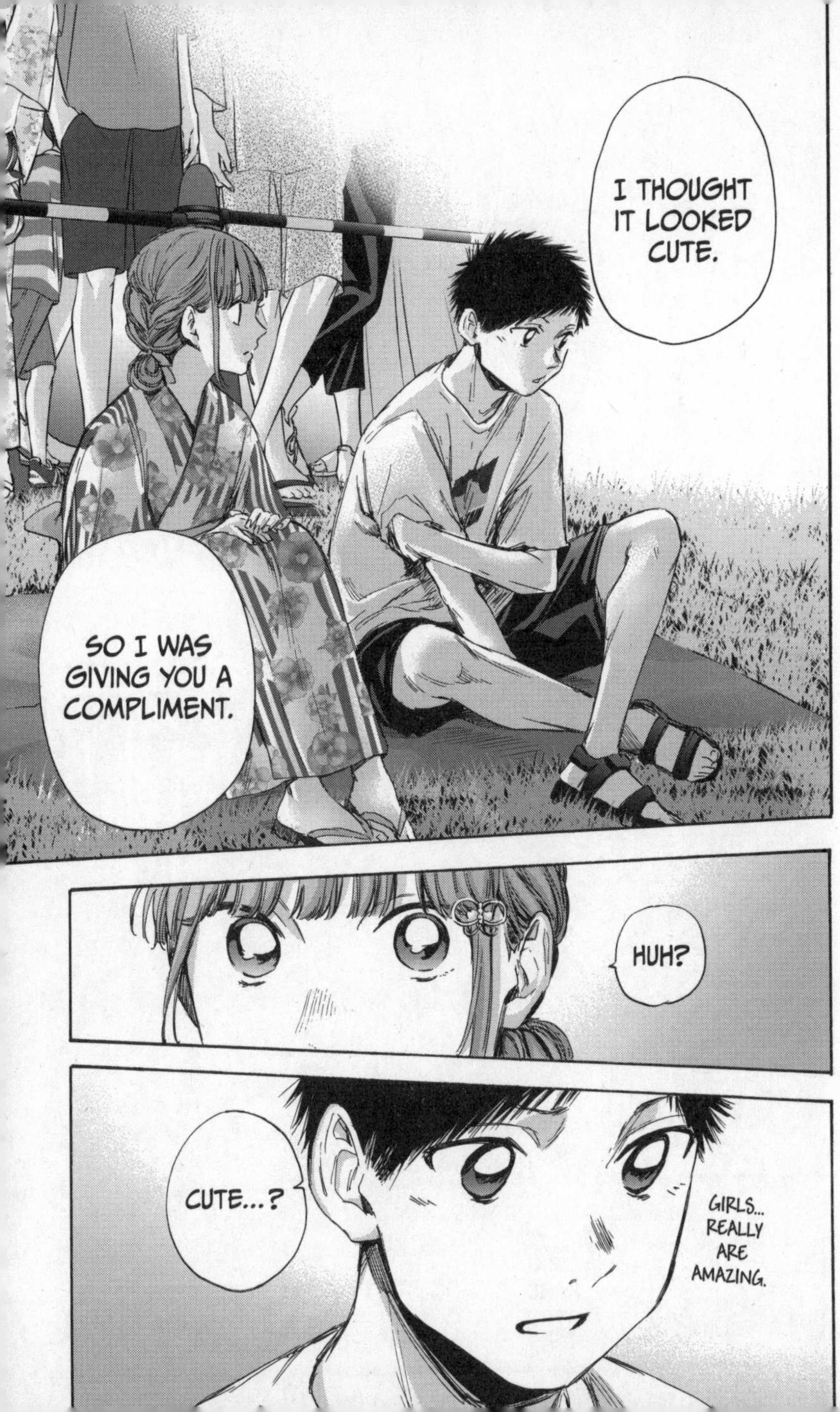
I THOUGHT IT LOOKED CUTE.
SO I WAS GIVING YOU A COMPLIMENT.
HUH?
CUTE...?
GIRLS... REALLY ARE AMAZING.

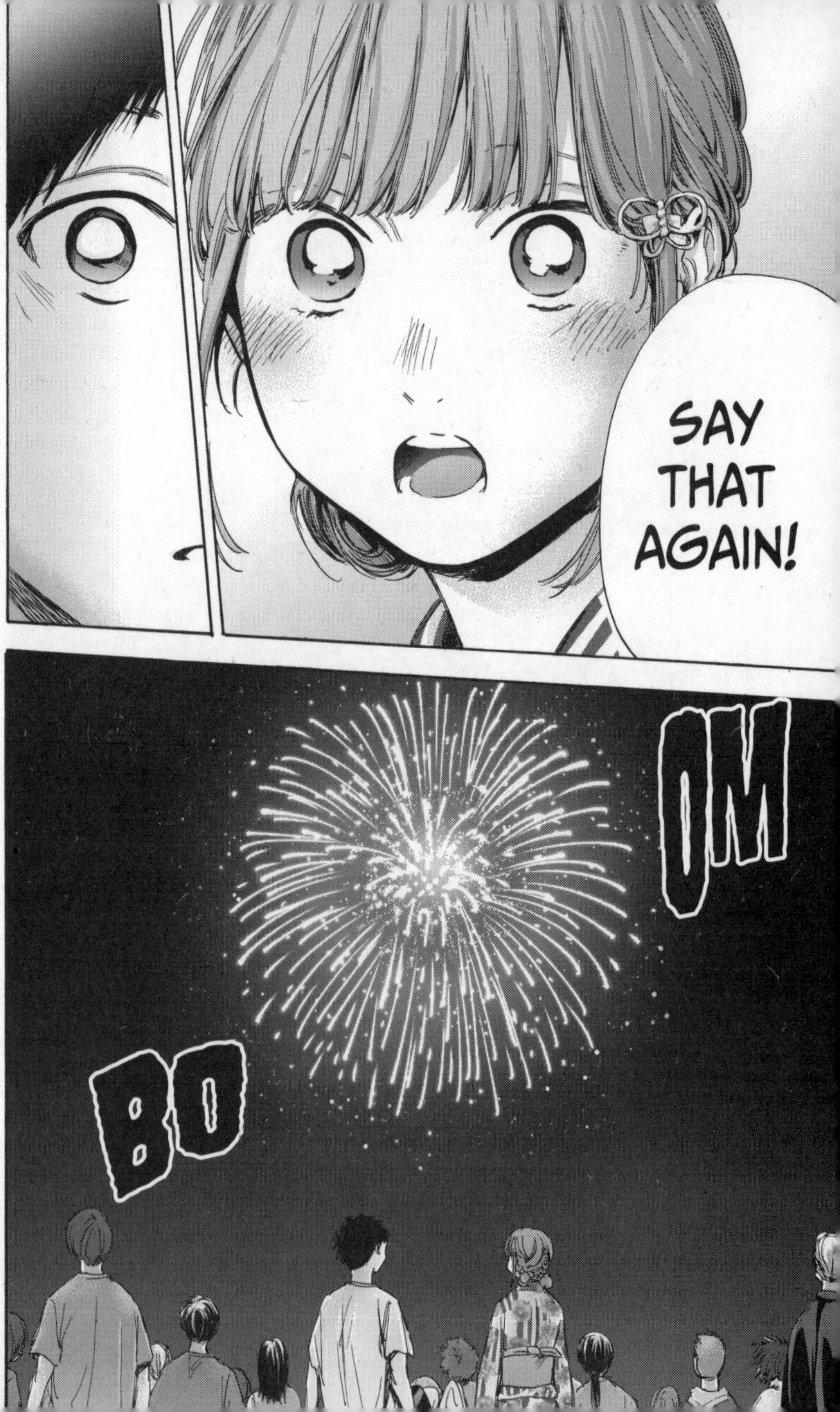
SAY THAT AGAIN!
BO
OM

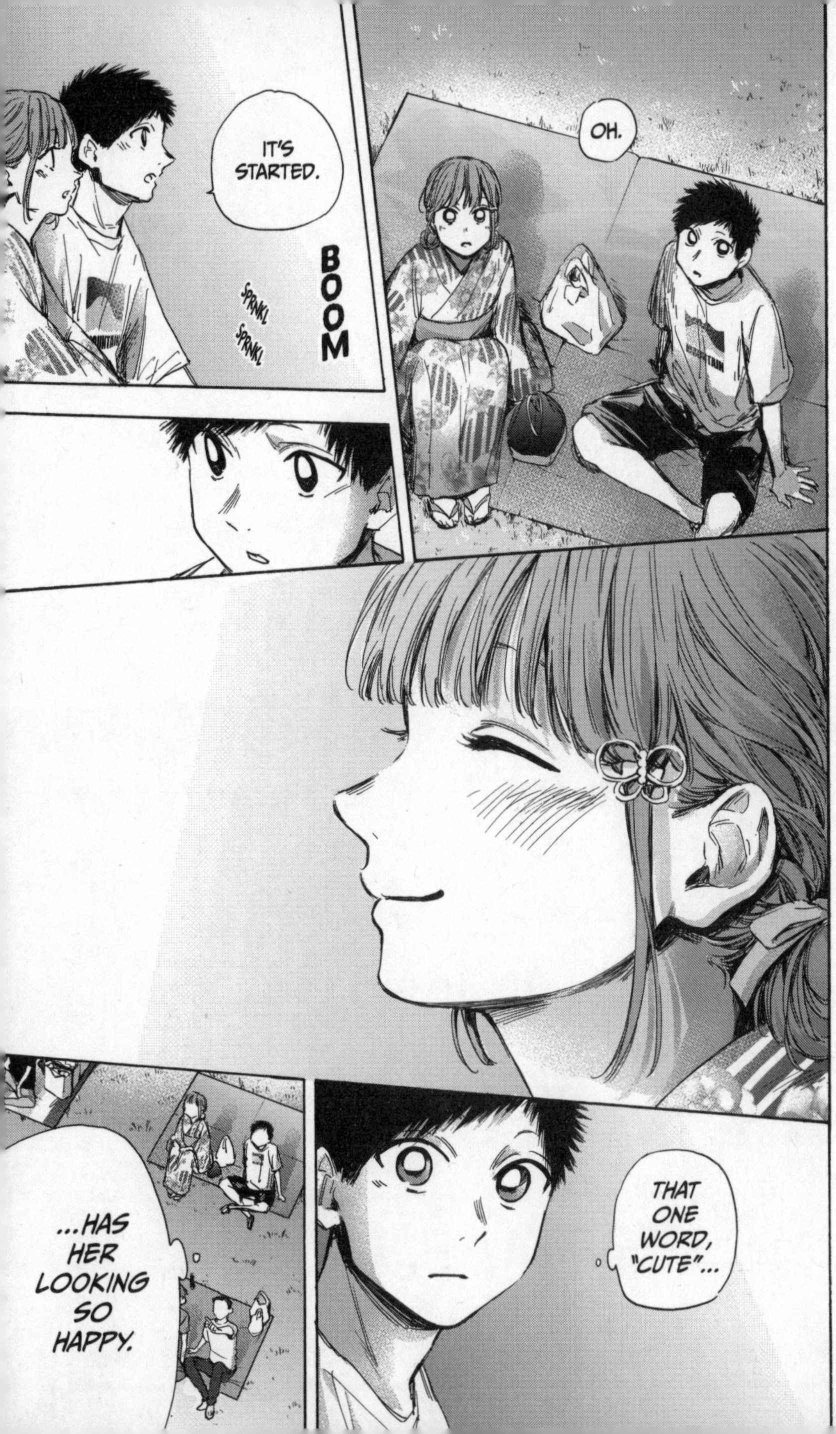
OH.
IT'S STARTED.
BOOM
SPRNKL
SPRNKL
THAT ONE WORD, "CUTE"...
...HAS HER LOOKING SO HAPPY.

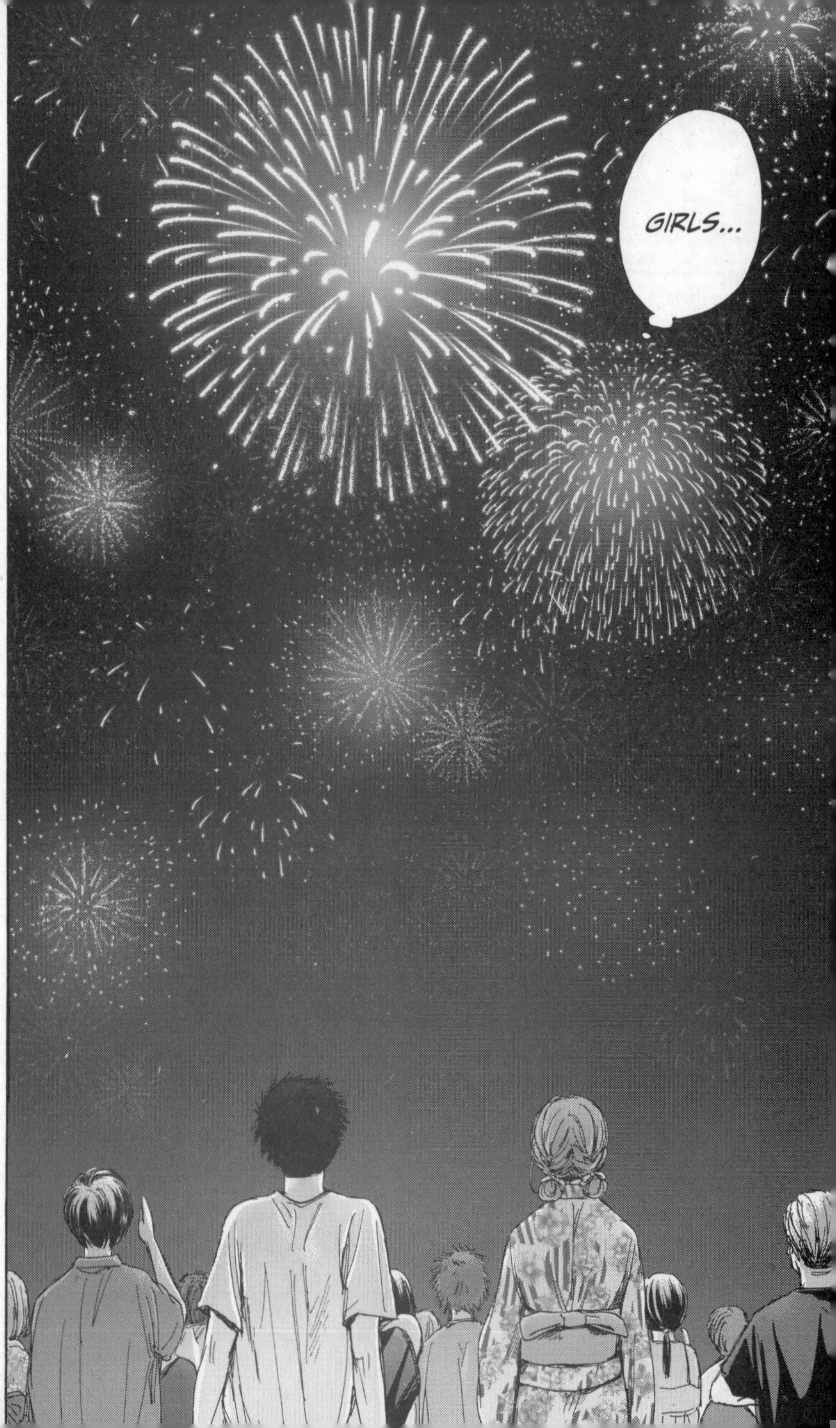
GIRLS...

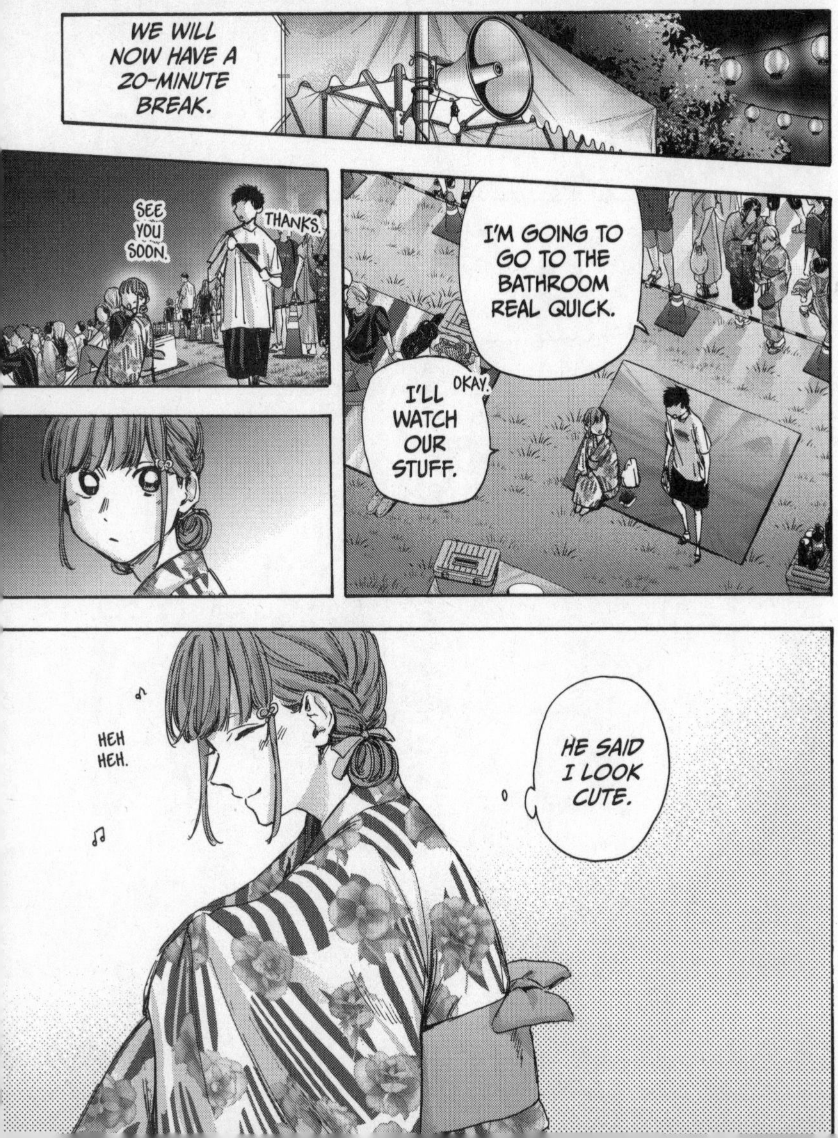
WE WILL NOW HAVE A 20-MINUTE BREAK.
I'M GOING TO GO TO THE BATHROOM REAL QUICK.
OKAY.
I'LL WATCH OUR STUFF.
THANKS.
SEE YOU SOON.
HE SAID I LOOK CUTE.
HEH HEH.

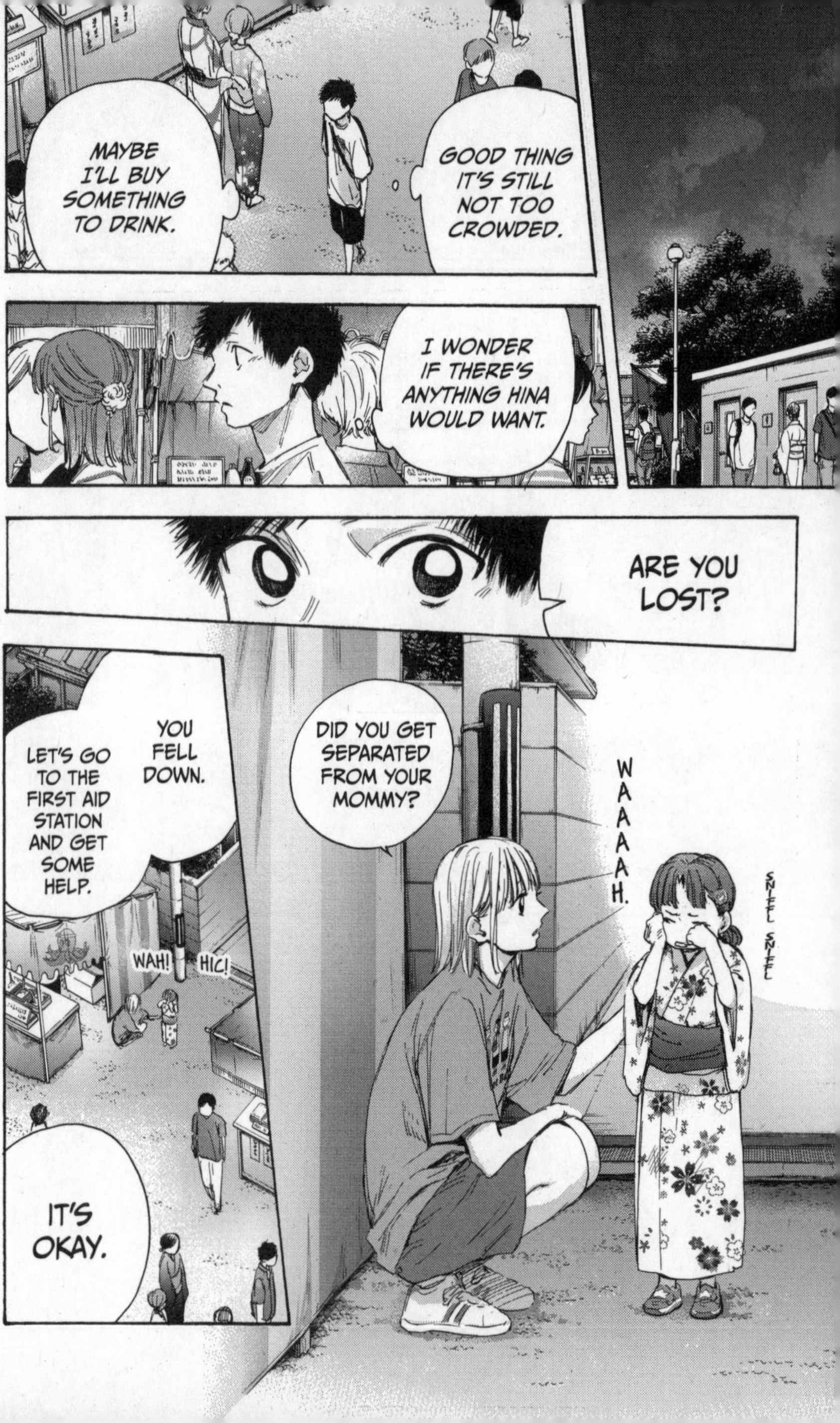
GOOD THING IT'S STILL NOT TOO CROWDED.
MAYBE I'LL BUY SOMETHING TO DRINK.
I WONDER IF THERE'S ANYTHING HINA WOULD WANT.
ARE YOU LOST?
WAAAAAH.
SNIFF SNIFF
DID YOU GET SEPARATED FROM YOUR MOMMY?
YOU FELL DOWN.
LET'S GO TO THE FIRST AID STATION AND GET SOME HELP.
HIC!
WAH!
IT'S OKAY.

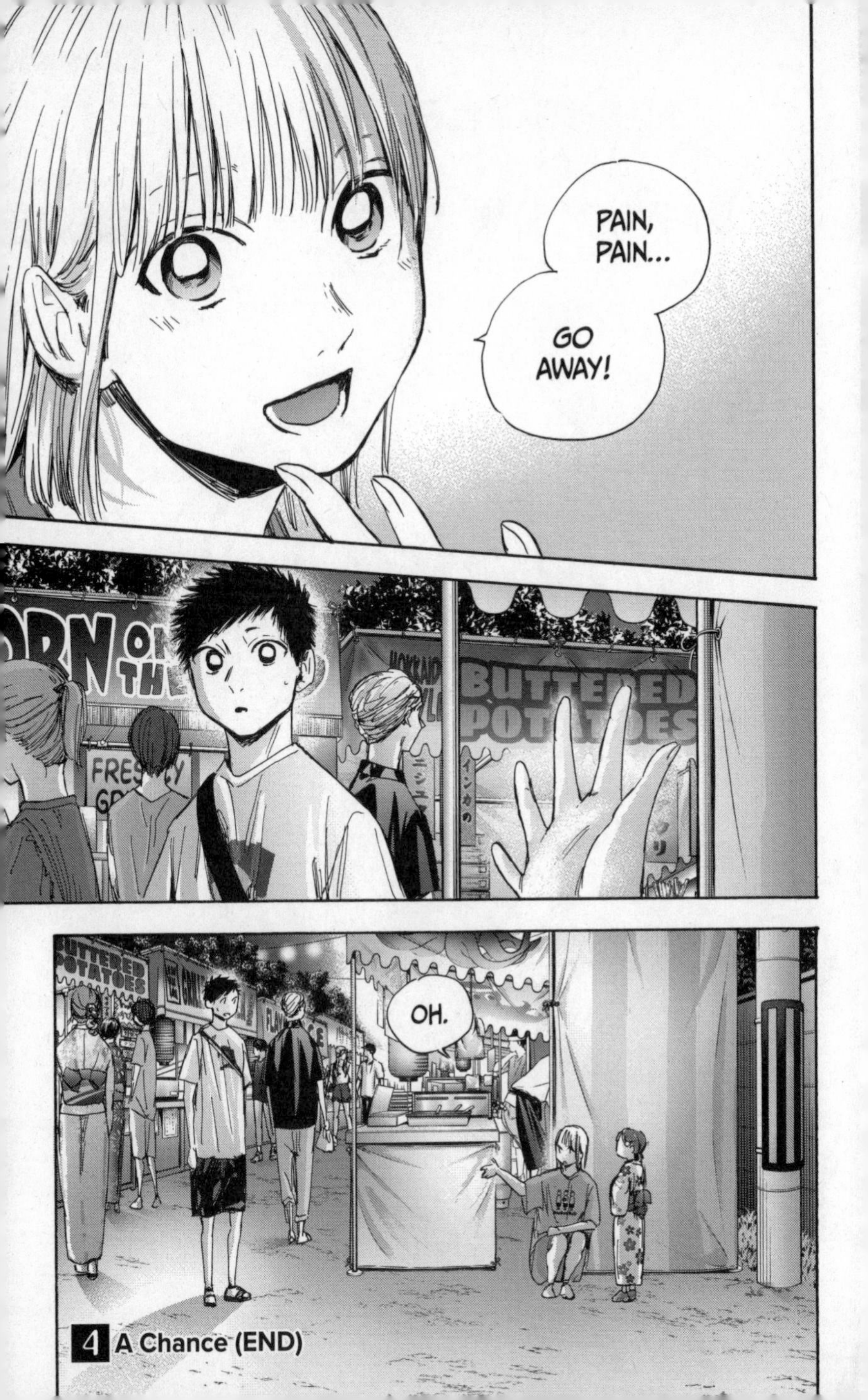
PAIN, PAIN...
GO AWAY!
BUTTERED POTATOES
OH.

4 A Chance (END)

THIS IS THE LAST PAGE

Blue Box has been printed in the original Japanese format to preserve the orientation of the artwork.

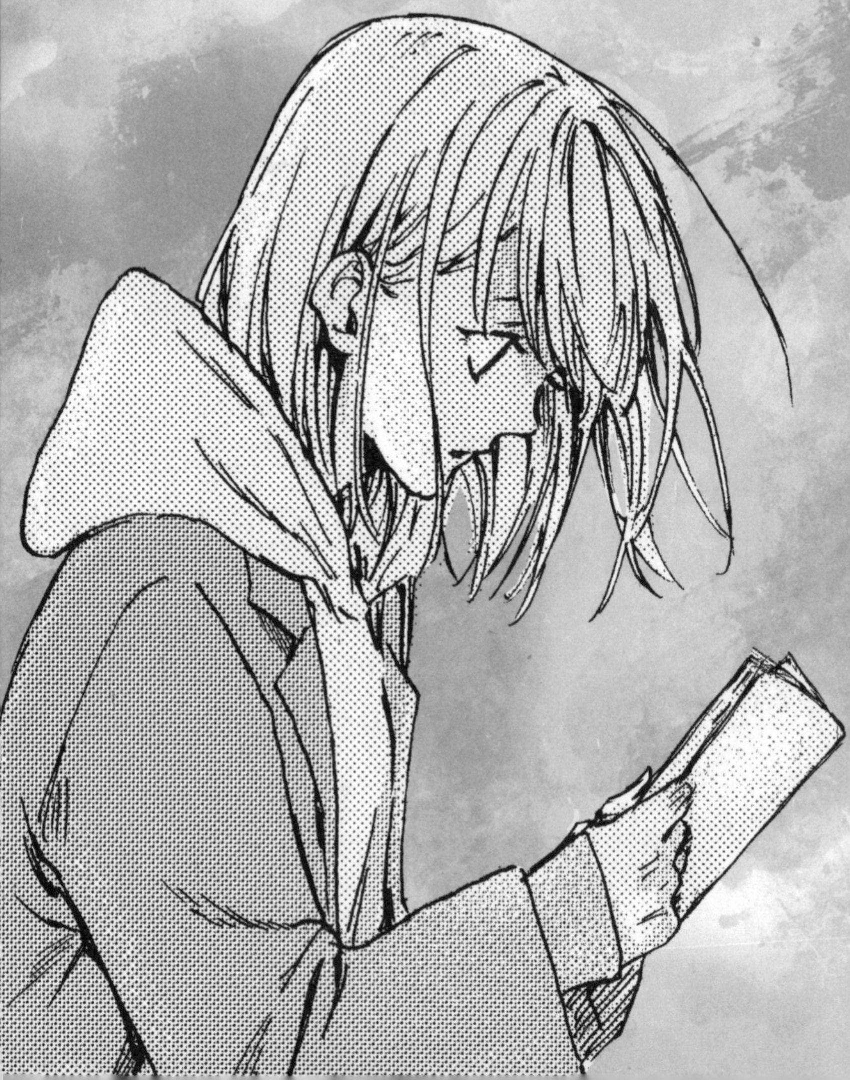